"Who Am I to Judge?"

"Who Am I to Judge?"

Homosexuality and the Catholic Church

Edited by
Stephan Goertz

Translated by
Alissa Jones Nelson

DE GRUYTER

ISBN 978-3-11-070502-7
e-ISBN (PDF) 978-3-11-070518-8
e-ISBN (EPUB) 978-3-11-070525-6

Library of Congress Control Number: 2021943329

Bibliographic information published by the Deutsche Nationalbibliothek
The Deutsche Nationalbibliothek lists this publication in the Deutsche Nationalbibliografie;
detailed bibliographic data are available on the Internet at http://dnb.dnb.de.

© 2022 Walter de Gruyter GmbH, Berlin/Boston

Cover image: Nacho Caballero / iStock / Getty Images Plus (Rainbow); franckreporter / iStock /
Getty Images Plus (St. Peter, Rom)
Title of the original publication: "Wer bin ich, ihn zu verurteilen?" Homosexualität und
katholische Kirche, edited by Stephan Goertz © 2015 Verlag Herder GmbH, Freiburg im Breisgau
Printing and binding: CPI books GmbH, Leck

www.degruyter.com

Table of Contents

Stephan Goertz
"Who Am I to Judge?"
 An Overview of the Context and the Themes of the Contributions —— **1**

Exegetical Substantiation

Thomas Hieke
Does the Old Testament Recognize and Condemn Homosexuality? —— **9**

Michael Theobald
Paul and Same-Sex Sexuality
 A Plea for a Sensible Approach to Scripture —— **43**

Insights from the Human and Social Sciences

Hartmut A. G. Bosinski
A Normal Variance of the Human Capacity for Bonding and Love
 Homosexuality from the Perspective of Sexual Medicine —— **75**

Melanie Caroline Steffens and Claudia Niedlich
Homosexuality Between Acceptance and Discrimination
 A Social-Science Perspective —— **113**

Theological and Ethical Debates

Magnus Striet
Creation Theology and Concepts of Homosexuality —— **139**

Stephan Goertz
From the Primacy of Nature to the Primacy of Love
 Phases in the Assessment of Homosexuality in Moral Theology and
 the Roman Magisterium —— **151**

Todd A. Salzman and Michael G. Lawler
Reconstructing Complementarity as a Foundational Catholic Sexual Ethical Principle —— 213

Socio-Ethical Challenges

Konrad Hilpert
Same-Sex Partnership and Marriage —— 235

Gerhard Marschütz
Same-Sex Parenthood
    Theological and Ethical Reflections on a Contentious Debate —— **259**

List of Contributors —— 287

Stephan Goertz

"Who Am I to Judge?"

An Overview of the Context and the Themes of the Contributions

In the liberal societies of the West, the idea of the universality of certain inalienable human rights has led to a historically unique process of emancipating sexual minorities and democratizing a variety of relationship structures. Globally, we see the ongoing decriminalization and depathologization of homosexuality, which began after World War II. While everyday discrimination is still widespread, it is increasingly losing its cultural legitimacy. At the same time, in some parts of the world, lesbian and gay people continue to face oppression and repression.

In the teaching and practice of the Catholic Church, however, same-sex sexuality remains grounds for exclusion. Magisterium documents disapprove of homosexual relationships in principle. Since there is no analogy between such relationships and marriage between a man and a woman, the blessing of homosexual unions is rejected as illicit, on the grounds that the Catholic Church has no authority to alter God's plans for men and women.[1] In essence, the devaluation and exclusion of homosexuality hinges on the conviction that same-sex sexuality operates outside the bounds of God's intended order of creation. Thus for Catholic moral teaching, homosexual orientation is and remains a problem.

This consistently negative view of homosexuality means that many homosexuals do not experience the Catholic Church as a place where they feel that their sexual orientation and partnerships are accepted or their identity is recognized. The Church explicitly opposes discrimination against homosexuals because this violates their dignity as persons. At the same time, however, it denies them the opportunity to practice their sexuality responsibly and lovingly. Church teaching has been caught in this dichotomy ever since 1986, when the Congregation for the Doctrine of the Faith in Rome first addressed the question of homosexuality in greater detail.[2]

---

1 Congregation for the Doctrine of the Faith, "Responsum to a dubium regarding the blessing of the unions of persons of the same sex" (February 22, 2021)", http://www.vatican.va/roman_curia/congregations/cfaith/documents/rc_con_cfaith_doc_20210222_responsum-dubium-unioni_en.html (accessed May 21, 2021).
2 Congregation for the Doctrine of the Faith, "Letter to the Bishops of the Catholic Church on the Pastoral Care for Homosexual Persons. *Homosexualis problema*," AAS 79 (1987): 543–554.

https://doi.org/10.1515/9783110705188-001

The evaluation of homosexuality and homosexual partnerships is developing into a crucial test for the Catholic Church, as has also been the case in other Christian churches and denominations.[3] For some, the negative evaluation of homosexuality is a necessary consequence of church tradition; for others, it is a an outrage against Christian principles of justice. The issue of the treatment of sexual minorities alienates many believers from their Church. This is not simply a Western issue, as is often assumed. Lesbian and gay people are also fighting for their emancipation and their rights for example in Africa and in many Eastern European countries. We should begin by attending to their experiences, and we should not simply be satisfied with the statement that homosexuality is incompatible with certain cultures or religious traditions.[4] Tradition should not be sacred to us for its own sake, but the human person, human dignity, and human rights should be.

The present volume is envisioned as a contribution to the ongoing self-reflection on the Catholic view of homosexuality. This effort can only succeed if we face up to the prejudices inherent in the classical Catholic evaluation of homosexuality, opening this perspective to interrogation from a human sciences perspective as well as to theological criticism. In 2013, after decades of gridlock in this area, Pope Francis raised hopes for a new Catholic attitude toward homosexuals with just a few sentences. In an interview, the pontiff said:

> In Buenos Aires I received letters from homosexual persons who are "socially wounded" because they always feel condemned by the Church. But the Church does not want that. On the flight back from Rio de Janeiro, I said that if a homosexual person has good will and seeks God, I am not the one to judge him. In this way, I said what is written in the Catechism. [...] God has set us free in creation: there must be no spiritual interference in personal life.[5]

Does this indicate a learning curve – a shift from the "casting off" way of thinking to the "reinstating" way of thinking, which Francis has spoken of so forceful-

---

3 Cf. Jeffrey S. Siker, ed., *Homosexuality and Religion. An Encyclopedia* (Westport/London: Greenwood Publishing Group, 2007).
4 See, for example, Makau Mutua, "Sexual Orientation and Human Rights: Putting Homophobia on Trial," in *African Sexualities. A Reader*, ed. Sylvia Tamale (Nairobi/Cape Town/Oxford: Pambazuka Press, 2011), 452–462.
5 Antonio Spadaro, *Das Interview mit Papst Franziskus*, ed. Andreas R. Batlogg (Freiburg im Breisgau: Herder, 2013), 49–50. The precise words which the Pope spoke on the return flight from Brazil on July 28, 2013 were: "If someone is gay and is searching for the Lord and has good will, then who am I to judge him (*ma chi sono io per giudicarla*)?" See http://www.vatican.va/content/francesco/en/speeches/2013/july/documents/papa-francesco_20130728_gmg-conferenza-stampa.html (accessed March 22, 2021).

ly?[6] At the same time – and this is what makes his statement about the Catholic position so difficult – the Pope, as a "son of the Church"[7], repeatedly refers to the Catechism, in which the condemnation of homosexual behavior stands alongside the criticism of discrimination. Should the homosexual person be protected from moral disgrace ("Who am I to judge him?"), while their sexuality and relationships are not? After all, despite the Catechism's assertion to the contrary, do we not see the old discriminatory prejudices against homosexuals' moral integrity lurking behind the Vatican's reservations regarding the ordination of homosexual candidates for the priesthood?[8] Violence against homosexual people has many faces. It can also be symbolic, denying them the opportunity to live out their sexuality in a humane manner. The "casting off" way of thinking will not change as long as the Church's moral teaching continues to view homosexual behavior as sin. At the present moment, it is impossible to know whether or not the Catholic Church will revise its teaching on this point. This assessment, given in the German-language first edition of this volume, is still valid.[9]

For all the controversy over the moral evaluation of homosexuality, we may be able to establish a theological consensus on the principles that could lead us to an ethically justified position. I would like to mention the following six principles, and at the same time to briefly introduce the contributions in this book.

First, according to the wishes of the most recent Council, the Bible – "the soul of all theology"[10] – should take its rightful, primary place in moral theology. This is not to be understood as a call for a direct biblical justification of our ethics. Moral norms must be justified on the basis of human reason. Christian ethics is confronted with the question of whether historically developed and time-tested moral standards can be biblically supported (not justified!). To put it succinct-

---

6 Holy Mass with the New Cardinals, Homily of His Holiness Pope Francis, Vatican Basilica, February 15, 2015, http://www.vatican.va/content/francesco/en/homilies/2015/documents/papa-francesco_20150215_omelia-nuovi-cardinali.html (accessed March 22, 2021).

7 Antonio Spadaro, *Das Interview mit Papst Franziskus*, 51.

8 Congregation for the Clergy, *The Gift of the Priestly Vocation: Ratio Fundamentalis Institutionis Sacerdotalis* (Rome: Vatican, 2016), nos. 199 – 201, http://www.clerus.va/content/dam/clerus/Ratio%20Fundamentalis/The%20Gift%20of%20the%20Priestly%20Vocation.pdf (accessed April 21, 2021).

9 Stephan Goertz, ed., *"Wer bin ich, ihn zu verurteilen?" Homosexualität und katholische Kirche* (Katholizismus im Umbruch 3; Freiburg im Breisgau: Herder, 2015).

10 Second Vatican Council, *Decree on Priestly Training: Optatam totius* (Rome: Vatican, 1965), no. 16, http://www.vatican.va/archive/hist_councils/ii_vatican_council/documents/vat-ii_decree_19651028_optatam-totius_en.html (accessed April 21, 2021).

ly: it is not the Bible that interprets morality, but morality that interprets the Bible.[11]

The Old and New Testament biblical passages that are often used as the ground upon which to condemn homosexuality must be examined exegetically prior to any ethical critique (see the contributions by Thomas Hieke and Michael Theobald). It is precisely the high theological esteem in which we hold Scripture that requires us to approach the texts with hermeneutical care. In doing so, it becomes apparent that the biblical authors, while condemning certain same-sex sexual acts from their respective points of view and in confrontation with their cultural and religious environments, are by no means generally concerned with homosexuality as we understand it today. The exegetical deconstruction of the idea that the Bible unequivocally condemns homosexuality has a liberating effect on the Christian approach to sexual minorities. An analysis of the concepts of purity evident in the book of Leviticus, the narrative of Sodom, and the Letter to the Romans shows that these sometimes drastic biblical condemnations cannot constitute a sufficient basis for a present-day evaluation of homosexuality. This insight is not fundamentally new[12], but it is still often ignored today.

Second, in making any ethical judgment, the Catholic Church expects that the earthly realities God created should be appreciated in their own right, "with their own stability, truth, [and] goodness."[13] The "rightful independence of science" must be respected.[14] This also applies to the understanding of what has been called homosexuality for almost one hundred and fifty years. A Catholic sexology would therefore contradict the Catholic self-understanding. Therefore, this volume gives expert voices from sexual medicine and the social sciences their say. On the one hand, these experts demonstrate that homosexuality should be understood as a variant of sexual orientation and relational capacity (see Hartmut Bosinski's contribution), and on the other hand, they show that social evaluations of homosexuality still oscillate between discrimination and acceptance (see Melanie Caroline Steffens and Claudia Niedlich's contribution). Religious convictions play a significant role in these processes.

---

11 Cf. Christof Breitsameter and Stephan Goertz, eds., *Bibel und Moral – ethische und exegetische Zugänge* (Jahrbuch für Moraltheologie 2; Freiburg im Breisgau: Herder, 2018).

12 Cf. Herman van de Spijker, *Die gleichgeschlechtliche Zuneigung* (Freiburg im Breisgau: Walter-Verlag, 1968); Martti Nissinen, *Homoeroticism in the biblical World: A Historical Perspective* (Minneapolis: Fortress, 1998).

13 Second Vatican Council, *Pastoral Constitution on the Church in the Modern World: Gaudium et spes* (Rome: Vatican, 1965), no. 36, http://www.vatican.va/archive/hist_councils/ii_vatican_council/documents/vat-ii_cons_19651207_gaudium-et-spes_en.html (accessed April 21, 2021).

14 Ibid.

Third, fundamental theological issues arise in the debate over the Christian evaluation of homosexuality. Some still claim that homosexuality contradicts not only biblical directives, but also the order of creation and thus God's will and God's law. Moreover, only marriage between a man and a woman can be considered sacred. But how can we recognize and verify God's will? What do we mean theologically when we speak of a sacrament in the context of partnership? What would a theology grounded on the foundation of the freedom of God and of humankind mean for the topic of homosexuality? These questions relate to the theology of creation and its impact on a wide range of ethical issues (see Magnus Striet's contribution).

Church tradition sees itself as a living transmission of the word of God into new situations and contexts. In the process, "there is a growth in the understanding of the realities and the words which have been handed down. This happens through the contemplation and study made by believers."[15] Thus *the tradition* is not simply identical with *traditions*. If it becomes apparent that interpretations have developed and practices have become established in the tradition which have led or continue to lead to the exclusion or persecution of homosexuals – those who, in the past, were called "sodomites" – then these traditions are no longer morally binding for us today.

Fourth, the teaching office of the Catholic Church "is not above the word of God, but serves it, teaching only what has been handed on."[16] The Christian heart of the word of God is believed to be God's self-revelation in Jesus Christ, in whom God, as the Council writes, "out of the abundance of His love speaks to men as friends."[17] This revelation presupposes freedom on the part of human beings. God desires a lively response, not a dead echo. The credibility of the Christian message, and thus also of doctrinal documents, depends on this respect for human maturity. If the faithful receive the Christian testimony on the basis of their own independent insight, then it acquires a special, binding theological force. Many church statements on homosexuality fail to achieve this independent reception of faith based on insight. The assumption is that this has to do with the documents' selective reception of scientific and theological insights, and their associated lack of persuasive argumentation (see my contribution). The resentment of same-sex love has become a theological offense today.

---

15 Second Vatican Council, *Dogmatic Constitution on Divine Revelation: Dei Verbum* (Rome: Vatican, 1965), no. 8, https://www.vatican.va/archive/hist_councils/ii_vatican_council/documents/vat-ii_const_19651118_dei-verbum_en.html (accessed April 21, 2021).
16 Ibid, no. 10.
17 Ibid, no. 2.

Fifth, as a fundamental principle for sexual morality, the Council has formulated the idea that sexuality should be "expressed in a manner which is truly human."[18] But what does this principle mean concretely? And does it only apply to sex between a man and a woman? Can homosexual behavior also be understood as behavior in which partners complement each other in love and interact in a just way? These questions relate to the theological idea of complementarity and its revision (see Todd A. Salzman's and Michael G. Lawler's contribution)?

Sixth, in addition to these exegetical, human scientific, theological, and ethical considerations on the status of same-sex relationships, we should not overlook two specific, controversial questions that affect the Church and the broader public in various countries. Christian ethics has always been interested in such concrete questions. The first concerns same-sex partnerships (see Konrad Hilpert's contribution). What is the relationship between such partnerships and marriage between a man and a woman? Which legal form is appropriate for same-sex relationships, so as not to discriminate against homosexuals and at the same time to take into account the specificity of such partnerships? Finally, the question of how to evaluate same-sex parenthood regularly leads to disputes (see Gerhard Marschütz's contribution). Do such family structures constitute a threat to the child's welfare? What ethically relevant findings might help shed light on these discussions?

Finally, I would like to express my gratitude to Alice Meroz, our editor at De Gruyter, without whose knowledgeable and prudent guidance this project could not have been realized. I am no less indebted to the expertise of our translator, Alissa Jones Nelson, for her excellent work on the texts. I would also like to thank Herder publishing house in Freiburg for making this English-language edition possible. For their meticulous management of and care for these contributions – which have been updated, revised, and partly rewritten for this edition – I offer my sincere gratitude to the staff at the Chair of Moral Theology in Mainz: Katharina Deutschle, Dr. Stephanie Höllinger, Franziska Rauh, and Johanna Schmitt.

Mainz, May 29, 2021

---

18 Second Vatican Council, *Gaudium et spes*, no. 49.

—

Exegetical Substantiation

Thomas Hieke
Does the Old Testament Recognize and Condemn Homosexuality?

You shall not lie with a male as with a woman;
it is an abomination.
– Leviticus 18:22[1]

1 Task and Hermeneutics

Does the Old Testament have a concept of homosexuality? And if so, does it condemn homosexuality? The answer to both of these questions is a resounding "No." This may be surprising, especially when we consider the verse quoted above, Leviticus 18:22. Is this not a perfectly clear, plainly formulated, categorical rejection of homosexual practices? Nevertheless, it is scholarship's task to take a closer look at supposedly self-evident facts and to put them to the test. The alleged certainty that Holy Scripture – or more precisely, the Hebrew Bible or the Old Testament[2] – condemns same-sex sexual acts in every respect also shapes the Roman Catholic Church's current teachings on homosexuality, as articulated in the Catechism, for example (on which see below). In the Second Vatican Council's Dogmatic Constitution on Divine Revelation (*Dei Verbum*, 1965), the same Roman Catholic Church calls on biblical scholars to "carefully investigate what meaning the sacred writers really intended, and what God wanted to manifest by means of their words."[3] In what follows, I aim to fulfill this task. For this purpose, we first need to clarify certain preconditions and terminology. Then it will be worthwhile to explore the ancient Near Eastern environment that provides the context for Israel's Holy Scriptures, which Christians have adopted as

---

1 Unless otherwise noted, all biblical references are taken from the New Revised Standard Version (NRSV).

2 The term Old Testament already implies the Christian reception of Israel's Bible (the Hebrew Bible) as the first part of the Christian Bible. Nevertheless, Christianity also views the "Old Testament" as having its very own message, "an intrinsic word with intrinsic value." See Erich Zenger and Christian Frevel, "Heilige Schrift der Juden und der Christen," in *Einleitung in das Alte Testament*, ed. Christian Frevel et al. (Stuttgart: Verlag W. Kohlhammer, 2015), 20.

3 Second Vatican Council, *Dogmatic Constitution on Divine Revelation: Dei verbum* (Rome: Vatican, 1965), no. 12, http://www.vatican.va/archive/hist_councils/ii_vatican_council/documents/vat-ii_const_19651118_dei-verbum_en.html (accessed April 21, 2021).

https://doi.org/10.1515/9783110705188-002

their "Old Testament." On this basis, and against their historical background and the social framework of the time, I will analyze the "legal" provisions in the book of Leviticus, together with certain narrative texts. The results of this exploration raise the question of whether the Roman Catholic Church's handling of the Holy Scriptures in its Catechism is appropriate. In the concluding section, I would like to comment on this position as a biblical scholar.

Before we begin, a few hermeneutical clarifications are necessary. One cannot write "neutrally" on the topic of homosexuality, even if one tries to maintain a scholarly distance.[4] The subsequent remarks are not intended to conceal a "hidden agenda" under a scientific cloak, so I would like to clarify my position in advance: I consider any ostracization or disparagement of homosexuality and homosexual persons to be inhumane and also a violation of basic human rights and human dignity. Supposedly religiously motivated campaigns against homosexual people and their expressions of sexual love constitute manifestations of a hollow homophobia, which is merely concealed by alleged Christian, Jewish, or Muslim traditions. My aim is to show that the Hebrew Bible or the Old Testament cannot and must not be used to support a homophobic agenda. This raises the second hermeneutical problem: a direct "application" of the biblical texts to today's questions of sexual morality is impossible. When such applications are made regardless, it is most often with the intent to support preconceived, usually homophobic views with "proof texts" from the "Holy Scriptures" – texts that have been detached from their literary and socio-historical contexts. This process is highly selective: those texts which fit the preconceived worldview are "taken literally," while other passages are ignored. In contrast, the scriptural hermeneutics I apply in this contribution take the Old Testament seriously as Holy Scripture, insofar as the focus is always directed toward the overall context and the historical background of the text. The extent to which this provides impetus for today's sexual-ethical debates is another matter – one which can only be approached in an interdisciplinary manner.

2 Prerequisites and Terminology

The conception of what homosexuality really is has undergone quite significant changes in recent decades, as a result of findings in both the human and the so-

---

4 As James E. Harding's *The Love of David and Jonathan. Ideology, Text, Reception* (BibleWorld; Sheffield: Equinox, 2013) convincingly shows with regard to the David and Jonathan story and its interpretation; cf. also Martti Nissinen, *Homoeroticism in the Biblical World: A Historical Perspective* (Minneapolis: Fortress Press, 1998), 6.

cial sciences. We must take this into account in two respects. On the one hand, we must recognize the considerable time it takes for scientific insights to penetrate the general consciousness among broader segments of the population and to provoke changes in mentalities and moral attitudes in that sphere – here, one must reckon not in terms of years, but in terms of generations. On the other hand, maintaining an outdated view of a certain phenomenon that is no longer tenable according to scientific standards cannot be used as a basis on which to argue for adherence to moral and/or ethical norms. The moral judgment and ethical normalization of human sexuality is thus inextricably linked to that which characterizes this particular human sexuality. When this link is broken, an institution or a society may try to regulate a phenomenon that exists only in its imagination, and not in reality – in such cases, the established rules inevitably forfeit their relevance, and in the worst-case scenario, the norm-setting community loses its credibility.

To avoid falling into this trap in what follows, and to ensure that the term homosexuality is used to describe the reality that actually stands behind it (according to the current state of the field in the human and social sciences), I must briefly state that homosexuality is neither a (mental) illness that can be treated, nor a voluntary deviation from essentially heterosexual behavior. The individual discovers same-sex sexual orientation in the course of their personal development, and like any other sexual orientation, this must be integrated into a coherent concept of life (an identity).[5] Sexuality should never be reduced merely to the sexual act, but should be understood as a multi-dimensional phenomenon, which on the one hand is interconnected with the community in which the individual lives (i.e., social dimensions), and on the other hand is connected to the individual's personality (character) as a whole (i.e., psychological dimensions). Thus homosexuality as we understand it today includes – as does heterosexuality, naturally – questions of partnership, responsibility for the other person(s) and to the larger community (family, group, society), accountability, emotionality, respect, and much more. If these aspects are ignored, or if the term homosexuality is limited to same-sex sexual acts (among men) – in the following sections, the term homosexuality will be deliberately rendered in quotation marks when it is intended to represent such one-sided views – then it would be better not to speak of "homosexuality" at all, but rather of anal sexual intercourse among men, for which there can be many reasons.[6]

---

5 See, for example, Nissinen, *Homoeroticism*, 10, as well as his remarks in chapter 1.

6 Nissinen suggests using the term homoeroticism as a broader term for same-sex practices undertaken for any reason; this term could then include the phenomena described in ancient texts,

3 "Homosexuality" in Ancient Israel's Cultural Context

In the light of the above clarification of terms, we can safely assert that antiquity had neither a concept nor a concrete understanding of homosexuality as an aspect of an individual's personality in which sexuality and identity are integrated.[7] The general understanding of sexuality has changed considerably since then.[8] One aspect of this is the fact that in antiquity, public and private spheres were not as strictly separated as they are today, and thus sexual acts were more often judged with reference to their social dimension than with reference to the act itself.[9] Thus same-sex anal intercourse between men ("penetration") is almost never seen as an expression of a love relationship, but rather as a demonstration of power (sometimes associated with explicit violence) which the "superior," penetrating man exercises over the "inferior," penetrated man, who takes

---

to which the narrower term homosexuality – when linked to its contemporary understandings – cannot usually be applied. See Nissinen, *Homoeroticism*, 17.

7 See also Thomas Römer, "Homosexuality in the Hebrew Bible? Some Thoughts on Lev 18 and 20; Gen 19 and the David-Jonathan Narrative," in *Ahavah. Die Liebe Gottes im Alten Testament*, ed. Manfred Oeming (Leipzig: Evangelische Verlagsanstalt, 2018), 213–231.

8 For an overview, see Nissinen, *Homoeroticism*, 35; Martti Nissinen, "Are There Homosexuals in Mesopotamian Literature?" *Journal of the American Oriental Society* 130 (2010): 73–77. See also Stefan Scholz, "Homosexualität (NT)," Das wissenschaftliche Bibellexikon im Internet, September 2012, Punkt 3.4.4., https://www.bibelwissenschaft.de/stichwort/46910/ (accessed August 25, 2020). One aspect of this is that female homosexuality plays almost no role. The reasons for this become clear in the subsequent discussion: female homosexuality is not about penetration, nor is it about questions of superiority or inferiority, nor "honor" or "shame," nor action and military might. This eliminates women from the few contexts in which same-sex acts among men are spoken of at all. On this point, Nissinen's (*Homoeroticism*, 43) comments on the Hebrew Bible are relevant: "The Holiness Code never mentions women's homoeroticism, nor does the Hebrew Bible anywhere."

9 For example, in the case of regulations on opposite-sex relationships, the focus was on the question of whether the child who could potentially result from such a relationship would grow up in "well-ordered" circumstances and be entitled to a share of the inheritance, or whether the social fabric of society would be unbalanced as a result of the child's birth. Furthermore, it was also a question of financial and property laws, as well as of the "honor" and "disgrace" (i.e., the social reputation) of the man or the family as a whole. This can be seen, for example, in the biblical prohibitions on incest in Lev 18 and 20; cf. Thomas Hieke, *Levitikus 16–27* (HThKAT; Freiburg im Breisgau: Herder, 2014), 653–654.

on the gender-stereotypical role of the woman. The following sections offer some examples of this.[10]

3.1 The Ancient Near East

Very few relevant records from the Hittite civilization (second millennium BCE) exist. Of all the numerous Hittite ritual regulations in the Ḫattusa cuneiform archive, only two are pertinent to our discussion here.

The first concerns Anniwiyani, who recorded two rites on a tablet (CTH 393), one of which describes how she performs the ritual of two tutelary deities (ᵈLAMMA *lulimi-* ["LAMMA the effeminate"] and ᵈLAMMA *innarawant-* ["LAMMA the manly"]). This ritual was presumably performed when a man had "suffered" the passive role in a homoerotic sexual encounter, and it was intended to restore the penetrated man's "masculinity" and to ensure fertility (especially the bearing of male offspring). If this interpretation of the ritual is correct, then male anal intercourse is not a homosexual act as we understand it today, but rather a practice which aims to humiliate the penetrated man as "inferior." When the community in which the man lives learns of this act, a satisfactory performance of the aforementioned ritual is necessary to restore his original social status and to cleanse the community after this "attack."[11] In general, the Hittites clearly condemned incest and zoophilia (sexual intercourse with animals), but they did not comment on same-sex ("homosexual") intercourse in legal texts. Presumably the latter was not tolerated as "normal behavior," but a deviation from the norm was also not considered terribly serious – no prohibition was formulated; instead, a purification rite for the penetrated man was established.[12] The problem with the penetrated man's passivity here is that he engages in behavior that runs counter to his social role as an active warrior: he behaves not as a fighter, but rather like a woman who stays home during war, while the man who performs the penetra-

---

10 The number of references is very small in comparison to other topics we find in ancient sources. I would like to sincerely thank my colleague Doris Prechel (Mainz) for her valuable suggestions in the field of ancient Near Eastern literature.

11 Cf. Ilan Peled, "Expelling the Demon of Effeminacy: Anniwiyani's Ritual and the Question of Homosexuality in Hittite Thought," *Journal of Ancient Near Eastern Religions* 10, no. 1 (2010): 69–81, esp. 76. On CTH 393, see also ‹D. Bawanypeck (ed.), hethiter.net/: CTH 393 (INTR 2016–03–31)› (introduction; copy the "citatio" between ‹ › to your web browser; see *translatio* for a German translation).

12 Cf. Peled, "Expelling," 77.

tion is active and does exactly what is expected of a warrior. Therefore this is not an issue of sexual morality, but rather a conflict of social roles.

Second, although Paskuwatti's Ritual (CTH 406) was previously interpreted as a ritual intended to overcome sexual impotence, a more recent analysis follows a similar vein to the ritual outlined above: in this new perspective, the ritual aims to "heal" the "patient's" passive homosexual inclination. The process of stepping into the role which cultural tradition ascribes to women, by allowing oneself to be penetrated by a man, must be reversed so that the individual can once again be considered an actively aggressive, dominant male.[13] Again, this is not a question of sexuality in the context of partnership, but rather a social-behavioral role – one which is not permitted to a man, or which is seen as deficient and pathological. The "patient" is "missing something" – namely, reproductive success and sexual desire for the other (female) sex – and the ritual is supposed to cure him of this "disease." In addition to the "disturbed" distribution of social roles, another main reason why homosexual sexual behavior is taboo and must be "cured" is that it does not produce offspring.[14] Finally, we must bear in mind that the interpretation of the ritual text I have just described is merely a suggestion, and it is impossible to achieve any greater certainty about the exact meaning and social background of the actions described.

Mesopotamian literature pays some attention to the relationship between Gilgamesh and Enkidu. Scholarly research disputes whether theirs is a "homosexual" relationship or the ideal image of a deep "male friendship."[15] In general,

---

13 Cf. Jared L. Miller, "Paskuwatti's Ritual: Remedy for Impotence or Antidote to Homosexuality?" *Journal of Ancient Near Eastern Religions* 10, no. 1 (2010): 83–89, esp. 85. On CTH 406, see also ‹A. Mouton (ed.), hethiter.net/: CTH 406 (INTR 2017–01–12)› (introduction; see *translatio* for a French translation).

14 Cf. Miller, "Paskuwatti's Ritual," 87.

15 On this topic, see Jerrold S. Cooper, "Buddies in Babylonia: Gilgamesh, Enkidu, and Mesopotamian Homosexuality," in *Riches Hidden in Secret Places: Ancient Near Eastern Studies in Memory of Thorkild Jacobsen*, ed. Tzvi Abusch (Winona Lake: Eisenbrauns, 2002), 73–85; see also Nissinen, *Homoeroticism*, 20–24. In his critical edition of the Babylonian Epic of Gilgamesh, A. R. George interprets the corresponding lines (96–99) on Tablet XII of the Akkadian version in the sense of a memory of a pleasurable experience of anal intercourse between Gilgamesh and Enkidu, and thus assumes a "homosexual" relationship between the two (see also the explanations on pp. 529 and 903; Tablet XII is an appendix to the eleven-tablet epic and consists of the Akkadian translation of the Sumerian text "Bilgames and the Underworld"). However, since both "heroes" in the epic narrative also have explicit sexual relations with women (particularly Enkidu, who only turns from a wild animal into a human by means of his sexual encounter with the prostitute Šamhat), the sexual pleasure of the two friends is only one narrative facet of their close friendship. See Andrew R. George, *The Babylonian Gilgamesh Epic: Intro-*

however, "homosexuality" does not seem to have been a significant issue or problem in Mesopotamia.[16] Among the Mesopotamian omen texts from the first millennium BCE, known as the *šumma ālu*, tablets 103 and 104 address human sexuality. The first clause in each sentence (*protasis*) describes a certain behavior, and the second clause (*apodosis*) describes a subsequent fate. These tablets do not address regulations for sexual intercourse, but rather constitute an "observation of nature" (in analogy, for example, to the practice of divination based on reading the entrails, and particularly the livers of sacrificial animals) by which one hoped to gain insight into the future. An example related to male sexuality is the following: "If a man ejaculates in his dream and is spattered with his semen – that man will find riches; he will have financial gain."[17] In the same context, the following omen appears quite unusual: "If a man has anal sex with his peer – that man will be foremost among his brothers and colleagues."[18] This paradox is typical of the omen texts: he who penetrates his peer from behind is placed ahead of him in the social order. Same-sex intercourse among men who are on the same social level is seen as a sign of particular self-assertion.[19] Thus the omen texts are not instructions for action: the magic "works" only as long as the people concerned have no knowledge of the context. As soon as one's own behavior is calculated to achieve the outcome described as positive, the text no longer acts as an omen (another paradox). More important than the positive information are the apotropaic rituals associated with the negative outcome, which seek to avert the evil foretold by means of simple acts.

In the Middle Assyrian Laws, two provisions (MAL A 19 and MAL A 20) address same-sex intercourse among (socially equal) men, but 19 concerns a false accusation (a partner is falsely called a "prostitute"), while 20 takes up the issue

---

duction, *Critical Edition and Cuneiform Texts* (Oxford: Oxford University Press, 2003); see also Nissinen, *Homoeroticism*, 24.

16 Cf. Cooper, "Buddies in Babylonia," 82; see also Jean Bottéro and Herbert Petschow, "Homosexualität," in *Reallexikon der Assyriologie und Vorderasiatischen Archäologie*, vol. 4, ed. Erich Ebeling, Ernst F. Weidner, and Dietz Otto Edzard (Berlin: De Gruyter, 1972–1975), 459–468.
17 Cf. Ann Kessler Guinan, "Erotomancy: Scripting the Erotic," in *Sex and Gender in the Ancient Near East. Proceedings of the 47th Rencontre Assyriologique Internationale, Helsinki, July 2–6, 2001*, ed. Simo Parpola and Robert M. Whiting (Helsinki: Helsinki University Press, 2002), 185–201, 188; see also Nissinen, *Homoeroticism*, 27 f.; Idan Dershowitz, "Revealing Nakedness and Concealing Homosexual Intercourse. Legal and Lexical Evolution in Leviticus 18," *Hebrew Bible and Ancient Israel* 6 (2017): 510–526, esp. 522.
18 Cf. Guinan, "Erotomancy," 189.
19 Cf. Cooper, "Buddies in Babylonia," 82, with a reference to p. 74 of an older essay by Thorkild Jacobsen, "How Did Gilgamesh Oppress Uruk?" *Acta Orientalia* 8 (1930): 62–74.

of rape.[20] "Homosexuality" as such is not condemned, although this is a controversial point even among scholars.[21] The problem here, as in the Greek thinking of the time, is that only a certain type of same-sex intercourse among men is criminalized: while active "homosexual" anal intercourse with male prostitutes or slaves was not a problem, it was socially unacceptable for a man to actively anally penetrate a citizen who was equal to him without his consent (!), because the latter constituted a deliberate act of humiliation.[22] Such an act endangers the complex social fabric of reciprocal relationships. Those who passively allowed this to happen to them without resisting thereby forfeited their civil rights.[23]

While the conditions in Assyria and Greece were very different, their attitudes toward homosexual acts are quite comparable: it is shameful to be penetrated by a man of equal status, and it is an act of assault to penetrate a fellow citizen. The omen quoted above also aligns with this: whoever penetrates a man of equal status proves himself to be assertive because he can humiliate others and no one opposes him.[24] None of this has anything to do with homosexuality in today's sense. Martti Nissinen summarizes his findings on Mesopotamian literature as follows:

> So are there homosexuals in Mesopotamian literature? This is ultimately something that can only be decided by the community using the category of homosexuality. If love between people of same sex, sexual coercion, random homoerotic encounters, and a gender-neutral sexual role are not considered expressions of homosexuality, as I believe they are not, then the answer is inevitably "no." Perhaps the most important outcome of the above discussion is how little sense it makes to strain "homosexual" lumps out of the gravy of ancient literature, even when this is done in order to find out how the modern concept of homosexuality works in texts to whose authors the whole concept was unknown.[25]

---

20 See, for example, Nissinen, *Homoeroticism*, 25.
21 Cf. Cooper, "Buddies in Babylonia," 83.
22 On this topic, see also Nissinen, *Homoeroticism*, 26–27, with further examples of anal penetration as an act of violence used to humiliate one's inferiors.
23 Cf. Cooper, "Buddies in Babylonia," 84, with reference to Kenneth Dover, *Greek Homosexuality* (London: Duckworth, 1978), 103; see also Nissinen, *Homoeroticism*, 57–69; cf. Scholz, "Homosexualität (NT)," Punkt 3.2.
24 Cf. Cooper, "Buddies in Babylonia," 85.
25 Nissinen, "Homosexuals," 76.

3.2 Ancient Egypt

In pharaonic Egypt,[26] only a few sources attest to sexual acts between same-sex couples (men), and these are exclusively textual. Most of these testimonies are linked to the myth of Horus and Seth. These two gods quarrel over the succession to the throne: after Seth kills his brother Osiris, he claims Osiris's throne, as does Horus, Osiris's son. One of the incidents, which the ancient Egyptian religious texts often allude to, is the sexual act between the gods, by means of which Seth seeks to triumph over Horus.

The most detailed elaboration of this episode has been preserved in Papyrus Chester Beatty I, recto (ca. 1140 BCE), which describes how Seth penetrates the young Horus and subsequently reports this to the "great Ennead." The gods' reaction clarifies their appraisal of this event: they "cry out loud" and "spit out before Horus."[27] The semen – which is described elsewhere as a poison, which one does not want to have in one's body[28] – plays an important role in this story. Luckily, Horus is able to catch Seth's semen before it enters his body, without Seth noticing it. Furthermore, Isis succeeds in transferring her son Horus's semen to a lettuce plant, and Seth eats the plant. Since Horus's semen comes out of Seth's body in the presence of the Ennead of the gods, in response to the god Thot's invocation, Horus thus proves that Seth is in fact the inferior of the two.[29] Although Horus emerges victorious from this event, he is nevertheless defiled by the humiliation of having been penetrated (see the discussion of the Hittite purification rite above). Both his hand, with which he caught Seth's semen, and his phallus need purification: when Horus holds out Seth's collected semen to his mother Isis with the words: "Come and see what Seth did to me," she cries out, cuts off his defiled hand, throws it into the water, grows him a new one, and cleanses his phallus with "soothing oil."

An older, fragmented text (Papyrus Kahun VI, ca. 1800 BCE) also describes how Horus and his mother thwart Seth's plans.[30] Due to the fact that the papyrus

---

26 The section on ancient Egypt was written by the Egyptologist Dr. Andrea Klug (Mainz).
27 Cf. Friedrich Junge, "Die Erzählung vom Streit der Götter Horus und Seth um die Herrschaft," in *Texte aus der Umwelt des Alten Testaments. Alte Folge*, vol. 3, ed. Otto Kaiser (Gütersloh: Gütersloher Verlagshaus Mohn, 1995), 930–950, esp. 944f; Miriam Lichtheim, *Ancient Egyptian Literature, vol. II: The New Kingdom* (Berkeley/Los Angeles/London: University of California Press, 1976), 214–223, esp. 220.
28 Cf. Wolfhart Westendorf, "Homosexualität," in *Lexikon der Ägyptologie*, vol. 2, ed. Wolfgang Helck (Wiesbaden: Harrassowitz Verlag, 1977), 1272.
29 Cf. Junge, "Streit der Götter," 945.
30 Cf. Frank Röpke, "Überlegungen zum 'Sitz im Leben' der Kahuner Homosexuellen Episode zwischen Horus und Seth (pKahun VI.12 = pUniversity College London 32158, rto.)," in *Das Er-

is in bad condition, we can only guess at the context of the scene. Ostensibly on the basis of sexual desire, Seth compliments Horus on his "beautiful buttocks" and "broad thighs," perhaps with the aim of disparaging his younger counterpart by assigning him female attributes. Against the background of the satirically constructed story in the Chester Beatty I papyrus, these statements may sound like sheer irony to our ears, as does Seth's claim that for him, the act was "sweeter than the sky is high." Before the act occurs, Horus tells his mother Isis that Seth is making sexual advances to him. She gives him three pieces of advice: 1) to keep away from Seth; 2) if this is not possible, to tell Seth that he is physically inferior to him and that such an act would be painful for him; 3) if the act cannot ultimately be prevented, to put his fingers between his buttocks during the course of it – again most probably with the aim of catching Seth's semen. The remaining passages, which mention semen and the phallus, among other things, are barely intelligible. They appear to refer to another of Seth's sexual advances to Horus, and in this way diverge from the version of the later papyrus, Chester Beatty I.[31]

These attestations indicate the one-sidedness of the sexual act, in contrast to the earliest evidence from the Pyramid Texts (PT 1036, ca. 2300 BCE), which speaks of reciprocity: "Seth shrieks (now) because of his testicles, after Horus has infused his semen into Seth's anus, after Seth has infused his semen into Horus's anus."[32] But here again superiority is the decisive factor, albeit an alternating superiority in this case.

Although space does not allow me to go into further details, the above-mentioned main textual witnesses to the sexual act between the gods Horus and Seth show that this act – as already stated above with regard to the ancient Near East-

---

zählen in frühen Hochkulturen I. Der Fall Ägypten, ed. Hubert Roeder (Munich: Fink, 2009), 239 – 290, esp. 249 f., 288 – 290; cf. Richard B. Parkinson, "'Homosexual' Desire and Middle Kingdom Literature," *The Journal of Egyptian Archaeology* 81 (1995): 57 – 76, esp. 70 f.

31 Cf. Röpke, "Überlegungen," 249 f. A passage in Papyrus Cairo JE 52000 (ca. 1290 BCE) also refers to the myth of Horus and Seth: it speaks of Seth's semen leaving Horus's belly again by means of a spell; cf. ibid, 260 f. Against the background of this evidence, and taking into account the textual remnants that precede the "homosexual episode" in the Kahun papyrus, Röpke arrives at a new interpretation of the Kahun text as a "magical"-therapeutic text connecting an abdominal infection ("poison in the abdomen") with the mythological story of Horus and Seth ("semen in the abdomen"); cf. ibid., 267.

32 Simplified after Röpke's translation in "Überlegungen," 262. Röpke believes that the reciprocal penetration in the Pyramid Text spell has no reference to Horus and Seth's disputes over the throne, which in his opinion were introduced only later. Instead he explains this reciprocity as "royal ideological dualism" in the context of a protective charm against snakebites; see ibid., 263 f.; cf. Parkinson, "'Homosexual' Desire," 65.

ern texts – has nothing to do with same-sex love, but rather indicate that one of the participants proves his superiority over the other by penetrating him. Any evaluation implied in the episode, which is obviously shaped differently in the various textual accounts, can only ever be considered text-immanently and thus contextually, and must not be misinterpreted as a general attitude.[33]

One fragmented text, which can be assigned to the genre of literature, seems to be about same-sex love. In Papyrus Chassinat I (ca. 700 BCE), a king named Neferkare is said to have sneaked out of the palace night after night to spend four hours in the home of his general, Sasenet, where he did "what he wanted with him."[34] Since this phrase is a euphemism for sexual intercourse, as confirmed by other parallels, the facts seem clear. However, because the text breaks off at this point, there are no explicit references to the detailed circumstances, the outcome, or the assessment of the encounter. The secrecy of the deed and the rumors swirling around it could suggest condemnation, and the document may be an effort to defame the king by telling this story.[35] On the other hand, there are convincing arguments that this episode is a parody of the repeated nightly union of the sun god Ra (= the king) and the god of the dead, Osiris (= the general), in the underworld,[36] which again qualifies this interpretation.

Among the religious texts, the first to mention is the evidence from the so-called Negative Confession in the Egyptian Book of the Dead (ca. 1500 BCE). In this declaration, which the deceased is to make in front of a tribunal of gods during the Judgment of the Dead, one of the wrongdoings that he assures them he has not committed is: "I have not penetrated (*nk*) a *nkk* (= a man on whom a sexual act is performed)" (BD, chapter 125b).[37] Thus we see that such an act clearly

---

33 Even if the reaction of the Ennead in the Chester Beatty I papyrus is intended to condemn Horus's passive position, we cannot therefore automatically deduce that the act itself and the active part of the connection are generally considered "neutral"; cf. Westendorf, "Homosexualität," 1272.

34 Frank Kammerzell, "Von der Affäre um König Nafirku'ri'a und seinen General," in *Texte aus der Umwelt des Alten Testaments. Alte Folge*, vol. 3, ed. Otto Kaiser (Gütersloh: Gütersloher Verlagshaus Mohn, 1995), 965–969, esp. 968 f. (Nafirku'ri'a Pijapij und Sisenet); Parkinson, "'Homosexual' Desire," 71–74.

35 See also Parkinson, "'Homosexual' Desire," 72–73; Westendorf, "Homosexualität," 1273.

36 Cf. Jacobus van Dijk, "The Nocturnal Wanderings of King Neferkarēᶜ," in *Hommages à Jean Leclant Vol. 4*, ed. Catherine Berger (LeCaire: Inst. Français d'Archéologie Orientale, 1994), 387–393.

37 Cf. Parkinson, "'Homosexual' Desire," 61–62. The repeatedly quoted phrase "I have not penetrated (*nk*) a *ḥm.t ṯȝy*," which is also found in the Negative Confession, should be translated as "a man's wife (= married woman)" rather than "a female man"; cf. Rainer Hannig, *Großes Handwörterbuch Ägyptisch-Deutsch (Marburger Edition)* (Kulturgeschichte der Antiken Welt 64; Mainz: von Zabern, 2006), 1016 f.

did not correspond to the official ideal, and thus not to the ancient Egyptian principle of Maat (cosmic order).[38] In the Coffin Texts (spell 635; CT VI, 258 f–g; ca. 2000 BCE), we find the following passage: "(the god) Atum has no power over NN (= the name of the deceased). NN penetrates (*nks*) his anus (*ꜥr.t*)."[39] This statement, which is difficult to interpret, can at least be understood to mean that the issue is once again the power one person exercised over another.

From the field of didactic literature, a passage in the thirty-second maxim of the Teaching of Ptahhotep (ca. 2000 BCE) must be consulted. Recent translations of the controversial phrase *jmj=k nk ḥm.t ẖrd* cast doubt on the interpretation as a fundamental rejection of a homosexual relationship.[40] In fact, it admonishes the recipient of the teaching not to engage in sexual contact with another person against his or her will: "You shall not copulate with a woman (or) a child (if) you have recognized the resistance to the seminal fluid (literally: water) on his (or her) forehead."[41]

Evidence of a complaint against a man who "defiled" (*ḥꜥ*) another man is preserved in Papyrus Turin 1887 (verso 3,4, ca. 1140 BCE).[42] However, there is no evidence for legal texts addressing the subject of "homosexuality," nor is there textual or other evidence for female "homosexuality." Moreover, the alleged pictorial evidence, which is repeatedly referenced, can be more convincingly explained in other ways.[43]

---

38 Cf. Parkinson, "'Homosexual' Desire," 62.

39 Cf. ibid., 64.

40 Cf., for example: "May you not have sex with a woman-boy;" Parkinson, "'Homosexual' Desire," 68.

41 Peter Dils, "Die Lehre des Ptahhotep, pPrisse = pBN 186–194 (Ptahhotep, Version P)," Thesaurus Linguae Aegyptiae, http://aaew.bbaw.de/tla/index.html (accessed August 27, 2020). This version is perhaps preferable to the original proposal, "with a woman or a boy"; cf. Frank Kammerzell and María Isabel Toro Rueda, "Nicht der Homosexuelle ist pervers. Die Zweiunddreißigste Maxime der Lehre des Ptahhotep," *Lingua Aegyptia* 22 (2003): 63–78, esp. 74.

42 Cf. Parkinson, "'Homosexual' Desire," 66; cf. Günter Vittmann, "Hieratic Texts," in *The Elephantine Papyri in English: Three Millennia of Cross-cultural Continuity and Change*, ed. Bezalel Porten (Atlanta: Society of Biblical Literature, 2011), 63–78, esp. 56.

43 See, for example, the unusual depictions of Niankhkhnum and Khnumhotep (ca. 2400 BCE), who are shown in their joint tomb at Saqqara in a close embrace, while depicted in other scenes with their wives, which rather suggests that they were probably twins; cf. Parkinson, "'Homosexual' Desire," 62; see also Richard B. Parkinson, *Little Gay History. Desire and Diversity Across the World* (London: British Museum Press, 2013), 39. Some of the discussions about the interpretation of these representations in particular have been very emotional in recent years, but there is not space to discuss this in detail here. The most recent literature, including drawings and photographs of the relevant scenes from the tomb, is accessible via Beryl Büma and Martin Fitzen-

The few extant sources[44] – which are explored here by means of their principal exemplars – which tend to be discussed with reference to the topic of ancient Egyptian homosexuality have as little to do with homosexuality as we understand it today as do the ancient Near Eastern sources. They constitute evidence of same-sex sexual intercourse among men (gods as well as humans), probably exclusively with the aim of suppressing the inferior partner. No general evaluation of same-sex relationships can be derived from this.

4 The Regulations in the Book of Leviticus

As an ancient document, the Hebrew Bible has no explicit concept of homosexuality either.[45] "Homosexuality" in the sense of same-sex anal intercourse is addressed in only two places, and in the same context: in the book of Leviticus. The regulations in Leviticus chapters 18 and 20 do not constitute a comprehensive concept of human sexual orientation, nor do they reflect a sophisticated sexual morality. Rather, under specific historical, social, and cultural circumstances, they take aim at individual acts, which are rejected and outlawed. To some extent these acts are accompanied by sanctions, the meaning and feasibility of which may be deliberately obscure. More detailed justifications are not explicitly

---

reiter, "'Spielt das Lied der beiden göttlichen Brüder': Erotische Ambiguität und 'große Nähe' zwischen Männern im Alten Reich," *Studien zur altägyptischen Kultur* 44 (2015): 19 – 42. With regard to Büma and Fitzenreiter's article, I would like to point out – after consulting new photographs, which Dr. Heimo Hohneck (Mainz) has kindly made available to me – that the reading of a part of the inscription, which accompanies a scene with a harpist, as "the two divine brothers" (*sn.wj nṯr.wj*) is in my opinion not correct, because there are in fact no dual strokes. Cf. the article by Hartwig Altenmüller, "Väter, Brüder und Götter – Bemerkungen zur Szene der Übergabe der Lotosblüte," in *"Zur Zierde gereicht …". Festschrift Bettina Schmitz zum 60. Geburtstag am 24. Juli 2008*, ed. Antje Spiekermann (Hildesheim: Gerstenberg, 2008), 17– 28, esp. 25 – 28, where he speaks of "the divine brother" ("*sn nṯrw*") and compares the inscription with texts found in other tombs.

44 For a discussion of further evidence, cf. Parkinson, "'Homosexual' Desire"; see also Alessia Amenta, "Some Reflections on the 'Homosexual' Intercourse Between Horus and Seth," *Göttinger Miszellen* 199 (2004): 7– 21; Beate Schukraft, "Homosexualität im Alten Ägypten," *Studien zur altägyptischen Kultur* 36 (2007): 297– 331.

45 The sources are very sparse and hardly allow one to draw any conclusions about the phenomenon of same-sex sexual behavior in ancient Israel; cf. Nissinen, *Homoeroticism*, 37. See also Innocent Himbaza, Adrian Schenker, and Jean-Baptiste Edart, *The Bible on the Question of Homosexuality* (Washington, DC: Catholic University of America Press, 2012), 5.

given, but these can be inferred from the order of the provisions, and thus from the context.[46]

The verse I cited at the beginning of this contribution, Leviticus 18:22, seems to prohibit "homosexual" acts between men with commendable clarity: "You shall not lie with a male as with a woman. It is an abomination."[47] This supposedly categorical rejection would be unprecedented and exceptional against the ancient Near Eastern background I have outlined above,[48] and it also functions

---

46 For further details, see the commentary in Hieke, *Levitikus*, 645–697, 770–813; see also Römer, "Homosexuality," 214–218.

47 On the following, see the commentary in Hieke, *Levitikus*, 688–690, with further evidence from the secondary literature. The wording in Lev 18:22 is clearly intended to be understood as same-sex anal intercourse between men, with one of the partners taking the "underdog" (in both senses of the word!) role of the "woman" – that is to say, this wording also follows "classic" gender role stereotypes: "active masculine and passive feminine gender roles"; see Nissinen, *Homoeroticism*, 44. With Nissinen (ibid.), we note: "it was the act that was condemned, not same-sex desire, the existence of which is not even acknowledged." Some scholars point out that these proscriptions were directed at the actions of the receptive rather than the penetrative party – that is, the text addresses the actions of the receptive party. See Jerome T. Walsh, "Leviticus 18:22 and 20:13: Who Is Doing What to Whom?" *JBL* 120 (2001): 201–209; George M. Hollenback, "Who Is Doing What to Whom Revisited: Another Look at Leviticus 18:22 and 20:13," *JBL* 136 (2017): 529–537. Dershowitz ("Nakedness," 510–520) suggests that Lev 18:14 originally read: "Do not uncover the nakedness of your father's brother." Hence this version prohibits a male same-sex relationship only if the partners are related by blood (in this case, between uncle and nephew). This wording would implicitly permit same-sex sexual intercourse among non-consanguineous males. A later redactor, however, edited the text according to the premises of the Holiness Code and changed the sense of the prohibition entirely by adding "do not approach his wife; she is your aunt." Thus the prohibited sexual intercourse refers to the aunt. This addition obscured the prohibition of same-sex relations between consanguineous males, but the same editor wanted to prohibit male same-sex anal intercourse in general. In order to do so, he added Lev 18:22 and 20:13 (p. 516), and thus created something new in the context of the ancient Near East. See Bruce Wells, "On the Beds of a Woman: The Leviticus Texts on Same-Sex Relations Reconsidered," in *Sexuality and Law in the Torah*, ed. Hilary Lipka and Bruce Wells (London: T & T Clark, 2020) 125–160, in which Wells argues that the phrase *miškəbê 'iššâ* in Leviticus 18:22 refers to the sexual domain of a woman, which "means that the men with whom the law's addressees may not have sex are qualified as males who are off limits by virtue of a relationship that they have with a particular woman. Sex with married men, therefore, would be forbidden as well as sex with any males who are under the guardianship of a woman within the community" (p. 158). Even according to this interpretation, Leviticus 18:22 and 20:13 do not refer to the modern concept of homosexuality.

48 Dershowitz ("Nakedness," 523–525) and Römer ("Homosexuality," 217) point out that this prohibition might be due to the influence of Persian laws. In the Avesta, the holy book of Zoroastrianism, one finds a passage that demonstrates considerable similarities with Lev 18:22, declaring that a man who lies with mankind as a man lies with womankind is a Daêva or worshipper of the Daêvas (evil deities or demons); Vendidad/Videvdad 8:32. See the English translation

in this way only when the sentence is extracted from its context. However, such neglect of the literary context in which this "prohibition" is handed down is both impossible from the perspective of general biblical hermeneutical principles (see above) and detrimental to an adequate literary understanding of the text. It is precisely the context that provides the key to understanding the prohibition in Leviticus 18:22, and thus its purview as well. Leviticus 18:21, the verse which comes immediately before the verse in question, concerns the prohibition of "giving one of one's descendants over to Molech" (my translation). This puzzling turn of phrase has often been and continues to be read as a prohibition on cultic child sacrifice. However, the context and the socio-historical situation of the post-exilic period (when the Persians ruled Judah/Jerusalem) as the text's original setting seems to suggest a more appropriate alternative: the "Molech" prohibition is a cipher for prohibiting Israelites from offer their children to the foreign occupying power (the Persian king, in Hebrew: *melek*[49]). Thus the priestly authors of Leviticus forbid a lucrative form of collaboration with the occupiers, which – from the authors' point of view – resulted in the loss of a young member of one's own religious community: in other words, whoever "gave his child over to Moloch" made the child available to the Persian officials, effectively giving the child away, so that the child learned and adopted a foreign religion and was thus lost to one's own community.[50]

The verse following Leviticus 18:22 addresses the prohibition on sexual intercourse with animals, for both men and women (Lev 18:23). Whether this was due to the fear of dangerous hybrids or demons is an open question. If one reads Leviticus 18:21–23 in context, then the common denominator is clear: these verses

---

by James Darmesteter, *The Zend-Avesta* (SBE04; Oxford: Clarendon Press, 1880), http://www.sacred-texts.com/zor/sbe04/sbe0414.htm (accessed August 6, 2020).

49 The Hebrew word for "king" has the same consonants as "Molech."

50 On this topic, see Hieke, *Levitikus*, 679–688; see also Thomas Hieke, "Das Verbot der Übergabe von Nachkommen an den 'Molech' in Lev 18 und 20. Ein neuer Deutungsversuch," *Die Welt des Orients* 41 (2011): 147–167; and Thomas Hieke, "The Prohibition of Transferring an Offspring to 'the Molech.' No Child Sacrifice in Leviticus 18 and 20," in *Writing a Commentary on Leviticus. Hermeneutics – Methodology – Themes*, ed. Christian Eberhart and Thomas Hieke (Göttingen: Vandenhoeck & Ruprecht, 2019), 171–199. If one subscribes to this interpretation, Nissinen's somewhat dubious assumptions (*Homoeroticism*, 39–41) about a cultic-theological background to the prohibition of same-sex practices are also invalid. Jan Joosten ("A New Interpretation of Leviticus 18:22 [Par. 20:13] and Its Ethical Implications," *The Journal of Theological Studies NS* 71 [2020]: 1–10, here 2 n. 4) states that the "implications of this prohibition [in Lev 18:21] are very unclear." According to my interpretation of the entire section of Leviticus 18 mentioned in the publications above, all the prescriptions relate to one and the same plausible theme: the production and protection of the community's offspring.

aim to prevent progeny being lost to one's own religious community, whether by child sacrifice (less likely) or by handing children over to the foreign occupying power (more likely); whether through engaging (exclusively) in same-sex anal intercourse among men; or whether through engaging (exclusively) in sexual intercourse with animals. In addition, and in the same vein, there is a prohibition against having sexual intercourse with a menstruating woman (Lev 18:19); in this case as well, procreation does not occur. Thus the goal of these prohibitions is to strengthen one's own community by having as many descendants as possible. For the very small community of YHWH worshippers in Jerusalem and the Persian province of Yehud in the historical epoch in which these texts were written, this was a question of survival. Thus there was no place for someone who evaded the duty to procreate and did not produce and raise offspring. In the overall context of the chapter, as well as in the specific socio-historical situation at the time of its composition, these verses made plausible sense. Since in this case the Bible was less interested in individual personal happiness or individual preferences than in the stability of the community, the text pronounces clear prohibitions in relation to a complex world.[51] Tensions between men as a result of disordered sexual activity should not be permitted to arise,[52] nor should male sexuality be unproductive.[53] All of this has little to do with the conditions in which we live today. Thus a direct transposition in the literal sense is impossible.[54] A categorical condemnation of homosexual practices or even inclinations

---

[51] See Himbaza, Schenker, and Edart, *Homosexuality*, 134–135.

[52] See, for example, Gérald Caron, "Le Lévitique condemnerait-il l'homosexualité? De l'exégèse à l'herméneutique," *Studies in Religion/Sciences Religieuses* 38 (2009): 27–49, esp. 34. The protection of the communal order shaped by familial structures and laws is very important for the interpretation of Leviticus 18 and 20. Joosten ("New Interpretation," 1–10) has argued convincingly in this direction. He demonstrates that the laws in Leviticus 18:22 and 20:13 prohibit homosexual intercourse involving a married man. One might debate the anachronistic use of the term homosexual here; I would rather suggest the neutral expression "same-sex." Joosten leaves open the question of why Leviticus prohibits same-sex relations in which at least one partner is a married man. In sum, his suggestion fits quite well with my observations on the texts, as I have explained them above.

[53] See also Himbaza, Schenker, and Edart, *Homosexuality*, 69–71 (A. Schenker).

[54] See also the question in Jay Sklar's article, "The Prohibitions against Homosexual Sex in Leviticus 18:22 and 20:13: Are They Relevant Today?" *Bulletin for Biblical Research* 28 (2018): 165–198. Sklar explores whether the prohibitions against homosexual sex in Leviticus 18:22 and 20:13 have ongoing relevance today. He begins by noting that the use of the term abomination in these verses does not settle the question. He then considers three different types of responses to the question: (1) the prohibitions do not apply today because Leviticus does not apply today; (2) the prohibitions do not apply today because the reason this activity was prohibited in Leviticus no longer applies today; or (3) the prohibitions do apply today because the rea-

is therefore also impossible to draw from this Bible verse (as well as its counterpart in Lev 20:13, on which see below).[55]

If we look at the conclusion of the verse in Leviticus 18:22, we see that same-sex anal intercourse is called an "abomination." In the Bible (e. g., Deuteronomy, Proverbs), this term is used to condemn the worship of foreign gods, the practice of magic, the use of false weights in measurement, and similar social and cultic offenses. The argument is as follows: the condemned behavior does not please God and therefore triggers God's wrath, and it is better to refrain from provoking God in this way. Thus it is not an issue of human judicial bodies or moral guardians being called to action; rather, it is a religious proscription of certain behavior, and it is left up to God to decide how to enact his wrath upon the person in question.[56] This textual nuance alone is sufficient to make it clear that the Bible can in no way be used to justify the criminal prosecution of homosexuals.[57]

Turning to Leviticus chapter 20, however, almost all the prohibitions in Leviticus 18 – most of which concern incestuous sexual unions – are linked with penalties. Leviticus 20:13 picks up Leviticus 18:22: "If a man lies with a male as with a woman, both of them have committed an abomination; they shall be put to death; their blood is upon them." The assumption of an alleged "death penalty" goes back to a problematic mistranslation: the phrase "they shall be

---

son this activity was prohibited in Leviticus still applies today. Thus Sklar puts to the test or even questions all the hermeneutical points of view that occur in discussions on these biblical passages today. The only point that ultimately remains to be made is that the book of Leviticus leans heavily on the gender roles evident in the creation story (Gen 1) and therefore retains its relevance on the basis of this biblical text. However, this raises two critical issues: First, the reference to Genesis 1 in Leviticus 18 and 20 is not very pronounced on a literary level; one might even say that it does not exist, at least not explicitly. Second, it is by no means proven that the statements about humankind's manifestation in two sexes (or genders?) in Genesis 1 permit sexual relations exclusively between a man and a woman. This assumption is thus a *petitio principii*.

55 Cf. Hieke, *Levitikus*, 690. Markus Zehnder's view – in "Homosexualität (AT)," Das wissenschaftliche Bibellexikon im Internet, March 2008, Punkt 3.5, https://www.bibelwissenschaft. de/stichwort/21490/ (accessed September 1, 2020) – that the verses in Leviticus concern "all kinds of sexual acts, including those which, according to a modern definition, are performed in mutual love by equal, consenting partners" is tenable only if one completely disregards their literary context. Isolating verses in this way, however, is problematic from a biblical hermeneutical point of view.

56 Cf. Caron, "Le Lévitique," 36.

57 In the long history of criminal punishment for homosexual behavior, the Bible has almost never been used as a legal argument. Justifications for such punishment have run along other lines, such as natural law, the common good, "public opinion," or "common sense."

put to death" must not simply be equated with a "death penalty."[58] The terminology in Leviticus 18:22 (the word "abomination") is more likely to call to mind God's punishment than human jurisdiction. A detailed examination of the Hebrew phrase *mot yumat*, which should be translated "he will certainly be killed" (and also occurs in the plural), has shown that, despite its many attestations, a death penalty in the modern sense can never be presumed. In cases in which a human being kills another human being (manslaughter or murder), the legal instrument of blood vengeance takes effect: the closest relative of the slain or murdered person must kill the one who committed manslaughter or murder. The relative then goes unpunished, since the blood of the slain perpetrator is upon the perpetrator themself (and no longer requires atonement), while the victim's spilled blood has been atoned for. In all other cases, rather than expressing a penal provision, the phrase is parenetic – it constitutes an urgent exhortation.[59] Thus there is no human authority behind the passive voice, but rather God himself (*passivum divinum*). As a kind of divine punishment, God himself will call the perpetrator or perpetrators to account and will ensure their death – by whatever means. What we find in Leviticus 20:13 is one such urgent admonition, not a penal provision.[60] The behavior proscribed as an "abomination" (that which displeases God) in Leviticus 18:22 is subject to God's punishment in Leviticus 20:13 and is thus presented with the greatest possible urgency (as are many other acts, incidentally) as something which absolutely must be avoided. Once again, it comes down to hermeneutics: while contemporary societies may share many of the incest prohibitions in Leviticus chapters 18 and 20 and we may see them similarly in our culture, this does not mean that the verses should be taken "literally," with no hermeneutical mediation. Every Bible verse requires careful interpretation; it is only in the case of the skin diseases discussed in Leviticus 13 or the animal sacrifices in Leviticus 1–7 that it becomes more obvious that these texts are not to be understood "literally." An appropriate hermeneutics must also take into account the conditions of life at the time the texts were written: a small religious community under foreign rule, with its identity under

---

58 For further details on this topic, see Thomas Hieke, "Das Alte Testament und die Todesstrafe," *Biblica* 85 (2004): 349–374. The term "death penalty," as used by Nissinen (*Homoeroticism*, 37) and many others, is thus most likely misleading.

59 Nissinen (*Homoeroticism*, 37) states this explicitly: "In no way can the [holiness] code be likened to civil or criminal law in the modern sense of the word. It might instead be compared to a catechism that teaches Israelites, especially adult males, God's will and, accordingly, the rules for just behavior."

60 Cf. Himbaza, Schenker, and Edart, *Homosexuality*, 63: "The death penalty is used as a warning, not as a penal norm" (A. Schenker).

threat, was in urgent need of descendants, and under the guidance of its priestly theologians it strives to live rightly, to ensure stability and order. The circumstances of our lives today are completely different; it is no longer a matter of "descendants at any price," and yet stability, reliability, order, loyalty, and responsibility are enduring values. A successful transformation of the biblical prohibition – one which takes the word of God in human words seriously, but not "literally"[61] – could go like this: the highest goal of the regulations in Leviticus 18 – 20 (and in the Torah more generally) is successful communal life (see the key verse in Lev 18:5), and every form of human sexual activity must take this into consideration. What best serves the cohesion, the peace, and the happiness of the individual and the community? Certainly not the homophobic terrorization of a minority which, in its specific sexual orientation and expression, cannot follow an imposed code of conduct. God's commandment is not a one-size-fits-all solution that "applies" in the same way always and everywhere, regardless of different life circumstances; it is the word of the living God, which speaks to different readers in different historical periods from the same textual vantage point, and which intends to lead them down the path to true life. According to this principle, Leviticus 18:22 and 20:13 call for responsible sexuality, taking into account the broader community and the social dimensions of sex, but not for a rigid prohibition of all homosexual behavior.

Let us reflect once again on these passages in Leviticus with reference to the question in the title of this contribution: "Does the Old Testament recognize and condemn homosexuality?" On the basis of the text, we have established that there is no mention of homosexuality as we understand it today, but only of same-sex anal intercourse with the ejaculation of semen, and that such mentions occur in a context dominated by the principle that the community requires descendants. Thus the Hebrew Bible (or the "Old Testament," if we want to emphasize the Christian perspective), as is the case across the whole of antiquity, does not recognize our contemporary concept of homosexuality and does not address the question of sexual identity or orientation. Therefore the Old Testament does not condemn homosexuality. What the text condemns are forms of sexual behavior that place one's own pleasure and sexual satisfaction above the good of the community, or that disregard the social dimensions of human sexuality.[62]

---

61 See Pinchas Lapide's well-known quotation: "There are basically only two ways of dealing with the Bible: one can take it literally, or one can take it seriously. The two together get along very poorly"; see Pinchas Lapide, *Ist die Bibel richtig übersetzt?* (Gütersloh: Gütersloher Verlagshaus Haus Mohn, 1987), 12.

62 On this topic, see also Thomas Pola, "'Und bei einem Manne sollst du nicht liegen, wie man bei einer Frau liegt: Ein Greuel ist es.' Der literarische und sozialgeschichtliche Zusammenhang

In this sense, the Bible still has much to teach us in terms of sexual morality today.[63]

5 Narrative Passages in the Hebrew Bible

In the history of biblical interpretation, four narrative passages in the Hebrew Bible have been heavily associated with same-sex sexuality between men. Yet this much we can say in advance: none of them have anything to do with homosexuality in today's sense.[64]

For much of history, "homosexuality" – more specifically anal intercourse among men – has been referred to as "sodomy."[65] This term is a reference to the story told in Genesis 19: Lot, living as a "stranger" in the city of Sodom, has taken into his home the two "messengers" (angels) sent by God to warn him of the city's destruction. In the evening, the men of Sodom ask Lot to bring out his guests so that they may "know them" (Gen 19:5). The Hebrew verb *yd'*, translated here as "to know," can also refer to sexual intercourse (the expression in the Greek text of the Septuagint is analogous). However, sex is not the men of Sodom's primary concern, because when Lot monstrously offers his virgin daughters as sexual objects in place of his guests, this makes the mob even more aggressive: the men now want to gain access to Lot's guests by force; his daughters do not interest them. If one rejects the absurd notion that all the men of Sodom were homosexual,[66] then it is clear that their actual goal is not to enjoy same-sex sexual intercourse, but to violently humiliate the foreigner

---

von Lev 18,22 und 20,13," *Theologische Beiträge* 46 (2015): 218–230; Caron, "Le Lévitique," 37–39.

63 See also Erin Dufault-Hunter, "Sexual Ethics," in *Dictionary of Scripture and Ethics*, ed. Joel B. Green (Grand Rapids: Baker Academic, 2011), 723–728, esp. 726 f.; Steffan Mathias, "Queering the Body. Un-Desiring Sex in Leviticus," in *The Body in Biblical, Christian and Jewish Texts*, ed. Joan E. Taylor (London: Bloomsbury T & T Clark, 2014), 17–40.

64 See Himbaza, Schenker, and Edart, *Homosexuality*, 42: "the reader can emphasize that the stories of Genesis 19 and Judges 19 denounce the violent nature of the intention of the inhabitants of Sodom and Gibeah, whereas in today's world homosexuality is seen in the context of mutual consent. On this precise point, the stories have nothing to say" (I. Himbaza).

65 Today the term sodomy is often colloquially understood as referring to sexual acts with animals (bestiality, zoophilia). The connection between "homosexual" acts and the "sin of Sodom" has no basis in the biblical text, as can be shown, but has nevertheless led to many centuries in which the sinfulness of homosexuality was asserted and homosexuals were persecuted accordingly; cf. Nissinen, *Homoeroticism*, 45–46; Römer, "Homosexuality," 218.

66 See also Himbaza, Schenker, and Edart, *Homosexuality*, 10 (I. Himbaza).

Lot, together with his suspicious guests. In keeping with the ancient Near Eastern parallels outlined above, anal penetration is a means to the end of humiliation; the object is not to obtain pleasure or to satisfy one's sex drive, but rather to suppress foreigners with violence.[67] Thus the sin committed by the men of Sodom is not their supposed homosexuality, but their attempt to violently refuse the foreigners' right to hospitality and to oppress them. The angels' supernatural powers prevent the worst from happening.

Moreover, in early reception history, the story is not understood as addressing homosexuality. Instead, "Sodom" stands for sinful behavior in general (e. g., exploiting the poor or committing violence, as in Ezekiel 16:49).[68] On the other hand, Josephus, in the context of his Hellenistic background, likens the men of Sodom's desire to pederasty: "But the Sodomites, on seeing these young men of remarkably fair appearance whom Lot had taken under his roof, were bent only on violence and outrage to their youthful beauty" (*Ant.* 1.200).[69] In *Contra Apionem* 2.199, Josephus sees same-sex sexual intercourse between men as a vice among other peoples – one which has nothing to do with the Jewish people, among whom such activity is punishable by death. Josephus regards same-sex anal intercourse among men as *para physin* ("against nature") (*C. Ap.* 2.273). Philo also lists same-sex intercourse among men, effeminacy, and the slide into indulgence and luxury among the Sodomites' vices.[70] In this way, Josephus and Philo also oppose pederasty – a practice which was accepted in their Hellenistic and Roman environments.[71] However, Philo in particular is not concerned with adults making rational decisions about their sexual orientation or preferences, but always with passion's unbridled addiction to sexual gratification (which is usually also encouraged by the consumption of alcoholic beverages, such as the wine at the symposium) – that is, with a complete loss of control. Philo shows no sign of reflecting on the possibility that sober people with a clear sense of reality could have a same-sex sexual orientation. Like all Jewish authors of his time, he assumes that there are two sexes (Gen 1:27) and that any deviation

---

67 Zehnder ("Homosexualität [AT]," Punkt 4.1) confirms this view, but notes that sexual desire must be added as a "secondary element" if rape is to function in this context.

68 Cf. Nissinen, *Homoeroticism*, 46–47.

69 See also Nissinen (*Homoeroticism*, 93), who points out the significance of the fact that, in retelling the parallel story in Judges 19, Josephus glosses over the Benjaminites' "homosexual" attack (Judg 19:22, see below).

70 Cf. Nissinen, *Homoeroticism*, 94–95; see also William R. G. Loader, *Making Sense of Sex: Attitudes Towards Sexuality in Early Jewish and Christian Literature* (Grand Rapids: William B. Eerdmans, 2013), 134.

71 Cf. Loader, *Making Sense*, 132–140, with further examples from early Jewish and early Christian literature.

from heterosexual practices is a deliberate denial and perversion of this "reality."[72]

In the same way as the Sodomites, "a perverse lot" (NRSV) or "a bunch of scoundrels" (NABRE) in the Benjamite city of Gibeah (Judg 19:22) demand that a guest be brought out to them so that they can "know" him. Here again, the sexual element of "to know" is implied, and again this has nothing to do with homosexuality: the men want to humiliate the guest (and thus his host) by means of anal penetration.[73] In this case the guest offers them his concubine, and the mob is satisfied with raping her all night long. The woman does not survive this. The narrative text condemns this atrocious outrage perpetrated by the Benjamites in the strongest possible terms (Judg 19:30), and in its aftermath a bloody civil war ensues (Judg 20–21). The narrative constellation is somewhat different from the one in Genesis 19, but there is nothing to be gleaned from either narrative on the topic of homosexuality beyond the ancient Near Eastern perspective I have already outlined.[74]

Some interpreters identify a "homosexual" component in the incident involving Ham and his father Noah (Gen 9:20–27), but this is absurd: Ham sees his father Noah lying drunk and naked outside his tent after drinking the first wine ever made. Instead of covering him, Ham tells his brothers about the incident, and they then cover Noah with their faces averted. Yet if one reads the text closely and considers its context, Ham's "offense" does not consist in any sexual act he commits,[75] but rather in the fact that Ham has not rendered the respect of the younger toward the elder which is necessary for social cohesion.[76]

---

72 Cf. ibid., 135; Josephus sees this quite similarly.

73 See also Himbaza, Schenker, and Edart, *Homosexuality*, 18 (I. Himbaza).

74 See also Nissinen, *Homoeroticism*, 49–52; and similarly Jeffrey S. Siker, "Homosexuality," in *Dictionary of Scripture and Ethics*, ed. Joel B. Green (Grand Rapids: Baker Academic, 2011), 371–374, here 371: "Certainly, homosexual rape is condemned, but it seems quite a step to condemn all forms of homosexual expression on the basis of this passage about sexual violence. ... [M]any ethicists and biblical scholars do not view Gen. 19 as having probative value for the debate over homosexuality in the modern world." Furthermore, Himbaza, Schenker, and Edart (*Homosexuality*, 22) argue that "we should not read into these stories homosexuality as it is known today. In these texts, there is no question of persons having a marked or exclusive attraction to members of the same sex. As we have stressed, we cannot call all of the inhabitants of Sodom homosexuals. Nor can we call the wicked men of Gibeah homosexuals either, since they raped a woman at some length. In these texts, homosexuality is limited to a one-time episode. It is not understood as a desire or as a constitutive feature of the psyche" (I. Himbaza). On Genesis 19 and Judges 19, see also Römer, "Homosexuality," 218–221.

75 This contradicts Nissinen's assumption in *Homoeroticism*, 52. Nissinen presumes that Ham intended to humiliate his father by means of a same-sex sexual act (analogously to the ancient Egyptian myth of Horus and Seth, for example). On the other hand, on the basis of certain phras-

Thus we are left with David and Jonathan, the two childhood friends (1 Sam 18–20; 2 Sam 1:26). The literature already written about them could fill entire bookshelves.[77] In their search for positive expressions of homoerotic relationships in the Bible, people have often pointed to the friendship between David and Jonathan, especially the phrase in David's lament for Saul and Jonathan in 2 Samuel 1:26: "I am distressed for you, my brother Jonathan; greatly beloved were you to me; your love to me was wonderful, passing the love of women." In this lament, the deep friendship between David and Saul's son Jonathan is expressed poetically, as it had already been presented in 1 Samuel 18:1–4:

> [1] When David had finished speaking to Saul, the soul of Jonathan was bound to the soul of David, and Jonathan loved him as his own soul. [2] Saul took him that day and would not let him return to his father's house. [3] Then Jonathan made a covenant with David, because he loved him as his own soul. [4] Jonathan stripped himself of the robe that he was wearing, and gave it to David, and his armor, and even his sword and his bow and his belt.

These are signs of affection and friendship, but they are also politically symbolic, and the phrase "he [Jonathan] loved him [David] as his own soul" is literally realized in the further course of the narrative: when Jonathan's father Saul begins to hate and persecute David, Jonathan holds on to his friendship with David at the risk of his own life, warns David of his father's plans, and supports David whenever and however he can.[78] In a dramatic farewell scene, they both

---

es in the story, John Sietze Bergsma and Scott Walker Hahn ("Noah's Nakedness and the Curse on Canaan," *Journal of Biblical Literature* 124, no. 1 [2005]: 25–40, esp. 39f.) identify an act of heterosexual incest between Ham and his mother, Noah's wife, which results in the birth of Canaan, whom Noah eventually also curses. Whether the text really supports these interpretations is an open question. In any case, a homosexual inclination on Ham's part is not the issue here.
76 Cf. Thomas Hieke, *Die Genealogien der Genesis* (HBS 39; Freiburg im Breisgau: Herder, 2003), 95.
77 Cf. Harding, *Love*, passim, esp. 51–121, in which the various proposals from past decades are presented and critically analyzed with regard to their respective ideological positioning; see also the selection of literature in Zehnder, "Homosexualität (AT)." Römer ("Homosexuality," 221–228) presents an interesting comparison of the David and Jonathan story with the friendship between Gilgamesh and Enkidu. The similarities might indicate that "the relationship between David and Jonathan looks more like a love story than a reading of 1 Samuel may suggest at first glance" (p. 227).
78 As Zehnder ("Homosexualität (AT)," Punkt 5.3) shows, this talk of love and covenant can have "theological and political overtones" in both the David and Jonathan story and its broader context. 1 Samuel 18:16 also tells us that "all Israel and Judah loved David."

weep over their distressing situation and kiss each other (1 Sam 20:41).[79] Shortly before this, Saul himself had reproached his son Jonathan for having "chosen the son of Jesse" (David), to his own shame and the shame of his mother's nakedness (1 Sam 20:30). It is possible that Saul's outburst is the narrator's attempt to suggest that David and Jonathan's extremely close friendship transcended what was typical of male friendships – just as David transcended boundaries and conventions in other areas and distinguished himself as exceptional in many ways. Thus one must admit that the Jonathan–David narrative does intend to give very particular weight to this male relationship, placing it among the many "unusual" things David did and accomplished. Precisely for this reason, however, it is rather unlikely that the narrative really has a homosexual relationship in mind.[80] In David's case, one would have to assume that he was "bisexual" in today's sense, because he had many (perhaps too many) women in his life, as becomes quite clear. David's relationship with Uriah's wife (Bathsheba) will have a decisively negative effect on his career. However, no text has been handed down in which Jonathan makes a statement comparable to David's statement in his prayer of lamentation (2 Sam 1:16), and there is no indication of homosexual activity on Jonathan's part: "Nothing indicates that David and Jonathan slept together 'as one sleeps with a woman.'"[81] There may be many reasons why David preferred Jonathan's love to that of women, but these can hardly be sexual, because it is not evident that David experienced less sexual pleasure with women. Perhaps it is the "wonderful" equality in his relationship with Jonathan, in which there is no "active" or "passive" role (unlike in the classical gender stereotypes of the man–woman relationship, in which – incidentally – the woman's "inferiority" in Gen 3:16 is interpreted as punishment and as a diminution of her existence, but not as the original will of the creator). Perhaps the story intends to suggest that there is still a little "paradise" in everyday life – and that the wonderful friendship between David and Jonathan is one example of this. The fact that readers of both sexes still wish to see the relationship between the two as a homosexual one is due to the openness of the text itself,[82]

---

79 Kissing as such is not an indication of a homoerotic relationship. It may refer to the installation of the future king, as we see in 1 Samuel 10:1. Cf. Zehnder, "Homosexualität (AT)," Punkt 5.2; Harding, *Love*, 107.
80 See also Himbaza, Schenker, and Edart, *Homosexuality*, 41 (I. Himbaza).
81 Nissinen, *Homoeroticism*, 55. Josephus also makes no mention of a sexual component in his retelling of David and Jonathan's relationship (*Antiquitates* 6.206, 241, 275–276; 7, 5.111); cf. Loader, *Making Sense*, 135–136.
82 Cf. the detailed discussion in Harding, *Love*, 122–273.

which does not place strict limits on the recipient's imagination.[83] The different ways of reading and interpreting the relationship between David and Jonathan are part of the process in which the modern conception of homosexuality itself came into being. Today it is almost impossible to read the texts that speak of the love between David and Jonathan without gaining at least a vague impression of a homoerotic or even a homosexual relationship.[84]

6 On the Treatment of the Old Testament Passages in Contemporary Catechism

The biblical passages discussed above are also referred to in statements the Roman Catholic Church has made on the subject of homosexuality. I will examine this treatment of the relevant Old Testament passages with reference to the Catechism of the Catholic Church (also called the "World Catechism") by way of example.[85]

The Catechism discusses homosexuality in the second section of Article 6 on the "Sixth Commandment," under the heading "Vocation to Chastity," numbers 2357 to 2359, and in number 2396 of the final section of the article, titled "In Brief." In number 2396, "homosexual practices" are described as "sins gravely contrary to chastity," along with masturbation, fornication (by which the text means extramarital sex), and pornography. Number 2357 takes a more differentiated approach: here the variety of forms homosexuality has taken historically are acknowledged, and its "psychological genesis" is presented as "largely unexplained." Then comes the scriptural argument: "Basing itself on Sacred Scripture, which presents homosexual acts as acts of grave depravity [cf. Gen

---

83 The David and Jonathan episode cannot be invoked as a narrative in which we find a "biblical legitimation" of homoerotic and homosexual practices, thus cancelling out Leviticus 18:22 and 20:13, as it were. It would be hermeneutically misguided to play the texts off against each other in this way. Nevertheless, some exegetes are palpably interested in identifying a homosexual relationship in this narrative, with the ultimate aim of using this as "biblical evidence" to condone homosexual practices; cf. the summary in Harding, *Love*, 403, and also 100. In this way, biblical texts are misused as alleged "evidence" to support one's own interests. But the same kind of abuse of the text takes place when Leviticus 18:22 and 20:13 are detached from their context and their social history, and interpreted as "absolute truths" which support a rigid sexual morality.
84 Cf. Harding, *Love*, 403–404.
85 Catechism of the Catholic Church (Rome: Vatican, 1993; rev. 1997), http://www.vatican.va/archive/ENG0015/_INDEX.HTM (accessed April 21, 2021).

19:1–29; Rom 1:24–27; 1 Cor 6:10; 1 Tim 1:10], tradition has always declared that 'homosexual acts are intrinsically disordered'."[86] However, as I have shown above, the passage cited (Gen 19:1–29) does not address homosexuality, but rather the Sodomites' attempt to humiliate Lot's foreign guests by means of anal penetration, thus demonstrating their superiority through rape. That such an approach should be rejected is beyond question. Yet the biblical passage is not a suitable basis on which to infer that the Holy Scriptures describe homosexuality as an "act of grave depravity." Therefore this claim in the Catechism is false; the Old Testament has no knowledge of the modern concept of homosexuality. The passages in the Torah (Lev 18:22 and 20:13) which are more relevant to the Catechism's argumentation are not mentioned. But in these cases as well, and again as I have shown above, we cannot derive any condemnation of homosexuality in the modern sense. The rest of the Catechism's argument for the rejection of homosexual practices is based on natural law. Number 2358 admonishes all Catholics: "Every sign of unjust discrimination in their regard should be avoided." Yet the Catechism itself practices unjust discrimination by declaring in the same paragraph that the homosexual inclination is "objectively disordered." Moreover, number 2359 states, "Homosexual persons are called to chastity," and hence to abstain completely from sexual activity. This statement has no reference to and no basis in the Bible, and it deeply contradicts human experience.

The 2006 statement of the United States Conference of Catholic Bishops (USCCB), entitled *Ministry to Persons with a Homosexual Inclination: Guidelines for Pastoral Care*, intends "to provide basic guidelines for pastoral ministry to persons with a homosexual inclination or tendency."[87] The statement clearly rejects as unjust any attempt to make such persons objects of scorn, hatred, or even violence. However, the text also reduces sexuality as such (i.e., all human sexuality) to a very limited spectrum:

> By its very nature, the sexual act finds its proper fulfillment in the marital bond. Any sexual act that takes place outside the bond of marriage does not fulfill the proper ends of human sexuality. Such an act is not directed toward the expression of marital love with an open-

---

86 Here the Catechism quotes from Congregation of the Doctrine of the Faith, *Persona Humana: Declaration on Certain Questions of Sexual Ethics* (Rome: Vatican, 1975), no. 8, http://www.vatican.va/roman_curia/congregations/cfaith/documents/rc_con_cfaith_doc_19751229_persona-humana_en.html (accessed April 21, 2021).

87 United States Conference of Catholic Bishops, *Ministry to Persons with a Homosexual Inclination: Guidelines for Pastoral Care* (Washington, DC: USCCB, 2006), 1, https://www.usccb.org/issues-and-action/human-life-and-dignity/homosexuality/upload/minstry-persons-homosexual-inclination-2006.pdf (accessed April 21, 2021).

ness to new life. It is disordered in that it is not in accord with this twofold end and is thus morally wrong.[88]

This approach makes things easy and complicated at the same time. It is easy in the sense that this statement prohibits any acts or expressions of sexuality apart from sexual intercourse between a married couple for the purpose of conceiving offspring. Yet it is complicated in the sense that this idea flies in the face of the lived experience of most human beings. One may ask whether wrenching the ideal and the reality so far apart is justified or wise.

The USCCB statement refers to the Old Testament on page 4: "Whenever homosexual acts are mentioned in the Old Testament, it is clear that they are disapproved of, as contrary to the will of God." Here the guidelines quote Genesis 19:1–19 and Leviticus 18:22 and 20:13 in the footnote. As I have demonstrated above, these passages do not refer to "homosexual acts" in the proper, modern sense. In Genesis 19:1–19, the Sodomites seek to humiliate Lot's guests – and thus the stranger Lot himself – by perpetrating violent acts. This chapter is about xenophobia and violence, and it is obvious that God disapproves of violent acts committed against foreigners. However, homosexuality in the contemporary, modern understanding is characterized by mutual consent and mutual love, as any human sexuality should be. Quoting Genesis 19 in the current debate about homosexuality and the Church constitutes terrible discrimination against people with a homosexual inclination, because it implicitly assumes that such people are prone to violence and oppression. As an Old Testament scholar and an advocate for the true word of God, I strongly recommend that Genesis 19 no longer be associated with the issue of homosexuality.

The Leviticus passages originate in the context of a community under threat and in urgent need of offspring; such a community cannot permit any sexual practices that do not result in new life (that is, progeny) and that might disturb the fragile order of a small society under the pressure of cultural change. Quoting Leviticus 18 and 20 in the current debate about homosexuality presupposes that we live in a period in which we are urgently dependent on the birth of more children, and in which cultural diversity is interpreted as a threat. Again, this flies in the face of most lived human experience. Today, there is no lack of human offspring on the planet, and cultural diversity is an enrichment. It is a hermeneutical flaw to isolate a biblical verse from its context and its socio-cultural setting. Such a practice can lead to absurd results. This way of referring to the Bible would necessitate the excommunication of all tattooed Catholics, since

---

88 Ibid., p. 3 – 4.

Leviticus 19:28 reads: "Do not lacerate your bodies for the dead, and do not tattoo yourselves."[89] Hence the references to the Old Testament in the USCCB statement are unacceptable. For further details on the references to the New Testament, the reader may consult Michael Theobald's contribution in this volume.

It is commendable that the USCCB statement praises training in virtue and the ideal of chastity. However, any virtue that derives from a necessity is no virtue at all, and any chastity that emerges from an untenable predicament is a displacement that might result in psychological harm (or in the abuse of power). If a person with a homosexual inclination freely chooses a life of sexual abstinence (chastity), then this choice deserves our deepest respect. However, it is highly unrealistic to demand such a high virtue of *all* human beings with a homosexual inclination. It is simply not fair that the Church demands such a high ideal from so many people when it knows they will fail. Striving for holiness and referring to several passages from Leviticus (11:44–45; 19:2; 20:7, 26) does not help in this case: once again, the verses are isolated from their context and setting, and the identification of holiness with sexual chastity devalues the concept of holiness. Holiness involves much, much more than one's sexual practices. It has to do with fairness in business; paying fair wages; transforming economic and social structures to prevent people from falling into poverty; providing equal opportunities for all human beings, regardless of their race, color, ethnic provenance, age, sex, or sexual orientation; and much more. In its entirety, Leviticus 19 provides only a few examples of what holiness is all about.

In sum, the Old Testament does not support the Church's current teaching on homosexuality, and thus we need an open, worldwide discussion of this issue. Alternatively, perhaps it would be even better to say nothing about this particular issue at all. It would suffice to urge Catholics to enact their sexuality in a reasonable and responsible way, with high respect for their partner, with consideration for the needs and structures of their social framework (family, community, state, church), and with mutual love and mutual consent. This is in fact what the Old Testament teaches.

---

89 Quoted from the New American Bible (rev. ed.; Washington, DC: The United States Conference of Catholic Bishops, 2011). The footnote to this verse reads: "This prohibition probably refers only to the common ancient Near Eastern practice of branding a slave with its owner's name as well as branding the devotees of a god with its name." Here the editors correctly stress the verse's socio-cultural background. This methodological practice should be applied to all biblical verses, and hence also to Leviticus 18:22 and 20:13.

7 Concluding Statement

Does the Old Testament recognize and condemn homosexuality? Our scholarly review of the texts has confirmed the double negative answer to this question which I provided at the beginning of this contribution. Indeed, the following points hold true for all of antiquity: (1) today's differentiated concept of homosexuality as a multi-dimensional phenomenon and an integrated component of one's personality was not understood in this way, and (2) the subject had nowhere near the significance it has in today's culture. Likewise, the Hebrew Bible – or in Christian reception, the Old Testament – has no concept of homosexuality in the sense in which we understand it today.[90] Only a very few passages provide any starting points for this debate. In the Torah, Leviticus 18:22 and 20:13 refer to a specific socio-historical situation and, in their context, address the pressing need for procreation. Without their literary and social contexts, these provisions hang in midair; therefore, for both literary and theological reasons, they must not be considered in isolation.[91] The narrative texts that describe the Sodomites (Gen 19) and "Gibeah's shameful deed" (Judg 19) do not address homosexuality, but rather the perpetration of male violence against inferior foreigners without regard for the law of hospitality. Anal penetration as a sign of humiliation is also evident in Israel's environment. The story of Noah and his son Ham (Gen 9:20 – 27) is about young people displaying a lack of respect for their elders; the presumption that (homo)sexual acts took place is not necessary to understand this text. Finally, the narrative passages describing David and Jonathan's relationship are left open and therefore often serve as a projection screen for the reader's desire to find a homoerotic or homosexual relationship between men in the Bible. The text itself by no means compels the reader to situate their friendship in the sexual realm, but it is open to this interpretation.[92]

Thus as a biblical scholar, I can state with confidence that a rejection of homosexuality as we understand it today finds no justification in the Old Testa-

---

90 See also Robert Karl Gnuse, *Trajectories of Justice. What the Bible Says about Slaves, Women, and Homosexuality* (Eugene: Wipf and Stock, 2015), 117– 141; Himbaza, Schenker, and Edart, *Homosexuality*, 132. Römer ("Homosexuality," 228) concludes: "No text of the Hebrew Bible (and also no text of the New Testament) speaks about homosexuality as a social phenomenon to describe loving and sexual same sex relations. As a result one has to seriously question the use of different biblical texts in contemporary and ecclesial debates."
91 Siker ("Homosexuality," 372) rightly and rhetorically asks: "Are modern people of faith to pick and choose among the various Levitical prohibitions and punishments? If so, on what basis?"
92 Cf. Harding, *Love*, 228; Römer, "Homosexuality," 228.

ment.[93] The argument that homosexually inclined people should be condemned to abstinence cannot be derived from the Old Testament. Social discrimination against or state criminal prosecution of such people constitutes a lack of mercy and a crime against human dignity – as the Roman Catholic Church's Catechism also clearly states.

Bibliography

Altenmüller, Hartwig. "Väter, Brüder und Götter – Bemerkungen zur Szene der Übergabe der Lotosblüte." In *"Zur Zierde gereicht …". Festschrift Bettina Schmitz zum 60. Geburtstag am 24. Juli 2008*, ed. Antje Spiekermann, 17–28. Hildesheim: Gerstenberg, 2008.

Amenta, Alessia. "Some Reflections on the 'Homosexual' Intercourse Between Horus and Seth." *Göttinger Miszellen* 199 (2004): 7–21.

Bergsma, John Sietze, and Scott Walker Hahn. "Noah's Nakedness and the Curse on Canaan." *Journal of Biblical Literature* 124, no. 1 (2005): 25–40.

Bottéro, Jean, and Herbert Petschow. "Homosexualität." In *Reallexikon der Assyriologie und Vorderasiatischen Archäologie*, vol. 4, ed. Erich Ebeling, Ernst F. Weidner, and Dietz Otto Edzard, 459–468. Berlin: De Gruyter, 1972–1975.

Büma, Beryl, and Martin Fitzenreiter. "'Spielt das Lied der beiden göttlichen Brüder': Erotische Ambiguität und 'große Nähe' zwischen Männern im Alten Reich." *Studien zur altägyptischen Kultur* 44 (2015): 19–42.

Caron, Gérald. "Le Lévitique condemnerait-il l'homosexualité? De l'exégèse à l'herméneutique." *Studies in Religion/Sciences Religieuses* 38 (2009): 27–49.

Catechism of the Catholic Church. Rome: Vatican, 1993; rev. 1997. http://www.vatican.va/archive/ENG0015/_INDEX.HTM. Accessed April 21, 2021.

Cooper, Jerrold S. "Buddies in Babylonia: Gilgamesh, Enkidu, and Mesopotamian Homosexuality." In *Riches Hidden in Secret Places: Ancient Near Eastern Studies in Memory of Thorkild Jacobsen*, ed. Tzvi Abusch, 73–85. Winona Lake: Eisenbrauns, 2002.

Congregation of the Doctrine of the Faith. *Persona Humana: Declaration on Certain Questions of Sexual Ethics*. Rome: Vatican, 1975. http://www.vatican.va/roman_curia/congregations/cfaith/documents/rc_con_cfaith_doc_19751229_persona-humana_en.html. Accessed April 21, 2021.

Darmesteter, James. *The Zend-Avesta*. SBE04. Oxford: Clarendon Press, 1880. http://www.sacred-texts.com/zor/sbe04/sbe0414.htm. Accessed August 6, 2020.

Dershowitz, Idan. "Revealing Nakedness and Concealing Homosexual Intercourse. Legal and Lexical Evolution in Leviticus 18." *Hebrew Bible and Ancient Israel* 6 (2017): 510–526.

van Dijk, Jacobus. "The Nocturnal Wanderings of King Neferkarēᶜ." In *Hommages à Jean Leclant Vol. 4*, ed. Catherine Berger, 387–393. LeCaire: Inst. Français d'Archéologie Orientale, 1994.

---

93 Cf. also Caron, "Le Lévitique," 45.

Dils, Peter. "Die Lehre des Ptahhotep, pPrisse = pBN 186–194 (Ptahhotep, Version P)" Thesaurus Linguae Aegyptiae. http://aaew.bbaw.de/tla/index.html. Accessed August 27, 2020.

Dover, Kenneth. *Greek Homosexuality.* London: Duckworth, 1978.

Dufault-Hunter, Erin. "Sexual Ethics." In *Dictionary of Scripture and Ethics*, ed. Joel B. Green, 723–728. Grand Rapids: Baker Academic, 2011.

George, Andrew R. *The Babylonian Gilgamesh Epic: Introduction, Critical Edition and Cuneiform Texts.* Oxford: Oxford University Press, 2003.

Gnuse, Robert Karl. *Trajectories of Justice. What the Bible Says about Slaves, Women, and Homosexuality.* Eugene: Wipf and Stock, 2015.

Guinan, Ann Kessler. "Erotomancy: Scripting the Erotic." In *Sex and Gender in the Ancient Near East. Proceedings of the 47th Rencontre Assyriologique Internationale, Helsinki, July 2–6, 2001*, ed. Simo Parpola and Robert M. Whiting, 185–201. Helsinki: Helsinki University Press, 2002.

Hannig, Rainer. *Großes Handwörterbuch Ägyptisch-Deutsch (Marburger Edition).* Kulturgeschichte der Antiken Welt 64. Mainz: von Zabern, 2006.

Harding, James E. *The Love of David and Jonathan. Ideology, Text, Reception.* BibleWorld. Sheffield: Equinox, 2013.

Hieke, Thomas. "Das Alte Testament und die Todesstrafe." *Biblica* 85 (2004): 349–374.

Hieke, Thomas. "Das Verbot der Übergabe von Nachkommen an den 'Molech' in Lev 18 und 20. Ein neuer Deutungsversuch." *Die Welt des Orients* 41 (2011): 147–167.

Hieke, Thomas. *Die Genealogien der Genesis.* HBS 39. Freiburg im Breisgau: Herder, 2003.

Hieke, Thomas. *Levitikus 16–27.* HThKAT. Freiburg im Breisgau: Herder, 2014.

Hieke, Thomas. "The Prohibition of Transferring an Offspring to 'the Molech.' No Child Sacrifice in Leviticus 18 and 20." In *Writing a Commentary on Leviticus. Hermeneutics – Methodology – Themes*, ed. Christian Eberhart and Thomas Hieke, 171–199. Göttingen: Vandenhoeck & Ruprecht, 2019.

Himbaza, Innocent, Adrian Schenker, and Jean-Baptiste Edart. *The Bible on the Question of Homosexuality.* Washington, DC: Catholic University of America Press, 2012.

Hollenback, George M. "Who Is Doing What to Whom Revisited: Another Look at Leviticus 18:22 and 20:13." *Journal of Biblical Literature* 136 (2017): 529–537.

Jacobsen, Thorkild. "How Did Gilgamesh Oppress Uruk?" *Acta Orientalia* 8 (1930): 62–74.

Joosten, Jan. "A New Interpretation of Leviticus 18:22 (Par. 20:13) and Its Ethical Implications." *The Journal of Theological Studies NS* 71 (2020): 1–10.

Josephus. *Jewish Antiquities.* Vol. 1: *Books 1–3.* Translated by H. St. J. Thackeray. Loeb Classical Library 242. Cambridge, MA: Harvard University Press, 1930.

Josephus. *The Life: Against Apion.* Translated by H. St. J. Thackeray. Loeb Classical Library 186. Cambridge, MA: Harvard University Press, 1926.

Junge, Friedrich. "Die Erzählung vom Streit der Götter Horus und Seth um die Herrschaft." In *Texte aus der Umwelt des Alten Testaments. Alte Folge*, vol. 3, ed. Otto Kaiser, 930–950. Gütersloh: Gütersloher Verlagshaus Mohn, 1995.

Kammerzell, Frank, and María Isabel Toro Rueda. "Nicht der Homosexuelle ist pervers. Die Zweiunddreißigste Maxime der Lehre des Ptahhotep." *Lingua Aegyptia* 22 (2003): 63–78.

Kammerzell, Frank. "Von der Affäre um König Nafirkuˀriˀa und seinen General." In *Texte aus der Umwelt des Alten Testaments. Alte Folge*, vol. 3, ed. Otto Kaiser, 965–969. Gütersloh: Gütersloher Verlagshaus Mohn, 1995.

Lapide, Pinchas. *Ist die Bibel richtig übersetzt?* Gütersloh: Gütersloher Verlagshaus Mohn, 1987.

Lichtheim, Miriam. *Ancient Egyptian Literature, vol. II: The New Kingdom.* Berkeley/Los Angeles/London: University of California Press, 1976.

Loader, William R. G. *Making Sense of Sex: Attitudes Towards Sexuality in Early Jewish and Christian Literature.* Grand Rapids: William B. Eerdmans, 2013.

Mathias, Steffan. "Queering the Body. Un-Desiring Sex in Leviticus." In *The Body in Biblical, Christian and Jewish Texts*, ed. Joan E. Taylor, 17–40. London: Bloomsbury T & T Clark, 2014.

Miller, Jared L. "Paskuwatti's Ritual: Remedy for Impotence or Antidote to Homosexuality?" *Journal of Ancient Near Eastern Religions* 10, no. 1 (2010): 83–89.

Nissinen, Martti. *Homoeroticism in the Biblical World: A Historical Perspective.* Minneapolis: Fortress Press, 1998.

Nissinen, Martti. "Are There Homosexuals in Mesopotamian Literature?" *Journal of the American Oriental Society* 130 (2010): 73–77.

Parkinson, Richard B. "'Homosexual' Desire and Middle Kingdom Literature." *The Journal of Egyptian Archaeology* 81 (1995): 57–76.

Parkinson, Richard B. *Little Gay History. Desire and Diversity Across the World.* London: British Museum Press, 2013.

Peled, Ilan. "Expelling the Demon of Effeminacy: Anniwiyani's Ritual and the Question of Homosexuality in Hittite Thought." *Journal of Ancient Near Eastern Religions* 10, no. 1 (2010): 69–81.

Pola, Thomas. "'Und bei einem Manne sollst du nicht liegen, wie man bei einer Frau liegt: Ein Greuel ist es.' Der literarische und sozialgeschichtliche Zusammenhang von Lev 18,22 und 20,13." *Theologische Beiträge* 46 (2015): 218–230.

Römer, Thomas. "Homosexuality in the Hebrew Bible? Some Thoughts on Lev 18 and 20; Gen 19 and the David-Jonathan Narrative." In *Ahavah. Die Liebe Gottes im Alten Testament*, ed. Manfred Oeming, 213–231. Leipzig: Evangelische Verlagsanstalt, 2018.

Röpke, Frank. "Überlegungen zum 'Sitz im Leben' der Kahuner Homosexuellen Episode zwischen Horus und Seth (pKahun VI.12 = pUniversity College London 32158, rto.)." In *Das Erzählen in frühen Hochkulturen I. Der Fall Ägypten*, ed. Hubert Roeder, 239–290. Munich: Fink, 2009.

Scholz, Stefan. "Homosexualität (NT)." Das wissenschaftliche Bibellexikon im Internet, September 2012. https://www.bibelwissenschaft.de/stichwort/46910/. Accessed August 25, 2020.

Schukraft, Beate. "Homosexualität im Alten Ägypten." *Studien zur altägyptischen Kultur* 36 (2007): 297–331.

Siker, Jeffrey S. "Homosexuality." In *Dictionary of Scripture and Ethics*, ed. Joel B. Green, 371–374. Grand Rapids: Baker Academic, 2011.

Sklar, Jay. "The Prohibitions against Homosexual Sex in Leviticus 18:22 and 20:13: Are They Relevant Today?" *Bulletin for Biblical Research* 28 (2018): 165–198.

United States Conference of Catholic Bishops. *Ministry to Persons with a Homosexual Inclination: Guidelines for Pastoral Care.* Washington, DC: USCCB, 2006. https://www.

usccb.org/issues-and-action/human-life-and-dignity/homosexuality/upload/minstry-per sons-homosexual-inclination-2006.pdf. Accessed April 21, 2021.

Vittmann, Günter. "Hieratic Texts." In *The Elephantine Papyri in English. Three Millennia of Cross-Cultural Continuity and Change*, ed. Bezalel Porten, 63–78. Atlanta: Society of Biblical Literature, 2nd rev. ed. 2011.

Walsh, Jerome T. "Leviticus 18:22 and 20:13: Who Is Doing What to Whom?" *Journal of Biblical Literature* 120 (2001): 201–209.

Wells, Bruce. "On the Beds of a Woman: The Leviticus Texts on Same-Sex Relations Reconsidered." In *Sexuality and Law in the Torah*, ed. Hilary Lipka and Bruce Wells, 125–160. London: T & T Clark, 2020.

Westendorf, Wolfhart. "Homosexualität." In *Lexikon der Ägyptologie 2*, ed. Wolfgang Helck, 1272. Wiesbaden: Harrassowitz Verlag, 1977.

Zehnder, Markus. "Homosexualität (AT)." Das wissenschaftliche Bibellexikon im Internet, March 2008. https://www.bibelwissenschaft.de/stichwort/21490/. Accessed September 1, 2020.

Zenger, Erich, and Christian Frevel. "Heilige Schrift der Juden und der Christen." In *Einleitung in das Alte Testament*, ed. Christian Frevel et al., 11–36. Stuttgart: Verlag W. Kohlhammer, 2015.

Michael Theobald
Paul and Same-Sex Sexuality
A Plea for a Sensible Approach to Scripture

In conversations about whether and how Christian churches might become a true home for people in same-sex partnerships, one regularly encounters the objection: "But Scripture says...!" And often enough, this is where the readiness to understand ends. With regard to "worldview" claims, such as the question of how the biblical creation narratives relate to scientific theories about the origin of the world, a biblicist approach to Scripture has long been obsolete; we have learned from what happened to Galileo. When it comes to ethical-anthropological controversies such as the one at hand, however, approaches to Scripture that have been painstakingly cultivated in other contexts are still not effectively applied. Yet such questions also require us to consider the cultural-historical character of the relevant texts and to look closely at which issues they address – and which they do not. For example, years ago Wolfgang Stegemann pointed out that Paul argues on the basis of an entirely different system of cultural values than that which we are accustomed to in modern Western societies, which is why his views on sexuality are also very different from ours.[1] It is reasonable to assume that Paul is not at all familiar with our problems, because our contemporary anthropological knowledge is quite different from that of his day, and therefore his views do not offer us much help. Thus it is to be expected that Scripture, once we have read it carefully, will then send us forth and expect us to develop our own ethical perspectives in the light of faith – which of course brings us back to Scripture and its wealth of encounters with God – in conversation with the human sciences, to put these perspectives to the test, and to verify them in the everyday pastoral life of the Church.

Only a few texts in the Holy Scriptures are directly relevant to our discussion here. There is no mention of "lesbian love" anywhere in the Bible – neither in the Old nor in the New Testament – a fact which hinges on the text's androcentric perspective.[2] In the New Testament, same-sex sexual activity is mentioned only in the Pauline corpus, in 1 Corinthians 6:9–11 and Romans 1:26–27, and

---

1 Wolfgang Stegemann, "Homosexualität – ein modernes Konzept," *ZNT* 2 (1998): 61–68.
2 For further reflections on this topic in the Old Testament, see Thomas Hieke's contribution in this volume.

https://doi.org/10.1515/9783110705188-003

once in the pseudo-Pauline pastoral letters, in 1 Timothy 1:9 – 11.[3] Of these three texts, the reference in the Letter to the Romans is certainly the most important, which is why in this contribution – after glancing at the other two texts – we will turn our attention primarily to Romans. I will begin with some preliminary remarks on the differences between the world of the New Testament and our world today, in terms of both culture and mindset.

1 The New Testament Texts: Witnesses to Another World

As Stegemann put it in the article I mentioned at the beginning, sexuality as we encounter it today, in the many ways in which it is perceived, is "a cultural construct of modern Western societies,"[4] a distinct, independent "concept" in the larger context of human scientific anthropology. It is guided by "the notion of a distinct realm of personal human identity defined by sexual desires, pleasure, and acts. And from here it becomes possible to assign to each individual human being an individual sexual 'orientation' that defines him or her as a homosexual or heterosexual or bisexual type."[5]

This modern "invention of sexuality as a separate area of human identity" manifests itself, for example, "in the fact that we distinguish sexual identity from gender affiliation" and "decouple types of sexual preferences from degrees of masculinity or femininity." This concept is what makes it possible for sexuality to be "the subject of physiological and psychological analyses or therapies."[6]

This account is supported by historical linguistic research. "The first occurrences of the terms homosexual and homosexuality can be traced to two pam-

---

3 William Loader (*Making Sense of Sex: Attitudes towards Sexuality in Early Jewish and Christian Literature* [Grand Rapids/Cambridge: Eerdmans, 2013], 138) also refers to Mark 9:42, "the only other probable reference to same-sex relations," although this is "limited to pederasty, where it makes best sense of the severe warning issued by Jesus against causing little ones to stumble, a common metaphor for sexual failing. In this case the issue is abuse of children and, while not explicitly mentioning sexual abuse, most likely has it in mind" (with reference to Mark 9:43 – 48 as well); see also William Loader, *The New Testament on Sexuality* (Grand Rapids/Cambridge: Eerdmans, 2012), 334; but cf. Rudolf Pesch's discussion in *Das Markusevangelium, II. Teil: Kommentar zu Kap. 8,27 – 16,20* (HThK.NT 2.2; Freiburg im Breisgau: Herder, 1977), 114 n. 3; based on a careful exegesis of Mark's text, Pesch considers the interpretation of Proverbs as a warning against sexual sin (homosexuality, onanism) to be absurd.
4 Stegemann, "Homosexualität," 62.
5 Ibid., 61.
6 Ibid., 62.

phlets, published anonymously in Leipzig in 1869, and probably became more widely known through their inclusion in the second edition of this book by Krafft-Ebbing" – a reference to *Psychopathia Sexualis*, published in 1887.[7] These terms have only been in use since the time when sexuality first began to be perceived as a separate sphere of private individual existence, and they correspond to this anthropological perception. If the Greek language – and thus also Hellenistic Judaism – has no terms corresponding to "homosexuality," which is an artificial compound word formed from a Greek and a Latin component,[8] then this alone constitutes a sufficient warning against projecting modern perceptions of sexuality back onto ancient texts. This caution applies to the Pauline texts as well.

Stegemann goes on to say that "[o]ne of the insights M. Foucault brought to the concept is that there was no autonomous, distinct realm of 'sexuality' in ancient societies. Sexual desire and lust were inextricably linked to the relations of power and domination that characterized the societies of the time."[9] In classical Athens, for example, "sexual roles [...] were isomorphic with status and gender roles; 'masculinity' combines the congruent functions of penetration, activity, dominance, and social superiority, while 'femininity' means being penetrated, passivity, submission, and social subordination."[10] Moreover, "[f]ree men stood on one side as active sexual partners, [while] women, slaves, and boys [stood] as passive on the other." It follows that "the issue of hetero- or homosexuality was not normative for sexual practice. The free Greek man could penetrate women, slaves (male and female), and boys, but not another free Greek man. This choice of partner was frowned upon because the other man would have had to assume the passive, subordinate, female role."[11]

What holds true for Greek culture – the view of sexuality as part of overarching discursive and institutional structures – also holds true analogously for the

---

7 Ibid., 61 (following David M. Halperin, *One Hundred Years of Homosexuality* [New York: Routledge, 1990]). The author of these two pamphlets was the Austro-Hungarian writer Karl Maria Kertbeny (1824–1882).

8 Karl Hoheisel, "Art. Homosexualität," in *RAC*, vol. 16, ed. Theodor Klauser (Stuttgart: Hiersemann, 1994), 289–364, esp. 299: "There are numerous Greek and Latin words that denote, are associated with, or imply homosexuality, depending on the context," such as παιδεραστία, παιδοφιλεῖν, παιδοπίπης, καταπύγων, and εὐρύπρωκτος, and later μαλακός, ἀνδρόγυνος, and πασχητιῶν/pathicus, among others; Hoheisel also provides a general overview of the ancient sources.

9 Stegemann, "Homosexualität," 62; cf. Michel Foucault, *The History of Sexuality*, 3 vols. (London: Allen Lane/Penguin, 1979/1990).

10 Stegemann, "Homosexualität," 62 (following Halperin, *Hundred Years*, 130).

11 Ibid., 62.

biblical and early Jewish tradition, for which, in addition to concepts of purity, the creation narratives provide the primary normative framework.[12] When Leviticus 18:22 and 20:13 prohibit "a man from 'using' another man as a woman, and thus transgressing the boundaries between the sexes"[13] which are grounded in creation, contextual evidence indicates that the prohibition is probably due to the "pressing need to produce offspring."[14] However, the way this prohibition

---

12 Cf. Loader, *Making Sense*, 9 – 31 ("In the Beginning"), 75 – 104 ("Sacred Space"). Loader has dealt extensively with this issue in recent years, resulting in a total of five monographs, of which his short work *Making Sense of Sex* offers a synopsis; only two of these works are mentioned here: William Loader, *Philo, Josephus, and the Testaments on Sexuality: Attitudes towards Sexuality in the Writings of Philo, Josephus, and the Testaments of the Twelve Patriarchs* (Grand Rapids/ Cambridge: Eerdmans, 2011); idem, *New Testament*.

13 Following Stegemann's paraphrase of the two regulations in "Homosexualität," 65. The history of the impact of these verses – especially of Leviticus 20:13 – is catastrophic (beginning with Philo's reception [see note 16 below]); Erhard S. Gerstenberger, *Das dritte Buch Mose: Leviticus* (ATD 6; Göttingen: Vandenhoeck & Ruprecht, 1993), 271: "In the Western legal tradition, sexual acts between persons of the same sex are still criminal offenses to some extent. The biblical condemnation of homosexuality has led to merciless persecution or ostracism of those with a disposition or inclination toward same-sex sexuality in church history." There is ongoing exegetical controversy over what exactly the directives in the book of Leviticus are directed against: (1) against forms of male cult prostitution, as Walter Kornfeld argues in *Leviticus* (NEB 6; Würzburg: Echter-Verlag, 1986), 71 f.; (2) against particular homosexual practices, as Stegemann argues in "Homosexualität," 63, with reference to Saul M. Olyan, "'And with a Male You Shall Not Lie the Lying Down of a Woman': On the Meaning and Significance of Leviticus 18:22 and 20:13," *Journal of the History of Sexuality* 4 (1994): 179 – 206: "Leviticus 18:22 and 20:13 obviously prohibit sexual intercourse (penetration) exclusively, while ignoring other possible sexual acts between men," and thus "[t]he problem, then, is that a man 'uses' another man as a woman, thereby transgressing the boundaries between the sexes, namely the distinctions between man and woman established at creation (Gen 1:27)"; or (3) against male "homosexual" practices in general, as Gerstenberger argues in *Leviticus*, 232, 271 f. Gerstenberger is inclined to think that "the total ban on male homosexuality was a late phenomenon, i. e., a feature of the early Jewish community," and that "[w]here the actual roots of this brutal rejection of homosexuality lie is obscure. Presumably, as in the case of many taboo regulations, they involve a fear of demons," which admittedly "have been considered overcome for centuries and are finally being replaced by uninhibited, philanthropic attitudes in the church as well." Thomas Hieke argues similarly in *Levitikus: Zweiter Teilband: 16 – 27* (HThK.AT; Freiburg im Breisgau: Herder, 2014), 688: "This categorical prohibition is singular in the Bible as well as in the ancient world." Admittedly, he does not want to exclude a limited interpretation according to which "same-sex relations are forbidden for a man only with certain of his relatives [...] precisely by analogy to the women mentioned [in Lev 18] (i. e., with father, son, brother, grandson, stepson) [...] Homosexual relations with other men would then be permitted"; ibid., 689.

14 See Thomas Hieke's contribution in this volume; idem., *Levitikus*, 2:688. The actual roots of the biblical repudiation are obscure; "nevertheless, the text as a whole offers a common thread. The context makes it clear that the key to understanding is the production of progeny. On the

is formulated also reveals the underlying problem for the standard social construction of roles: in the "feminization" of a man through another man's "lying with him as with a woman" (Lev 18:22; 20:13). This also explains why "this prohibition in the Torah applies only to men – not to women."[15]

A brief survey of the writings of Philo of Alexandria – who takes up the prohibition in the Torah, expands upon it, and extends it to apply to pederasty – demonstrates the importance of both of these aspects from the Jewish perspective: the commandment to procreate (cf. Gen 1:28) and the distinction of the sexes in the sense of the creation narrative, which would preclude the "feminization" of a man. According to Philo, whoever violates this prohibition – and this applies to both the active and the (in Philo's terminology) "feminized man (ὁ ἀνδρόγυνος)" – deserves to be put to death, and he invokes Leviticus 20:13c to support this view.[16] The text does not address same-sex sexual acts between women,[17] as such acts are mentioned only rarely in early Jewish tradition –

---

one hand, Lev 18 is concerned with preventing incestuous and illegitimate progeny [...], on the other hand, it is concerned with preventing sexual practices that do not lead to progeny; here the social dimension and function of sexuality once again becomes clear."

15 Stegemann, "Homosexualität," 63; Hieke, *Levitikus* 2:689: "Women's homosexual behavior was well known but is not addressed and, since there is no semen involved and it does not concern men's social status, was probably not considered a problem."

16 Cf. Philo, *Spec. Laws* 3.37–42, 38–39: "And it is natural for those who obey the law to consider such persons worthy of death, since the law commands that the man-woman (τὸν ἀνδρόγυνον), who adulterates the precious coinage of his nature (τὸ φύσεως νόμισμα), shall die without redemption, not allowing him to live a single day, or even a single hour, as he is a disgrace to himself, and to his family, and to his country, and to the whole race of mankind. And let the man who is devoted to the love of boys (ὁ παιδεραστής) submit to the same punishment, since he pursues that pleasure which is contrary to nature (τὴν παρὰ φύσιν ἡδονήν), and since, as far as depends upon him, he would make the cities desolate, and void, and empty of all inhabitants, wasting his power of propagating his species"; see also *Spec. Laws* 1.325; *QG* 2.49; *Abraham* 135f.; *Contempl. Life* 59–62; and also Josephus (see note 48 below); cf. Hoheisel, "Art. Homosexualität," 334f. As far as Leviticus 20:13c is concerned, recent exegesis judges differently: "The qualification as an 'abomination' marks the act as something that triggers God's displeasure and wrath, and is therefore to be refrained from to the extent possible. This terminology itself indicates the strongly parenetic character of these texts, and therefore it is only logical to see the punitive *mot* clause not as a 'death penalty' to be imposed and executed by human courts, but as a warning against God's punishment, whatever that might look like"; Hieke, *Levitikus*, 2:797, with reference to Adrian Schenker.

17 In contrast to Loader, *Making Sense*, 134: "He [Philo] reads the prohibitions in Lev 18:22 and 20:13 as targeting both pederasty and adult consensual sex, both male and female." Loader seems to infer the latter from *Virt.* 20–21, although the text there only addresses men and women who do not dress "in keeping with nature" (19). For details on Philo, see Loader, *Philo*, 2–258.

for example, in the "didactic poem" by an unknown Hellenistic Jew from Alexandria, which has been handed down under the name of Phocylides.[18] The same holds true for the Greek–Hellenistic tradition.[19] Moreover, this finding is also relevant to the interpretation of Romans 1:26.

The early Jewish reception of Leviticus 18:22 and 20:13 also includes the reflexive move of demarcating Jewish life from the pagan way of life,[20] understanding sexual transgressions – such as the "exchange of the sexes" (Wisdom 14:26) – as both a symptom and a consequence of idolatry. The Book of Wisdom[21] and the Testaments of the Twelve Patriarchs, for example, provide material that illustrates this point: "For a pit unto the soul is the sin of fornication, separating it from God, and bringing it near to idols" (Testament of Reuben 4:6; cf. Testament of Simeon 5:3; Testament of Judah 23:2).[22] Thus "the nexus between perverted un-

---

18 Cf. Pseudo-Phocylides 190 – 192: "Go not beyond natural sexual unions for illicit passion; unions between males are not pleasing even to beasts. *Let not women mimic the sexual role of men at all.*" As Nikolaus Walter notes, we can assume that the didactic poem was composed in Alexandria; as for the dating, "one must think of the time between 100 BCE [at the earliest] and ca. 100 CE [at the latest]. The termination of openly Hellenistic Judaism in Alexandria soon after 100 [...] is to be regarded as the *terminus ante quem*"; see Walter, "Pseudepigraphische jüdisch-hellenistische Dichtung," in *JSHRZ*, vol. 4.3, ed. Werner Georg Kümmel (Gütersloh: Gütersloher Verlagshaus, 1983), 173 – 276, here 193. Further evidence from later rabbinic tradition is provided in Pieter W. van der Horst, *The Sentences of Pseudo-Phocylides. With Introduction and Commentary* (SVTP 4; Leiden: Brill, 1978), 239 f.

19 But cf. Plato, *Leg.* 636c, in which the Athenian's speech reads: "one certainly should not fail to observe that when male unites with female for procreation (τῇ θηλείᾳ καὶ τῇ τῶν ἀρρένων φύσει εἰς κοινωνίαν ἰούσῃ τῇ γεννήσεως) the pleasure experienced is held to be due to nature (κατὰ φύσιν), but contrary to nature (παρὰ φύσιν) when male mates with male (ἀρρένων δὲ πρὸς ἄρρενας) or female with female (θηλειῶν πρὸς θηλείᾳ), and that those first guilty of such enormities were impelled by their slavery to pleasure." See also note 56 below.

20 This is already programmatic in Leviticus 18:1 – 5: "(3) You shall not do as they do in the land of Egypt, where you lived, and you shall not do as they do in the land of Canaan, to which I am bringing you. You shall not follow their statutes. (4) My ordinances you shall observe and my statutes you shall keep, following them: I am the Lord your God."

21 Cf. Wisdom 14:12: "For the idea of making idols was the beginning of fornication, and the invention of them was the corruption of life"; Wisdom 14:26 – 27: "confusion over what is good, forgetfulness of favors, defiling of souls, exchange of sexes (γενέσεως ἐναλλαγή), disorder in marriages, adultery, and debauchery. For the worship of idols not to be named is the beginning and cause and end of every evil."

22 The Testament of Levi 17:11 offers a catalogue of vices of the kind that is familiar to us from the New Testament: "And in the seventh week shall become priests, (who are) idolaters, adulterers, lovers of money, proud, lawless, lascivious, abusers of children and beasts." On the topic of same-sex sexuality in the Testaments of the Twelve Patriarchs, particularly in the Testament of Naphtali, see Hoheisel, "Art. Homosexualität," 333 f.; Loader, *Philo*, 415 – 419; see also Matthias Konradt, "'Fliehet die Unzucht!' (TestRub 5,5): Sexualethische Perspektiven in den Testa-

derstandings of God and perverted sexual behaviour, present in Wisdom, inspired the same connection made by Paul in Romans 1."[23] Here as well, it becomes clear how apt the observation made at the beginning of this contribution is – namely that in antiquity, sexuality is not yet perceived as an independent anthropological sphere, but always in the context of overarching discourses, be they discourses of power, structures of domination and dependence, or – as in Paul's corpus and in Hellenistic Judaism – discourses demarcating Israel's true religion from pagan idolatry.

2 Where Paul's Heart Is Not In It: The Apostle on Traditional Paths

Anyone who seeks the beating heart of Pauline ethics inevitably comes across the directive to love in the apostle's ethical instructions and discourses: "Love does no wrong to a neighbor; therefore love is the fulfilling of the law" (Rom 13:10). Or again: "For in Christ Jesus neither circumcision nor uncircumcision counts for anything; the only thing that counts is faith working through love" (Gal 5:6). This is where the apostle's heart is! And when he indicates that he is open to other values, as in Philippians 4:8 – "Whatever is true, whatever is honorable, whatever is just, whatever is pure, whatever is pleasing, whatever is commendable, if there is any excellence and if there is anything worthy of praise, think about these things!" – all of this is ultimately oriented toward concretizing and realizing *agape*. His ethos is certainly Jewish–Hellenistic in terms of both mindset and culture[24] – as is also confirmed by his statements on "same-sex" sexual practice – but this imprint stands under the banner of *agape*, even though his directives, rules, and parenetic remarks, which are usually situational, do not often make this explicit.

In the case of the three texts I will discuss in this contribution, this preconception is already evident in the traditional linguistic form of the catalogue of

---

menten der zwölf Patriarchen," in *Anthropologie und Ethik im Frühjudentum und im Neuen Testament: Wechselseitige Wahrnehmungen. Internationales Symposium in Verbindung mit dem Projekt CJHNT, 17.–20. Mai 2012, Heidelberg*, ed. Matthias Konradt and Esther Schläpfer (WUNT 322; Tübingen: Mohr Siebeck, 2014), 249–282; on the early Jewish texts, see also Martin Stowasser, "Homosexualität und Bibel: Exegetische und hermeneutische Überlegungen zu einem schwierigen Thema," *NTS* 43 (1997): 503–526.

23 Loader, *Making Sense*, 133.

24 See also the contributions in the volume edited by Matthias Konradt and Esther Schläpfer (cited in note 22 above).

vices, which constitutes the setting in which the topic appears in each case (1 Cor 6:9 – 11; 1 Tim 1:9 – 11; cf. also Rom 1:28 – 32). This does not diminish the importance of this topic for the authors, but it does show that they are treading conventional paths here. Moreover, the discourse in Romans 1:18 – 32 places the topic in a subordinate position, insofar as it serves to illustrate a superordinate thesis with regard to contemporary pagan culture as the Jews perceived it. The function of this topic as a subordinate argument in a limited perspective is in itself extremely important for a reflective hermeneutical approach to the text.

2.1 He Will Not Inherit the Kingdom of God: Observations on the Catalogue of Vices in 1 Corinthians 6:9 – 11

1 Corinthians 6:9 – 11 offers a traditional catalogue of vices framed by references to the "heir of the kingdom of God" (1 Cor 6:9b, 10e). Paul did not "invent" this reference either, but adopted it as a discourse formula (cf. 1 Cor 15:50; Eph 5:5; James 2:5; cf. also Mark 10:17). While the term βασιλεία τοῦ θεοῦ is not typical of Paul's texts, his catalogue follows well-trodden ground. With this expression he concludes his treatment of a specific incident in Corinth, which he sums up as follows: "When any of you has a grievance against another, do you dare to take it to court before the unrighteous, instead of taking it before the saints?" (1 Cor 6:1). "Law and its renunciation in the Christian community" is the theme here.[25] At the end, in 1 Corinthians 6:11, he assures his addressees that they have been "sanctified," even "justified in the name of the Lord Jesus Christ." Within the guidelines set by these concepts – "justified" versus "unrighteous" – the catalogue fleshes out the ethical consequences of the addressees' new status before God. If we include the framing device, the text reads:

9 a Or do you not know
  b *that the unrighteous will not inherit the kingdom of God?*
  c Do not deceive yourselves!
  d   Neither the sexually licentious, nor idolators,
  e   nor adulterers,
      nor the effeminate (μαλακοί), nor those who sleep/lie with men (ἀρσενοκοῖται),[26]

---

25 Andreas Lindemann, *Der erste Korintherbrief* (HNT 9.1; Tübingen: Mohr Siebeck, 2000), 133; see also Michael Theobald, "Vom Werden des Rechts in der Kirche: Beobachtungen zur Sprachform von Weisungen im Corpus Pastorale und bei Paulus," *ZNW* 106 (2015): 65 – 95.
26 The NRSV/CE version has "male prostitutes" and "sodomites," and thus transports massive value judgments into the text. It is in urgent need of revision.

10 a   nor thieves, nor those who covet,
  b   not drunkards,
  c   not blasphemers,
  d   not scoundrels
  e   *Shall inherit the kingdom of God.*
11 a   And such were some of you!

"The unrighteous will not inherit the kingdom of God!" To illustrate what "unrighteous" (ἀδικία) means concretely, the catalogue offers ten examples – vices that are "consistently considered reprehensible, also according to Hellenistic–Roman moral standards."[27]

At issue is the translation of the phrase in verse 9d, which is of interest here: μαλακοὶ οὔτε ἀρσενοκοῖται. Whereas μαλακός occurs often in extra-biblical Greek, albeit with quite different meanings,[28] ἀρσενοκοίτης is not attested prior to Paul's use of the term. It is a neologism based on Leviticus 20:13 in the Septuagint: "And whoever lies with a man (ἄρσενος) sexual intercourse (as) with a woman (κοίτην γυναικός), both have committed an abomination" (we find the same terminology in Lev 18:22). In extra-biblical Greek, the expression first occurs in the imperial period.[29] If the term μαλακός denotes the passive role in homoerotic sexual practice, then ἀρσενοκοίτης denotes the active role. However, it is unclear whether this is a reference specifically to pederasty (boy love),[30] or whether such a limitation of the restriction is not intended. The fact

---

27 Lindemann, *1 Kor*, 140: "including the sphere of homoeroticism" (with reference to Hans Herter, "Art. Effeminatus," in *RAC*, vol. 4, 620 – 642); but there are also "critical statements" about homosexual practices in Greek literature, as an example of which Lindemann refers to *Anthologia Graeca* IX 686: "The wanderer who comes to Thessalonica reads in a gate inscription that it is a well-governed city (βάρβαρον οὐ τρομέεις, οὐκ ἄρρενας ἀρρενοκοίτας) and need fear neither barbarians nor men who espouse men." See also note 54 below.

28 See the discussion in note 8 above; μαλακός = soft. In extra-biblical Greek, the word refers to men who act like women; in Latin: *effeminatus*.

29 Cf. Wolfgang Schrage, *Der erste Brief an die Korinther (1 Kor 1,1 – 6,11)* (EKK 7.1; Zürich: Benziger/Neukirchener, 1991), 430 – 432.

30 Jacob Kremer, *Der erste Brief an die Korinther* (RNT; Regensburg: Pustet, 1997), 116: The terms μαλακοί and ἀρσενοκοῖται both, "according to most interpreters, denote those men–women are never mentioned in this context – who passively (invitingly) or actively engage in same-sex intercourse. The widespread translation of μαλακοί and ἀρσενοκοῖται as 'catamites' and 'pederasts' rightly assumes that these are 'merely' references to offenses with adolescents (pederasty, the love of boys, was very common in the pagan environment and often praised as the ideal). (On the other hand, only Rom 1:27 [cf. Lev 18:22; 20:13] speaks unequivocally of 'men with men')"; Lindemann, *1 Kor*, 133 has: "neither effiminates nor pederasts." In fact, pederasty was the dominant form of homosexual contact in antiquity; see Robin Scroggs, *The New Testament and Homosexuality: Contextual Background for Contemporary Debate* (Philadelphia: Fortress Press, 1983), 29 – 62.

that this neologism is grounded in the directives in Leviticus 18:22 and 20:13 speaks in favor of the second hypothesis.[31]

Verse 11a is a remarkable conclusion to this list, demonstrating that Paul is looking at "the behavior, not at the underlying predisposition. Otherwise he could not say: 'And such were some of you! '"[32]

2.2 The Torah Is for the Lawless: Observations on the Catalogue of Vices in 1 Timothy 1:8–11

Closely related to 1 Corinthians 6:9–11 is 1 Timothy 1:8–11, where once again we find the term ἀρσενοκοίτης in the context of a traditional catalogue of vices, with a total of fourteen vices or perverse attitudes. As the parallel columns in the following synopsis illustrate, there is some evidence to suggest that Pseudo-Paul arranged the vices – some of which occur in pairs, and some individually – in accordance with the Decalogue. The fact that verses 9f–10c refer to commandments five through ten is undisputed, but the theory that verses 9c–e refer to the first four commandments is not. "Direct terminological echoes of the Decalogue" are not present in either case.[33] While the wider context concerns the proper use of the Torah (cf. v. 8c) – a question about which our author is in dispute with his opponents (cf. 1 Tim 1:3–7 immediately prior to the passage we are considering here) – verses 9–10 make clear that he ascribes to the Torah an ordering function for moral life, with a particular focus on the Decalogue. The idea that he un-

---

31 Dieter Zeller, *Der erste Brief an die Korinther* (KEK 5; Göttingen: Vandenhoeck & Ruprecht, 2010), 217: "Attempts to restrict the Pauline statements to prostitution or pederasty fail on the basis of the general expression ἀρσενοκοῖται, which is oriented to the OT, and which in the parallel in Rom 1:26f. is also extended to same-sex intercourse among women." I agree with the first part of this statement, but not with the second (see below on Rom 1:26–27). See Loader, *New Testament*, 331, which asserts that it is "certainly not limited to the latter (= pederasty)"; see also William L. Petersen, "Can ARSENOKOITAI be translated by 'Homosexuals'? (1 Cor 6.9; 1 Tim 1.10)," *VigChr* 40 (1986): 187–191.

32 See Zeller, *1 Kor*, 218. He continues: "Thus [Paul] does not do justice to the complex biological, psychological, and social conditions of homosexuality." See also Kremer (*1 Cor*, 116), who argues: "The widespread designation 'homosexuals' is in any case unsuitable in this instance, especially since this term, according to the modern view, includes not only perpetrators [*sic!*], but also those predisposed [*sic!*] to it."

33 Jürgen Roloff, *Der erste Brief an Timotheus* (EKK 15; Zürich: Benziger/Neukirchener, 1988), 75f: "Lists of vices that paralleled the commandments on the second tablet of the Decalogue were widespread in Judaism."

derstands the Decalogue "as a normative codification of the divine law," however, cannot be inferred from the text.[34]

1 Timothy 1:8 – 11	*References to the Decalogue*

8 a Now we know
  b that *the law* is good,
  c   if one uses it legitimately.
9 a This means understanding
  b that *the law* is laid down not for the innocent
  c   but for the lawless and disobedient,   Offenses against the
  d   for the godless and sinful,   realm of the divine
  e   for the unholy and profane,   (first four commandments?)
  f   for those who kill their father or mother,   Fifth commandment
  g   for murderers,   Sixth commandment
10 a   for those who sleep with males (ἀρσενοκοῖται),   Seventh commandment
  b   slave traders,   Eighth commandment
  c   liars, perjurers,   Ninth commandment
  d and whatever else is contrary to the sound teaching
11 a that conforms to the *glorious gospel* of the blessed God,
  b which he entrusted to me.

The question of translation, which is pernicious in 1 Corinthians 6:9, also arises in 1 Timothy 1:10a. Again, the fact that the neologism ἀρσενοκοίτης is a reference to Leviticus 18:22 and 20:13 speaks against the widespread understanding in the sense of pederasty,[35] as was also the case with 1 Corinthians 6:9 above. This is particularly clear here because the term occurs in a(nother) vice catalogue and stands under the banner of the Torah. It is also noteworthy that the author indi-

---

34 Ibid., 75 f.: "What speaks against this assumption [that the text also refers to the first tablet, and hence to the Decalogue as a whole], besides the fact that neither Jewish–Hellenistic nor NT catalogues take up the first tablet of the Decalogue, is the observation that nowhere in the NT is there an attempt to introduce the Decalogue into the paraenesis as a normative factor. There is only a reception of the Ten Commandments 'in the context of central theological statements' [H. Hübner], but not for the sake of the Decalogue itself. Thus here as well, the Ten Commandments seem to serve little more than a merely heuristic function. They are not yet understood as the sum total of God's enduring law."

35 Roloff (*1 Tim* 60) translates this as: "Knabenschänder." Here we also note that many English translations render this phrase with the term "sodomites" or "homosexuals." The King James Version translates the phrase as: "them that defile themselves with mankind," while the New International Version has: "those practicing homosexuality." See also Philip H. Towner (*The Letters to Timothy and Titus*, NICNT [Grand Rapids/Cambridge: Eerdmans, 2006], 122), who renders the phrase: "for those practicing homosexuality." The term "homosexuality" in translations should be avoided at all costs because it introduces modern concepts into the ancient texts.

rectly connects Leviticus 18:22 and 20:13 to the seventh commandment in the Decalogue, thus giving high priority to the directives of the "Torah of Holiness."

On the other hand, from a hermeneutical point of view, we should bear in mind that in Paul's teaching – including here in 1 Timothy – the "law" is also brought into relationship with the "gospel" (v. 11). As Jürgen Roloff points out:

> the pastoral epistles have tried to hold on to the Pauline heritage, insofar as they proclaimed – with Paul – believers' fundamental freedom from the law. [...] Their answer to the inevitable question of where the law, if its salvific function is rejected, finds a place as a regulatory function for Christians, is that the sound doctrine that originates from the gospel fulfills this regulatory function. This does not happen in the law's manner of coercion and threat, but in that the gospel creates a new possibility of salvific, communal life for believers, namely *love*. The gospel points to the existing orders of the world and society, not by threatening, and still less by establishing a meritorious principle of achievement, but by bestowing and enabling.[36]

These remarks are based on 1 Timothy 1:5, immediately prior to our passage, in which Pseudo-Paul programmatically declares with respect to the law: "But the aim of all such instruction (τῆς παραγγελίας) is love that comes from a pure heart, a good conscience, and sincere faith."

These rather general hermeneutical considerations are important in addressing the catalogue of vices in 1 Timothy. If the Torah in general or the Decalogue in particular displays a rather defensive, negative character – "the law is laid down not for the innocent but for the lawless and disobedient" (v. 9b–c) – then love prevails positively, as the power of salvation. Love is the fundamental principle that governs the moral conduct of the just. Individual norms must be subordinated to and measured by this principle.

2.3 "Against Nature": On the Argumentation in Romans 1:26–27

In the case of Rom 1:26–27 – which the most important passage in relation to our topic, along with Leviticus 18:22 and 20:3 – the context in which the verse is placed is crucial, which is why we must turn to this issue first.[37]

---

36 Roloff, *1 Tim*, 81 (emphasis in the original).
37 Hardly any other passage in Romans has been the subject of so many studies in recent years as Romans 1:26–27; see Michael Theobald, *Der Römerbrief* (EdF 294; Darmstadt: Wissenschaftliche Buchgesellschaft, 2000), 142–145, namely the excursus on "Das Argument 'contra naturam' und die Homosexualität (1,26f.). Zur ethischen Normativität der Schöpfungsordnung"

It is striking that Paul does not address the topic in the parenetic, moral-exhortatory part of his letter (Rom 12 – 15:13), but in the argumentative, introductory part. Same-sex sexual practices do not seem to have been a "pastoral problem" among the letter's addressees. Moreover, when we consider the argumentation in Romans 1:16 – 31, the topic ranks quite low in terms of the logic employed. Let us therefore take a closer look at the structure of this argumentation.

Romans 1:26 – 27 form part of a kind of prophetic judgment speech in which Paul exposes humankind's sinful, fallen nature: in Romans 1:18 – 32 that of the ἔθνη, the the nations,[38] and in Romans 2 that of his own people, the Jews. Why does Paul attach such importance to demonstrating the sinful depravity of all humankind? We find the answer in the letter's main theme, formulated in the central thesis in Romans 1:16 – 17: only the gospel of Jesus Christ can save people – whether Jew or Gentile – from the calamity of the world. This gospel is justification and life. However, this means that all people – and, according to Paul, especially the Jews – are entangled in the calamities of this world, or as it says toward the end of the prophetic judgment speech in Romans 3:9: "all are

---

(with references); as well as the list in Michael Wolter, *Der Brief an die Römer (Teilband 1: Röm 1 – 8)* (EKK 6.1; Neukirchen-Vluyn: Neukirchener Theologie/Patmos, 2014), 133 f.; see also Loader, *New Testament* 293 – 326; Diana M. Swancutt, "'The Disease of Effemination': The Charge of Effeminacy and the Verdict of God (Romans 1:18 – 2:16)," in *New Testament Masculinities*, ed. Stephen D. Moore and Janice Capel Anderson (SBL Semeia Studies 45; Atlanta: Society of Biblical Literature, 2003), 193 – 233; Robert Jewett, *Romans: A Commentary* (Hermeneia; Minneapolis: Fortress Press, 2007), 172 – 181; Richard N. Longenecker, *The Epistle to the Romans: A Commentary on the Greek Text* (NIGTC; Grand Rapids: Eerdmans, 2016), 217 – 219, 229 f.; David J. Murphy, "More Evidence Pertaining to 'Their Females' in Romans 1:26," *JBL* 138 (2019): 221 – 240; Martin Ebner, "Verbietet das Neue Testament 'Homosexualität'? Neutestamentliche Grundlagen zu einer aktuellen Streitfrage," *Lebendige Seelsorge* 70 (2019): 55 – 60; Ansgar Wucherpfennig, *Sexualität bei Paulus* (Freiburg im Breisgau: Herder, 2020).

38 In Romans 1:18, however, which constitutes the "heading" of the whole argument in 1:19 – 3:20, Paul avoids the word ἔθνη and instead speaks *in principle* of "men." On the one hand, this can be ascribed to the function of this verse as a "heading"; on the other hand, it is a clever rhetorical device, because this speech – which is peculiarly detached and addresses men's transgressions and their just consequences in the third person – is intended for an interlocutor who has been steeped in *Jewish* thought. This interlocutor can only agree with the remarks in 1:18 – 32, since Paul, in accordance with his own religious background, presents humankind's situation from an entirely Jewish perspective, as the hopeless situation of *others* – that is, the Gentiles. The attentive reader will have already recognized that Paul is up to something here by the fact that he turns the tables in 2:1, so that the one who has already applauded this prophetic judgment speech is afflicted with his own guilt, and thus has already pronounced judgment on himself. In contrast to Jewish apocalyptic literature, Paul refuses to divide humankind into the pious and the godless: "There is *no one* who is righteous, *not even one*," he declares in Romans 3:10, taking up Ecclesiastes 7:20 LXX.

under the power of sin." Paul defines sin (ἡ ἁμαρτία) in the introduction to the whole judgment speech in Romans 1:18, namely "ungodliness and wickedness" – the refusal to acknowledge God as God, and thus also the rejection of his will, which demands justice in human coexistence. According to Paul's thesis in Romans 1:18, such doubly determinate behavior – negating the creator as well as the fellow human being – has always been subject to God's wrath: that is, to the threat of his judgment. Paul explicates this point in what follows. On the one hand, he declares that anyone who denies the creator is culpable, and he justifies this assertion on the grounds that people always had the chance to recognize him through his works (Rom 1:19 – 20).[39] On the other hand, he shows this denial of the creator – for which the offender is culpable – leads to punishment, which consists in the fact that God "gives them up" to the depths of their impure hearts (Rom 1:24, 26, 28), so that the punishment takes the form of new offenses against his will. Three times Paul expounds on this connection between guilt and punishment with great rhetorical force (Rom 1:21 – 24, 25 – 27, 28 – 31).[40] Paul's description of their guilt becomes shorter and shorter, while his description of their punishment becomes longer and longer. The reader is left with the impression of a cycle of sin in which people are inexcusably (Rom 1:20) but also inescapably involved. The second description in verses 25 – 27 is of particular interest for our purposes here:

25 a because they [the people] *exchanged* the truth about God for a lie
 b and worshipped and served the creature rather than the Creator,
 c who is blessed forever! Amen.
26 a *For this reason* (διὰ τοῦτο) God gave them [the people] up to degrading passions.
 b *Then* (γάρ) *their females* exchanged *natural* [use] (τὴν φυσικὴν χρῆσιν) for *unnatural* (παρὰ φύσιν),
27 a in the same way (ὁμοίως) also *the males*, giving up the *natural* use of femaleness (τὴν φυσικὴν χρῆσιν τῆς θηλείας),
 b were consumed with passion for one another.
 c *Males* committed shameless acts with *males* (ἄρσενες ἐν ἄρσεσιν)
 d and received in their own persons the due penalty for their error.

The text evinces a stereotypical manner of speech and thought. The fact that people "exchanged the truth about God for a lie and worshipped and served the creature rather than the Creator" – as stated in the preceding verse 25a – b, which the *berakha* "who is blessed forever" further underscores rhetorically –

---

39 In his summary of this argument in verse 21a–c: "for though they knew God, they did not honor him as God or give thanks to him (ηὐχαρίστησαν)" (cf. verse 25), he also hints at humankind's basic sin, which amounts to "not wanting to thank the Creator."
40 Cf. the diagram with details of the respective parallel formulations in Wolter, *Röm I*, 135.

takes aim at pagan idolatry as the worship of creation (cf. Rom 1:23). Thus this verse reproduces the familiar Jewish prejudice against pagan depravity. Those in the Greek tradition who sought God – such as Socrates and Plato, to name just a few – are left out, without this becoming a problem in any way.

The subsequent presentation of God's punishment in verses 26–27 is also stereotypical: the perversion of sexuality as a consequence of idolatry,[41] which also establishes a linguistic correspondence between the "exchange" of "natural intercourse" for intercourse that is "unnatural"[42] and the previous "exchange" through which the creature is worshipped in place of the Creator.[43]

It is important for the logic of the argument and the significance of the passage that Paul once again formulates a kind of subheading in verse 26a, which he then explains in verses 26b–27, indicated by a justificatory γάρ: "For this reason God gave them [the people] up to degrading passions." As all-encompassing as this heading sounds, the explanation that follows is equally all-encompassing, for it was probably not true of all pagans that "*their females* exchanged *natural* [use] (τὴν φυσικὴν χρῆσιν) for *unnatural* (παρὰ φύσιν)" (v. 26c), and likewise that all "*the males*" gave up the "*natural* use of *femaleness* (τὴν φυσικὴν χρῆσιν τῆς θηλείας)." The terminology here is significant. By using the substantive adjectives αἱ θήλειαι ("the females") and οἱ ἄρσενες ("the males") here, rather than the standard nouns αἱ γυναῖκες ("the women") und οἱ ἄνδρες ("the men"), Paul signals that he is concerned with "biological gender identity" (sex) and that "social gender identity" (gender) takes a back seat. "Even where the sexual practices of men and women are negotiated in terms of their conformity with or deviation from "nature' outside the New Testament, these adjectives are generally used."[44] This alone indicates the distance between this text and the modern concept of homosexuality as an aspect of personal identity. The meaning of the first statement about "the females" in verse 26b is controversial. How are we to interpret this?

---

41 See above, notes 21 and 22.

42 See the Testament of Naphtali 3:4–5: "But ye shall not be so, my children, recognizing in the firmament, in the earth, and in the sea, and in all created things, the Lord who made all things, that ye become not as Sodom, which *changed the order of nature* (ἐνήλλαξεν τάξιν φύσεως αὐτῆς)." Order (τάξις) is a key word in the Testament of Naphtali; see 2:8, 9; 3:2, 4; 8:9, 10.

43 Behind this correspondence between deed and punishment is the Jewish principle of appropriate retribution, in accordance with the link between what one does and who one becomes.

44 Wolter, *Röm I*, 149 (with references).

The idea that Paul had lesbian relationships in mind here – which is the common interpretation[45] – is not convincing, because early Judaism hardly considers such relationships worth mentioning, and the Old Testament does not address them anywhere.[46] The primary weakness of this interpretation is that it interprets verse 26b along the same lines as the subsequent verse, but there is no formulation in 26b which corresponds to verse 27c – that is, whereas 27c has "male with male," there is nothing in 26b about "female with female." So what does Paul mean by "natural" and "unnatural" here? If he does not have lesbian relationships in mind, then the most plausible of the interpretations offered seems to be the idea that women exchanged their natural sexual practice for an "unnatural" one in which they practice heterosexual but non-coital sexual intercourse for contraceptive purposes.[47] In this case, the natural practice of female sexuality is determined by the Jewish conviction (which also partly overlaps with Greek–Hellenistic ideas[48]) that the "natural" purpose of sexual union is procreation – in line with the exhortation in Genesis 1:28: "Be fruitful and multiply."[49] This interpretation is supported by the fact that Romans 1:18–32 is measured against the order of creation in other respects,[50] and also

---

45 Zeller, *1 Kor*, 217; see more recently Loader, *Making Sense*, 137 f.; and Jewett, *Romans* 176. Wucherpfennig (*Sexualität* 124) does not exclude this interpretation.
46 See notes 15, 18, and also 19 above.
47 See also James E. Miller, "The Practices of Romans 1:26: Homosexual or Heterosexual?," *NT* 37 (1995): 1–11; Roy Bowen Ward, "Why Unnatural? The Tradition behind Romans 1:26–27," *HThR* 90 (1997): 263–284; Murphy, "More Evidence" (with illuminating references to patristic exegesis), 221: "Although it is the interpretation attested first in the church, AO [= the view that the females took up anal and/or oral sex with men] has been revived only recently."
48 Cf. Ward, "Why Unnatural," 269–277 (on Philo and Pseudo-Phocylides); cf. also Josephus, *C. Ap.* 2.199: "But, then, what are our laws about marriage? That law owns no other mixture of sexes but that *which nature hath appointed* (κατὰ φύσιν), of a man with his wife, and that this be used only *for the procreation of children* (εἰ μέλλοι τέκνων ἕνεκα γίνεσθαι). But it abhors the mixture of a male with a male (τὴν δὲ πρὸς ἄρρενας ἀρρένων); and if any one do that, death is its punishment"; see also 2.273–275.
49 Ward ("Why Unnatural," 264–267) points out that the κατὰ (παρὰ) φύσιν terminology is taken from the Timaeus creation myth: "Femaleness is defined by procreation in which the female of the species is the passive receptor of the male seed. The active/passive dichotomy, representing male citizens and women respectively, was already the cultural norm in Plato's time, yet he did offer an innovative rationale for this dichotomy and gave it normative value *in the order of creation* as κατὰ φύσιν" (267, my emphasis). See also note 19 above, as well as the example in Plato, *Leg.* 836c, where he describes intercourse among males as "unnatural" (τὸ μὴ φύσει τοῦτο εἶναι).
50 See verses 19, 23, and 25. See also Stowasser, "Homosexualität," 518: "The formulation of Romans 1:23 is largely inspired by the order of creatin in Genesis 1:26–7, which is in any case rounded off in Genesis 1:28 with the mandate to multiply. The theme of creation is also present

by the specific terminology I have already mentioned – "the female" and "the male" – which unilaterally emphasizes biological sex and accentuates procreation and childbearing.[51]

This interpretation of verse 26b suits the subsequent verse 27 quite well. There is a good reason why the word ὁμοίως (meaning "just the same") is used to link these two verses: "just as" "the females" violate the exclusively procreative purpose of sexuality by "using" their sexuality as described in the text,[52] "the males" do the same when they turn to same-sex sexual practices.

An orientation around the traditional purpose of marriage – namely procreation – thus connects the two statements about women and men. Both are sweeping statements, and while the one about women lacks any specificity, the one about men has "little or nothing" to do with the circumstances obtaining in the non-Jewish sphere. It was not the case that

> "the" – i.e., all – men abandoned "normal" heterosexual sexual intercourse, nor were heterosexual and homosexual relationships mutually exclusive. Moreover, Paul's presentation of inter-male sexual practice in v. 27b–c as a relationship characterized by reciprocal egalitarianism [they "were consumed with passion for one another"; "males with males"] does not correspond to reality in such a sweeping way, because like every sexual relationship,

---

in Romans 1:25; the designation of wrongdoing as παρὰ τὸν κτίσαντα even created a linguistic approximation to that of 1:26: παρὰ φύσιν"; and similarly Loader, *New Testament*, 313–315. One must also keep in mind that Leviticus 18:22 and 20:13 are to be understood in terms of the guiding principle of procreation; see note 14 above.

51 Cf. Genesis 1:27, 5:2 LXX; Mark 10:6 = Matthew 19:4; Galatians 3:28. The same terminology is also found in Plato (cf. Ward, "Why Unnatural," 264–267: "θῆλυ differs from γυνή inasmuch as the former denotes one who bears and nurses offspring, whether human or animal, while γυνή refers to any human woman." Wucherpfennig (*Sexualität*, 108) denies this connection, though without compelling reasons: "The idea that sexual activity acquires its natural legitimacy only through the production of offspring is not to be found in him [Paul]." Evaluating the conclusion that a condemnation of lesbian relations in Jewish literature is first attested in Pseudo-Phocylides (see note 18 above), Klaus Haacker (*Der Brief des Paulus an die Römer* [ThHK 6; Leipzig: Evangelische Verlagsanstalt, 1999]) argues that "the generally held formulation in v. 26 is very difficult to explain as an allusion to a tradition presumed to be known and recognized. [...] I therefore understand it as incorporating the warning against sexual intercourse with animals which immediately follows the condemnation of intercourse between men in Lev 18:23, and which expressly includes women." But why then does Paul allude to Leviticus 18:23 and 24 in reverse order? Thus we see that Haacker's alternative interpretation is also too narrow.

52 This is also true of intercourse which takes place between "females," but Paul does not address this in v. 26b (see above).

such relationships was also based on the distinction between active and passive roles, and thereby mapped social hierarchies.[53]

Thus Paul declares that which was forbidden by the Jewish moral law according to Leviticus 18:22 and 20:13 – namely same-sex sexual relations between men – to be a behavior typical of ἔθνη, the people of the nations.[54] Here he uses this Jewish anti-pagan stereotype to illustrate the fact that all people, concretely the "Gentiles," are entangled in the calamity burdening the world – thus operating on the lowest level of his argumentation, so to speak, by reproducing this cliché for rhetorical effect, exploiting his readers' expected consent. Both of these factors prevent us from placing Romans 1:26–27 at the center of Paul's ethics.

3 On the Need to Reform the Catechism of the Catholic Church

Are the Pauline statements on same-sex sexual practice – especially in Romans 1:26–27 – still applicable to contemporary discussions of the topic? As is well known, the 1993 Catechism of the Catholic Church (revised in 1997) answers this question in the affirmative, referring to Paul – and specifically to Romans 1:26–27 – as the basis for the teaching "that homosexual acts are intrinsically disordered" and "are contrary to the natural law" because "they close the sexual

---

53 Wolter, *Röm I*, 152; with reference to verse 26b, Wolter abstains from any further interpretation: "Paul merely says that there are women who exchange 'natural' sexual intercourse for the 'unnatural' – he leaves open what it is they do."

54 The *Letter of Aristeas* puts it as follows: "For *most of the rest of humankind* defile themselves when they have associations, committing great injustice [...] For not only do they procure males, but also they defile mothers and even still daughters. We, however, have been kept apart from these things" (*Let. Aris.* 152–153). We should note, with Roloff, that same-sex love in the Greek world was "by no means universally morally accepted, despite its prevalence"; Roloff, *1 Tim*, 77, with reference to Hans Licht, *Die Homoerotik in der griechischen Literatur* (Abhandlungen aus dem Gebiet der Sexualforschung 3.3; Bonn: Marcus & Weber, 1921). According to Swancutt ("Disease"), Paul has Stoic philosophers in mind in Romans 1:18–32. Wucherpfennig (*Sexualität*) adopts this view and states with reference to 1:27: "It means that Stoic teachers humiliated their students through homosexual activity" (125). But there is no indication that this sweeping statement should be limited in this way; moreover, Romans 2:1 (about which Wucherpfennig claims: "Here Paul overturns the socially dominant philosophy with a caricature of the self-righteous Stoic sage") does not permit such a specification, since Paul says: "Therefore you have no excuse, whoever you are, when you judge others."

act to the gift of life" (no. 2357). The corresponding note on this text also includes Genesis 19, thus transmitting an uncritical moral disqualification of "homosexual acts" as sodomy.[55] As for Romans 1:26–27, the Catechism uses these verses indiscriminately to develop its own doctrine of natural law, ignoring their context and disregarding their rhetorical character. There are three main arguments against such a use of Scripture.

First, for Paul, same-sex sexual practices would connote a deliberate turning away from "natural intercourse with women," which is why he also understands such practices as sin – irrespective of the overriding idea that they are also a vehicle for God's punishment. In the Greek tradition, we occasionally encounter voices that are aware of the possibility of same-sex sexual practice based on a predisposition,[56] but in the case of Paul's Jewish perspective, such a concept

---

55 Here the Catechism aligns itself with a long tradition stretching back to antiquity; cf. Hoheisel, "Art. Homosexualität," 329 f. The 1986 "letter" to the bishops from the Congregation for the Doctrine of the Faith (*Letter to the Bishops of the Catholic Church on the Pastoral Care of Homosexual Persons* [Rome: Vatican, 1986], no. 6, http://www.vatican.va/roman_curia/congregations/cfaith/documents/rc_con_cfaith_doc_19861001_homosexual-persons_en.html [accessed April 21, 2021]), is even more explicit: "Thus, in Genesis 19:1–11, the deterioration due to sin [since the fall] continues in the story of the men of Sodom. There can be no doubt of the moral judgement made there against homosexual relations." The "letter" also gives an account of the underlying hermeneutics. Number 5 acknowledges that "it is quite true that the Biblical literature owes to the different epochs in which it was written a good deal of its varied patterns of thought and expression (*Dei Verbum* 12)," but it counters this by noting "a clear consistency within the Scriptures themselves on the moral issue of homosexual behaviour," which it adopts as "the solid foundation of a constant Biblical testimony" on which Church tradition, unbroken to this day, "is thus based." Moreover, "it is likewise essential to recognize that the Scriptures are not properly understood when they are interpreted in a way which contradicts the Church's living Tradition."

56 Aristotle, for example, speaks of pederasty as a behavior which arises "in some cases from natural disposition, and in others from habit, as with those who have been abused from childhood"; *Nicomachean Ethics* 7.5, 1148b. See also Plato, *Symp.* 191d–193d: "Thus, each of us is the matching half of a human being, since we have been severed like a flatfish, two coming from one, and each part is always seeking its other half [...] Those women who are split from a woman, however, have no interest at all in men, but rather are oriented toward women [...] Those who are split from the male (ἄρρενος) pursue males (τὰ ἄρρενα). While they are boys, since they are a slice of a male, they are fond of men and enjoy lying with men and becoming entwined with them. These are the best of the boys and young men, and at the same time they are the most manly in nature (φύσει). Anyone who says they are shameless is mistaken, for they do this, not from shamelessness, but from courage, manliness, and masculinity, welcoming what is like themselves. There is a definite proof of this: Only men of this sort are completely successful in the affairs of the city. When they become men, they are lovers of boys and by nature (φύσει) are not interested in marriage and having children, though they are forced into it by cus-

is not even a distant possibility.[57] But if contemporary human sciences substantiate the existence of permanent same-sex sexual orientations or predispositions, due to whatever factors, then the Pauline texts can no longer be used as an argumentative authority for a serious theological anthropology that is in conversation with the human sciences. With Stegemann and others, I argue that it is anachronistic to read the biblical texts along the hermeneutical lines of what we understand as "homosexuality" today.[58]

Second, in the context of his Jewish tradition, Paul only speaks of same-sex sexual practices;[59] he is not able to conceive of them as an expression of person-

---

tom (ὑπὸ τοῦ νόμου). They would be satisfied to live all the time with one another without marrying." Cf. Hoheisel, "Art. Homosexualität," 310 f.; see also Zeller, *1 Kor*, 218 n. 140.

57 In contrast, Haacker (*Brief des Paulus*, 54) observes: "It is widely overlooked [...] that Paul, under the auspice of παρέδωκεν αὐτούς, alludes to an irresistible, fateful homosexual inclination, which he interprets theologically, while other ancient sources explain the phenomenon astrologically. Thus one cannot solve the hermeneutical problem of the relevant biblical texts by claiming that antiquity did not yet recognize the phenomenon of 'constitutional' homoerotic inclinations." On the other hand, it must be said that the wording in Romans 1 does not intend to abrogate a person's responsibility for their actions. Otherwise the speech, which seeks to hold its readers responsible for their actions, would lose its argumentative force (see note 39 above). See also Jewett (*Romans*, 173), who argues: "In contrast to traditional moralizing based on this passage, sexual perversion is, in Paul's view, 'the result of God's wrath, not the reason for it' (Käsemann)."

58 See section 1 above. It is precisely such an anachronistic reading that characterizes the Catholic Church's documents. The Council of the Evangelical Church in Germany is more advanced than the Catechism in this area and has issued a much more nuanced document on the subject: *Mit Spannungen leben: Eine Orientierungshilfe des Rates der Evangelischen Kirche in Deutschland zum Thema 'Homosexualität'* (Living with Tension: The Council of the Evangelical Church in Germany's Guide to the Topic of "Homosexuality"), EKD 57 (February 26, 1996), https://archiv.ekd.de/EKD-Texte/44736.html (accessed December 15, 2020). Concerning the biblical evidence (in chapter 2), on the one hand this "guide" states: "The thesis that there is no (explicit) mention of predispositional, premeditated homosexuality in the Bible is true, but says nothing about whether and to what extent such a view of homosexuality would modify or correct the respective biblical statements"; see 2.3. But can this really be a matter of modification or correction, and not rather a dismissal of the biblical passages in question? On the other hand, after appraising Jesus's ethos, for example, the document arrives at the following assessment of the issue, which admittedly still seems fractured: "based on the overall testimony of the Bible, it must be said that in forming a homosexual relationship (as with any other interpersonal relationship), the decisive factor is whether it is lived out in love for God and for humankind, which also means: whether it encompasses a readiness to accept the burdens of a relationship. The tension between the biblical opposition to homosexual practice as such and the affirmation of its ethical formation according to the will of God does not therefore disappear, but can be understood and endured on this basis." Obviously the principle of *sola scriptura* plays an obstructive role here.

59 Cf. note 44 above.

al identity. In our contemporary context, however, the issue in many ways is one of personal dignity and the rights of people in same-sex partnerships,[60] on the basis of which we must draw the conclusion that Paul is simply not an appropriate discussion partner for us today – at least as far as Romans 1:26–27 is concerned.

Third, while Paul orients himself in Romans 1 as a Jewish theologian concerned with the order of creation, exegetical analysis also demonstrates that the way in which he sets the "natural" in opposition to the "unnatural" is at the same time part of a "rhetorical strategy" that is "solely intended to discredit behaviors that contradict (one's own) cultural conventions."[61] However, his theological classification of the topic under the order of creation does not simply dissolve into rhetoric, which is why this passage calls for a theological hermeneutics. What Catholic doctrine describes as an immutable "law of nature" must be rethought from the perspective of a historically oriented theological anthropology.[62] Sexuality is always also a social construct.[63] Therefore the question is

---

60 When the Catechism of the Catholic Church states that "homosexual persons are called to chastity" (no. 2359), it demonstrates its inability to consider the issue from the position of holistic personhood. This is also demonstrated in the revealing statement on "homosexual acts" (no. 2357): "They do not proceed from a genuine affective and sexual complementarity." The Catechism considers the immutability of the Church's moral teaching more important than addressing the real-life circumstances of same-sex oriented people who demand answers from the faith. Thus it states: "tradition has always declared that 'homosexual acts are intrinsically disordered'" (no. 2357). This *topos* of a constant, unchanging church doctrine which determines all church documents could become a snare for us today.

61 Wolter, *Röm I*, 153. He continues: "What has always been considered 'natural' is what the majority does, while deviation from the norm has been devalued as 'unnatural.' Such argumentation is always solely concerned with marginalizing people who deviate from the socially prevailing norm. What people deem 'natural' and 'unnatural' is therefore in reality nothing more than a cultural construct." Moreover, because "people's sexual practice [...] is always embedded (in) culturally mediated and learned patterns of perception and behavior," from this perspective it is also "impossible to distinguish between 'natural' and 'unnatural' approaches to human sexuality." See also Jewett, *Romans*, 177: "Paul is raising a cultural norm to the level of a 'natural' and thus biological principle, which would probably have to be formulated differently today." Longenecker (*Romans*, 230) takes a different approach. In a major scholarly commentary (with Charles Talbert) in 2016, under the heading "Contextualization for Today," he succinctly declares: "if homosexual acts are wrong, those committing them are sinners, like the rest of us, who are in need of a Savior. So Christians are called to show Christ's love to them, not a radical intolerance."

62 The Congregation for the Doctrine of the Faith's *Letter to the Bishops of the Catholic Church* (see note 55), however, pulls the rug out from under this possibility by starting from a doctrine of creation interpreted in terms of natural law: "Providing a basic plan for understanding this entire discussion of homosexuality is the theology of creation we find in Genesis. God, in his in-

whether theological anthropology, in conversation with the human sciences, should perhaps come to consider homosexual and heterosexual predispositions as variants of sexuality and as a gift – as a sign of the diversity of God's good creation. This would require an approach that places the human person, with all of their characteristics and possibilities, at the center of theological discourse.

As the author of Romans 1:26–27 (as well as 1 Cor 6:9), for the three reasons mentioned above, Paul may no longer be an authoritative interlocutor for us today. Nevertheless, he offers important insights elsewhere that support us in our question regarding the theological grounds on which we might situate the Church as a true home for gay and lesbian people. In particular, Galatians 3:28 is a text to which we must turn our attention as we conclude.

4 The Significance of Galatians 3:28 for an Ecclesiastical Accommodation of Different Personal Identities and Orientations

As we have seen in our discussion above, Romans 1:26–27 certainly does not stand at the center of the gospel. The maxim in Galatians 3:28, however, is of the utmost importance for Pauline ecclesiology, as demonstrated not only by its high significance in the overall argumentation of the Letter to the Galatians, but also by the fact that it is reiterated in 1 Corinthians 12:13 and Colossians 3:11. It is possible that Paul did not formulate it himself, but learned it – along with other gospel principles – from the church in Antioch and subsequently adopted it. It reads:

---

finite wisdom and love, brings into existence all of reality as a reflection of his goodness. He fashions mankind, male and female, in his own image and likeness. Human beings, therefore, are nothing less than the work of God himself; and in the complementarity of the sexes, they are called to reflect the inner unity of the Creator. They do this in a striking way in their cooperation with him in the transmission of life by a mutual donation of the self to the other"; see no. 6. The proposition derived from this, which is also decisive for other moral-theological questions currently being debated, therefore reads as follows: "It is only in the marital relationship that the use of the sexual faculty can be morally good"; see no. 7. It follows that "[a] person engaging in homosexual behaviour therefore acts immorally." The same applies to a second marriage: according to this logic, if the first marriage was a sacramental one, then the second can only be considered an extramarital and therefore immoral "use of the sexual faculty." These issues are interrelated and together call for the further development of church teaching.
63 See section 1 above.

a There is no longer Jew or (οὐδέ) Greek,
b   there is no longer slave or (οὐδέ) free,
c   there is no longer male and female (ἄρσεν καὶ θῆλυ; cf. Gen 1:27 LXX);
d for all of you are one in Christ Jesus.

The immediate context of the maxim in Galatians 3:26–27 signals its "Sitz im Leben" and thus also the experiential background against which it should be understood: "For in Christ Jesus you are all children of God through faith. As many of you as were baptized into Christ have clothed yourselves with Christ." The experience of conversion culminates in the convert's baptism and first Eucharistic meal with their new community[64] – an experience in which the new believer leaves behind the former world, with all of its faults, hierarchies, and discord: "So if anyone is in Christ, there is a new creation: everything old has passed away; see, everything has become new!" (2 Cor 5:17).

People who are as different as the polar opposites described in this maxim come together, practice table fellowship, accept one another, and are freed from the constraint of having to assert themselves over against one another. They put their religious (v. 28a), social (v. 28b), and cultural identities (v. 28c) to rest in view of the fact that in Christ Jesus, they can each conceive of themselves as holding an equal position before God: Jews and Greeks (i.e., the people of the nations), slaves and free persons, men and women.

It is not only the first, but also the third dyad that is formulated from a Jewish perspective, specifically on the basis of Genesis 1:27, which says: "So God created humankind in his image, in the image of God he created them; *male and female* (ἄρσεν καὶ θῆλυ) he created them."[65] Particularly the first creation narrative, of which Genesis 1:27 is part – in contrast to the second, Genesis 2:4b–3:24, with its hierarchical sequence (first Adam, then Eve[66]) – contains an emancipatory potential, which also repeatedly been brought to bear in the text's reception history.[67] Galatians 3:28 also makes use of this potential, although Joel 2:28–29, a significant text for the early church, may also play into it.[68]

---

64 Hans-Ulrich Weidemann, *Taufe und Mahlgemeinschaft. Studien zur Vorgeschichte der altkirchlichen Taufeucharistie* (WUNT 338; Tübingen: Mohr Siebeck, 2014).

65 The contrast between the οὐδέ in Paul's first two pairings and the καί in his third pairing permits us to speak of a clear allusion to Genesis 1:27.

66 Cf. 1 Tim 2:11–14: "Let a woman learn in silence with full submission. I permit no woman to teach or to have authority over a man; she is to keep silent. For Adam was formed *first, then* Eve; and Adam was not deceived, but the woman was deceived and became a transgressor."

67 Valuable information on the reception of this text in the early church can be found in Gerhard Dautzenberg, "'Da ist nicht männlich und weiblich'. Zur Interpretation von Gal 3,28," in *Studien zur paulinischen Theologie und zur frühchristlichen Rezeption des Alten Testaments*, ed. Gerhard Dautzenberg and Dieter Sänger (Gießen: Selbstverlag des Fachbereichs, Evangelische

From a contemporary perspective, this maxim might also have consequences for the determination of the range of seemingly temporally remote but undoubtedly culturally shaped arguments from "nature," since Paul employs them along the lines of traditional anthropology in Romans 1:26–27. He ascribes decisive – though admittedly, as I have shown above, argumentatively subordinate – importance to the "proper" classification of the two sexes, from the perspective of the reproduction of humankind, in terms of their relationship to God, when he lists deviations from this classification under the category of "sin" and as a consequence of "God's wrath." According to Galatians 3:28, however, this does not apply, which is why the two texts stand in tension with one another: "Rom 1:26 f. stands in tension with Gal 3:28: in Rom 1:26 f. maleness and femaleness are of ultimate significance, whereas in Gal 3:28 they are of no significance."[69] This is also linked to the fact that Romans 1:26–27 is formulated from a creation-theological perspective, while Galatians 3:28 takes an eschatological view. Paul himself – unmarried and, in view of the (supposed) dawn of the end times, "anxious about the affairs of the Lord" (1 Cor 7:32) above all else[70] – speaks from a worldview in which marriage and the associated task of raising offspring are no longer the top priority, because "the present form of this world is passing away" (1 Cor 7:31), and "the ends of the ages have come" upon us (1 Cor 10:11). Thus Paul is completely consumed with the wish that "all were as I myself am" (1 Cor 7:7) – that is, unmarried![71]

Theologie und Katholische Theologie und deren Didaktik der Justus-Liebig-Universität, 1999), 69–99.

68 Joel 2:28–29: "Then afterward I will pour out my spirit on all flesh; *your sons and your daughters* shall prophesy, your old men shall dream dreams, and your young men shall see visions. Even on *the male and female slaves*, in those days, I will pour out my spirit." Cf. Acts 2:16–21.

69 Bernadette J. Brooten, *Love between Women: Early Christian Responses to Female Homoeroticism* (Chicago: University of Chicago Press, 1996), 265.

70 Solely because – from his personal perspective – he raises contrasts such as the following: "I want you to be free from anxieties. The unmarried man is anxious about the affairs of the Lord, how to please the Lord; but the married man is anxious about the affairs of the world, how to please his wife, and his interests are divided" (1 Cor 7:32–34).

71 Cf. Michael Theobald, "Die Ehetheologie des Epheserbriefs (Eph 5,21–33). Literarhistorischer Kontext und kanontheologische Relevanz," in *Ehe und Familie: Wege zum Gelingen aus katholischer Perspektive*, ed. George Augustin and Ingo Proft (Theologie im Dialog 13; Freiburg im Breisgau: Herder, 2014), 121–147, here 124–134 on 1 Corinthians 7 (see "Paulus – Patron der Enkratiten," among others). Although the Congregation for the Doctrine of the Faith's *Letter to the Bishops of the Catholic Church* (see note 55), no. 6, states: "Against the background of this exposition of theocratic law [in Lev 18:22 and 20:13], an *eschatological* perspective is developed by St. Paul when, in I Cor 6:9, he proposes the same doctrine and lists those who behave in a

Yet Galatians 3:28 does not simply declare that the factual differences between "Jews and Greeks," "slaves and free," or men and women do not exist; rather, it strips them of their soteriological relevance, which has concrete consequences for the effort to live together "in Christ": Jews should still be able to adhere to their traditions in the ecclesia – for example, to have their sons circumcised – but they must not and can no longer make this the *casus stantis et cadentis ecclesiae* and seek to impose it on others. Furthermore, slaves are not promised a revolt against their contemporary slaveholding society, but their masters are taken to task and told that social relations in the *oikos* must be determined by Christian love (see the Letter to Philemon). Likewise, relations between the sexes – their differences and classifications as Paul sees them, and indeed as large parts of society at that time saw them – are still valid, but they should not and must no longer play a role in the ecclesia: man and woman are equal, and the "charisms" (including κυβέρνησις or "forms of leadership" in the church; see 1 Cor 12:28) are solely the free gifts of the Holy Spirit (cf. 1 Cor 12; Rom 12) and are thus independent of characteristics such as age, sex, or origin.[72] Admittedly Paul occasionally finds these topics difficult, and his various statements on the subject do not always fit together seamlessly.[73]

Thus it should be all the more important to take the maxim in Galatians 3:28, which Paul himself declares to be a high priority in his Letter to the Galatians, theologically seriously.[74] On this basis, according to our contemporary hermeneut-

---

homosexual fashion among those who shall not enter the Kingdom of God," the letter nevertheless leaves it to the reader to discern what is meant by "eschatological perspective."

72 The pastoral letters, however, are different; they are orientated toward the second creation narrative (cf. note 65 above), and they reverse not only the emancipatory tendencies of the first churches Paul planted, but also the breadth of his doctrine of charisms to a significant extent.

73 1 Corinthians 11:2–16 remains a difficult text; it is by no means seamlessly argued, and it evinces a strong pragmatic orientation, since Paul seeks to use this letter to counter those emancipatory tendencies in Corinth which he finds unpleasant. Cf. Hans-Josef Klauck, *1. Korintherbrief* (NEB 7; Würzburg: Echter Verlag, 1984), 77–80; Klauck speaks of the "theological weaknesses of these speculations" (referring to v. 10), which Paul would be aware of and which he attempts to "correct" in v. 11–12 (see p. 79).

74 In the *Dogmatic Constitution of the Church: Lumen Gentium* (Rome: Vatican, 1964), no. 32, http://www.vatican.va/archive/hist_councils/ii_vatican_council/documents/vat-ii_const_19641121_lumen-gentium_en.html (accessed April 21, 2021), the Second Vatican Council pays particular attention to Galatians 3:28: "There is, therefore, in Christ and in the Church no inequality on the basis of race or nationality, social condition or sex, because 'there is neither Jew nor Greek: there is neither bond nor free: there is neither male nor female. For you are all "one" in Christ Jesus' (Gal 3:28; cf. Col 3:11). Therefore, from divine choice the laity have Christ for their brothers who though He is the Lord of all, came not to be served but to serve

ical premises, one would then conclude that different personal identities and orientations are also irrelevant when it comes to sex.[75] As Romans 1:26–27 insinuates, under no circumstances may one ascribe to a certain anthropological view of sexual classification a relevance that impacts upon one's relationship with God (the keyword here is "sin"). As Michael Wolter explains in his recent commentary on Romans:

> Gal 3:28 is relevant for the different sexual identities, insofar as cultural identity attributions play no role in this world of meaning which, for those who believe in Christ, constitutes God's "new creation" (2 Cor 5:17; Gal 6:15). When Paul writes: "for you are all one in Christ Jesus," this applies not only to the everyday worldly differences between "Jew and Greek," "slave and free," "male and female," but also to the difference between "homosexual" and "heterosexual."[76]

"Welcome one another, therefore, just as Christ has welcomed you, for the glory of God" – so the apostle writes in Romans 15:7, with an eye to the cultural and religious imprinting of the various house churches in Rome, thus formulating his "ecclesiological constitution."[77] When gay and lesbian partnerships are welcomed into the Church without prejudice, it is precisely this "ecclesiological constitution" – according to which others are accepted with all of their differences – that is at stake. Where else should it be possible to experience God's unconditional acceptance of every human being, if not first and foremost in the congregations that invoke on the name of Jesus?

However, simply invoking this principle in Church practice remains insufficient if it is not simultaneously accompanied by Church doctrine that also breaks

---

(cf. 2 Pet 1:1)." In the *Decree on Ecumenism: Unitatis Redintegratio*, no. 2, the second occurrence of this passage in the conciliar textual corpus (this verse is encountered nowhere else), the quotation from Galatians 3:28 is shortened, and these concrete oppositions are left out; see http://www.vatican.va/archive/hist_councils/ii_vatican_council/documents/vat-ii_decree_19641121_unitatis-redintegratio_en.html (accessed April 21, 2021).

75 See Peter von der Osten-Sacken, "Paulinisches Evangelium und Homosexualität," in *Evangelium und Tora: Aufsätze zu Paulus,* ed. Peter von der Osten-Sacken (TB 77; Munich: Kaiser, 1987), 210–236, esp. 236.

76 Wolter, *Röm I,* 153 f.

77 It constitutes an ecclesiological constitution because it concerns the mutual acceptance of those in the church who think differently, here in concrete terms: that is, Jewish–Christian and Gentile–Christian church members. Moreover, the structure of the sentence is indicative and imperative, the latter grounded in the former (καθώς has a justificatory sense: cf. John 13:15, 34; and also Matt 18:33 [ὡς καγώ;]). The indicative itself fully circumscribes the christological salvific event according to its soteriological as well as its theocentric aspects (εἰς δόξαν τοῦ θεοῦ'), whereas the imperative draws from this the appropriate ecclesiological conclusion: mutual acceptance.

new ground. We need a profound revision of the "Catechism of the Catholic Church,"[78] and until this takes place, the problem will continue to smolder.[79] Fundamentalist appeals to Scripture contradict the very essence of the Catholic hermeneutic. So let us approach Scripture sensibly and listen to what it truly calls us to do – for the sake of our salvation!

Bibliography

Aristotle. *Nicomachean Ethics*. Vol. 19. Translated by H. Rackham. Loeb Classical Library 73. Cambridge, MA: Harvard University Press, 1926.

Brooten, Bernadette J. *Love between Women: Early Christian Responses to Female Homoeroticism*. Chicago: University of Chicago Press, 1996.

Congregation for the Doctrine of the Faith. *Letter to the Bishops of the Catholic Church on the Pastoral Care of Homosexual Persons*. Rome: Vatican, 1986. http://www.vatican.va/ roman_curia/congregations/cfaith/documents/rc_con_cfaith_doc_19861001_homosexual-persons_en.html. Accessed April 21, 2021.

Dautzenberg, Gerhard. "'Da ist nicht männlich und weiblich': Zur Interpretation von Gal 3,28." In *Studien zur paulinischen Theologie und zur frühchristlichen Rezeption des Alten Testaments*, ed. Gerhard Dautzenberg and Dieter Sänger, 69–99. Gießen: Selbstverlag des Fachbereichs, Evangelische Theologie und Katholische Theologie und deren Didaktik der Justus-Liebig-Universität, 1999.

Ebner, Martin. "Verbietet das Neue Testament 'Homosexualität'? Neutestamentliche Grundlagen zu einer aktuellen Streitfrage." *Lebendige Seelsorge* 70 (2019): 55–60.

Foucault, Michel. *The History of Sexuality*. 3 vols. London: Allen Lane/Penguin, 1979/1990.

Gerstenberger, Erhard S. *Das dritte Buch Mose: Leviticus*. ATD 6. Göttingen: Vandenhoeck & Ruprecht, 1993.

Haacker, Klaus. *Der Brief des Paulus an die Römer*. ThHK 6. Leipzig: Evangelische Verlagsanstalt, 1999.

Halperin, David M. *One Hundred Years of Homosexuality*. New York: Routledge, 1990.

Herter, Hans. "Art. Effeminatus." In *Reallexikon für Antike und Christentum*, vol. 4, ed. Theodor Klauser, 620–642. Stuttgart: Hiersemann, 1959.

---

78 Over against this, of course, stands an antiquated fundamental-theological concept of church "doctrine" that seeks to present it as rigid, unchanging, and unshakable (cf. note 60 above), out of fear that Church authority could be damaged if doctrinal "changes" occur. In the process, one must close one's eyes to the alarming, repeatedly statistically verified fact that the *diastasis* of "doctrine" and "practice," as well as the tendency of the faithful to reject the Church's decisions, has been eroding Rome's authority for quite some time. The days when Karl Rahner spoke of the necessity of dogmatic-historical doctrinal development have been forgotten.

79 See Hansjürgen Verweyen, *Der Weltkatechismus: Therapie oder Symptom einer kranken Kirche?* (Düsseldorf: Patmos-Verlag, 1993).

Hieke, Thomas. *Levitikus: Zweiter Teilband: 16–27*. HThK.AT. Freiburg im Breisgau: Herder, 2014.

Hoheisel, Karl. "Art. Homosexualität." In *Reallexikon für Antike und Christentum*, vol. 16, ed. Theodor Klauser, 289–364. Stuttgart: Hiersemann, 1994.

Jewett, Robert. *Romans: A Commentary*. Hermeneia. Minneapolis: Fortress Press, 2007.

Josephus. *The Works of Flavius Josephus*. Translated by William Whiston. London: George Routledge, 1892.

Klauck, Hans-Josef. *1. Korintherbrief*. NEB 7. Würzburg: Echter Verlag, 1984.

Konradt, Matthias, and Esther Schläpfer, eds. *Anthropologie und Ethik im Frühjudentum und im Neuen Testament: Wechselseitige Wahrnehmungen. Internationales Symposium in Verbindung mit dem Projekt CJHNT, 17.–20. Mai 2012, Heidelberg*. WUNT 322. Tübingen: Mohr Siebeck, 2014.

Konradt, Matthias. "'Fliehet die Unzucht!' (TestRub 5,5): Sexualethische Perspektiven in den Testamenten der zwölf Patriarchen." In *Anthropologie und Ethik im Frühjudentum und im Neuen Testament: Wechselseitige Wahrnehmungen. Internationales Symposium in Verbindung mit dem Projekt CJHNT, 17.–20. Mai 2012, Heidelberg*, ed. Matthias Konradt and Esther Schläpfer, 249–282. WUNT 322. Tübingen: Mohr Siebeck, 2014.

Kornfeld, Walter. *Leviticus*. NEB 6. Würzburg: Echter-Verlag, 1986.

Kraus, Wolfgang, and Martin Karrer, eds. *Septuaginta Deutsch: Das griechische Alte Testament in deutscher Übersetzung*. Stuttgart: Deutsche Bibelgesellschaft, 2009.

Kremer, Jacob. *Der erste Brief an die Korinther*. RNT. Regensburg: Pustet, 1997.

Licht, Hans. *Die Homoerotik in der griechischen Literatur*. Abhandlungen aus dem Gebiet der Sexualforschung 3.3. Bonn: Marcus & Weber, 1921.

Lindemann, Andreas. *Der erste Korintherbrief*. HNT 9.1. Tübingen: Mohr Siebeck, 2000.

Loader, William. *Philo, Josephus, and the Testaments on Sexuality: Attitudes towards Sexuality in the Writings of Philo, Josephus, and the Testaments of the Twelve Patriarchs*. Grand Rapids/Cambridge: Eerdmans, 2011.

Loader, William. *The New Testament on Sexuality*. Grand Rapids/Cambridge: Eerdmans, 2012.

Loader, William. *Making Sense of Sex: Attitudes towards Sexuality in Early Jewish and Christian Literature*. Grand Rapids/Cambridge: Eerdmans, 2013.

Longenecker, Richard N. *The Epistle to the Romans: A Commentary on the Greek Text*. NIGTC. Grand Rapids: Eerdmans, 2016.

Miller, James E. "The Practices of Romans 1:26: Homosexual or Heterosexual?" *NT* 37 (1995): 1–11.

Murphy, David J. "More Evidence pertaining to 'Their Females' in Romans 1:26." *JBL* 138 (2019): 221–240.

Olyan, Saul M. "'And with a Male You Shall Not Lie the Lying Down of a Woman': On the Meaning and Significance of Leviticus 18:22 and 20:13." *Journal of the History of Sexuality* 4 (1994): 179–206.

Osten-Sacken, Peter von der. "Paulinisches Evangelium und Homosexualität." In *Evangelium und Tora: Aufsätze zu Paulus*, ed. Peter von der Osten-Sacken, 210–236. TB 77. Munich: Kaiser, 1987.

Pesch, Rudolf. *Das Markusevangelium, II. Teil: Kommentar zu Kap. 8,27–16,20*. HThK.NT 2.2. Freiburg im Breisgau: Herder, 1977.

Petersen, William L. "Can ARSENOKOITAI be translated by 'Homosexuals'? (1 Cor 6.9; 1 Tim 1.10)." *VigChr* 40 (1986): 187–191.

Philo. *On the Special Laws, On the Virtues, On Rewards and Punishments.* Vol. 8. Loeb Classical Library 341. Cambridge, MA: Harvard University Press, 1939.

Plato. *Laws.* 2 vols. Translated by R. G. Bury. Loeb Classical Library 187/192. Cambridge, MA: Harvard University Press, 1926.

Plato. *The Symposium and the Phaedrus: Plato's Erotic Dialogues.* Translated by William S. Cobb. Albany: SUNY Press, 1993.

Rat der evangelischen Kirche. *Mit Spannungen leben: Eine Orientierungshilfe des Rates der Evangelischen Kirche in Deutschland zum Thema 'Homosexualität' (26.2.1996).* EKD 57. https://archiv.ekd.de/EKD-Texte/44736.html. Accessed December 15, 2020.

Roloff, Jürgen. *Der erste Brief an Timotheus.* EKK 15. Zürich: Benziger/Neukirchener, 1988.

Schrage, Wolfgang. *Der erste Brief an die Korinther (1 Kor 1,1–6,11).* EKK 7.1. Zürich: Benziger/Neukirchener, 1991.

Scroggs, Robin. *The New Testament and Homosexuality: Contextual Background for Contemporary Debate.* Philadelphia: Fortress Press, 1983.

Second Vatican Council. *Decree on Ecumenism: Unitatis Redintegratio.* Rome: Vatican, 1964. http://www.vatican.va/archive/hist_councils/ii_vatican_council/documents/vat-ii_decree_19641121_unitatis-redintegratio_en.html. Accessed April 21, 2021.

Second Vatican Council. *Dogmatic Constitution of the Church: Lumen Gentium.* Rome: Vatican, 1964. http://www.vatican.va/archive/hist_councils/ii_vatican_council/documents/vat-ii_const_19641121_lumen-gentium_en.html. Accessed April 21, 2021.

Stegemann, Wolfgang. "Homosexualität – ein modernes Konzept." *ZNT* 2 (1998): 61–68.

Stowasser, Martin. "Homosexualität und Bibel: Exegetische und hermeneutische Überlegungen zu einem schwierigen Thema." *NTS* 43 (1997): 503–526.

Swancutt, Diana M. "'The Disease of Effemination': The Charge of Effeminacy and the Verdict of God (Romans 1:18–2:16)." In *New Testament Masculinities*, ed. Stephen D. Moore and Janice Capel Anderson, 193–233. SBL Semeia Studies 45. Atlanta: Society of Biblical Literature, 2003.

The Testaments of the Twelve Patriarchs. Translated by R. H. Charles. London: Wentworth Press, 1907/2019.

Theobald, Michael. *Der Römerbrief.* EdF 294. Darmstadt: Wissenschaftliche Buchgesellschaft, 2000.

Theobald, Michael. "Die Ehetheologie des Epheserbriefs (Eph 5,21–33): Literarhistorischer Kontext und kanontheologische Relevanz." In *Ehe und Familie: Wege zum Gelingen aus katholischer Perspektive*, ed. George Augustin and Ingo Proft, 121–147. Theologie im Dialog 13. Freiburg im Breisgau: Herder, 2014.

Theobald, Michael. "Vom Werden des Rechts in der Kirche: Beobachtungen zur Sprachform von Weisungen im Corpus Pastorale und bei Paulus." *ZNW* 106 (2015): 65–95.

Towner, Philip H. *The Letters to Timothy and Titus.* NICNT. Grand Rapids/Cambridge: Eerdmans, 2006.

Van der Horst, Pieter W. *The Sentences of Pseudo-Phocylides: With Introduction and Commentary.* SVTP 4. Leiden: Brill, 1978.

Verweyen, Hansjürgen. *Der Weltkatechismus: Therapie oder Symptom einer kranken Kirche?* Düsseldorf: Patmos-Verlag, 1993.

Walter, Nikolaus. "Pseudepigraphische jüdisch-hellenistische Dichtung." In *Jüdische Schriften aus hellenistisch-römischer Zeit*, vol. 4.3, ed. Werner Georg Kümmel, 173–276. Gütersloh: Gütersloher Verlagshaus, 1983.

Ward, Roy Bowen. "Why Unnatural? The Tradition behind Romans 1:26–27." *HThR* 90 (1997): 263–284.

Weidemann, Hans-Ulrich. *Taufe und Mahlgemeinschaft: Studien zur Vorgeschichte der altkirchlichen Taufeucharistie.* WUNT 338. Tübingen: Mohr Siebeck, 2014.

Wilson, Walter T. *The Sentences of Pseudo-Phocylides.* Commentaries on Early Jewish Literature. Berlin/New York: De Gruyter, 2005.

Wolter, Michael. *Der Brief an die Römer (Teilband 1: Röm 1–8).* EKK 6.1. Neukirchen-Vluyn: Neukirchener Theologie/Patmos, 2014.

Wright, Benjamin G. *The Letter of Aristeas: "Aristeas to Philocrates" or "On the Translation of the Law of the Jews."* Commentaries on Early Jewish Literature. Berlin/Boston: De Gruyter, 2015.

Wucherpfennig, Ansgar. *Sexualität bei Paulus.* Freiburg im Breisgau: Herder, 2020.

Zeller, Dieter. *Der erste Brief an die Korinther.* KEK 5. Göttingen: Vandenhoeck & Ruprecht, 2010.

Insights from the Human and Social Sciences

Hartmut A. G. Bosinski
A Normal Variance of the Human Capacity for Bonding and Love
Homosexuality from the Perspective of Sexual Medicine

1 Sexual Orientation: Definition and Frequency

For heuristic reasons, understanding the causes and developmental paths of homosexuality necessarily requires one to consider the entire range of human sexual orientation. Sexual orientation is a lifelong, deeply anchored sexual-erotic attraction to and orientation toward members of one's own sex, the opposite sex, or both sexes. The simplest indicator may be to answer the following question: Given a free choice, with members of which sex would a person have a sexual relationship?

A person's *real sexual behavior* does not necessarily have to be a reliable indicator of his oder her sexual orientation: under conditions of monosexual isolation (for example, in prisons), a large number of people who are in fact exclusively heterosexual are capable of homosexual acts – just as conversely, under repressive conditions in which homosexuality is prohibited or condemned, a large number of homosexually oriented people can perform heterosexual acts (for example, in arranged marriages). In both cases, such acts usually involve mobilizing accompanying fantasies to imagine acts corresponding to the person's actual sexual orientation (e.g., the male prison partner is reimagined as a woman, or the wife of the homosexual man as a male lover etc.).

Even a person's *self-definition* as heterosexual, bisexual, or homosexual (e.g., gay or lesbian) is not a sufficient indicator: On the one hand, it presupposes the corresponding conscious self-classification, which is not always easily possible for everyone. Second, it presupposes that such a categorization exists at all. The term homosexuality is only about 140 years old. It was coined in 1869 by the Austro-Hungarian physician Karl-Maria Benkert, alias Kertbeny. Prior to this, all same-sex sexual behavior was indiscriminately labeled and stigmatized as "sodomy," "unnatural fornication," "effeminacy," or "contrary sexual instinct." Moreover, some non-European cultures do not even have a term for same-sex love – although such love exists in these cultures as well (see below).

Thus while sexual behavior and even self-definition may vary, longitudinal studies have shown that sexual orientation (defined as sexual-erotic attraction to

https://doi.org/10.1515/9783110705188-004

members of one's own sex, the opposite sex, or both sexes) is a stable personality trait.[1] Moreover, studies undertaken by our research group in Kiel have
shown that a person's sexual orientation is anchored in his or her brain.[2]
Using magnetic resonance imaging (MRI), we found that men's and women's
brains respond (in fractions of a second which makes conscious control impossible) to the presentation of images of naked men and women, depending on
their own sexual orientation – heterosexual men and homosexual women respond in the same way, with the same brain areas, to images of women, while
homosexual men and heterosexual women respond in the same way when images of men are presented. This finding has been replicated by other researchers.[3] The difference in relation to sexual orientation was so clear that it was possible to determine the respective subject's sexual orientation solely on the basis
of their brain activity.[4]

Ever since Kinsey conducted his groundbreaking research,[5] however, we
know that "heterosexuality" and "homosexuality" are not dichotomous, unrelat-
ed entities, but rather that they present along a spectrum of more or less fluid
combinations. Kinsey therefore formulated the seven-level scale of sexual orientation which bears his name (the "Kinsey-Scale"):

Kinsey 0: Exclusively heterosexual
Kinsey 1: Predominantly heterosexual, only incidentally homosexual
Kinsey 2: Predominantly heterosexual, but more than incidentally homosexual
Kinsey 3: Equally heterosexual and homosexual
Kinsey 4: Predominantly homosexual, but more than incidentally heterosexual
Kinsey 5: Predominantly homosexual, only incidentally heterosexual
Kinsey 6: Exclusively homosexual

---

1 Cf. Nigel Dickson, Charlotte Paul, and Peter Herbison, "Same-sex attraction in a birth cohort:
Prevalence and persistence in early adulthood," *Social Science & Medicine* 56, no. 8 (2003): 1607–
1615; Ritch C. Savin-Williams, Kara Joyner, and Gerulf Rieger, "Prevalence and stability of self-
reported sexual orientation identity during young adulthood," *Arch Sex Behav* 41, no. 1 (2012):
103–110.
2 Cf. Jorge Ponseti et al., "A functional endophenotype for sexual orientation in humans," *Neuroimage* 33, no. 3 (2006): 825–833.
3 See the overview in Adam Safron et al., "Neural Correlates of Sexual Orientation in Heterosexual, Bisexual, and Homosexual Men," *Scientific Reports* 7 (2017): 1–15; Adam Safron et al., "Neural Correlates of Sexual Orientation in Heterosexual, Bisexual, and Homosexual Women," *Scientific Reports* 8, no. 1 (2018): 673–687.
4 Cf. Jorge Ponseti et al., "Hirnanatomie und sexuelle Orientierung," *Sexuologie* 16, no. 3–4
(2009): 83–89.
5 Cf. Alfred C. Kinsey, Wardell B. Pomeroy, and Clyde E. Martin, *Sexual Behavior in the human
male* (Philadelphia: Saunders, 1948).

Based on his data at the time (which were biased due to a distorted sample), Kinsey presumed that there is a continuous distribution from heterosexuality (Kinsey 0 – the majority of his test subjects) via bisexuality (which meant 1–5 on the Kinsey scale, and 2–4 in other publications) to exclusively homosexually oriented people (Kinsey 6 – the minority); thus bisexuality was presumed to be more frequent than homosexuality. Although more recent studies have clearly relativized Kinsey's figures, the basic point – that sexual orientation follows a statistical pattern of distribution between the poles of "heterosexuality" and "homosexuality" – has not changed. Data on the numeric distribution of sexual orientation sometimes diverge. There are several reasons for this: all sexual behavior surveys suffer from the fact that this topic is often taboo; survey methods and the extent to which survey respondents are representative of the broader sexual sphere often vary; and distinguishing between whether it is a matter of individual sexual acts, whatever the subject's motivation, or of sexual orientation is often difficult when it comes to questions of data collection. Nevertheless, large-scale random studies on the distribution of sexual attraction, the frequency of opposite-sex and/or same-sex sexual contacts, and self-classification as heterosexual, bisexual, or homosexual are now available.[6] Tables 1.1–1.5 list the results of some of these studies.

---

6 Cf. Edward O. Laumann et al., *The social organization of sexuality. Sexual practices in the United States* (Chicago: University of Chicago Press, 1994); Anne Johnson et al., *Sexual attitudes and lifestyles* (Oxford: Blackwell, 1994); Randall L. Sell, James A. Wells, and David Wypij, "The prevalence of homosexual behavior and attraction in the United States, the United Kingdom and France: Results of national population-based samples," *Arch Sex Behav* 24 (1995): 235–248; Catherine H. Mercer et al., "Changes in sexual attitudes and lifestyles in Britain through the life course and over time: Findings from the National Surveys of Sexual Attitudes and Lifestyles (Natsal)," *Lancet* 382, no. 9907 (2013): 1781–1794; Anjani Chandra et al., "Sexual behavior, sexual attraction, and sexual identity in the United States: Data from the 2006–2008 National Survey of Family Growth," *National Health Statistics Report* 36 (2011): 1–36; YouGov, "Kinsey Scale. Fieldwork Dates: 11th – 12th June 2018," (2018): https://d25d2506sfb94s.cloudfront.net/cumulus_up loads/document/forf2v7ra9/Results%20for%20Editorial%20(Kinsey%20Scale)%20131%2012.6. 2018.pdf (accessed October 29, 2020).

Table 1.1: Distribution of heterosexual, bisexual, and homosexual attraction, sexual self-definition, and lifetime experience of same-sex sexual contact (based on Chandra et al., 2011). (Data presented as % of n)

	Women (n = 56,032)	Men (n = 55,556)
Sexual attraction		
Exclusively to the opposite sex	83.3	93.5
Predominantly to the opposite sex	11.9	3.7
Equally to the opposite sex and the same sex	2.8	0.5
Predominantly to the same sex	0.6	0.7
Exclusively to the same sex	0.8	1.2
Unsure	0.7	0.4
Self-definition		
Heterosexual	93.7	95.7
Bisexual	3.5	1.1
Homosexual	1.1	1.7
Have ever had same-sex sexual contact	**Women (n = 61,865)**	**Men (n = 62,199)**
	12.5	5.2

Computer-assisted interview data collected from US citizens of both sexes, aged 18 to 44 years between 2006 and 2008, as part of the Centers for Disease Control and Prevention (CDC) National Survey of Family Growth (NSFG).

Table 1.2: Distribution of heterosexual, bisexual, and homosexual attraction, sexual self-definition, and sex of previous sexual partners (based on Laumann et al., 1994). (Data presented as % of n)

	Women (n = 1,731)	Men (n = 1,404)
Sexual attraction		
Exclusively to the opposite sex	95.6	93.8
Predominantly to the opposite sex	2.7	2.6
Equally to the opposite sex and the same sex	0.8	0.6
Predominantly to the same sex	0.6	0.7
Exclusively to the same sex	0.3	2.4
Self-definition	**Women (n = 1,732)**	**Men (n = 1,401)**
Heterosexual	98.6	96.9
Bisexual	0.5	0.8
Homosexual	0.9	2.0
Other	0.1	0.3
Sexual partners since puberty	**Women (n = 1,678)**	**Men (n = 1,334)**
Only opposite sex	94.3	90.3
Both men and women	3.3	5.8
Only same sex	0.2	0.6
None	2.2	3.3

Representative sample of face-to-face interviews with US citizens of both sexes, aged 18 to 59 years.

Table 1.3: Distribution of self-definition in terms of sexual orientation and lifetime experience of same-sex sexual contact (based on Mercer et al., 2013). (Data presented as % of n)

	Women (n = 8,869)	Men (n = 6,293)
Self-definition		
Heterosexual	97.3	97.1
Bisexual	1.4	1.0
Homosexual	1.0	1.5
Other	0.3	0.3
Have ever had same-sex sexual contact	11.5	8.0

Representative, computer-assisted interview data, UK citizens aged 16 to 74 years between 2010 to 2012, (part of the National Survey of Sexual Attitudes and Lifestyles (NATSAL–III).

Table 1.4: Distribution of sexual attraction and sexual behavior from age 15 years onward (based on Sell et al., 1995). (Data presented as % of n)

	Women			*Men*		
	USA (n = 674)	UK (n = 696)	France (n = 788)	USA (n = 1,288)	UK (n = 1,137)	France (n = 1,506)
Sexual attraction						
also or exclusively to persons of the same sex, but no sexual contact	11.1	8.6	11.7	8.7	7.9	8.5
Sex of sexual partners						
Only persons of the opposite sex	86.0	88.1	87.0	83.9	82.5	80.1
Persons of both sexes	3.3	1.6	3.2	5.4	3.4	10.0
Only persons of the same sex	0.3	0.5	0.1	0.8	1.1	0.7
No sexual partners	10.4	9.8	9.7	9.9	13.0	9.2
Neither sexual contact nor sexual attraction to persons of the same sex	82.2	81.4	81.6	79.2	83.7	81.5

Representative, interviewer-assisted anonymous questionnaire using identical methodology in all three countries, with respondents aged 16 to 50 years in
1988.

Table 1.5: Distribution of self-definition in terms of sexual orientation and lifelong experience of same-sex sexual contact (based on YouGov, 2018). (Data presented as % of n)

	Total *(n = 1,096)*	*Women* *(n = 553)*	*Men* *(n = 543)*
Self-classification			
Heterosexual	86	87	84
Homosexual	2	3	5
Bisexual	3	4	3
Other	1	1	1
No information provided	5	5	6
Kinsey 0	69	69	70
Kinsey 1	8	8	9
Kinsey 2	3	4	3
Kinsey 3	5	6	3
Kinsey 4	3	2	4
Kinsey 5	1	2	1
Kinsey 6	5	4	7
Unsure	5	5	4
Sexual experience			
Have ever had sex with a same-sex partner	18	18	18
Have never had sex with a same-sex partner	79	78	79

Representative, anonymous email survey based on a US census sample (total
n = 1.2 million) of adults (i.e., those over 18 years), survey period June 11–12,
2018.

2 Sexual Orientation as a Sex-Typical Difference

Based on this distribution pattern – sexual attraction exclusively to men (i.e., androphilia), to men and women (i.e., gynandrophilia), or exclusively to women
(i.e., gynephilia) – we can classify sexual orientation as a sex-typical difference.
These are differences that occure only in comparisons between the sexes on the
group level – that is, differences in physical, psychological, or social characteristics and functions which occur more frequently and/or with greater intensity in
one sex group than in the other, and/or for which the differences in the mean
values within a given sex group are smaller than the differences between the

two groups. I.e., these are only statistical differences. Deviation from the mean value of the group and an overlap with the distribution in the other sex group is constitutive for these types of sex differences. Hence, one can only consider that a person statistically belongs to a male-like or female-like distribution for a certain characteristic in question. It says nothing about his or her gender in general.[7]

Such sex-typical differences are found across a wide variety of parameters. The best known are differences in physique: at 1.78 meters, men are on average 13 centimeters taller than women (at 1.65 meters).[8] Yet no one would seriously consider denying the masculinity of a man who is 1.64 meters tall or the femininity of a woman who is 1.81 meters tall (which is incidentally the height of many supermodels).

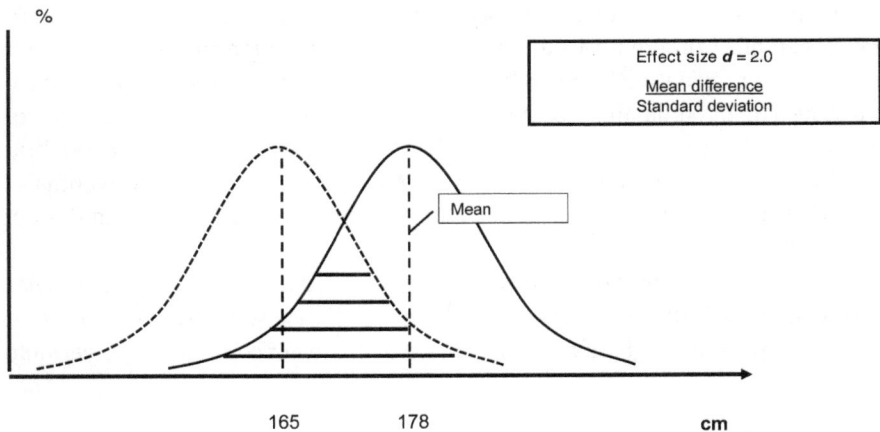

Figure 1: Diagram depicting sex-typical body-size distribution (the dotted line represents women; the solid line represents men)

Sex-typical body-proportion distributions are even more striking. Among the multitude of confirmed sex-typical differences in body proportions, we could mention the so-called 2:4 digit ratio (or 2D:4D ratio), which has been well re-

---

7 For further details, see Hartmut A. G. Bosinski, "Determinanten der Geschlechtsidentität – Neue Befunde zu einem alten Streit," *Sexuologie* 7 (2000): 96–140.
8 Cf. Statistisches Bundesamt, "Körpermaße nach Altersgruppen und Geschlecht für das Jahr 2013," figure 1, https://www.destatis.de/DE/ZahlenFakten/GesellschaftStaat/Gesundheit/Ge sundheitszustandRelevantesVerhalten/Tabellen/Koerpermasse.html?nn=50798 (accessed August 18, 2020).

searched and attested: men's ring fingers are on average longer than their index fingers (hence, in a group comparison, the 2D:4D ratio is < 1.0), while women's index and ring fingers are about the same length (thus their 2D:4D ratio is 1.0 on average). This difference is already apparent in fetuses in the last trimester of pregnancy.[9]

A number of structural and functional sex-typical differences are now recognized in the brain as well.[10] Women have smaller brains than men in absolute terms, but the relative size of women's brains in relation to their height does not differ from men's brain size/height ratio. Moreover, women's smaller brain size is counterbalanced by the fact that their grey matter (the neurons and synapses that form the cortex responsible for cognitive processes) is more densely packed, thicker, and more pronounced compared to the white matter (the nerve fibers that connect different areas of the cortex) than is the case for men.[11] For the purposes of our discussion here, it is worth pointing out an important sex-typical difference in the hypothalamus, the region in the midbrain responsible for regulating basal functions such as hunger, thirst, and sexual reproduction. The hypothalamus contains a large number of nuclei – collections of nerve cells that are connected to each other and to different areas of the cerebral cortex. These include four so-called interstitial nuclei of the anterior hypothalamus (INAH 1–4), of which the third (INAH 3) is three times larger in men than in women.[12]

Neurological functions also exhibit sex-typical differences.[13] One particular example are so-called otoacoustic emissions (OAE). These are sounds produced by the inner ear throughout a person's life, which are not consciously perceivable

---

9 Cf. John T. Manning, *Digit ratio. A pointer to fertility, behavior, and health* (New Brunswick: Rutgers University Press, 2002).

10 For further details, see Akira Matsumoto, ed., *Sexual differentiation of the Brain* (Boca Raton: CRC Press, 1999); Melissa Hines, *Brain Gender* (Oxford: Oxford University Press, 2004).

11 Cf. the overview in John S. Allen et al., "Sexual dimorphism and asymmetries in the grey-white composition of human cerebrum," *Neuroimage* 18 (2003): 880–894.

12 Cf. Laura S. Allen et al., "Two sexually dimorphic cell groups in the human brain," *The Journal of Neuroscience* 9, no. 2 (1989): 497–506; Simon LeVay, "A difference in hypothalamic structure between heterosexual and homosexual men," *Science* 253 (1991): 1034–1037; William Byne et al., "The interstitial nuclei of the human anterior hypothalamus: An investigation of sexual variation in volume and cell size, number and density," *Brain Research* 856, no. 1–2 (2000): 254–258.

13 See the overview in Doreen Kimura, *Sex and cognition* (Cambridge, MA: MIT Press, 2000).

but are measurable, and which are significantly more frequent in women than in men, whether spontaneously occurring (SOAE) or evoked by clicks (COAE).[14]

Proven sex-typical differences in the psychological domain are particularly interesting when it comes to understanding the development of sexual orientation. Such differences have been the subject of extensive meta-analytical studies for approximately the last 50 years, with hundreds of studies conducted on thousands of men and women. These studies have shown that the majority of potential behaviors do not differ in their statistical distribution between men and women.[15] Nevertheless, significant differences were found in cognitive, emotional, and behavioral parameters.

Effect size d, which is calculated as the quotient of mean differences divided by standard deviation, is used to measure the extent of a sex-typical difference. For the difference in height between men and women, d is ~ 2.0. In psychological sex comparisons, effect sizes in which d is less than or equal to 0.20 are generally considered negligible, those between 0.21 and 0.50 are considered minor, those between 0.51 and 0.80 are considered moderate, and those over 0.80 are considered pronounced.[16] One must always pay attention to the specific testing conditions and the methods employed, which may well produce sex-differentiated results. According to convention, characteristics that are more pronounced among men than among women are assigned a positive prefix (+), while those that are more pronounced among women are assigned a negative prefix (-).

In the following section, I will discuss some significant sex-typical differences in behavior, cognition and emotion: As a group, men score higher on aggressive behavior (d +0.33 to +0.84) than women.[17] This difference can already be observed in childhood, when boys play wild, rough-and-tumble games more often on average than girls. In group comparisons, men have better spatial orientation and are, for example, better able to "rotate" a three-dimensional object in their minds – that is, to assign it correctly from different perspectives.[18] On average,

---

14 See the overview in John C. Loehlin and Dennis McFadden, "Otoacoustic emissions, auditory evoked potentials, and traits related to sex and sexual orientation," *Arch Sex Behav* 32, no. 2 (2003): 115–127.

15 See the overview in Janet Shibley Hyde, "The gender similarities hypothesis," *American Psychology* 60, no. 6 (2005): 581–592; Lee Ellis, *Sex Differences: Summarizing More than a Century of Scientific Research* (New York: Psychology Press, 2008).

16 Cf. Jacob Cohen, *Statistical power analysis for the behavioral sciences* (Hillsdale: Erlbaum, 1988).

17 Cf. John Archer, "Sex Differences in Aggression in Real-World Settings – A Meta-Analytic Review," *Review of General Psychology* 8, no. 4 (2004): 291–322.

18 This is the so-called Mental Rotation Test (MRT); cf. Daniel Voyer, Susan Voyer, and M. Phillip Bryden, "Magnitude of sex differences in spatial abilities: A meta-analysis and consideration

women have better fine motor coordination than men (d -0.75 to -1.37),[19] and they demonstrate better word association and fluency – for example, they can generate more synonyms for a term or more words with the same initial letter faster than men (d -1.2; this does not concern the number of words spoken per day, however – there is definitely no difference between the sexes on that score!).[20]

The most pronounced sex-typical differences are found in the domain of sexuality: men masturbate more frequently than women (d +0.86)[21] and, according to a worldwide group comparison, show a significantly more pronounced interest in casual, noncommittal sexual encounters than women (depending on the world region, d +0.48 [Africa] to +1.20 [Southeast Asia]),[22] while women's sexuality is on average much more context- and relationship-dependent (incidentally, this explains why women use male prostitutes only infrequently and consume much less pornography than men). Furthermore, men are sexually interested in women (gynephilic) far more often than women are sexually interested in women (d +6,0);[23] conversely, women are sexually interested in men (androphilic) far more often than men are – this is precisely what we mean by sexual orientation. Figure 2 compares these differences in sexual interest as a sex-typically distributed difference: the x-axis plots women's and men's sexual orientation, while the y-axis plots the percentages.

3 Causes of Sex-Typical Differences

The causes of sex-typical differences in physique are relatively well researched: although absolute differences in body size are also influenced by social conditions (such as nutrition and medical care) to a certain extent, they are essentially

of critical variable," *Psychological Bulletin* 117, no. 2 (1995): 250–270 (d +0.56); Marcia C. Linn and Anne C. Petersen, "Emergence and characterization of sex differences in spatial abilities: A meta-analysis," *Child Development* 56 (1985): 1479–1498 (d +0.73).

19 Measured using the Purdue Pegboard Test (PPT); cf. Geoff Sanders and Tom Walsh, "Testing Predictions from the Hunter-Gatherer Hypothesis – 1: Sex Differences in the Motor Control of Hand and Arm," *Evolutionary Psychology* 5, no. 3 (2007): 653–665.

20 Cf. Melissa Hines, "Gonadal hormones and human cognitive development," in *Hormones, brain and behavior in vertebrates*, ed. Jacques Balthazart (Basel: Karger, 1990), 51–63.

21 Cf. Mary Beth Oliver and Janet S. Hyde, "Gender differences in sexuality: A meta-analysis," *Psychol Bulletin* 114 (1993): 29–51.

22 Cf. David P. Schmitt et al., "Universal sex differences in the desire for sexual variety: Tests from 52 nations, 6 continents, and 13 islands," *Journal of Personality and Social Psychology* 85, no. 1 (2003): 85–104.

23 Cf. Hines, *Brain Gender*.

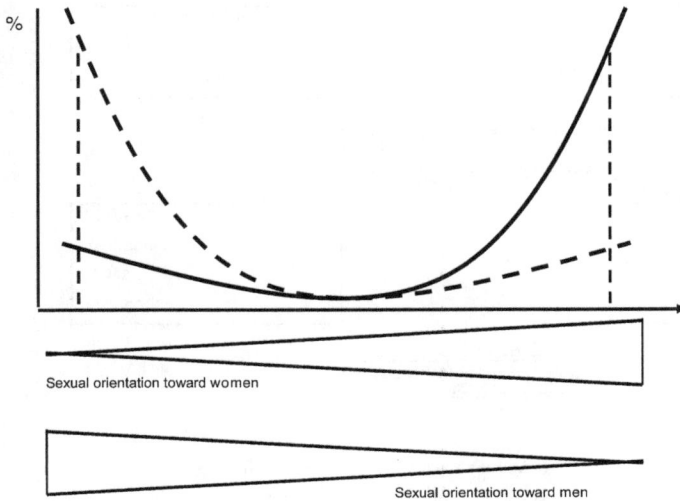

Figure 2: Diagram depicting sex-typical sexual-orientation distribution (the dotted line represents women; the solid line represents men)

genetically determined and hormonally mediated. Proof of such biological causes of psychological (cognitive, emotional, or behavioral) sex differences – and thus also of sexual orientation – is much more complicated. It is true that our day-to-day thought is all too easily inclined not only to overemphasize such differences, but also to simplistically attribute them to biological causes for the simple reason that such differences are associated with a different biological sex. However, such a view fails to recognize the following points:

First, as human beings, we are not merely products of biological evolution, but also of decades-long cultural evolution. Human behavior, thought, feeling, and perception are the result of a highly complex bio-psycho-social development process (on which see below).

Second, even the apparently unambiguous *topos* of biological sex turns out to be a highly multilayered, complex phenomenon on closer examination: even on the somatic level, we can distinguish a chromosomal, a gonadal and endocrine, a gonoductal, a genital, and presumably also a cerebral sex.

In contrast to sex-typical differences these biological sex differences are *sex-specific*. They develop prenatally as part of a cascading process known as somatosexual differentiation, which requires a brief explanation (see figure 3):

Male Embryo 46; XY, SRY +		Female Embryo 46; XX, SRY -

Bipotent Gonadal System

5th – 7th week of pregnancy

TESTES		OVARIES
[Androgen +]		Androgen -
[AMH +]		AMH -
		Estrogen (+)

Bipotent Gonoductal System

11th – 14th week of pregnancy

⇩

Epididymis ⇐	↓ Müller's Duct ↑	⇒ Fallopian Tubes
Vas deferens ⇐	↑ Wolffian Duct ↓	⇒ Uterus
Seminal vesicles ⇐		⇒ Vagina
Prostate ⇐		(cranial aspect)

DHT

Bipotent External Genitalia

[5-α-Reductase2]

12th – 16th week of pregnancy

⇩

Corpus cavernosa	⇐ Genital tubercule ⇒	Clitoris
Scrotum	⇐ Labioscrotal swelling ⇒	Labia majora
Corpus spongiosum	⇐ Urogenital fold ⇒	Labia minora
Urethra (penile aspect)	⇐ Urogenital sinus ⇒	Vulval vestibule
?		

? Hypothalamus ?

16th week of pregnancy –

perinatal

(perhaps until 3 or 4

years of age?)

↑ ⇐ "male erotic center" ⇒ ↓
↓ ⇐ "female erotic center" ⇒ ↑

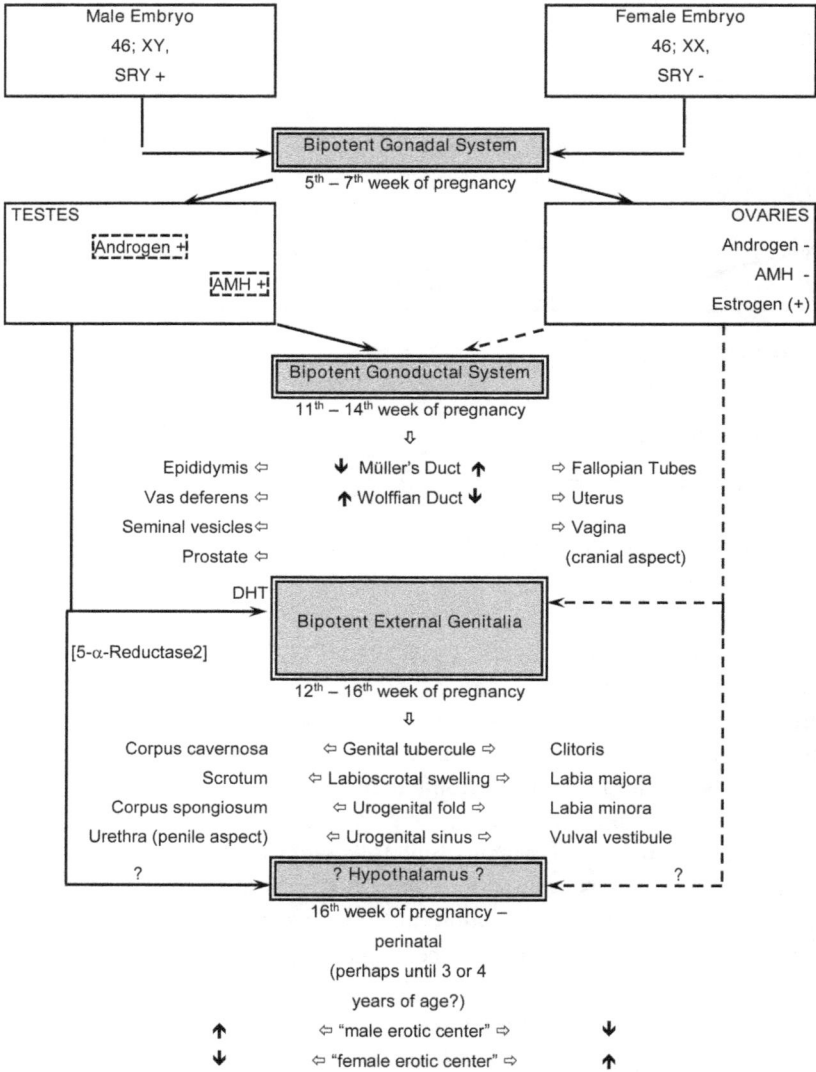

Figure 3: Diagram depicting prenatal somatosexual differentiation
SRY = Sex-determining region of the Y chromosome
AMH = Anti-Müllerian hormone
- = Substance is missing or inactive
+ = Substance is present or active
↑ = Substrate develops/becomes differentiated
↓ = Substrate does not develop/disappears
? = Hypothetical process

3.1 Chromosomal Differentiation Level

At conception, the fusion of the sperm's haploid chromosome set (22 autosomes and 1 gonosome/sex chromosome, either a Y or an X chromosome) with that of the egg (22 autosomes and 1 gonosome, always an X chromosome) determines the genetic sex of the embryo. For the female sex, the diploid chromosome set of 44 autosomes and two X gonosomes (46, XX) is characteristic, while for the male sex the constellation is 46, XY. The embryo's further somatosexual differentiation is determined by whether a Y chromosome (which always originates from the father) with a functional so-called SRY gene is present (SRY stands for "sex-determining region of the Y-gene"). If the SRY gene is missing – which is typically the case in genetically female embryos, but also in patients with certain intersex syndromes – then the embryo's further development proceeds in the female direction. If the SRY gene is present – typically in genetically male embryos with a Y chromosome – then further somatosexual differentiation proceeds in the male direction.

3.2 Gonadal Differentiation Level

Until the fifth week of pregnancy, gonads are sexually undifferentiated. Under the influence of the SRY gene, testes differentiate from the medulla of a "bipotent" gonadal anlage, which bears the ability to differentiate either in male or in female direction; in the absence of SRY, the cortex of this "gonadal anlage" differentiates into ovaries. In steps that follow somatosexual development is now under the influence of the gonads and the hormones produced there. In a genetically male embryo, the fetal testes produce considerable quantities of androgens – especially testosterone – as early as the ninth week of gestation, which up to the eighteenth week of gestation correspond to the hormone levels of adult males, in relation to the size of the embryo. The so-called Anti-Müllerian Hormone (AMH) is produced in the Sertoli cells (on which see below). In a genetically female embryo, however, the ovaries produce hardly any significant quantities of hormones during this phase of differentiation.

3.3 Gonoductal Differentiation Level

The differentiation of gonoducts (i.e., the internal genitalia structures) also originates from a bipotent system, which consists of the Wolffian and Müllerian ducts. When adequately differentiated and functioning testes exist, under the influence of testicular AMH Müller's duct atrophies in male embryos from the twelfth week of gestation. This defeminization is complemented by the testosterone-dependent masculinization of the Wolffian duct, from which the epididymis, vas deferens, vesicular gland, and prostate develop. Since both testosterone and AMH are nearly absent in the female embryo, the Wolffian duct atrophies (= demasculinization), whereas the Müllerian duct is differentiated into the fallopian tube, uterus, and upper part of the vagina (= femininization). To the best of our knowledge, this appears to occur in the female embryo independently of the influence of any particular substance.

3.4 Genital Differentiation Level

The differentiation of the external genitalia, which is initially regarded at birth as the decisive sex characteristic (the so-called "midwife's sex"), takes place after the developmental steps discussed above. Here again we find a bipotent system with a genital tubercule, a labioscrotal swelling, a urogenital fold, and a urogenital sinus. In female fetuses, differentiation of the external genitalia occurs without the influence of additional substances. However, this process can be pushed in a masculine direction with somewhat pronounced genital virilization by the prenatal influence of either increased androgens as a result of disease (e.g., in Congenital Adrenal Hyperplasia, CAH) or by externally iatrogenically supplied androgenic substances. The development of the external genital system in a male direction is again tied to several preconditions (sufficient testicular testosterone production, sufficient quantity and quality of certain enzymes, and sufficient quantity and quality of cellular androgen receptors).

Thus the following four fundamental principles become apparent:

1. The principle of bipotency: A system develops in a male or female direction only through the determining action of certain substances.
2. The principle of reciprocity: Parallel processes of masculinization and defeminization (usually in the genetically male embryo) or feminization and demasculinization (usually in the genetically female embryo) occur. However, in intersex syndromes) – i.e., disorders of sex development (DSD) – demonstrate that these processes can also be uncoupled.
3. The "Adam principle": Male somatosexual development always requires larger biological investment ("You always have to add something to produce a male"), while female development is primary and proceeds without the intervention of particular substances (genes, enzymes, hormones). Thus from a biological point of view, Adam springs from Eve's rib rather than the other way around.
4. The principle of organization and activation in sensitive phases: These are short timeframes in which otherwise marginal internal or external factors organizising pre- or perina-

tally structures and/or functions via gene or hormones that are activated only later in life (mostly after puberty) and hence have a life-long impact on individual development.

Somatosexual differentiation leads to the formation of sex-specific differences. In contrast to sex-typical differences, sex-specific differences are distributed according to the either–or principle – that is, bipolar-dichotomously. In standard cases, somatosexual development is only possible as either male or female. Again unlike sex-typical differences, this means that – at the chromosomal, gonadal, gonoductal, or genital level of sexuality – on an individual base it is possibly to determine, if a single person belongs either to the male or the female sex. Transitions do occur, but in such cases – so-called intersex syndromes – these are characterized as disorders of sex development.

Although peristatic factors also play a role in the somatosexual development of sex-specific differences, these are essentially biologically determined. The development of sex-typical differences in feeling, behavior, or perception is a different matter. To prove the connex between sex-typical and sex-specific difference, i.e. to asks for biological predispositions for the first, we need to address the following questions here:

1. The interspecies aspect: Is a particular sex-typical difference also found in the animal kingdom, particularly in mammals?
2. The transcultural aspect: Is a particular sex-typical difference found in all human cultures?
3. The socialization aspect: Is a particular sex-typical difference independent of the conditions of socialization, or at least not reversible by means of socialization?
4. The intraspecies aspect: Are there correlations in human beings between an atypical expression of certain sex-typical differences (e.g., sexual orientation) in relation to biological sex and biological parameters, which would point to a similar alignment of sex-typically distributed characteristics and thus to a similar variation in prenatal somatosexual differentiation? Conversely, are there people with known variations in sex-specific somatosexual differentiation who also show an equally atypical expression of sex-typically distributed traits? Do such people exhibit differences in identifiable genetic characteristics? In other words, is there evidence for a hereditary component of sexual orientation?
5. The evolutionary aspect: Does divergence from the particular sex-typical trait in question serve an evolutionary-adaptive function?

Given the long history of the exclusion, condemnation, criminalization, and/or pathologization of homosexuality, it should not be surprising that for more than 100 years, a multitude of researchers (at the forefront of which stood the German physician and sexologist Magnus Hirschfeld) have addressed these questions, particularly with regard to sexual orientation. The results of this research already fill whole libraries, and I only have space to summarize them in what follows.[24]

4 Five Aspects of Biologically Determined Sex-Typical Differences

4.1 On the Interspecies Aspect

There is no doubt that the vast majority of male animals are mating with females, and the vast majority of female animals are mating with males. However, as many extensive overviews have convincingly demonstrated,[25] the formation of same-sex pairs with sexual contact is by no means a rarity in the animal kingdom. In most cases, this is a matter of "communities of purpose" that last for a significant period of time, or even for life – for example, lower-ranking males who have no access to females may open up resources for themselves by forming pairs to compete with stronger members of the same species. In primates, homosexual contacts between females or between males to reduce group tension and aggression (such as in Bonobos), or in some cases even preferential pair formations between females, are frequently found, since this facilitates increased gratification and status gains (in certain macaque groups). Lifelong preferential selection of same-sex sexual partners has been described in rams,[26] 7 to 10 percent of which spurn breeding females and mate only with other rams – a phenomenon that has also been extensively studied (see below) because it poses a real problem for breeders, as these rams cannot be bred.

In sum, these animal behavior research findings indicate that designating homosexuality as "unnatural fornication" is absurd. Significantly, while there are examples of homosexuality in the animal kingdom, there is no indication of sexual

---

24 For further details, see William Byne and Bruce Parsons, "Human sexual orientation. The biological theories reappraised," *Archives of General Psychiatry* 50 (1993): 228–239; Glenn Wilson and Qazi Rahman, *Born Gay. The Psychobiology of Sex Orientation* (London: Peter Owen, 2005); Simon LeVay, *Gay, straight, and the reason why. The science of sexual orientation* (Oxford: Oxford University Press, 2011).

25 Cf. Bruce Bagemihl, *Biological exuberance: Animal homosexuality and natural diversity* (New York: St. Martin's Press, 1999); Volker Sommer and Paul L. Vasey, *Homosexual Behaviour in Animals: An Evolutionary Perspective* (Cambridge: Cambridge University Press, 2006).

26 Cf. Chuck Roselli, Radhika C. Reddy, and Katherine R. Kaufman, "The development of male-oriented behavior in rams," *Frontiers in Neuroendocrinology* 32, no. 2 (2011): 164–169.

preference disorders (i.e., paraphilia), which exist only in humans. This impressive-ly demonstrates the naturalness of homosexual orientation. However, if "unnatu-ral" simply refers to sexuality's reproductive function, then not only the animal be-havior described above would also be considered "unnatural", but also the sexual behavior of childless human couples.

4.2 On the Transcultural Aspect

Although it is difficult to prove empirically that "homosexuality" – and especial-ly the broad range of "sexual orientations" – existed in previous cultures, since these are very recent concepts, and although same-sex sexuality and partner se-lection have been subject to penalization for centuries,[27] reports about male–male love, partnership, and sexuality in ancient writings are nevertheless legion. Love and sexuality between women, on the other hand, was almost never a topic of in-depth discussion due to the inferior role assigned to women in all spheres at that time – including women's sexuality, the existence of which was often de-nied . Modern transcultural surveys which include non-European cultures have shown that, alongside the predominance of heterosexual partner selection, ho-mosexual partner selection is also attested in all cultures. In the case of the Phil-ippines, Milton Diamond's study has indicated that around 2 percent of men and 0.7 percent of women describe themselves as homosexual; in Thailand, 0.2 per-cent of men and 0.9 percent of women exhibit lifelong homosexual behavior; in China, 7.6 percent of all subjects of both sexes reported homosexual experience or attraction, and around 2 percent described themselves as homosexual.[28] The information contained in the Standard Cross-Cultural Sample and the Human Relationship Area Files (HRAF) on the behaviors, norms, and values in a total of 200 cultures worldwide (including recent Neolithic cultures) is particularly meaningful. Gwen Broude and Sarah J. Green have analyzed this immense data-base, compiled by ethnologists and anthropologists over decades, by focusing on attitudes toward and frequencies of homosexuality (although we must cautiously point to the fact that no distinction was made between "behavior" and "attrac-tion" in the source data, and the data presumably refer exclusively to men).[29]

---

27 See Gisela Bleibtreu-Ehrenberg, *Homosexualität. Die Geschichte eines Vorurteils* (Frankfurt am Main: Fischer, 1981).
28 Cf. Milton Diamond, "Homosexuality and bisexuality in different populations," *Arch Sex Behav* 22, no. 4 (1993): 291–310.
29 Cf. Gwen Broude and Sarah J. Green, "Crosscultural codes on twenty sexual attitudes and practices," *Ethnology* 15 (1976): 409–428.

With regard to "attitudes toward homosexuality," data were collected for 42 cultures (= 21% of 200); with regard to "frequency of homosexuality," data were collected for 70 cultures (= 35%). Tables 2.1 and 2.2 present the corresponding results.

Table 2.1: Attitudes toward homosexuality in 42 (of 200) cultures (based on Broude and Green, 1976).

Item: "Homosexuality is..."	No. of Cultures	%
Accepted, ignored	9	21.4
Mocked but not penalized	6	14.3
Depracated and undesirable, but not penalized	5	11.9
Strongly deprecated and penalized	17	40.9
No concept of homosexuality	5	11.9
Total	42	100.0

Table 2.2: Data on the frequency of homosexuality in 70 (of 200) cultures (based on Broude and Green, 1976).

Item: "Homosexuality is..."	No. of Cultures	%
Not present or very rare	41	58.6
Present, not uncommon	29	41.4
Total	70	100.0

Of the 41 cultures in which homosexuality is supposedly not present or very rare:
-   1 culture accepts or ignores homosexuality;
-   5 cultures have no concept of homosexuality;
-   3 cultures mock homosexuality but do not penalize it;
-   2 cultures reject homosexuality and consider it undesirable, but do not penalize it;
-   9 cultures condemn and penalize homosexuality; and
-   21 cultures demonstrate no codification of "attitudes toward homosexuality."

Of the 29 cultures in which homosexuality is supposedly present and/or not uncommon:
-   8 cultures accept or ignore homosexuality;
-   3 cultures mock homosexuality but do not penalize it;
-   2 cultures reject homosexuality and consider it undesirable, but do not penalize it;

- 6 cultures condemn and penalize homosexuality;
- 10 cultures demonstrate no codification of "attitudes toward homosexuality"; and
- none of the cultures in which homosexuality is supposedly present and/or not uncommon has no concept of homosexuality.

Thus the occurrence or the ethnographic description of "homosexuality" (whatever is meant by this term) is inversely proportional to a (mild or rigid) rejection of homosexuality or a lack of information on attitudes toward homosexuality.

Ritualized male–male sexual customs in which sexual acts occur between older and prospective warriors can be identified in Melanesian cultures,[30] in which the "transfer of semen" via fellatio or anal intercourse supposedly promotes manhood and warriorhood – which is why such acts are not viewed as promoting individual sexual pleasure, but rather as strengthening the tribal community, and are thus obligatory. Male–male pair formations in the sense of a "teacher–pupil" relationship which includes sexual contact are also found in other warrior cultures, such as among the Samurai in Japan, the Siwans in Libya, and the Azande in sub-Saharan Africa. From a historical perspective, the teacher–pupil relationships described in Greek antiquity could also be included here; such pedagogical relationships were permitted exclusively between adult men and "free" (i.e., unenslaved) boys entrusted to them for education – same-sex sexual contact between free adult men was taboo.

Based on their evaluation of the available ethnographic data, Raymond Hames and his colleagues conclude that homosexuality is a cross-cultural universal, but its expression is strongly influenced by the social context in which it occurs.[31]

In sum, homosexual attraction and homosexual behavior has existed and continues to exist in all cultures. Such behavior often played or plays a role in rites of passage. The development of a homosexual, bisexual, or heterosexual orientation is neither prevented nor encouraged by social norms, but the expression of this orientation and the establishment of a corresponding (lesbian, gay, bisexual) identity is considerably influenced by the respective social norms.

---

30 Cf. Gilbert Herdt, *Guardians of the flute* (Chicago: University of Chicago Press, 1994); idem, *Same sex, different cultures. Gays and lesbians across cultures* (Boulder: Westview Press, 1997).
31 Raymond Hames, Zachary Garfield, and Melissa Garfield, "Is Male Androphilia a Context-Dependent Cross-Cultural Universal?" *Arch Sex Behav* 46, no. 1 (2017): 63–71.

4.3 On the Socialization Aspect

A large number of studies have searched in vain for typical family constellations, patterns of upbringing, or developmental experiences to which homosexually oriented people have been exposed, in contrast to those which heterosexually oriented people have experienced. Alan Bell and his colleagues conducted the most comprehensive and methodologically demanding of these studies.[32] The authors interviewed 676 homosexual men and 292 homosexual women, as well as 337 heterosexual men and 140 heterosexual women in the USA in the 1970s about their childhood and adolescence; their parental, sibling, and family situations; their relationship with their father and mother; and their socio-economic, religious, and emotional situations, among other things. These data were subjected to an elaborate statistical (path-analytical) model to test relevant psychogenetic theories about sexual orientation. The authors – who were sociologists and psychologists – found no pattern in the retrospective data that would allow one to make statements about homosexual men's and women's "typical" socialization conditions. They themselves concluded that a biological explanatory approach to homosexual orientation would not only not contradict their data, but might make the data more plausible.

Conversely, in the South Pacific cultures described above, in which sexual acts regularly occur between older warriors and young men, cases of exclusively homosexual attraction are reported as extremely rarely.[33] Even those who grew up in single-sex accommodation (such as boarding schools or all-boys or all-girls schools), who often initially experience same-sex sexual contact due to a lack of other opportunities to gain sexual experience, do not become homosexual more often than average (otherwise there would have been a much higher number of homosexually oriented people in previous eras than there are today, but there is no evidence for this whatsoever). Follow-up studies of men who experienced sexual abuse by men in childhood or adolescents provided no evidence for an above-average frequency of homosexual orientation later in life among those affected.[34] Conversely, homosexual men and women report above-average frequency of prepubescent sexual experiences with older members of their own sex. However, one has to consider the fact that postpubescent

---

32 Cf. Alan Bell, Martin S. Weinberg, and Sue Kiefer Hammersmith, *Sexual preference: Its development in men and women* (New York: Indiana University Press, 1981).

33 The fact that such cases nevertheless exist is demonstrated by the research presented in Broude and Green, "Crosscultural codes," 409–428.

34 See, for example, Joseph H. Beitchman et al., "A review of the long-term effects of child sexual abuse," *Child Abuse & Neglect* 16 (1992): 101–118.

homosexually oriented people retrospectively report that even before puberty, they felt wistful or erotic rather than explicitly sexual attraction to members of their own sex, just as postpubescent heterosexually oriented people describe with regard to persons of the opposite sex. At this juncture, we must explicitly point out that pedophilia (i.e., sexual orientation to prepubescent children) and homosexuality have as much or as little to do with one another as do pedophilia and heterosexuality: the primary attraction for the pedophile is the child's immaturity, not the child's sex. In the case of homo-pedophilia, after the prepubescent boy, it is the prepubescent girl (and not the adult man) who elicits the strongest sexual response; and in the case of hetero-pedophilia, after the prepubescent girl, it is the prepubescent boy (and not the mature woman).

In sum, a wealth of research has shown that there are no specific socialization conditions which lead to the development of either heterosexuality or homosexuality. One can be educated, forced, or seduced into to homosexual or heterosexual acts, but not homosexual or heterosexual orientation.

4.4 On the Intraspecies Aspect

Empirical studies on the expression of different (somatic or psychological) sex-typical differences in homosexuals as compared to heterosexuals are already legion, and for reasons of space, I can only summarize them here. They offer a varied picture. In exclusively homosexually oriented individuals, the distribution of *aggressive behavior* in childhood (not in adulthood!) and of *spatial abilities* (in adulthood) demonstrates a gender-atypical pattern when compared with exclusively heterosexually oriented individuals – that is, the distribution of these two variables in homosexual men is more similar to that found in heterosexual women, and the distribution in homosexual women is more similar to that found in heterosexual men. *Fine motor coordination* and *speech fluency* are much less frequently studied but nevertheless demonstrate that homosexual men in particular occupy an intermediate position when the groups are compared. With regard to *interest in casual sex*, however, homosexuals display the typical distribution of their sex: heterosexual and homosexual men are highly interested in such contacts, while heterosexual and homosexual women are less interested. This finding also provides an explanation for the fact that homosexual men report having more sexual partners than heterosexual men on average over the course of their lives: their higher (male) interest in casual sex meets with an equally high interest among their male partners, while heterosexual men's (equally high) interest in women falls short as a result of women's significantly lower interest in noncommittal sexual contacts. If heterosexual men could do as they wished, they would have similarly high numbers of female partners as their homosexual counterparts have male partners. In addition, this high partner variability is not a phenomenon common to all homosexual men, but rather occurs among a small "high-end group" – for example, if only 1 percent of all homosexual men have more than 100 sexual partners per year, then logically the average number of partners for homosexual men as a group increases. In addition, there are also indications that taboos and the exclusion of homosexual behavior force homosexual men to escape into an anonymous "underground." In other words, gay men who visit dark rooms or "cruise" are representative of homosexual men as a group to the same extent that men who visit brothels, strip clubs, or sports bars are of all heterosexual men.

When it comes to understanding the development of sexual orientation, it is remarkable that the sex-typically distributed parameters in which homosexually oriented individuals correspond most closely to the distribution pattern of the opposite biological sex – that is, as shown above, aggressive behavior in childhood and spatial abilities in adulthood – are the same psychological traits that have been shown to be decisively influenced by the effects of prenatal androgens. Animal experiments have demonstrated that,[35] in correspondingly sensitive developmental phases, treating pre- or perinatal females fetuses with testosterone – possibly only for a short time – leads to a clear, sustained increase in postnatal aggressive behavior (so-called "play fighting") and also to a clear improvement in spatial orientation (in a maze test) in females (which show a lower expression in these two domains when untreated, just like human females). In contrast, decreasing pre- or perinatal testosterone levels in male fetuses leads to a permanent reduction in play-fighting behavior and maze orientation in males. Moreover, animals who receive such treatment also show an inversion in sexual mating behavior: the androgenized females mate with other females after puberty, and the deandrogenized males present themselves to other males for copulation in a position typical of females.

The amount of these findings prompted the development of the so-called prenatal brain androgenization model.[36] It is presumed that after gonadal differentiation, the brain is partially organized in a sex-typical manner, depending on prenatal androgen levels in sensitive phases: when prenatally (possibly only briefly) high levels of androgen and responsive receptors are present (i.e., normally in the male sex), the masculinization and defeminization of certain

---

35 Cf. the overview in Elizabeth Adkins-Reagan, "Sex hormones and sexual orientation in animals," *Psychobiology* 16 (1988): 335–347.
36 Cf. the overview in Matsumoto, *Sexual differentiation*; see also Hines, *Brain Gender*; LeVay, *Gay, straight*.

brain structures occur, including in the hypothalamus (INAH3). A postnatal or postpubescent activation of these cerebral structures then occurs, resulting in gender-typical male behaviors and cognitive performance. In the case of low androgen levels (i.e., normally in the female sex) or missing/unresponsive androgen receptors, a partial demasculinization/feminization of certain brain structures and functions occurs, and correspondingly a more feminine expression of cognitive, emotional, and behavioral characteristics results. This model is supported not only by the above-mentioned findings in animal experiments, but also by the fact that such prenatally treated animals' hypothalamuses, in a structure corresponding to INAH3 in the human hypothalamus, (the so-called SDN–MPOA), morphologically present in a way that is typical of the opposite sex: in prenatally androgenized females, this area is as small as it is in untreated males, and in prenatally deandrogenized males, it is as large as in untreated females. What is more, in rams that spontaneously engage in "homosexual" behavior, the size and shape of this hypothalamic nuclear area correspond to the typical female structure, even without hormone treatment.[37]

In addition to the similar alignment of many sex-atypical distributions (in aggressive behavior, spatial orientation, verbal fluency, and fine motor skills) in homosexuals, there is also further evidence to support the validity of the androgenization model in humans:

First, women with Congenital Adrenal Hyperplasia (CAH), who were exposed to markedly elevated androgen levels in utero due to a hereditary disorder affecting adrenal cortex activity (which can be adjusted by medication after birth), have a more masculine 2D:4D ratio (< 1.0),[38] exhibit a masculine pattern of (lower) spontaneous OAE production,[39] and exhibit significantly increased levels of "boyish" behavior in childhood, particularly rough-and-tumble play, as well as higher (i.e., more male-typical) spatial abilities.[40] In addition, compared to

---

37 Cf. Roselli, Reddy, and Kaufmann, "Male-oriented behavior in rams," 164–169.
38 Cf. M. P. Rivas et al., "New studies of second and fourth digit ratio as a morphogenetic trait in subjects with congenital adrenal hyperplasia," *American Journal of Human Biology* 26, no. 4 (2014): 559–561.
39 Cf. Amy B. Wisniewski et al., "Otoacoustic emissions, auditory evoked potentials and self-reported gender in people affected by disorders of sex development (DSD)," *Hormones and Behavior* 66, no. 3 (2014): 467–474.
40 Cf. Sheri A. Berenbaum and Melissa Hines, "Early androgens are related to childhood sex-typed toy preferences," *Psychological Science* 3 (1992): 203–206; Sheri A. Berenbaum, "Cognitive function in congenital adrenal hyperplasia (CAH)," *Endocrinology and Metabolism Clinics of North America* 30 (2001): 173–192; Melissa Hines et al., "Spatial abilities following prenatal androgen abnormality: Targeting and mental rotations performance in individuals with congenital adrenal hyperplasia," *Psychoneuroendocrinology* 28, no. 8 (2003): 1010–1026; J. Michael Bailey,

women without CAH, they show an increased rate of bi- and homosexual orientation, the expression of which also depends on prenatal androgen levels.[41] Conversely, genetically male individuals who experienced a prenatal receptor-related androgen deficiency (known as androgen insensitivity syndrome or AIS) exhibit a feminine 2D:4D ratio (= 1.0),[42] a feminized pattern of (higher) OAE production,[43] girl-typical play with low rates of aggressive behavior, poorer (also girl-typical) spatial orientation, and an androphilic homosexual orientation, relative to their genetic sex.[44]

Second, among other sexually dimorphic body proportions distributed in a sex-atypical manner, homosexually orientated men and women tend to have a sex-atypical 2D:4D ratio – that is, lesbian women exhibit an average value of < 1.0, while gay men exhibit an average value around of around 1.0.[45]

Third, homosexually orientated women exhibit an OAE-pattern that is more in line with the male sex (whereas homosexual men do not exhibit a pattern which can be clearly differentiated from that of heterosexual men).[46]

Fourth, in homosexual men, the structure of the hypothalamic INAH3 corresponds to that of heterosexual women (it is larger than that found in heterosexual men).[47] In lesbian women, our own studies found that grey matter density in certain brain regions is more in line with the male sex.[48]

Kathleen T. Bechtold, and Sheri A. Berenbaum, "Who are tomboys and why should we study them?" *Arch Sex Behav* 31, no. 4 (2002): 333–341.

41 Cf. Heino F. Meyer-Bahlburg et al., "Sexual orientation in women with classical or non-classical congenital adrenal hyperplasia as a function of degree of prenatal androgen excess," *Arch Sex Behav* 37, no. 1 (2008): 85–99.

42 Cf. Sheri A. Berenbaum et al., "Fingers as a marker of prenatal androgen exposure," *Endocrinology* 150, no. 11 (2009): 5119–5124.

43 Cf. Wisniewski et al., "Otoacoustic emissions," 467–474.

44 Cf. the overview in Hartmut A. G. Bosinski, "Psychosexuelle Probleme bei Intersex-Syndromen," *Sexuologie* 12 (2005): 31–59.

45 Cf. Teresa Grimbos et al., "Sexual orientation and the second to fourth finger length ratio: A meta-analysis in men and women," *Behavioral Neuroscience* 124, no. 2 (2010): 278–287.

46 Cf. Dennis McFadden, "Sexual orientation and the auditory system," *Frontiers in Neuroendocrinology* 32, no. 2 (2011): 201–213.

47 Cf. LeVay, "Difference in hypothalamic structure," 1034–1037; William Byne et al., "The interstitial nuclei of the human anterior hypothalamus: An investigation of variation with sex, sexual orientation, and HIV status," *Hormones and Behavior* 40 (2001): 86–92.

48 Cf. Jorge Ponseti et al., "Homosexual women have less grey matter in perirhinal cortex than heterosexual women," *PLoS ONE* 2, no. 8 (2007): e762.

Fifth, the brains of homosexual men and women respond to visual[49] and olfactory stimuli[50] in the same way as members of the opposite sex, respectively.

Sixth, in an attempt to clarify whether a genetic basis for androphilic or gynephilic sexual orientation exists, a large number of studies have been conducted on the familial occurrence of homosexuality, particularly among largely genetically identical monozygotic twins and dizygotic twins who differ genetically, like other siblings.[51] Due to the complex statistical methods employed, the data supported the hypothesis of an environmentally independent heritability factor of 30 to 50 percent. Research on the alignment of sexual orientation among identical twins who grew up separately, which is the "gold standard" of proof for a hereditary basis, has encountered understandable difficulties in view of the statistical rarity of both factors of interest (of finding identical twins who grew up separately, at least one of whom is homosexual). The only available study found a respective accordance in five out of six pairs of male twins.[52]

Seventh, in the course of the search for an indisputable genetic basis, various gene candidates have been identified,[53] proving that no single gene contributes to the development of a homosexual orientation, but presumably several

---

49 Cf. Jorge Ponseti et al., "Assessment of sexual orientation using the hemodynamic brain response to visual sexual stimuli," *The Journal of Sexual Medicine* 6, no. 6 (2009): 1628–1634; Ponseti et al., "Functional endophenotype," 825–833.

50 Cf. Ivanka Savic et al., "Brain response to putative pheromones in homosexual men," *Proceedings of the National Academy of Sciences USA* 102, no. 20 (2005): 7356–7361; Hans Berglund, Per Lindstrom, and Ivanka Savic, "Brain response to putative pheromones in lesbian women," *Proc Natl Acad Sci USA* 103, no. 21 (2006): 8269–8274.

51 Cf. the overview in Geoff Puterbaugh, ed., *Twins and homosexuality. A casebook* (New York: Garland, 1990); see also Frederick L. Whitam, Milton Diamond, and James Martin, "Homosexual orientation in twins: A report on 61 pairs and three triplet sets," *Arch Sex Behav* 22, no. 3 (1993): 187–206; J. Michael Bailey and Michael P. Dunne, "Genetic and environmental influences on sexual orientation and its correlates in an Australian twin sample," *J Pers Soc Psychol* 78, no. 3 (2000): 524–536; Kenneth S. Kendler et al., "Sexual orientation in a U.S. national sample of twin and nontwin sibling pairs," *The American Journal of Psychiatry* 157, no. 11 (2000): 1843–1846; Katarina Alanko et al., "Common Genetic Effects of Gender Atypical Behavior in Childhood and Sexual Orientation in Adulthood: A Study of Finnish Twins," *Arch Sex Behav* 39, no. 1 (2010): 81–92; Niklas Langstrom et al., "Genetic and environmental effects on same-sex sexual behavior: A population study of twins in Sweden," *Arch Sex Behav* 39, no. 1 (2010): 75–80; Andrea Burri, Tim Spector, and Qazi Rahman, "Common Genetic Factors among Sexual Orientation, Gender Nonconformity, and Number of Sex Partners in Female Twins: Implications of the Evolution of Homosexuality," *Journal of Sexual Medicine* 12, no. 4 (2015): 1004–1011.

52 Cf. Elke D. Eckert et al., "Homosexuality in monozygotic twins reared apart," *The British Journal of Psychiatry* 148 (1986): 421–425.

53 Cf. the overview in LeVay, *Gay, straight.*

genes located on different chromosomes. Furthermore, there are indications that such an orientation is inherited via the maternal lineage.

Finally, extensive meta-analytical studies with thousands of test subjects in different regions of the world have found that homosexual men are on average more likely to have older brothers than non-homosexual men, while there is no difference in the number of sisters or younger brothers.[54] From a purely statistical point of view, every seventh homosexual man owes his androphilic sexual orientation to the number of his older brothers, and each older brother increases the probability that a man will become homosexual by about 33 percent.[55] This phenomenon, which is known as the Fraternal Birth Order Effect (FBOE), is not found among lesbian women and cannot be explained with reference to psychosocial factors (such as child-rearing practices), since it is only evidenced among biological brothers with the same mother, not among paternal stepbrothers or adoptive brothers.[56] It has been postulated that a male fetus (which is genetically different from the mother) activates the maternal immune system more strongly, resulting in an intrauterine reduction in the responsiveness of the androgen receptors in some male embryos, due to maternal factors which are still unknown.[57]

4.5 On the Evolutionary Aspect

Homosexuality itself is a "Darwinian paradox": How can homosexuality, which through lack of procreation makes no direct contribution to reproduction (i.e., to the preservation of the species), be genetically preserved and passed on? A large number of studies have shown that the human species has a "bisexual potency" that contributes a great deal to increasing the species' reproductive prospects via

---

54 Cf. the overview in Ray Blanchard and Doug P. VanderLaan, "Commentary on Kishida and Rahman (2015), Including a Meta-analysis of Relevant Studies on Fraternal Birth Order and Sexual Orientation in Men," *Arch Sex Behav* 44, no. 5 (2015): 1503–1509; Ray Blanchard, "Older Brothers and Older Sisters Odds Ratios in 36 Samples of Homosexual Males," *Arch Sex Behav* 47, no. 4 (2018): 829–832.
55 Cf. James M. Cantor et al., "How many gay men owe their sexual orientation to fraternal birth order?" *Arch Sex Behav* 31, no. 1 (2002): 63–71.
56 Cf. Anthony F. Bogaert, "Biological versus nonbiological older brothers and men's sexual orientation," *Proceedings of the National Academy of Science USA* 103, no. 28 (2006): 10771–10774.
57 Cf. Ray Blanchard, "Fraternal Birth Order and the Maternal Immune Hypothesis of Male Homosexuality," *Hormones and Behavior* 40, no. 2 (2001): 105–114.

improved social cooperation,[58] or rather, given the high likelihood of polygenetic predisposition to homosexuality, that there are genes which increase an individual's fertility when they are heterozygous (unpaired), which more than compensates for the minimal or absent reproductive contribution of those relatives in whom the same gene is homozygous (paired) and who are therefore homosexual.[59]

In sum, a variety of research results have proven that homosexual orientation – as well as some other sex-atypically distributed differences in physical or psychological parameters, with which there is a partially high coherence – is biologically, prenatally predisposed by atypically low (in the case of homosexual men) or atypically high (in the case of homosexual women) androgenic effects on the developing brain. The causes of this sex-atypical androgenic effects may be genetic or epigenetic (that is, they may be hereditary, or they may be due to the effects of peristatic factors on gene expression in the womb). Furthermore, it has become clear that there is no unilinear relationship between these biological predispositions (e.g., genetic configuration, androgenic effect) and the expression of sexual orientation – otherwise every pair of identical twins would be concordant in their sexual orientation, for example, or all women who have CAH would be gynephilic (i.e., homosexual or bisexual).

---

58 For an introduction to this topic, see Hartmut A. G. Bosinski, "Geschlechtlichkeit und Sexualität unter dem Aspekt der Biopsychosozialität des Menschen," in *Interdisziplinäre Aspekte der Geschlechterverhältnisse in einer sich wandelnden Zeit,* ed. Karl-Friedrich Wessel (Bielefeld: Kleine, 1992), 121–142.

59 See Michael King et al., "Family size in white gay and heterosexual men," *Arch Sex Behav* 34, no. 1 (2005): 117–122; Doug P. Vanderlaan and Paul L. Vasey, "Male Sexual Orientation in Independent Samoa: Evidence for Fraternal Birth Order and Maternal Fecundity Effects," *Arch Sex Behav* 40, no. 3 (2011): 495–503; Andrea Camperio Ciani and Elena Pellizzari, "Fecundity of Paternal and Maternal Non-Parental Female Relatives of Homosexual and Heterosexual Men," *PLoS ONE* 7, no. 12 (2012): e51088; Andrea Camperio Ciani, Francesca Corna, and Claudio Capiluppi, "Evidence for maternally inherited factors favouring male homosexuality and promoting female fecundity," *Proc Biol Sci* 271, no. 1554 (2004): 2217–2221; Francesca Iemmola and Andrea Camperio Ciani, "New evidence of genetic factors influencing sexual orientation in men: Female fecundity increase in the maternal line," *Arch Sex Behav* 38, no. 3 (2009): 393–399; Andrea Camperio Ciani, Paolo Cermelli, and Giovanni Zanzotto, "Sexually antagonistic selection in human male homosexuality," *PLoS ONE* 3, no. 6 (2008): e2282; Francisco R. G. Jiménez, Scott W. Semenyna, and Paul L. Vasey, "Offspring Production Among the Relatives of Istmo Zapotec Men and Muxes," *Arch Sex Behav* 49 (2020): 581–594; Vincent Savolainen and Jason Hodgson, "Evolution of Homosexuality," in *Encyclopedia of Evolutionary Psychological Science,* ed. Todd K. Shackelford and Viviana A. Weeks-Shackelford (Cham: Springer, 2016), https://link.springer.com/referenceworkentry/10.1007/978-3-319-16999-6_3403-1 (accessed August 20, 2020).

5 Summary

Based on all of these findings, there can be no reasonable doubt about the existence of a biological predisposition to sexual orientation, whether heterosexual or homosexual. These predispositions constitute a field of possibilities – anything that is not found within this field cannot develop. Conversely, these predispositions also require "enabling" factors in the developing individual's environment. Neither of these mechanisms are mutually exclusive; rather, they are necessarily complementary, even conditional. Thus from the very beginning, the child influences the parents' reactions and behaviors simply by existing and acting in certain ways, through the child's vigilance, expressibility, and temperament (among other factors), which initially largely adhere to these predispositions. These predispositions in turn are shaped to a considerable extent by expectations regarding how a boy or a girl should behave, and thus by cultural gender role expectations. Cerebral biological predispositions act as a kind of grid through which one grasps reality, and this grid in turn changes through the individual's assimilation of reality in the process of ontogenesis itself. Thus the child simultaneously organizes and is organized by their environment. This interaction of biological predispositions, sociocultural expectations, norms, and reactions – among other factors – as well as their implementation via psychological processes, takes place in the developing brain, which differentiates gender-typically until after puberty under the influence of the interplay among environmental factors, genes, and hormones, and thus constitutes the "central switchboard" connecting prenatally gender-specific differentiation processes and postnatally gender-typically expressed psychological (cognitive, emotional, and behavioral) differences. In this way, a complex system of bio-psycho-social interdependencies is established (see figure 4).

As is typical of such complex, developing systems, the time factor is essential. In the interplay between stability and lability, a change in an otherwise marginal structural element can permanently alter the conditional structure of the entire system in certain periods of development. Such sensitive phases represent nodes or intersections for the interactions of biological, psychological, and social factors.

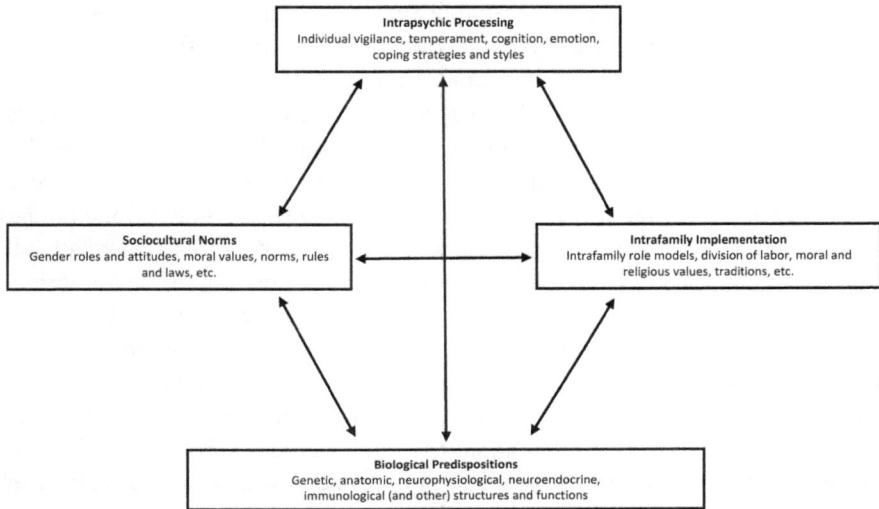

Figure 4: Diagram depicting the bio-psycho-social conditional structure of human individual development

6 An Essential Digression: The Question of Therapy

A whole century's worth of research has conclusively answered the question of whether homosexual orientation is pathological in the negative. In fact, by definition, a certain (e.g., homosexual) expression of sexual orientation cannot be pathological. This is, first, because deviation from the mean is a constituent of sex-typical difference, and second, because the standard definition of a pathological disorder are stress " and "impairment". That means, that a person suffers from an abnormal mental or physical condition. People who have a homosexual orientation do not suffer from the expression of their sexual orientation, but rather from the consequences of a social norm regarding which sexual orientation is "normal" and which is "sinful," "unnatural," or "pathological." Human sexuality is characterized by its multidimensionality: the phylogenetically oldest *reproductive dimension* is usually given priority in medical contexts. Yet this dimension has ultimately become optional in modern industrial societies, due to the availability of diverse contraceptive methods. Together with the *dimension of sexual lust*, which serves to gratify and reinforce sexual behavior (of whatever type), both dimensions are embedded in an overarching *communicative sexual dimension*, which serves not the simple satisfaction of hedonistic needs, but rather the basic human need for relational love. The tremendous importance of this communicative, relationship-oriented dimension of sexuality (which is already inherent in our closest biological relatives, non-human primates) results from the fact that humans are made for bonding and that their basic need for things such as acceptance, closeness, skin contact, and security – needs which are present from the very beginning of a person's life – are fulfilled in relationships. In the sexual encounter, which always addresses this relational dimension, the human being satisfies their basic psychosocial needs for acceptance, security, and closeness. Understanding human sexuality from a communicative perspective means considering the partners' ability to love and to form a relationship, not their genitalia. With regard to this relational dimension, studies have demonstrated that people with a homosexual orientation do not differ from people with a heterosexual orientation. The coincidental occurrence of homosexual orientation and various psychopathological abnormalities, as described in older studies, proved to be the result of exclusion and "attempts to cure" rather than of sexual orientation per se.

In this respect, there is a certain parallel to research on right- and left-handedness. Until the 1930s, left-handedness was considered a pathological disorder (for example in the USA), since a large number of psychopathological abnormalities were found in left-handed people. Thus children were forced to use the "fine hand." Once researchers recognized that there is a continuous distribution along a spectrum from exclusive right-handedness via ambidexterity to exclusive left-handedness, which moreover is caused by certain functional organizations of the brain, left-handedness came to be seen as a per se unproblematic variance of the norm, which need not be "cured," but to be accepted. As a result, the pathological symptoms in left-handed people also disappeared – they had been an expression of attempts at "pole reversal." Today, as we all know, a left-handed person can become president of the United States of America.

Homosexual orientation thus represents a normal variance of the human capacity for bonding and love. That is why, in 1973, the American Psychiatric Association removed its classification of "homosexuality" as a mental disorder and deleted the corresponding diagnosis code from the psychiatric classification system (the DSM). The WHO proceeded similarly with its ICD-10 classification of mental and behavioral disorders in 1994.

On this basis alone, it is clear that there is nothing about homosexual orientation that requires treatment. Yet attempts to "cure" homosexual people are legion. They were often cruel, and they always fail spectacularly. A desire for same-sex love that is "wired" in the brain and anchored in the personality cannot be eradicated any more than a desire for opposite-sex love.

This observation also applies to the "results" of so-called "conversion" or "reparation therapy" which fundamentalist circles have claimed in recent years. Such "therapy" is aimed at people who wish to be "freed" from their homosexuality on the basis of moral scruples or religious convictions. Yet these results have turned out to be errors at best, and often outright fraud. In 2003, the American psychiatrist Robert Spitzer (who played a key role in the depathologization of homosexuality in the USA in 1974!) believed he could prove the success of this "conversion therapy" on the basis of 200 test subjects,[60] but he has since recognized the various methodological and content-related errors in this study and has withdrawn the results.[61] A much more extensive study involving 1,612 participants[62] proved not only that the subjects' homosexual orientation remained unchanged by such "conversion attempts", but also that the goal of this "therapy" – namely, the eradication of the subjects' homosexuality – had psychologically disastrous consequences for the subjects, the most extreme of which was increased suicidal tendencies. Such tendencies are already significantly higher in adolescents who "come out" as homosexual,[63] since many young people do not want to be "different from others," and they increase dramatically when the young person is told that he or she is "sick" or "disturbed" and can and must be cured. For this reason, the leading psychotherapeutic, psychiatric, and pediatric professional societies (e.g., the American Psychiatric Association and the American Psychological Association) have made clear public statements in which they speak out against "conversion therapy" – which have been proven to do no good and can certainly do much harm – denouncing them as unethical and demanding that therapists and counselors help adolescents and adults to identify, accept, and responsibly express their respective sexual orientations.[64]

---

60 Cf. Robert L. Spitzer, "Can some gay men and lesbians change their sexual orientation? 200 participants reporting a change from homosexual to heterosexual orientation," *Arch Sex Behav* 32, no. 5 (2003): 403–417, as well as the discussion on pp. 419–472.
61 Cf. Robert L. Spitzer, "Spitzer reassesses his 2003 study of reparative therapy of homosexuality," *Arch Sex Behav* 41, no. 4 (2012): 757.
62 Cf. John P. Dehlin et al., "Sexual Orientation Change Efforts Among Current or Former LDS Church Members," *Journal of Counseling Psychology* 62, no. 2 (2014): 95–105.
63 Cf. Martin Plöderl et al., "Suicide Risk and Sexual Orientation: A Critical Review," *Arch Sex Behav* 42, no. 5 (2013): 715–727.
64 Cf. American Psychiatric Association, "Position statement on psychiatric treatment and sexual orientation," *The American Journal of Psychiatry* 156 (1999): 1131; American Psychiatric Association, "Position statement on therapies focused on attempts to change sexual orientation (reparative or conversion therapies)," *The American Journal of Psychiatry* 157 (2000): 1719–1721; American Psychological Association, "Appropriate Therapeutic Responses to Sexual Orienta-

In this respect, the new German "law for the protection against conversion therapy" (BT-Drucksache 234/20), passed in May 2020, is a welcome development. However, from the point of view of sexual medicine and medical ethics, it is regrettable that in the course of this development, the prohibition of treatments aimed at preventing transsexual development of children and adolescents with gender dysphoria was also included in this law. In fact, a large number of prospective and retrospective studies have shown that the vast majority (ca. 75%) of children with gender identity disorders – i.e., pronounced gender-atypical behavior and the desire to belong to the opposite sex – are homosexual once they emerge from puberty. Only in a minority of cases (ca. 20–25%) does gender dysphoria persist and develop into transsexuality.[65] The problem is that it is not possible to identify in childhood which group the child belongs to, whether to the majority of "desisters" in whom gender dysphoria disappears during puberty with the development of the adolescent's first erotic-sexual fantasies and experiences, and who subsequently evince a homosexual orientation, or to the minority of "persisters" in whom childhood gender dysphoria develops into transsexuality. The use of hormone blockers during puberty among children with gender dysphoria, a practice which has been propagated for some years, prevents homosexual development and paves the way for (risky and irreversible) hormonal and surgical "gender transformation treatment," thus constituting the conversion of *in statu nascendi* homosexuality into transsexuality.

Bibliography

Adkins-Reagan, Elizabeth. "Sex hormones and sexual orientation in animals." *Psychobiology* 16 (1988): 335–347.
Alanko, Katarina, et al. "Common Genetic Effects of Gender Atypical Behavior in Childhood and Sexual Orientation in Adulthood: A Study of Finnish Twins." *Arch Sex Behav* 39, no. 1 (2010): 81–92.

---

tion," 2009, http:// www.apa.org/pi/lgbt/resources/sexual-orientation.aspx (accessed August 20, 2020); American Psychological Association et al., "Just facts about sexual orientation and youth," 2008, http://www.apa.org/pi/lgbt/resources/just-the-facts.aspx (accessed August 20, 2020).

65 For an overview, see Alexander Korte et al., "Geschlechtsidentitätsstörungen im Kindes- und Jugendalter. Zur aktuellen Kontroverse um unterschiedliche Konzepte und Behandlungsstrategien," *Dtsch Arztebl Int* 105, no. 48 (2008): 834–841; see also Hartmut A. G. Bosinski, "Geschlechtsidentitätsstörungen / Geschlechtsdysphorie im Kindesalter," *Forum der Kinder- und Jugendpsychiatrie, Psychosomatik und Psychotherapie* 23, no. 2 (2013): 3–25.

Allen, John S., et al. "Sexual dimorphism and asymmetries in the grey-white composition of human cerebrum." *Neuroimage* 18 (2003): 880–894.

Allen, Laura S., et al. "Two sexually dimorphic cell groups in the human brain." *The Journal of Neuroscience* 9, no. 2 (1989): 497–506.

American Psychiatric Association. "Position statement on psychiatric treatment and sexual orientation." *The American Journal of Psychiatry* 156 (1999): 1131.

American Psychiatric Association. "Position statement on therapies focused on attempts to change sexual orientation (reparative or conversion therapies)." *The American Journal of Psychiatry* 157 (2000): 1719–1721.

American Psychological Association. "Appropriate Therapeutic Responses to Sexual Orientation." 2009. http://www.apa.org/pi/lgbt/resources/sexual-orientation.aspx. Accessed August 20, 2020.

American Psychological Association et al. "Just facts about sexual orientation and youth." 2008. http://www.apa.org/pi/lgbt/resources/just-the-facts.aspx. Accessed August 20, 2020.

Archer, John. "Sex Differences in Aggression in Real-World Settings – A Meta-Analytic Review." *Review of General Psychology* 8, no. 4 (2004): 291–322.

Bagemihl, Bruce. *Biological exuberance: Animal homosexuality and natural diversity.* New York: St. Martin's Press, 1999.

Bailey, J. Michael, and Michael P. Dunne. "Genetic and environmental influences on sexual orientation and its correlates in an Australian twin sample." *J Pers Soc Psychol* 78, no. 3 (2000): 524–536.

Bailey, J. Michael, Kathleen T. Bechtold, and Sheri A. Berenbaum. "Who are tomboys and why should we study them?" *Arch Sex Behav* 31, no. 4 (2002): 333–341.

Beitchman, Joseph H., et al. "A review of the long-term effects of child sexual abuse." *Child Abuse & Neglect* 16 (1992): 101–118.

Bell, Alan, Martin S. Weinberg, and Sue Kiefer Hammersmith. *Sexual preference: Its development in men and women.* New York: Indiana University Press, 1981.

Berenbaum, Sheri A. "Cognitive function in congenital adrenal hyperplasia (CAH)." *Endocrinology and Metabolism Clinics of North America* 30 (2001): 173–192.

Berenbaum, Sheri A., and Melissa Hines. "Early androgens are related to childhood sex-typed toy preferences." *Psychological Science* 3 (1992): 203–206.

Berenbaum, Sheri A., et al. "Fingers as a marker of prenatal androgen exposure." *Endocrinology* 150, no. 11 (2009): 5119–5124.

Berglund, Hans, Per Lindstrom, and Ivanka Savic. "Brain response to putative pheromones in lesbian women." *Proc Natl Acad Sci USA* 103, no. 21 (2006): 8269–8274.

Blanchard, Ray, and Doug P. VanderLaan. "Commentary on Kishida and Rahman (2015), Including a Meta-analysis of Relevant Studies on Fraternal Birth Order and Sexual Orientation in Men." *Arch Sex Behav* 44, no. 5 (2015): 1503–1509.

Blanchard, Ray. "Fraternal Birth Order and the Maternal Immune Hypothesis of Male Homosexuality." *Hormones and Behavior* 40, no. 2 (2001): 105–114.

Blanchard, Ray. "Older Brothers and Older Sisters Odds Ratios in 36 Samples of Homosexual Males." *Arch Sex Behav* 47, no. 4 (2018): 829–832.

Bleibtreu-Ehrenberg, Gisela. *Homosexualität. Die Geschichte eines Vorurteils.* Frankfurt am Main: Fischer Verlag, 1981.

Bogaert, Anthony F. "Biological versus nonbiological older brothers and men's sexual orientation." *Proceedings of the National Academy of Science USA* 103, no. 28 (2006): 10771–10774.

Bosinski, Hartmut A. G. "Determinanten der Geschlechtsidentität – Neue Befunde zu einem alten Streit." *Sexuologie* 7 (2000): 96–140.

Bosinski, Hartmut A. G. "Geschlechtlichkeit und Sexualität unter dem Aspekt der Biopsychosozialität des Menschen." In *Interdisziplinäre Aspekte der Geschlechterverhältnisse in einer sich wandelnden Zeit,* ed. Karl-Friedrich Wessel, 121–142. Bielefeld: Kleine, 1992.

Bosinski, Hartmut A. G. "Geschlechtsidentitätsstörungen / Geschlechtsdysphorie im Kindesalter." *Forum der Kinder- und Jugendpsychiatrie, Psychosomatik und Psychotherapie* 23, no. 2 (2013): 3–25.

Bosinski, Hartmut A. G. "Psychosexuelle Probleme bei Intersex-Syndromen." *Sexuologie* 12 (2005): 31–59.

Broude, Gwen, and Sarah J. Green. "Crosscultural codes on twenty sexual attitudes and practices." *Ethnology* 15 (1976): 409–428.

Burri, Andrea, Tim Spector, and Qazi Rahman. "Common Genetic Factors among Sexual Orientation, Gender Nonconformity, and Number of Sex Partners in Female Twins: Implications of the Evolution of Homosexuality." *Journal of Sexual Medicine* 12, no. 4 (2015): 1004–1011.

Byne, William, and Bruce Parsons. "Human sexual orientation. The biological theories reappraised." *Archives of General Psychiatry* 50 (1993): 228–239.

Byne, William, et al. "The interstitial nuclei of the human anterior hypothalamus: An investigation of sexual variation in volume and cell size, number and density." *Brain Research* 856, no. 1–2 (2000): 254–258.

Byne, William, et al. "The interstitial nuclei of the human anterior hypothalamus: An investigation of variation with sex, sexual orientation, and HIV status." *Hormones and Behavior* 40 (2001): 86–92.

Camperio Ciani, Andrea, and Elena Pellizzari. "Fecundity of Paternal and Maternal Non-Parental Female Relatives of Homosexual and Heterosexual Men." *PLoS ONE* 7, no. 12 (2012): e51088.

Camperio Ciani, Andrea, Paolo Cermelli, and Giovanni Zanzotto. "Sexually antagonistic selection in human male homosexuality." *PLoS ONE* 3, no. 6 (2008): e2282.

Camperio Ciani, Andrea, Francesca Corna, and Claudio Capiluppi. "Evidence for maternally inherited factors favouring male homosexuality and promoting female fecundity." *Proc Biol Sci* 271, no. 1554 (2004): 2217–2221.

Cantor, James M., et al. "How many gay men owe their sexual orientation to fraternal birth order?" *Arch Sex Behav* 31, no. 1 (2002): 63–71.

Chandra, Anjani, et al. "Sexual behavior, sexual attraction, and sexual identity in the United States: Data from the 2006–2008 National Survey of Family Growth." *National Health Statistics Report* 36 (2011): 1–36.

Cohen, Jacob. *Statistical power analysis for the behavioral sciences.* Hillsdale: Erlbaum, 1988.

Dehlin, John P., et al. "Sexual Orientation Change Efforts Among Current or Former LDS Church Members." *Journal of Counseling Psychology* 62, no. 2 (2014): 95–105.

Diamond, Milton. "Homosexuality and bisexuality in different populations." *Arch Sex Behav* 22, no. 4 (1993): 291–310.

Dickson, Nigel, Charlotte Paul, and Peter Herbison. "Same-sex attraction in a birth cohort: Prevalence and persistence in early adulthood." *Social Science & Medicine* 56, no. 8 (2003): 1607–1615.

Eckert, Elke D., et al. "Homosexuality in monozygotic twins reared apart." *The British Journal of Psychiatry* 148 (1986): 421–425.

Ellis, Lee. *Sex Differences: Summarizing More than a Century of Scientific Research*. New York: Psychology Press, 2008.

Grimbos, Teresa, et al. "Sexual orientation and the second to fourth finger length ratio: A meta-analysis in men and women." *Behavioral Neuroscience* 124, no. 2 (2010): 278–287.

Hames, Raymond, Zachary Garfield, and Melissa Garfield. "Is Male Androphilia a Context-Dependent Cross-Cultural Universal?" *Arch Sex Behav* 46, no. 1 (2017): 63–71.

Herdt, Gilbert. *Guardians of the flute*. Chicago: University of Chicago Press, 1994.

Herdt, Gilbert. *Same sex, different cultures. Gays and lesbians across cultures*. Boulder: Westview Press, 1997.

Hines, Melissa. *Brain Gender*. Oxford: Oxford University Press, 2004.

Hines, Melissa, et al. "Spatial abilities following prenatal androgen abnormality: Targeting and mental rotations performance in individuals with congenital adrenal hyperplasia." *Psychoneuroendocrinology* 28, no. 8 (2003): 1010–1026.

Hines, Melissa. "Gonadal hormones and human cognitive development." In *Hormones, brain and behavior in vertebrates*, ed. Jacques Balthazart, 51–63. Basel: Karger, 1990.

Iemmola, Francesca, and Andrea Camperio Ciani. "New evidence of genetic factors influencing sexual orientation in men: Female fecundity increase in the maternal line." *Arch Sex Behav* 38, no. 3 (2009): 393–399.

Jiménez, Francisco R. G., Scott W. Semenyna, and Paul L. Vasey. "Offspring Production Among the Relatives of Istmo Zapotec Men and Muxes." *Arch Sex Behav* 49 (2020): 581–594.

Johnson, Anne, et al. *Sexual attitudes and lifestyles*. Oxford: Blackwell, 1994.

Kendler, Kenneth S., et al. "Sexual orientation in a U.S. national sample of twin and nontwin sibling pairs." *The American Journal of Psychiatry* 157, no. 11 (2000): 1843–1846.

Kimura, Doreen. *Sex and cognition*. Cambridge, MA: MIT Press, 2000.

King, Michael, et al. "Family size in white gay and heterosexual men." *Arch Sex Behav* 34, no. 1 (2005): 117–122.

Kinsey, Alfred C., Wardell B. Pomeroy, and Clyde E. Martin. *Sexual Behavior in the human male*. Philadelphia: Saunders, 1948.

Korte, Alexander, et al. "Geschlechtsidentitätsstörungen im Kindes- und Jugendalter. Zur aktuellen Kontroverse um unterschiedliche Konzepte und Behandlungsstrategien." *Dtsch Arztebl Int* 105, no. 48 (2008): 834–841.

Langstrom, Niklas, et al. "Genetic and environmental effects on same-sex sexual behavior: a population study of twins in Sweden." *Arch Sex Behav* 39, no. 1 (2010): 75–80.

Laumann; Edward O., et al. *The social organization of sexuality. Sexual practices in the United States*. Chicago: University of Chicago Press, 1994.

LeVay, Simon. "A difference in hypothalamic structure between heterosexual and homosexual men." *Science* 253 (1991): 1034–1037.

LeVay, Simon. *Gay, straight, and the reason why. The science of sexual orientation*. Oxford: Oxford University Press, 2011.

Linn, Marcia C., and Anne C. Petersen. "Emergence and characterization of sex differences in spatial abilities: A meta-analysis." *Child Development* 56 (1985): 1479–1498.

Loehlin, John C., and Dennis McFadden. "Otoacoustic emissions, auditory evoked potentials, and traits related to sex and sexual orientation." *Arch Sex Behav* 32, no. 2 (2003): 115–127.

Manning, John T. *Digit ratio. A pointer to fertility, behavior, and health.* New Brunswick: Rutgers University Press, 2002.

Matsumoto, Akira, ed. *Sexual differentiation of the Brain.* Boca Raton: CRC Press, 1999.

McFadden, Dennis. "Sexual orientation and the auditory system." *Frontiers in Neuroendocrinology* 32, no. 2 (2011): 201–213.

Mercer, Catherine H., et al. "Changes in sexual attitudes and lifestyles in Britain through the life course and over time: Findings from the National Surveys of Sexual Attitudes and Lifestyles (Natsal)." *Lancet* 382, no. 9907 (2013): 1781–1794.

Meyer-Bahlburg, Heino F., et al. "Sexual orientation in women with classical or non-classical congenital adrenal hyperplasia as a function of degree of prenatal androgen excess." *Arch Sex Behav* 37, no. 1 (2008): 85–99.

Oliver, Mary Beth, and Janet S. Hyde. "Gender differences in sexuality: A meta-analysis." *Psychol Bulletin* 114 (1993): 29–51.

Plöderl, Martin, et al. "Suicide Risk and Sexual Orientation: A Critical Review." *Arch Sex Behav* 42, no. 5 (2013): 715–727.

Ponseti, Jorge, et al. "A functional endophenotype for sexual orientation in humans." *Neuroimage* 33, no. 3 (2006): 825–833.

Ponseti, Jorge, et al. "Assessment of sexual orientation using the hemodynamic brain response to visual sexual stimuli." *The Journal of Sexual Medicine* 6, no. 6 (2009): 1628–1634.

Ponseti, Jorge, et al. "Hirnanatomie und sexuelle Orientierung." *Sexuologie* 16, no. 3–4 (2009): 83–89.

Ponseti, Jorge, et al. "Homosexual women have less grey matter in perirhinal cortex than heterosexual women." *PLoS ONE* 2, no. 8 (2007): e762.

Puterbaugh, Geoff, ed. *Twins and homosexuality. A casebook.* New York: Garland, 1990.

Rivas, M. P., et al. "New studies of second and fourth digit ratio as a morphogenetic trait in subjects with congenital adrenal hyperplasia." *American Journal of Human Biology* 26, no. 4 (2014): 559–561.

Roselli, Chuck, Radhika C. Reddy, and Katherine R. Kaufman. "The development of male-oriented behavior in rams." *Frontiers in Neuroendocrinology* 32, no. 2 (2011): 164–169.

Safron, Adam, et al. "Neural Correlates of Sexual Orientation in Heterosexual, Bisexual, and Homosexual Men." *Scientific Reports* 7 (2017): 1–15.

Safron, Adam, et al. "Neural Correlates of Sexual Orientation in Heterosexual, Bisexual, and Homosexual Women." *Scientific Reports* 8, no. 1 (2018): 673–687.

Sanders, Geoff, and Tom Walsh. "Testing Predictions from the Hunter-Gatherer Hypothesis – 1: Sex Differences in the Motor Control of Hand and Arm." *Evolutionary Psychology* 5, no. 3 (2007): 653–665.

Savic, Ivanka, et al. "Brain response to putative pheromones in homosexual men." *Proceedings of the National Academy of Sciences USA* 102, no. 20 (2005): 7356–7361.

Savin-Williams, Ritch C., Kara Joyner, and Gerulf Rieger. "Prevalence and stability of self-reported sexual orientation identity during young adulthood." *Arch Sex Behav* 41, no. 1 (2012): 103–110.

Savolainen, Vincent, and Jason Hodgson. "Evolution of Homosexuality." In *Encyclopedia of Evolutionary Psychological Science*, ed. Todd K. Shackelford and Viviana A. Weeks-Shackelford. Cham: Springer, 2016. https://link.springer.com/referenceworkentry/10.1007/978-3-319-16999-6_3403-1. Accessed August 20, 2020.

Schmitt, David P., et al. "Universal sex differences in the desire for sexual variety: Tests from 52 nations, 6 continents, and 13 islands." *Journal of Personality and Social Psychology* 85, no. 1 (2003): 85–104.

Sell, Randall L., James A. Wells, and David Wypij. "The prevalence of homosexual behavior and attraction in the United States, the United Kingdom and France: Results of national population-based samples." *Arch Sex Behav* 24 (1995): 235–248.

Sommer, Volker, and Paul L. Vasey. *Homosexual Behaviour in Animals: An Evolutionary Perspective*. Cambridge: Cambridge University Press, 2006.

Spitzer, Robert L. "Can some gay men and lesbians change their sexual orientation? 200 participants reporting a change from homosexual to heterosexual orientation." *Arch Sex Behav* 32, no. 5 (2003): 403–417.

Spitzer, Robert L. "Spitzer reassesses his 2003 study of reparative therapy of homosexuality." *Arch Sex Behav* 41, no. 4 (2012): 757.

Statistisches Bundesamt. "Körpermaße nach Altersgruppen und Geschlecht für das Jahr 2013." https://www.destatis.de/DE/ZahlenFakten/GesellschaftStaat/Gesundheit/Gesundheitszustand RelevantesVerhalten/Tabellen/Koerpermasse.html?nn=50798. Accessed August 18, 2020.

Vanderlaan, Doug P., and Paul L. Vasey. "Male Sexual Orientation in Independent Samoa: Evidence for Fraternal Birth Order and Maternal Fecundity Effects." *Arch Sex Behav* 40, no. 3 (2011): 495–503.

Voyer, Daniel, Susan Voyer, and M. Phillip Bryden. "Magnitude of sex differences in spatial abilities: A meta-analysis and consideration of critical variable." *Psychological Bulletin* 117, no. 2 (1995): 250–270.

Whitam, Frederick L., Milton Diamond, and James Martin. "Homosexual orientation in twins: A report on 61 pairs and three triplet sets." *Arch Sex Behav* 22, no. 3 (1993): 187–206.

Wilson, Glenn, and Qazi Rahman. *Born Gay. The Psychobiology of Sex Orientation*. London: Peter Owen Publishers, 2005.

Wisniewski, Amy B., et al. "Otoacoustic emissions, auditory evoked potentials and self-reported gender in people affected by disorders of sex development (DSD)." *Hormones and Behavior* 66, no. 3 (2014): 467–474.

YouGov. "Kinsey Scale. Fieldwork Dates: 11th – 12th June 2018." 2018. https://d25d2506sfb94s.cloudfront.net/cumulus_uploads/document/forf2v7ra9/Results%20for%20Editorial%20(Kinsey%20Scale)%20131%2012.6.2018.pdf. Accessed October 29, 2020.

Melanie Caroline Steffens and Claudia Niedlich

Homosexuality Between Acceptance and Discrimination

A Social-Science Perspective

Today and in recent decades, the social perception of homosexuality has oscillated between acceptance and discrimination. In this process, the Catholic Church plays the role of an authority that sets basic moral standards. The perceived societal position of the Catholic Church is aptly captured in the following quote from 2010: "Why exactly does the church presume to dictate which sexuality one is allowed to live?"[1] The opportunity for dialogue with a leading member of the Catholic Church, as well as open opposition to its moral beliefs in relation to homosexuality, are the result of an enormous social change regarding the situation of lesbians and gay men in German-speaking and other European countries.[2] To illustrate this point: About 60 years ago, the famous British mathematician Alan Turing was convicted on a criminal charge of having a sexual relationship with a man. This was a punishable offense in many countries at that time. To avoid imprisonment,[3] Turing underwent estrogen therapy.[4] To date, there is no convincing evidence that sexual orientation can be influenced by therapy. During the twentieth century, numerous "therapies" have been test-

---

Note: We would like to thank Jeanine Plessing and Nele Nau for their support in translating this chapter.

1 This question was posed by Anne Will on her German political talk show, in which Bishop Franz-Josef Overbeck and film director Rosa von Praunheim engaged in a controversial discussion on the value of love, sexuality, marriage, and family. Rosa von Praunheim released the film *It's Not the Homosexual Who Is Perverse, but the Situation in Which He Lives* in 1971 and is regarded as one of the co-founders of the German lesbian and gay movement. Since 2010, Bishop Overbeck has revised his stance and called on the Church to change its views on homosexuality; see Franz-Josef Overbeck, "Vorurteile überwinden!" *Herder Korrespondenz* 73 (2019): 6.

2 For an overview, see Lisette Kuyper, Jurjen Iedema, and Saskia Keuzenkamp, *Towards Tolerance: Exploring Changes and Explaining Differences in Attitudes Towards Homosexuality Across Europe* (The Hague: The Netherlands Institute for Social Research, 2013).

3 See Melanie C. Steffens and Erin M. Thompson, "Verruchte – Perverse – Kranke – Unsichtbare: Der historische Blick," in *Anders ver-rückt?! Lesben und Schwule in der Psychiatrie*, ed. Ulrich Biechele, Philipp Hammelstein, and Thomas Heinrich (Jahrbuch Lesben – Schwule – Psychologie 2006; Lengerich: Pabst Science Publishers, 2006), 13–22.

4 Estrogen leads to a loss of libido. Furthermore, it has significant side effects, which include weight gain and breast growth.

https://doi.org/10.1515/9783110705188-005

ed with the intention of changing people's sexual orientation (e.g., hormone treatment or electroshock therapy). None of these treatments were able to withstand a critical review by the scientific community. It is not surprising that some "patients" report having (temporarily) suppressed their homosexual behavior. After all, such "therapy" reinforces and internalizes thoughts of rejecting one's own sexuality. Turing himself became depressed after the "therapy" he endured and committed suicide shortly thereafter.

Less than 50 years later, several top German politicians disclosed their homosexuality – starting with the mayor of Berlin, Klaus Wowereit – and Germany has confronted the international community with a gay Minister of Foreign Affairs (Guido Westerwelle) and currently a gay Minister of Health (Jens Spahn). Over these 50 years, the legal situation regarding homosexual behavior and same-sex partnerships has changed dramatically: homosexual behavior was decriminalized, and after the turn of the millennium, lesbians and gay men were granted certain legal rights via the law on registered partnerships (2001) and the General Equal Treatment Act (2006).[5] Yet compared to other countries in Europe, Germany has not played a pioneering role. It was only in 2017 that same-sex marriage and same-sex couples' right to adopt children together became legal in Germany, following in the footsteps of Scandinavia, France, and Spain. In 2018, the German Constitutional Court introduced the option of a third gender for people who do not identify as male or female. In 2019 – far too late – a legal ban on using conversion therapy to attempt to change people's sexual orientation was put in place.

Medical and social-scientific research reflects these social changes: while lesbians and gay men were classified as "ill" as recently as the middle of the previous century, and scientific research focused on homosexuality through this lens, the tables turned in the 1970s, when social-scientific research began to focus on the possible reasons for discrimination against and negative attitudes toward lesbians and gay men – it was "homophobia" rather than homosexuality that was said to be in need of explanation.[6] Today, both current scientific discourses and the legal and social situations of lesbians and gay men contradict the Catholic Church's position.

The aim of the present contribution is to provide an up-to-date overview of research on the social situations of lesbians and gay men. We will present both

---

5 See Melanie C. Steffens and Christof Wagner, "Diskriminierung von Lesben, Schwulen und Bisexuellen," in *Diskriminierung und Toleranz: Psychologische Grundlagen und Anwendungsperspektiven*, ed. Andreas Beelmann and Kai J. Jonas (Wiesbaden: VS Verlag für Sozialwissenschaften, 2009), 241–262.
6 See Celia Kitzinger, *The Social Construction of Lesbianism* (London: SAGE Publications, 1987).

the internal perspective – (To what degree) Do lesbians and gay men feel discriminated against? – and the external perspective: What characterizes people who have negative attitudes toward homosexuality, and how can these be explained? Both perspectives include considerations of religious affiliations, religiosity, and the role of the church.

1 Attitudes Toward Lesbians and Gay Men

Even though the term homophobia is popular worldwide, it is not an appropriate designation because it suggests an individual psychological disease (an irrational fear). Instead, "homophobia" consists in socially mediated negative attitudes toward lesbians and gay men that are learned over the course of a lifetime. In psychology, negative attitudes are often measured by self-reporting via questionnaires, and they include emotions ("affective attitudes," i.e., "On a scale from 1–7, how unpleasant/pleasant is the following situation for you: A gay couple is kissing near me?") and beliefs ("cognitive attitudes," i.e., "How strongly do you agree with the following statement: 'Lesbian couples should be allowed to adopt children to the same extent as heterosexual couples are'?").[7] Attitudes such as these are socio-culturally acquired and are part of broader values and belief systems.[8] Negative attitudes toward lesbians and gay men can lead to discriminatory behavior.[9]

Research shows that "between acceptance and discrimination" is an appropriate description for the current life situations of lesbians and gay men in Western and Northern Europe, while there is less acceptance in Southern and especially in Eastern Europe. In recent decades, there has been an overall improvement in attitudes across all European states. In Germany in 1981, 45 % of respondents indicated that homosexuality is always wrong, whereas in 2008 only 17 % shared this opinion.[10] Over the same time period, consent to the same statement also decreased in one of the most tolerant states – the Nether-

---

7 All examples are taken from the questionnaire in Jan Seise, Rainer Banse, and Franz J. Neyer, "Individuelle Unterschiede in impliziten und expliziten Einstellungen zur Homosexualität: Eine empirische Studie," *Zeitschrift für Sexualforschung* 15 (2002): 21–42.
8 See Gregory M. Herek and Kevin A. McLemore, "Sexual Prejudice," *Annual Review of Psychology* 64 (2013): 309–333.
9 See, for example, Melinda B. Goodman and Bonnie Moradi, "Attitudes and Behaviors Toward Lesbian and Gay Persons: Critical Correlates and Mediated Relations," *Journal of Counseling Psychology* 55 (2008): 371–384.
10 See Kuyper, Iedema, and Keuzenkamp, *Towards Tolerance*, 17.

lands – from 25% to 8%, while in a less tolerant state – Poland – it dropped from 77% in 1990 to 53% in 2008 (no data were available from Poland in 1981). Unfortunately, big international surveys such as the European Values Study contained only a few and often strange statements measuring attitudes toward homosexuality.[11] Since 1990, this survey has included a question asking which individuals one would not want to be one's neighbors, and in addition to drug abusers and criminals, there was the option to choose homosexuals. In 1990, 34% of Germans chose this answer, while in 2008, 17% still did so (in Austria, the percentages were 43% and 24%, respectively). In Europe (where the overall average is 25%), the numbers varied in 2008 from 2% (Ireland) to 67% (Lithuania). Another large-scale survey, the European Social Survey, contains a question asking whether one shares the opinion that gay men and lesbians should be free to live their lives as they wish. On a five-point scale, the attitudes of Northern and Western Europeans are close to 4 ("agree") on average, while in Southern Europe they are a bit lower, and in Eastern Europe the average is 3 ("neither agree nor disagree"). In Germany in 2010, 83% agreed (the variation across Europe ranged from 43% in Estonia to 93% in the Netherlands). For comparison: in the Russian federation, only 29% agreed. Lisette Kuyper and her colleagues discuss that, especially during the 1990s, attitudes toward lesbians and gay men became more tolerant across all of Europe.

The level of acceptance with regard to homosexuality depends on the concrete content of the statement. In Germany in 2003,[12] 65% of respondents agreed that "homosexuals should be allowed to marry" (in 2016 it was 83%,[13] while in Austria in 2003 it was 48%, in Switzerland 65%, and the EU average was 53%; in the 15 "old" EU states it was 57%, and in the 13 countries then acceding to the EU it was 23%).[14] Regarding the statement: "Homosexual couples in Europe should be allowed to adopt children," 57% agreed in Germany (33% in Austria, and 47% in Switzerland; the EU average was 38%, with the 15 "old" EU-states at 42%, and the 13 countries then acceding at 17%).[15] In 2020,[16] very low percen-

---

11 European Values Study, http://www.europeanvaluesstudy.eu/ (accessed December 8, 2020).
12 See Gallup Europe, "Homosexual Marriage, Child Adoption by Homosexual Couples: Is the Public Ready?" 2003, https://www.rklambda.at/archiv/dokumente/news_2003/News-PA-031015-Gallup-Umfrage-Text.pdf (accessed March 19, 2021).
13 See Beate Küpper, Ulrich Klocke, and Lena-Carlotta Hoffmann, *Einstellungen gegenüber lesbischen, schwulen und bisexuellen Menschen in Deutschland: Ergebnisse einer bevölkerungsrepräsentativen Umfrage* (Baden-Baden: Nomos, 2017).
14 See Kuyper, Iedema, and Keuzenkamp, *Towards Tolerance*.
15 There is no evidence in social science research that growing up with a same-sex couple has a detrimental effect on children; see Elke Jansen and Melanie C. Steffens, "Lesbische Mütter, schwule Väter und ihre Kinder im Spiegel psychosozialer Forschung," *Verhaltenstherapie und*

tages of respondents in Russia (12% and 3%), Lithuania (20% and 4%), and Hungary (27% and 11%) agreed or strongly agreed with this statement. The highest levels of agreement were found in the Netherlands (69%), Iceland (68%), France (66%), and Sweden (66%). While international comparisons tend to present individual countries as relatively homogenous, a closer look indicates considerable differences between social groups. The results of a representative telephone survey in Germany with 2,000 heterosexual participants can be summarized as follows:[17] the most positive attitudes toward lesbians and gay men (as well as bisexual men and women) were reported by persons who were under 30 years old, were female, lived in a larger city, were highly educated and rather politically left-wing, and counted homosexuals among their friends and acquaintances. The 2020 survey supports these findings across countries, regardless of whether or not the country in question recognizes the legal rights of LGBTI people. Religiosity was not assessed in this survey, but in many studies it is related to negative attitudes toward lesbians and gay men.[18]

Moreover, attitudes toward lesbians and gay men as distinct groups differ. Typically the most negative attitudes are reported by heterosexual men toward gay men.[19] Before we discuss the social-scientific reasons for this, we will look at the question of how lesbians and gay men experience their current social situations.

Psychosoziale Praxis: Sonderheft Psychotherapie mit Lesben, Schwulen und Bisexuellen 38 (2006): 643–656; Marina Rupp, ed., *Die Lebenssituation von Kindern in gleichgeschlechtlichen Lebenspartnerschaften* (Cologne: Bundesanzeiger Verlag, 2009). See also Gerhard Marschütz's contribution in this volume.

16 See Giulia M. Dotti Sani and Mario Quaranta, "Let Them Be, Not Adopt: General Attitudes Towards Gays and Lesbians and Specific Attitudes towards Adoption by Same-Sex Couples in 22 European Countries," *Social Indicators Research* 150 (2020): 351–373.

17 See Melanie C. Steffens and Christof Wagner, "Attitudes Towards Lesbians, Gay Men, Bisexual Women, and Bisexual Men in Germany," *Journal of Sex Research* 41 (2004): 137–149.

18 See, for example, Bernd Simon, "Einstellungen zur Homosexualität: Ausprägungen und psychologische Korrelate bei Jugendlichen mit und ohne Migrationshintergrund (ehemalige UdSSR und Türkei)," *Zeitschrift für Entwicklungspsychologie und Pädagogische Psychologie* 40 (2008): 87–99; Melanie C. Steffens, Kai J. Jonas, and Lisa Denger, "Male Role Endorsement Explains Negative Attitudes Toward Lesbians and Gay Men Among Students in Mexico More Than in Germany," *Journal of Sex Research* 52 (2015): 898–911, DOI:10.1080/00224499.2014.966047; Bernard E. Whitley, Jr., "Religiosity and Attitudes Toward Lesbians and Gay Men: A Meta-Analysis," *International Journal for the Psychology of Religion* 19 (2009): 21–38.

19 See Melanie A. Morrison and Todd G. Morrison, "Sexual Orientation Bias Toward Gay Men and Lesbian Women: Modern Homonegative Attitudes and Their Association with Discriminatory Behavioral Intentions," *Journal of Applied Social Psychology* 41 (2011): 2573–2599; Steffens and Wagner, "Attitudes Towards Lesbians," 137–149.

2 Discrimination Against Lesbians and Gay Men

When people in Europe were asked about their sexual orientation, the numbers differed between countries. Compared to other countries, Germany, Spain, and Great Britain saw the highest percentage of people who stated they were lesbian or gay (7%), followed by the Netherlands (6%). Hungary came in last, with only 2% identifying as lesbian or gay.[20] The different proportions of lesbians and gay men in different European countries proportions show that reservations and fear hinder people from being open about their sexual orientation. This indicates that scientific studies run the risk that not all participants will openly state their sexual orientation. Nevertheless, telephone interviews lead to more precise estimates than any other method.

A survey sample is representative if it is commensurate with the overall population in all relevant characteristics. To determine whether this is the case, of course, one needs to know the overall population. However, if a minority experiences discrimination and has the option of living "in the closet" (by not making their homosexuality public), then this overall population is unknown. This poses a major challenge for research. Alternatively, it is possible to survey a random sample of the entire population and to make it as easy as possible to state one's true sexual orientation. As one can imagine, this method is very complicated and expensive. We conducted such a survey in 2001.[21] When we reached someone by phone, we asked to speak to the person in the household whose birthday was next (to make sure that persons who often answer the phone were not overrepresented in the survey). Almost 15,000 persons were willing to state their sexual orientation ("Please answer with 'one' if you are heterosexual, say 'two' if you are bisexual, and say 'three' if you are homosexual."). All the lesbian/gay and bisexual persons (about 600 in total) were then asked about their experiences of discrimination: 55% of the gay men and 26% of the lesbians agreed with the statement: "I have been insulted because of my sexual orientation"; 21% of the gay men and 2% of the lesbians had experienced being threatened in everyday life; while 14% of gay men and 10% of lesbians had experienced insults at work.

---

20 See Bastian Brauns, "So homosexuell ist Europa," *Die Zeit Online*, Teilchen (Blog), October 19, 2016, https://blog.zeit.de/teilchen/2016/10/19/so-schwul-ist-europa/?wt_ref=https%3A%2F%2F2F (accessed February 11, 2021).
21 See Steffens and Wagner, "Attitudes Towards Lesbians"; Steffens and Wagner, "Diskriminierung von Lesben."

Thus it becomes obvious that gay men report more discrimination than lesbians (and also more than bisexual men and women). When interpreting the figures, one should bear in mind that sexual orientation – unlike, for example, ethnic origin – is a minority status that can potentially be concealed: if one feels insecure in a certain environment, one often has the choice not to reveal one's sexual orientation. Many lesbians and gay men make use of this option. Against this background, the numbers given above are alarming. To our knowledge, few other studies have used similar random samples (which is not surprising, given the costs outlined above). Gay men and lesbians with and without migrant backgrounds participated in another study.[22] Regarding whether they were "out" at work, about one-third of participants reported that nobody or almost nobody knew about their sexual orientation. Women stated that they had "come out" at work less often than men. About one-third of the participants stated that they had been verbally threatened or abused because of their sexual orientation, regardless of their migrant background. However, lesbians and gay men who were immigrants experienced discrimination on the basis of their sexual orientation within the family more often than autochthonous Germans. All the participants found discrimination based on their sexual orientation to be a very stressful experience.

Experiences of discrimination at work play a significant role in people's well-being. Work life is an important part of everyday life and is deeply connected to one's identity. Different studies show that between 82% and 94% of the persons interviewed consider their job a very important part of their life. With regard to (homo)sexuality, people often assume that the workplace is an "asexual space" from which private romantic relationships can be excluded. This is linked to the expectation that sexual orientation does not play a role in work life and is not relevant to work-related processes. Two brief examples illustrate that this is not the case, and indeed they might seem familiar: 1) Mr. Krause, a nurse, returns from his vacation and is asked how he spent it. He happily describes his wonderful experiences. 2) Ms. Müller was hired as a bank consultant. While she is setting up her office, she puts a photo of her family on her desk, and a ring glints on her left (or right) ring finger.

Both examples make it clear that these situations would require Mr. Krause or Ms. Müller to disclose their sexual orientation. When reading these examples,

---

22 See Melanie C. Steffens, Michael Bergert, and Stephanie Heinecke, "Studie Lebenssituation von Lesben und Schwulen mit Migrationshintergrund," in *Doppelt diskriminiert oder gut integriert? Lebenssituation von Lesben und Schwulen mit Migrationshintergrund in Deutschland,* ed. Familien- und Sozialverein des Lesben- und Schwulenverbandes in Deutschland (LSVD) e.V. (Cologne: LSVD, 2010), 13–107.

you probably assumed that Mr. Krause was accompanied by his wife. You may have imagined that the photo which Ms. Müller put on her desk depicted her with her husband and her children. If you have excluded the possibility that same-sex partners might be involved, then you have adopted a "heteronormative perspective." Heteronormativity means that heterosexuality is seen as the norm and as natural. Assuming that everyone one meets is heterosexual is a heterosexist practice. Gregory Herek defines heterosexism as a system that rejects and stigmatizes all forms of non-heterosexual behavior, identities, relationships, and communities.[23] Heterosexism is integrated into our daily behavior and our institutions, as well as into religion.[24] Heterosexuals can disclose their sexual orientation in their work life by talking about their experiences on vacation as well as through various symbols (such as wedding rings and family photos).[25] These symbols are considered everyday aspects of social life. If lesbians and gay men want to share this information in the same way, they often have to be careful at first, checking whether their work environment is open to their sexual orientation. Furthermore, information about their private life may be interpreted not as exclusively social, but as sexual information, and thus as "too much."[26] Scientific findings show that lesbian and gay employees use different strategies and show different levels of openness, or hide their sexual orientation either partly or completely.[27] This concealment, with the concurrent concerns that someone "might have noticed something after all"; the use of exclusively "heterosexual examples" in discussions; and efforts not to appear "stereotypically lesbian" or "stereotypically gay" require additional cognitive resources. As a result, these workers are exposed to additional stress. They cannot participate in work-

---

23 Gregory M. Herek, "The Context of Anti-Gay Violence: Notes on Cultural and Psychological Heterosexism," *Journal of Interpersonal Violence* 5 (1990): 316–333, http://jiv.sagepub.com/content/5/3/316.full.pdf+html.
24 See Judith A. Clair, Joy E. Beatty, and Tammy L. MacLean, "Out of Sight But Not Out of Mind: Managing Invisible Social Identities in the Workplace," *Academy of Management Review* 30 (2005): 78–95.
25 See Christopher Knoll, Manfred Edinger, and Günter Reisbeck, *Grenzgänge: Schwule und Lesben in der Arbeitswelt* (Munich/Vienna: Profil-Verlag, 1997).
26 See Gregory M. Herek, "Stigma, Prejudice, and Violence Against Lesbians and Gay Men," in *Homosexuality: Research Implications for Public Policy*, ed. John C. Gonsiorek and James D. Weinrich (Thousand Oaks, CA: SAGE Publications, 1991), 60–80; Knoll, Edinger, and Reisbeck, *Grenzgänge*; Thomas Köllen, "Privatsache und unerheblich für Unternehmen? Der Stand der Personalforschung zur 'sexuellen Orientierung'," *Zeitschrift für Personalforschung* 26 (2012): 143–166.
27 See Knoll, Edinger, and Reisbeck, *Grenzgänge*; Claudia Niedlich and Melanie C. Steffens, *Minoritätenstress von Lesben und Schwulen im Arbeitsleben* (unpublished manuscript, 2015).

related processes as whole persons and thus do not exploit their full potential. In sociopsychological research, this additional stress is called "minority stress."[28]

Different studies indicate a differentiated picture of how often lesbians and gay men experience discrimination in their work life and what effects this has on their psychological well-being. As early as 1997, Christopher Knoll and his colleagues reported the most common forms of discrimination lesbians and gay men face in Germany. In what follows, we compare these forms with studies conducted in 2013[29] and 2017[30] using a similar questionnaire: unpleasant lesbian and gay jokes (1997: 54%; 2013: 22%; 2017: 27%), talking behind one's back (1997: 48%; 2013: 34%; 2017: 49%), unpleasant interest in private life (1997: 36%; 2013: 22%; 2017: 36%), and unpleasant sexual allusions (1997: 26%; 2013: 21%; 2017: 28%) are the most common forms of discrimination lesbians and gay men experience. A study conducted by Dominic Frohn[31] reports similar findings: the data suggest that discrimination on the basis of sexual orientation in work life is a problem lesbians and gay men face every day. Hiding one's homosexuality in one's work life is considered a consistent problem in these studies (1997: 92%; 2007: 60%; 2013: 54%). Some employees decide not to talk to any of their colleagues about their sexual orientation (1997: 28%; 2007: 10%, 2013: 12%; 2017: 7%). The resulting minority stress may manifest in the form of psychosomatic symptoms. A recent study in Germany (2020) shows that discrimination in the workplace persists: although non-heterosexuals have a better education than heterosexuals on average, 30% still report experiencing discrimination in their work life, and a further 30% are not fully open with their colleagues about their sexual orientation. The problem is more apparent in work environments where lesbians and gay men are underrepresented.[32] Across Europe, 51% of lesbian and gay employees responded that they were very open about their sexual orientation at work (in Denmark, it was 61%; in the Netherlands, 44%; in Portugal, 54%; in Roma-

---

28 See Ilan H. Meyer, "Prejudice, Social Stress, and Mental Health in Lesbian, Gay, and Bisexual Populations: Conceptual Issues and Research Evidence," *Psychological Bulletin* 129 (2003): 674–697.

29 Niedlich and Steffens, *Minoritätenstress*.

30 See Dominic Frohn, Florian Meinhold, and Christina Schmidt, *"Out im Office?!" Sexuelle Identität und Geschlechtsidentität, (Anti-)Diskriminierung und Diversity am Arbeitsplatz* (Cologne: Institut für Diversity- und Antidiskriminierungsforschung, 2017), https://www.dominicfrohn.de/downloads/IDA_Out_im_Office_2017.pdf (accessed February 18, 2021).

31 See Dominic Frohn, "Out im Office?!" Sexuelle Identität, (Anti-) Diskriminierung und Diversity am Arbeitsplatz, Köln 2007

32 See Lisa de Vries et al., "LGBTQI*-Menschen am Arbeitsmarkt: hoch gebildet und oftmals diskriminiert," *Deutsches Institut für Wirtschaftsforschung Wochenbericht* 36 (2020): 619–627, DOI:10.18723/diw_wb:2020–36–1.

nia, 59%).[33] All of these studies indicate that people who report more intense experiences of discrimination also experience more health problems (i.e., headache, dizziness, back pain). "Discrimination makes you sick" is the message that Knoll and his colleagues were already sending in 1997. With regard to the ecclesiastical context, the following results can be observed in connection with work life: 12% of the respondents stated that they had avoided applying or refused to apply to a particular employer because of their sexual orientation, and 58% of these named a denominational institution when asked about the context of the job in question. In this respect, we can assume that church institutions represent a working environment that lesbian and gay employees often avoid. Thus a proportion of highly qualified employees decide not to contribute their qualifications and skills to work in church institutions. Furthermore, we can assume that a proportion of the employees in church institutions are exposed to minority stress, since in church contexts one might feel a particularly strong need to conceal one's sexual orientation.

In addition to the complex sampling mentioned above, there are other factors that make it difficult to obtain reliable statements regarding discrimination against social minorities. A second important factor is the ambiguity of most human experiences. In our survey, when asked: "Did you lose or not get a job because of discrimination?", 3% of the lesbians and gay men with migrant backgrounds responded that this had happened because of their sexual orientation, and 14% said it was because of their origin.[34] It would be surprising if any of the employers had explicitly cited one of these reasons. Instead, these answers are the result of the subjective interpretations of the persons concerned. But how well can people assess whether they have been discriminated against? And could it be that they forget such experiences? Psychological research provides reasons to believe that people may either underestimate or overestimate how often they are discriminated against. Underestimation can occur because people usually prefer to see themselves as active architects of their lives rather than as powerless beings helplessly exposed to others.[35] In contrast, overestimation is possible because attributing one's failures to one's own weaknesses can have negative consequences for one's self-esteem. In this respect, it can be less pain-

---

33 LGBTI Survey Data Explorer, 2019, https://fra.europa.eu/en/data-and-maps/2020/lgbti-survey-data-explorer (accessed April 21, 2021).

34 See Steffens, Bergert, and Heinecke, "Studie Lebenssituation."

35 A current overview is provided in Manuela Barreto and Naomi Ellemers, "Detecting and Experiencing Prejudice: New Answers to Old Questions," in *Advances in Experimental Social Psychology*, vol. 52, ed. James M. Olson and Mark P. Zanna (Waltham, MA: Academic Press, 2015), 139–219, DOI: 10.1016/bs.aesp.2015.02.001.

ful to assume: "They don't want gay people there!" than to admit: "The other applicant was simply better than me." In short, if 14% of gay men report having been insulted at work, this indicates the presence of a problem, but this method cannot indicate whether this number is an under- or an overestimation.

In addition to self-reporting in surveys, the social sciences have developed other ways to assess discrimination.[36] With regard to application processes, the following is one experimental approach: Identical application documents are created, and only one characteristic is changed – for example, the applicant's sexual orientation. One applicant could claim to have "experience as a treasurer for the gay student group," while this line is missing from another, otherwise identical application.[37] Each application is sent out many times, and the number of positive responses (e. g., invitations to interviews) is counted. An early study in Ontario, Canada showed that gay and lesbian activists received only half as many invitations to job interviews in law offices as persons with identical applications which did not contain any information on such activism. In this way, discrimination can be quantified.[38]

Psychological studies employ a similar procedure to test, for example, how the impression of a person's competence changes if just one characteristic in the documents is changed. If the same application documents lead to a higher impression of competence when they contain a male first name than when they contain a female first name, then the researchers conclude that male stereotypes are associated with higher competence than female stereotypes.[39] We used this approach in our studies to check whether same-sex couples are the most likely group to be discriminated against in adoption applications, as survey research suggests.[40] Participants were asked whether they would take part in a short

---

36 See also Melanie C. Steffens and Sabine Preuß, "Measuring Attitudes Toward LGBTI* Individuals: Theoretical and Practical Considerations," in *Oxford Encyclopedia of LGBT Politics and Policy*, ed. Don Haider-Markel and Gary Mucciaroni (New York: Oxford University Press, 2021).

37 For a detailed discussion, see András Tilcsik, "Pride and Prejudice: Employment Discrimination Against Openly Gay Men in the United States," *American Journal of Sociology* 117 (2011): 586–626.

38 Barry D. Adam, "Stigma and Employability: Discrimination by Sex and Sexual Orientation in the Ontario Legal Profession," *Canadian Review of Sociology and Anthropology* 18 (1981): 216–221.

39 For a comprehensive overview of this research, see Melanie C. Steffens and Ma. Àngels Viladot, *Gender at Work: A Social-Psychological Perspective* (New York: Peter Lang, 2015).

40 See Melanie C. Steffens, Kai J. Jonas, and Thérèse Scali, "Putting Prejudice into Perspective. Does Perceived Suitability for Adoption Depend on Sexual Orientation More than on Other Applicant Features?" *Sensoria: A Journal of Mind, Brain & Culture* 11 (2015): 41–57.

study and then received a fictitious adoption application. The application included the standard information which is usually expected by the relevant offices (age, occupation, income, housing conditions). The applicants were either a heterosexual, a gay, or a lesbian couple. In addition, the couple was listed as either in their early 30s or their early 50s, and their occupation(s), income, and the size of their accommodation suggested either high or low socioeconomic status. The results showed that gay male (but not lesbian) couples were considered less suitable as adoptive parents than heterosexual couples. A second study demonstrated that this was due to the fact that men correspond less to the stereotypical image of adoptive parents than women do. Older couples were also considered less suitable than younger couples. However, socioeconomic status was the most important factor in evaluating the applications: couples with a high income, a large apartment, and their own garden were considered particularly suitable. In other words, a gay couple – a dentist and a journalist – were considered more suitable than a heterosexual couple in which the wife was a secretary and the husband was unemployed. Another study indicated that assessments of suitability also depended on the child's characteristics when the child's sex and age were provided.[41] For the adoption of female teenagers, gay male couples were preferred over all other constellations. Apparently the respondents were concerned about child sexual abuse and believed that young girls were best situated in a household where no one could have a sexual interest in them (i.e., the gay male family). Overall, the results indicated that reservations about same-sex couples as adoptive parents are not always as significant as survey research suggests. A representative survey corroborating this theory showed that 43% of respondents in Germany believed that the children of lesbian and gay parents develop just as well as the children of heterosexual parents.[42] People think that the overall family constellation is what matters, and this can be an advantage for gay and lesbian couples.

Much of the research employing a comparable paradigm has investigated work-related discrimination on the basis of sexual orientation. The main question is whether applicants with different sexual orientations have equal chances of being hired for an advertised position, and whether they are considered capable of succeeding in the respective profession. Here again, the application materials of heterosexual and lesbian or gay applicants are identical except for their sexual orientation. Studies show that lesbians and gay men are often rated more

---

41 See Melanie C. Steffens and Kai J. Jonas, "Attitudes Towards Adoptive Parents, Child Age, and Child Gender: The Role of Applicants' Sexual Orientation," *Zeitschrift für Familienforschung*, special issue 7 (2010): 205–219.
42 See Küpper, Klocke, and Hoffmann, *Einstellungen*.

negatively than heterosexuals. This primarily depends on the broader social climate with regard to homosexuality – that is, discrimination was found in Greece or the US Midwest, but not in Belgium or in large US cities.[43] The results of one of our own studies indicate that lesbians are presumed to be more competent than heterosexual women.[44] However, this was only the case if both applicants acted in accordance with the stereotype of the traditional woman – both stated that they had moved and applied for the job in question because their new place of residence offered better work opportunities for their (female or male) partner. In subsequent studies, we found that lesbians and gay men were assessed as more competent in comparison to equally qualified heterosexual men and women.[45] In addition, gay male applicants were rated as having superior social skills but as less masculine than heterosexual male applicants. This pattern indicating a positive impression of lesbians and gay men in application processes was found in different occupational contexts (i.e., police, primary school, engineering). If someone is rated as highly competent, then this should lead to higher chances of being hired. However, for lesbians and gay men being considered for leadership positions, higher ascriptions of competence did not correlate with a greater likelihood of being hired.[46] This indicates discrimination based on sexual orientation: heterosexual applicants had equal chances of being hired as lesbians and gay men did, despite higher ascriptions of competence to the latter.

Taken together, these studies indicate that the decisions which influence a person's career opportunities are not made exclusively on the basis of that person's actual skills. Lesbians and gay men may experience discrimination on the basis of their sexual orientation; however, in terms of ascribed competence, lesbians and gay men may occasionally have an advantage. Stereotypes of lesbians, gay men, and heterosexuals apparently affect (simulated) career opportunities.

---

43 An overview is provided in Melanie C. Steffens, Claudia Niedlich, and Franziska Ehrke, "Discrimination at Work on the Basis of Sexual Orientation: Subjective Experience, Experimental Evidence, and Interventions," in *Sexual Orientation and Transgender Issues in Organizations: Global Perspectives on LGBT Workforce Diversity*, ed. Thomas Köllen (Heidelberg/New York: Springer, 2015), 367–388.

44 See Claudia Niedlich et al., "Ironic Effects of Sexual Minority Group Membership: Are Lesbians Less Susceptible to Invoking Negative Female Stereotypes than Heterosexual Women?" *Archives of Sexual Behavior* 44 (2015): 1439–1447, DOI:10.1007/s10508–014–0412–1.

45 See Claudia Niedlich and Melanie C. Steffens, "On the Interplay of (Positive) Stereotypes and Prejudice: Impressions of Lesbian and Gay Applicants for Leadership Positions," *Sensoria: A Journal of Mind, Brain & Culture* 11 (2015), https://www.researchgate.net/publication/275648569.

46 See Melanie C. Steffens et al., "Do Positive and Negative Stereotypes of Gay and Heterosexual Men Affect Job-Related Impressions?" *Sex Roles* 80 (2019): 9–10, DOI:10.1007/s11199-018-0963-z.

Such stereotypes can also provide explanations for negative attitudes, which we discuss in the following section.

3 Explaining Negative Attitudes

As we mentioned at the beginning, attitudes toward lesbians and gay men are not primarily seen as psychological phenomena, but rather as socially and culturally acquired, and as components of broader values and belief systems.[47] This explains why younger people have more positive attitudes toward lesbians and gay man than older people do: they have grown up with less restrictive belief systems. One such belief system is the Gender Belief System[48] – interrelated beliefs about what women and men are like, how they should (and should not) behave, which social roles they should adopt, and so on. Stereotypes (i. e., socially shared beliefs about the characteristics of various social groups) regarding lesbians and gay men involve the transgression of gender roles: lesbians are considered to be more masculine than heterosexual women, while gay men are considered to be more feminine than heterosexual men.[49] According to this theory, negative attitudes toward lesbians and gay men are based on the fact that people make strict demands on women and men to behave in accordance with certain gender roles. At the same time, lesbians and gay men are expected to transgress these boundaries. The finding that heterosexual men have more negative attitudes toward gay men and lesbians compared to heterosexual women can be explained by the fact that these men have stricter ideas about appropriate gender roles than women do.[50]

If one compares attitudes toward gender roles with attitudes toward gay men and lesbians, one finds a strong correlation across European countries.[51] Attitudes toward homosexuality are most positive in those countries which also have the most liberal gender roles: Denmark, Norway, Sweden, Iceland, and the Netherlands. Attitudes toward homosexuality are most negative in those

---

47 See Herek and McLemore, "Sexual Prejudice," 309–333.
48 See Kay Deaux and Brenda Major, "Putting Gender Into Context: An Interactive Model of Gender-Related Behavior," *Psychological Review* 94 (1987): 369–389.
49 See Bernard E. Whitley, Jr., "Gender-Role Variables and Attitudes toward Homosexuality," *Sex Roles* 45 (2001): 691–721.
50 As shown in Mary E. Kite and Bernard E. Whitley, Jr., "Sex Differences in Attitudes Toward Homosexual Persons, Behaviors, and Civil Rights: A Meta-Analysis," *Personality and Social Psychology Bulletin* 22 (1996): 336–353.
51 See Kuyper, Iedema, and Keuzenkamp, *Towards Tolerance*.

countries with the most restrictive gender roles: Turkey, Moldova, Georgia, and Ukraine. Countries like Spain, where attitudes toward lesbians and gay men are surprisingly positive compared to other countries in Southern Europe, also evince the most liberal gender roles relative to other countries in the region. In one of our own studies, we recently tested which psychological variables might explain negative attitudes toward lesbians and gay men among students in Mexico.[52] Among other things, we asked which norms the participants applied to the male gender role (e. g., "It is very important for a man that all persons who know him respect and admire him," and "I think it is silly and embarrassing if a friend is crying because of a sad love scene in a movie"). We statistically tested which of the constructs we asked about could explain negative attitudes toward lesbians and gay men (so-called multiple regression analysis). In the Mexican sample, only male role norms explained these negative attitudes: those Mexican students who had restrictive, traditional ideas about how men should (and should not) behave had the most negative attitudes toward lesbians and gay men. These and many other findings support the assumption that attitudes toward homosexuality are embedded in larger belief systems regarding gender-appropriate behavior. In this study, we also collected the same questionnaires from students in Germany for comparison. The German sample also indicated that those students who adhered to traditional norms of masculinity had the most negative attitudes toward lesbians and gay men. However, three other psychological constructs also played a role: attitudes were more negative when students had less contact with lesbians and gay men, when they felt it was less important not to hold prejudicial attitudes toward minorities, and the more religious they were. Hundreds of socio-psychological studies show that contact with minorities can make a significant contribution to reducing prejudice.[53] Like the above-mentioned beliefs about gender roles, religious values are major belief systems that can also explain attitudes toward homosexual behavior.

4 Religion and Negative Attitudes

If one considers the role religious value systems play in negative attitudes toward lesbians and gay men, then one should make a distinction between religious affiliation and religiosity. We talk about religious affiliation when we dis-

---

52 See Steffens, Jonas, and Denger, "Male Role Endorsement."
53 See, for instance, Gregory M. Herek and John P. Capitanio, "'Some of My Best Friends': Intergroup Contact, Concealable Stigma, and Heterosexuals' Attitudes Toward Gay Men and Lesbians," *Personality and Social Psychology Bulletin* 22 (1996): 412–424.

tinguish different religions – such as Jews, Christians, and Muslims. Confessional differences between Catholic, Protestant, or Orthodox Christians are also relevant. We define religiosity as the extent to which people see their religious affiliation as an important part of their lives. This is measured, for example, using scales that assess the degree of agreement with statements such as: "I believe in God." As numerous studies – most of them from the USA – have shown, people who are more religious report more negative attitudes toward lesbians and gay men.[54] A study from Germany also supports these findings, showing that non-denominational and less religious people are more likely to have positive attitudes toward lesbians and gay men than people who belong to a denomination.[55] This may seem surprising at first sight, because religious teachings often include acceptance and tolerance, but "[t]he role of religion is paradoxical. It makes prejudice and it unmakes prejudice [...] The sublimity of religious ideals is offset by the horrors of persecution in the name of these same ideals."[56]

In many religions, acceptance of others is not unconditional, but is limited to certain groups of people. In addition, certain writers or theological ideas in the Jewish and Christian traditions are considered to be explanatory factors for negative attitudes toward homosexuality.[57] Religiosity is understood by social-science researchers as a multidimensional construct.[58] In an analysis based on Christians, the first aspect is *religious fundamentalism:* the extent to which someone assumes the absolute superiority of their own truth claim, the corresponding lifestyles, and the extent to which they defend these. The second aspect is *[Christian] orthodoxy:* the extent to which one agrees with central Christian doctrines. The third aspect is *intrinsic religious motives:* the extent to which a person is a believer. The fourth aspect is *extrinsic religious motives:* the extent to which one uses religion to achieve non-religious goals (i. e., being part of a community). Each of these aspects is differently related to negative attitudes toward homosexual behavior. Religious fundamentalism makes the most important contribution to explaining negative attitudes toward homosexuality. The more fun-

---

54 An overview of international studies is provided in Whitley, Jr., "Religiosity," 21–38.
55 See Küpper, Klocke, and Hoffmann, *Einstellungen.*
56 Gordon W. Allport, *The Nature of Prejudice* (Reading, MA: Addison-Wesley, 1954), 413; quotation taken from Thomas E. Ford et al., "The Unmaking of Prejudice: How Christian Beliefs Relate to Attitudes Toward Homosexuals," *Journal for the Scientific Study of Religion* 48 (2009): 146–160, here 146.
57 See Wade C. Rowatt et al., "Associations Among Religiousness, Social Attitudes, and Prejudice in a National Random Sample of American Adults," *Psychology of Religion and Spirituality* 1 (2009): 14–24.
58 The subsequent explanations follow Whitley, Jr., "Religiosity," 21–38.

damentalist people are, the more negative their attitudes.[59] This is also related to the fact that religiously fundamentalist persons generally tend to have a so-called authoritarian personality: they seek conformity, safety, and tend to deny everything that is "different" and "strange." In contrast to religious fundamentalism, higher levels of Christian orthodoxy were related to positive attitudes toward homosexuality.[60] When looking at the connections between religiosity and attitudes toward homosexuality, one cannot ignore religious affiliation, because religious teachings differ in the extent to which they condemn homosexual behavior.[61] In an international study that included data from countries on different continents, Muslims displayed the most negative attitudes toward homosexuality.[62] In comparison, the following groups displayed more positive attitudes: non-religious people, Catholics, and Jews. No (statistically significant) differences were found between Muslims and Protestants, Hindus and Buddhists. The comparison between Catholics and Protestants depends on the country in focus. Protestantism in particular is conservative to different degrees, depending on social contexts.[63] The predominant religious affiliation in a country can be an indicator of negative attitudes toward homosexuality in that country.[64] Where a religion that condemns homosexuality prevails in a particular country, this appears to influence culture, politics, and public debate, so that the attitudes of people who do not adhere to this religion are also more negative than in other social contexts.

The negative attitudes toward homosexuals that prevail among Muslims appear worrying to many people in Germany. In a large study of young people in Berlin, Bernd Simon examined differences between young people with and without migrant backgrounds (from the former USSR and Turkey).[65] Both groups with

---

59 See, for instance, Wilson Vincent, Dominic J. Parrott, and John L. Peterson, "Effects of Traditional Gender Role Norms and Religious Fundamentalism on Self-Identified Heterosexual Men's Attitudes, Anger, and Aggression Toward Gay Men and Lesbians," *Psychology of Men and Masculinities* 12 (2011): 383–400.

60 See Ford et al., "Unmaking"; Eunike Jonathan, "The Influence of Religious Fundamentalism, Right-Wing Authoritarianism, and Christian Orthodoxy on Explicit and Implicit Measures of Attitudes Toward Homosexuals," *The International Journal for the Psychology of Religion* 18 (2008): 316–329.

61 See Amy Adamczyk and Cassady Pitt, "Shaping Attitudes About Homosexuality: The Role of Religion and Cultural Context," *Social Science Research* 38 (2009): 338–351.

62 Adamczyk and Pitt, "Shaping Attitudes."

63 See Kuyper, Iedema, and Keuzenkamp, *Towards Tolerance.*

64 See Adamczyk and Pitt, "Shaping Attitudes"; Aleksander Stulhofer and Ivan Rimac, "Determinants of Homonegativity in Europe," *Journal of Sex Research* 46 (2009): 24–32.

65 See Simon, "Einstellungen zur Homosexualität," 87–99.

migrant backgrounds held more negative attitudes than young people without a migrant background. In both groups with migrant backgrounds, religiosity was related to attitudes such as traditional norms of masculinity, in addition to the variables already mentioned: the more religious the young people were, the more negative their attitudes toward gay men and lesbians. If some religious affiliations are associated with more negative attitudes toward homosexuality than others, the question of whether these attitudes are conveyed by the same or by different processes arises. We investigated this question in a study in which Muslim and Christian young men in Germany participated.[66] Comparable to Simon's findings on young people, we found more negative attitudes toward gay men among Muslims than among Christians. In statistical analyses, we found evidence of two underlying beliefs: attitudes toward gay men were more negative when the stereotype of gay men was less masculine in the eyes of the participants, and when they felt that gay men threatened their own masculinity. More negative attitudes among Muslims than among Christians could thus be attributed to the beliefs about gender introduced above, which were more traditional among the Muslims. One aspect that distinguishes lesbians and gay men from other social minorities is that they have usually grown up in heterosexual families and typically form their identities as members of sexual minorities in their youth or early adulthood.[67] In our aforementioned study, which focused on lesbians and gay men with migrant backgrounds, we also asked about religious affiliation.[68] Among respondents with migrant backgrounds, 35% stated that they were Christian, and 15% were Muslim (39% stated that they had no religious affiliation, and the remaining participants adhered to other religions). We asked the participants how much they agreed with the statement: "I think it is difficult to reconcile my sexuality with my religion." Almost half of those who claimed to have a religious affiliation agreed with this statement. This illustrates the difficult situation in which lesbians and gay men find themselves if they re-

---

66 See Gerhard Reese, Melanie C. Steffens, and Kai J. Jonas, "Religious Affiliation and Attitudes Towards Gay Men: On the Mediating Role of Masculinity Threat," *Journal of Community & Applied Social Psychology* 24 (2014): 340–355.

67 Furthermore, there are instances of "late coming out," a term that refers to coming out as gay, lesbian, or bisexual after a phase of life in which one has had heterosexual relationships; see Melanie C. Steffens and Janine Dieckmann, "Der Umgang von Familienangehörigen mit einem späten Coming-out in der Familie," in *Homosexualität in der Familie: Handbuch für familienbezogenes Fachpersonal*, ed. Familien- und Sozialverein des Lesben- und Schwulenverbandes in Deutschland (LSVD) e.V. (Cologne: LSVD, 2014), 58–76.

68 See Steffens, Bergert, and Heinecke, "Studie Lebenssituation."

gard religion as an important part of their lives but feel excluded by their own religion.

5 Conclusion

The findings we have presented here illustrate the fact that the social contexts in which lesbians and gay men live and work are increasingly shifting toward broader acceptance. Fortunately, in 2020 the pope advocated appreciation and certain legal rights for lesbians and gay men: "Homosexual people have a right to be in a family. They are children of God and have a right to a family. Nobody should be thrown out or be made miserable over it. [...] What we have to create is a civil union law. That way they are legally covered."[69]

With regard to the Catholic Church, one could say that lesbians and gay men are confronted with doctrine and structures that make it difficult for them to find acceptance of their own lifestyles. This is harmful to their sense of belonging to their religious community. The same applies to persons who are accepting of homosexuality and who have close family relationships and friendships with lesbians and gay men. Both of these groups account for people leaving the Catholic Church with reference to its public attitude toward homosexuality. As we mentioned at the beginning of this chapter, we think the Church's doctrinal authority should refrain from the (presumptuous) idea that the Church can stipulate what the "right" sexuality is and how adults should practice it. Furthermore, autonomy and self-determination should also be established as basic moral values for (homo)sexuality within Catholicism. Social-science findings show that, regardless of the partners' gender, fulfillment in marriage and family is possible, and that tolerance is good for society's growth. On the basis of social-scientific findings, approaching acceptance and moving away from discrimination seems to be a requirement for the Catholic Church, so that it can be(come) a meaningful institution for lesbians and gay men; for their relatives, friends, and supporters; and so it can further bridge the increasing gap between the Church and legal and social realities.

---

69 This statement (made in 2019) is recorded in the film *Francesco*, directed by Evgeny Afineevsky; see Jason Horowitz, "In Shift for Church, Pope Francis Voices Support for Same-Sex Civil Unions," *The New York Times*, October 21, 2020, https://www.nytimes.com/2020/10/21/world/europe/pope-francis-same-sex-civil-unions.html (accessed March 19, 2021).

Bibliography

Adam, Barry D. "Stigma and Employability: Discrimination by Sex and Sexual Orientation in the Ontario Legal Profession." *Canadian Review of Sociology and Anthropology* 18 (1981): 216–221.

Adamczyk, Amy, and Cassady Pitt. "Shaping Attitudes About Homosexuality: The Role of Religion and Cultural Context." *Social Science Research* 38 (2009): 338–351.

Allport, Gordon W. *The Nature of Prejudice*. Reading, MA: Addison-Wesley, 1954.

Barreto, Manuela, and Naomi Ellemers. "Detecting and Experiencing Prejudice: New Answers to Old Questions." In *Advances in Experimental Social Psychology*, vol. 52, ed. James M. Olson and Mark P. Zanna, 139–219. Waltham, MA: Academic Press, 2015. DOI: 10.1016/bs.aesp.2015.02.001.

Brauns, Bastian. "So homosexuell ist Europa." *Die Zeit Online*, Teilchen (Blog), October 19, 2016. https://blog.zeit.de/teilchen/2016/10/19/so-schwul-ist-europa/?wt_ref=https%3A%2F%2F. Accessed February 11, 2021.

Clair, Judith A., Joy E. Beatty, and Tammy L. MacLean. "Out of Sight But Not Out of Mind: Managing Invisible Social Identities in the Workplace." *Academy of Management Review* 30 (2005): 78–95.

Deaux, Kay, and Brenda Major. "Putting Gender Into Context: An Interactive Model of Gender-Related Behavior." *Psychological Review* 94 (1987): 369–389.

Dotti Sani, Giulia M., and Mario Quaranta. "Let Them Be, Not Adopt: General Attitudes Towards Gays and Lesbians and Specific Attitudes Towards Adoption by Same-Sex Couples in 22 European Countries." *Social Indicators Research* 150 (2020): 351–373.

European Values Study. http://www.europeanvaluesstudy.eu/. Accessed December 8, 2020.

Ford, Thomas E., et al. "The Unmaking of Prejudice: How Christian Beliefs Relate to Attitudes Toward Homosexuals." *Journal for the Scientific Study of Religion* 48 (2009): 146–160.

Frohn, Dominic, Florian Meinhold, and Christina Schmidt. *"Out im Office?!" Sexuelle Identität und Geschlechtsidentität, (Anti-)Diskriminierung und Diversity am Arbeitsplatz*. Cologne: Institut für Diversity- und Antidiskriminierungsforschung, 2017. https://www.dominicfrohn.de/downloads/IDA_Out_im_Office_2017.pdf. Accessed February 18, 2021.

Gallup Europe. "Homosexual Marriage, Child Adoption by Homosexual Couples: Is the Public Ready?" 2003. https://www.rklambda.at/archiv/dokumente/news_2003/News-PA-031015-Gallup-Umfrage-Text.pdf. Accessed March 19, 2021.

Goodman, Melinda B., and Bonnie Moradi. "Attitudes and Behaviors Toward Lesbian and Gay Persons: Critical Correlates and Mediated Relations." *Journal of Counseling Psychology* 55 (2008): 371–384.

Herek, Gregory M. "The Context of Anti-Gay Violence: Notes on Cultural and Psychological Heterosexism." *Journal of Interpersonal Violence* 5 (1990): 316–333. http://jiv.sagepub.com/content/5/3/316.full.pdf+html.

Herek, Gregory M. "Stigma, Prejudice, and Violence Against Lesbians and Gay Men." In *Homosexuality: Research Implications for Public Policy*, ed. John C. Gonsiorek and James D. Weinrich, 60–80. Thousand Oaks, CA: SAGE Publications, 1991.

Herek, Gregory M., and John P. Capitanio. "'Some of My Best Friends': Intergroup Contact, Concealable Stigma, and Heterosexuals' Attitudes Toward Gay Men and Lesbians." *Personality and Social Psychology Bulletin* 22 (1996): 412–424.

Herek, Gregory M., and Kevin A. McLemore. "Sexual Prejudice." *Annual Review of Psychology* 64 (2013): 309–333.

Horowitz, Jason. "In Shift for Church, Pope Francis Voices Support for Same-Sex Civil Unions." *The New York Times*, October 21, 2020. https://www.nytimes.com/2020/10/21/world/europe/pope-francis-same-sex-civil-unions.html. Accessed March 19, 2021.

Jansen, Elke, and Melanie C. Steffens. "Lesbische Mütter, schwule Väter und ihre Kinder im Spiegel psychosozialer Forschung." *Verhaltenstherapie und Psychosoziale Praxis: Sonderheft Psychotherapie mit Lesben, Schwulen und Bisexuellen* 38 (2006): 643–656.

Jonathan, Eunike. "The Influence of Religious Fundamentalism, Right-Wing Authoritarianism, and Christian Orthodoxy on Explicit and Implicit Measures of Attitudes Toward Homosexuals." *The International Journal for the Psychology of Religion* 18 (2008): 316–329.

Kite, Mary E., and Bernard E. Whitley, Jr. "Sex Differences in Attitudes Toward Homosexual Persons, Behaviors, and Civil Rights: A Meta-Analysis." *Personality and Social Psychology Bulletin* 22 (1996): 336–353.

Kitzinger, Celia. *The Social Construction of Lesbianism*. London: SAGE Publications, 1987.

Knoll, Christopher, Manfred Edinger, and Günter Reisbeck. *Grenzgänge: Schwule und Lesben in der Arbeitswelt*. Munich/Vienna: Profil-Verlag, 1997.

Köllen, Thomas. "Privatsache und unerheblich für Unternehmen? Der Stand der Personalforschung zur 'sexuellen Orientierung'." *Zeitschrift für Personalforschung* 26 (2012): 143–166.

Küpper, Beate, Ulrich Klocke, and Lena-Carlotta Hoffmann. *Einstellungen gegenüber lesbischen, schwulen und bisexuellen Menschen in Deutschland: Ergebnisse einer bevölkerungsrepräsentativen Umfrage*. Baden-Baden: Nomos, 2017. https://www.antidiskriminierungsstelle.de/SharedDocs/Downloads/DE/publikationen/Umfragen/umfrage_einstellungen_geg_lesb_schwulen_und_bisex_menschen_de.html. Accessed March 19, 2021.

Kuyper, Lisette, Jurjen Iedema, and Saskia Keuzenkamp. *Towards Tolerance: Exploring Changes and Explaining Differences in Attitudes Towards Homosexuality Across Europe*. The Hague: The Netherlands Institute for Social Research, 2013.

Meyer, Ilan H. "Prejudice, Social Stress, and Mental Health in Lesbian, Gay, and Bisexual Populations: Conceptual Issues and Research Evidence." *Psychological Bulletin* 129 (2003): 674–697.

Morrison, Melanie A., and Todd G. Morrison. "Sexual Orientation Bias Toward Gay Men and Lesbian Women: Modern Homonegative Attitudes and Their Association with Discriminatory Behavioral Intentions." *Journal of Applied Social Psychology* 41 (2011): 2573–2599.

Niedlich, Claudia, and Melanie C. Steffens. *Minoritätenstress von Lesben und Schwulen im Arbeitsleben*. Unpublished manuscript, 2015.

Niedlich, Claudia, and Melanie C. Steffens. "On the Interplay of (Positive) Stereotypes and Prejudice: Impressions of Lesbian and Gay Applicants for Leadership Positions." *Sensoria: A Journal of Mind, Brain & Culture* 11 (2015): https://www.researchgate.net/publication/275648569.

Niedlich, Claudia, et al. "Ironic Effects of Sexual Minority Group Membership: Are Lesbians Less Susceptible to Invoking Negative Female Stereotypes than Heterosexual Women?" *Archives of Sexual Behavior* 44 (2015): 1439–1447. DOI:10.1007/s10508–014–0412–1.

Overbeck, Franz-Josef. "Vorurteile überwinden!" *Herder Korrespondenz* 73 (2019): 6.

Reese, Gerhard, Melanie C. Steffens, and Kai J. Jonas. "Religious Affiliation and Attitudes Towards Gay Men: On the Mediating Role of Masculinity Threat." *Journal of Community & Applied Social Psychology* 24 (2014): 340–355.

Rowatt, Wade C., et al. "Associations Among Religiousness, Social Attitudes, and Prejudice in a National Random Sample of American Adults." *Psychology of Religion and Spirituality* 1 (2009): 14–24.

Rupp, Marina, ed. *Die Lebenssituation von Kindern in gleichgeschlechtlichen Lebenspartnerschaften.* Cologne: Bundesanzeiger Verlag, 2009.

Seise, Jan, Rainer Banse, and Franz J. Neyer. "Individuelle Unterschiede in impliziten und expliziten Einstellungen zur Homosexualität: Eine empirische Studie." *Zeitschrift für Sexualforschung* 15 (2002): 21–42.

Simon, Bernd. "Einstellungen zur Homosexualität: Ausprägungen und psychologische Korrelate bei Jugendlichen mit und ohne Migrationshintergrund (ehemalige UdSSR und Türkei)." *Zeitschrift für Entwicklungspsychologie und Pädagogische Psychologie* 40 (2008): 87–99.

Steffens, Melanie C., and Christof Wagner. "Attitudes Towards Lesbians, Gay Men, Bisexual Women, and Bisexual Men in Germany." *Journal of Sex Research* 41 (2004): 137–149.

Steffens, Melanie C., and Erin M. Thompson. "Verruchte – Perverse – Kranke – Unsichtbare: Der historische Blick." In *Anders ver-rückt?! Lesben und Schwule in der Psychiatrie*, ed. Ulrich Biechele, Philipp Hammelstein, and Thomas Heinrich, 13–22. Jahrbuch Lesben – Schwule – Psychologie 2006. Lengerich: Pabst Science Publishers, 2006.

Steffens, Melanie C., and Christof Wagner. "Diskriminierung von Lesben, Schwulen und Bisexuellen." In *Diskriminierung und Toleranz: Psychologische Grundlagen und Anwendungsperspektiven*, ed. Andreas Beelmann and Kai J. Jonas, 241–262. Wiesbaden: VS Verlag für Sozialwissenschaften, 2009.

Steffens, Melanie C., Michael Bergert, and Stephanie Heinecke. "Studie Lebenssituation von Lesben und Schwulen mit Migrationshintergrund." In *Doppelt diskriminiert oder gut integriert? Lebenssituation von Lesben und Schwulen mit Migrationshintergrund in Deutschland*, ed. Familien- und Sozialverein des Lesben- und Schwulenverbandes in Deutschland (LSVD) e.V., 13–107. Cologne: LSVD, 2010.

Steffens, Melanie C., and Kai J. Jonas. "Attitudes Towards Adoptive Parents, Child Age, and Child Gender: The Role of Applicants' Sexual Orientation." *Zeitschrift für Familienforschung*, special issue 7 (2010): 205–219.

Steffens, Melanie C., and Janine Dieckmann. "Der Umgang von Familienangehörigen mit einem späten Coming-out in der Familie." In *Homosexualität in der Familie: Handbuch für familienbezogenes Fachpersonal*, ed. Familien- und Sozialverein des Lesben- und Schwulenverbandes in Deutschland (LSVD) e.V., 58–76. Cologne: LSVD, 2014.

Steffens, Melanie C., Kai J. Jonas, and Lisa Denger. "Male Role Endorsement Explains Negative Attitudes Toward Lesbians and Gay Men Among Students in Mexico More Than in Germany." *Journal of Sex Research* 52 (2015): 898–911. DOI:10.1080/00224499.2014.966047.

Steffens, Melanie C., Kai J. Jonas, and Thérèse Scali. "Putting Prejudice into Perspective. Does Perceived Suitability for Adoption Depend on Sexual Orientation More than on Other Applicant Features?" *Sensoria: A Journal of Mind, Brain & Culture* 11 (2015): 41–57.

Steffens, Melanie C., Claudia Niedlich, and Franziska Ehrke. "Discrimination at Work on the Basis of Sexual Orientation: Subjective Experience, Experimental Evidence, and Interventions." In *Sexual Orientation and Transgender Issues in Organizations: Global Perspectives on LGBT Workforce Diversity*, ed. Thomas Köllen, 367–388. Heidelberg/New York: Springer, 2015.

Steffens, Melanie C., and Ma. Àngels Viladot. *Gender at Work: A Social-Psychological Perspective.* New York: Peter Lang, 2015.

Steffens, Melanie C., et al. "Do Positive and Negative Stereotypes of Gay and Heterosexual Men Affect Job-Related Impressions?" *Sex Roles* 80 (2019): 9–10. DOI:10.1007/s11199–018–0963-z.

Steffens, Melanie C., and Sabine Preuß. "Measuring Attitudes Toward LGBTI* Individuals: Theoretical and Practical Considerations." In *Oxford Encyclopedia of LGBT Politics and Policy*, ed. Don Haider-Markel and Gary Mucciaroni. New York: Oxford University Press, 2021.

Stulhofer, Aleksander, and Ivan Rimac. "Determinants of Homonegativity in Europe." *Journal of Sex Research* 46 (2009): 24–32.

Tilcsik, András. "Pride and Prejudice: Employment Discrimination Against Openly Gay Men in the United States." *American Journal of Sociology* 117 (2011): 586–626.

Vincent, Wilson, Dominic J. Parrott, and John L. Peterson. "Effects of Traditional Gender Role Norms and Religious Fundamentalism on Self-Identified Heterosexual Men's Attitudes, Anger, and Aggression Toward Gay Men and Lesbians." *Psychology of Men and Masculinities* 12 (2011): 383–400.

de Vries, Lisa, et al. "LGBTQI*-Menschen am Arbeitsmarkt: hoch gebildet und oftmals diskriminiert." *Deutsches Institut für Wirtschaftsforschung Wochenbericht* 36 (2020): 619–627. DOI:10.18723/diw_wb:2020–36–1.

Whitley, Bernard E., Jr. "Gender-Role Variables and Attitudes toward Homosexuality." *Sex Roles* 45 (2001): 691–721.

Whitley, Bernard E., Jr. "Religiosity and Attitudes Toward Lesbians and Gay Men: A Meta-Analysis." *International Journal for the Psychology of Religion* 19 (2009): 21–38.

Theological and Ethical Debates

Magnus Striet
Creation Theology and Concepts of Homosexuality

1 The Current State of Affairs

There is hardly a more controversial topic in the religious arena than that of homosexuality. In contemporary liberal societies, one often has the impression that the normative exclusion of any sexual orientation that does not conform to a heteronormative pattern is a form of identity politics pursued by groups that are insecure in their own identities. This discourse of normality is an attempt to gain stability in the context of a sociocultural modernity that recognizes self-determined as opposed to essentialist identities. Thus religion – with its appealing offer of eternal truths –becomes an attractive option if one wants to lend one's own concept of normality a veneer of legitimacy.

The following reflections focus on disputes around the topic of homosexuality in the Catholic tradition. Even today, it is extremely difficult to address the fact that homosexually oriented people exist within this tradition. However, one must differentiate. While significant revisions have been made (whether behind the scenes or in the open) in the academic theology evaluation of homosexuality, the Magisterium – and the theology it represents – still thinks it must insist that homosexual partnerships should not be accepted. It is true that the pastoral tone has changed. After all, one now encounters an insistence that homosexual people must be respected on the grounds of unconditional respect for human dignity. Nevertheless, homosexual domestic partnerships are still not accepted on the doctrinal level. At the same time, on the level of Church life, open clashes increasingly occur when active homosexuals who live in loving relationships and feel they are Christian believers claim the right to self-determination (which is granted in liberal societies) and also ask for God's blessing on their relationship – that is, they want to place their relationship under the banner of God's blessing within the context of Church fellowship, and thus with explicit reference to the God who, according to the Christian faith, made himself manifest in the life of the Jewish man Jesus of Nazareth.[1] According to magisterial logic, while these people describe themselves as Christians, they are in fact living

---

1 Cf. Stephan Goertz, "Streitfall Diskriminierung. Die Kirche und die neue Politik der Menschenrechte," *Herder Korrespondenz* 67 (2013): 78–83.

https://doi.org/10.1515/9783110705188-006

in grave sin, because a homosexual predisposition is considered "objectively disordered" and therefore may not be actively pursued. The Church may not bless that which cannot be consecrated.

The Congregation for the Doctrine of the Faith reaffirmed this teaching in a *Responsum ad Dubium* dated March 15, 2021.[2] In response to the question of whether the Church has "the power to give the blessing to unions of persons of the same sex," the apodictic answer is "no." This "no" is justified by the fact that, "in addition to the right intention of those who participate" in a blessing, "it is necessary that what is blessed be objectively and positively ordered to receive and express grace, according to the designs of God inscribed in creation, and fully revealed by Christ the Lord." Therefore no blessing should be given to any relationship or partnership "that involve[s] sexual activity outside of marriage (i. e., outside the indissoluble union of a man and a woman open in itself to the transmission of life), as is the case of the unions between persons of the same sex." This has nothing to do with discrimination, because such blessings constitute only "a reminder of the truth of the liturgical rite," and thus "the very nature of the sacramentals, as the Church understands them."

The *Responsum* contains no new arguments in addition to those the Magisterium has previously presented. What is clear, however, is that the essence of the sacramentals – as recognized by the Magisterium and invoked by the Congregation – is no longer understood in certain segments of the Catholic Church, which is why the Congregation felt compelled to clarify the matter. This effort does not seem to have been very convincing. In any case, a storm of indignation and protest immediately arose, and open resistance in the form of a refusal to observe the ban on the blessing of same-sex couples was not only announced, but also practiced. Although this fact alone does not indicate that the acceptance and blessing of same-sex relationships and partnerships is possible, it nevertheless provides food for thought. The following considerations are intended to demonstrate that there is a fundamental shift in theological thinking on questions of sexual morality in the offing. This conflict is another instance of the fundamental theological disagreement – one which broke out immediately after the Second Vatican Council – over whether there is such a thing as a divinely established order (as identified by the ordinary and universal Magisterium) which is superior to humankind and to which humankind must obediently submit, or

---

2 Congregation for the Doctrine of the Faith, Responsum *to a* dubium *regarding the blessing of the unions of persons of the same sex* (Rome: Vatican, 2021), https://www.vatican.va/roman_curia/congregations/cfaith/documents/rc_con_cfaith_doc_20210222_responsum-dubium-un ioni_en.html (accessed June 7, 2021).

whether it is precisely the right to free self-determination which the free God desires to see realized as a human right in social relations.[3]

If we think strictly in terms of the theory of freedom, then the theological possibility of introducing the concept of sacramental partnership certainly opens up. This concept has an integrative effect insofar as it is not normatively bound to the criterion of heterosexuality. It theologically dignifies and legitimizes a relationship which a person attempts to practice in a committed, loving way – and this under the auspices of the God who is love, who loves freedom, and who places himself specifically on the side of those who are socially stigmatized, even for religious reasons. Partnered life would then no be longer subject to gradations of value by being calibrated against the *a priori* norm of heterosexual partnership.

2 The Basis for Magisterial Theological Approaches to Homosexuality

Before I undertake this attempt at a systematic approach, we must examine the Magisterium's theology more precisely, particularly with regard to its argumentative rigor. As I have already indicated, the magisterial statements on homosexual inclination have been modified since they were originally made. Since homosexuality began to be described as a variant of human sexuality in the nineteenth century, the magisterial tone has changed. However, the Magisterium has not become more favorable in its basic assessment of homosexual inclination. The persons – that is, the people who are homosexual – are to be respected, but their lifestyle is not valued with appreciation. Such lifestyles continue to be measured against an objective norm, which according to magisterial theology is the cohabitation of a man and a woman. Based on this logic, homosexual inclination is interpreted as unnatural. In contrast, that which is natural is that which is believed to be willed and established by God himself. One cannot overlook the fact that this constitutes not only a naturalistic fallacy, but also tautological reasoning.

It would be interesting to know the basis on which the Magisterium has established that people who "have deep-seated homosexual tendencies" do in fact

---

3 On this point, see my own analysis in "Ius divinum – Freiheitsrechte. Nominalistische Dekonstruktionen in konstruktiver Absicht," in *Nach dem Gesetz Gottes. Autonomie als christliches Prinzip*, ed. Stephan Goertz and Magnus Striet (Katholizismus im Umbruch 2; Freiburg im Breisgau: Herder, 2014), 91–128.

exist.[4] When something is not only described but also judged as "objectively disordered"[5], one would like to know how this objective disorder comes into a world which – theologically – is depicted as God's good creation. There are not many logical options here. In the end, there is in fact only one – but if I see it correctly, this option is presented extremely cautiously. If God himself has not brought this alleged disorder into the world – a conclusion which would strain the concept of God to the breaking point – then the only other option is the human being, which would mean that homosexual inclination and any practice corresponding to this inclination can be nothing other than a consequence of sin. This is the devastating legacy of a theology brought to bear primarily by Augustine, which is still in effect in the magisterial theological system today. For Augustine, sexual pleasure is nothing more or less than an expression of sin. He asks God for a "more abundant grace to quench even the impure motions of [his] sleep."[6]

Today, the human sciences have made various attempts to explain a person's inclination to the same sex. There is one point, however, on which all such explanatory attempts agree: no one can be held responsible for their attraction to another sex, or even to the same sex. Factual variants of desire exist, and it is also quite possible that such desire is modified over the course of one's life – that another partner of the same biological sex fascinates a person and triggers feelings that can no longer, or only with difficulty, be forcibly repressed. In view of the existential significance these phenomena have for human beings, one would like to ask those who speak of an "objective disorder" how they explain a human being's attraction to a person of the same sex. Of course, anyone who reckons they can refer back to Original sin in the present day sets themself against the sum total of evolutionary-biological, human-scientific, and psychological "knowledge" (I place this term in quotation marks because, under the present epistemic conditions, all knowledge creation is no more than hypothesis formation).

However, the self-contradiction in which such a theological position becomes entangled is an even more serious issue. If a lifestyle – that is, the self-selection of freedom and thus a liberal life praxis – is described as immoral,

---

4 Catechism of the Catholic Church (Rome: Vatican, 1993), no. 2358, https://www.vatican.va/archive/ENG0015/__P85.HTM (accessed June 7, 2021).
5 Ibid.
6 Augustine, *Confessions* 10.30: "Numquid non potens est manus tua, deus omnipotens, sanare omnes languores animae meae atque abundantiore gratia tua lascivos motus etiam mei soporis extinguere?" For the English translation, see *The Confessions of Saint Augustine*, trans. Edward B. Pusey (Grand Rapids: Christian Classics Ethereal Library, 1999), 243, https://ccel.org/ccel/a/augustine/confess/cache/confess.pdf (accessed June 7, 2021).

then one must clarify the origin of this norm as well as how such a judgment is justified. Scripture and tradition are repeatedly invoked as sources of theological knowledge. This is certainly not wrong, but one would have to establish precisely what this means, as well as how Scripture and tradition become sources of theological normativity. However, it is not appropriate to apply the biblical texts which address "homosexuality" to today's questions *verbatim et literatim*. This is particularly the case because the biblical texts are not simply the word of God, but are first and foremost the result of theological and therefore human reflection. But even the textual findings as such cannot be used to condemn sexual practices between same-sex lovers.

The Old Testament contains harsh condemnations of same-sex practices among males, but these exist against a completely different background than the concept of homosexual desire, which is the subject of our considerations here. At the time when the Old Testament Scriptures were written, men were supposed to beget children and thus fulfill their duty as men so that their clan could survive. This is not a matter of men's same-sex inclinations, and there is no mention of women at all. That is why lesbian love plays no role at all in these texts; it does not appear simply because it cannot be brought into focus in the context of a patriarchal society.[7] Moreover, the historical context within which the thematization of homosexual practices takes place in the book of Genesis (the judgment on Sodom in Genesis 19) is completely different from contemporary society. What this text condemns is the sexual degradation of men by men. This concerns the defense of the right to hospitality and protection, but not the phenomenon of mutual same-sex inclination. In addition, while biblical theology repeatedly justifies its assessment of homosexuality from the perspective of creation theology, by citing God's creation of humankind as man and woman, and on this basis arguing that only heterosexual relationships can be legitimate, this argument overlooks the historical context of Genesis 1:26–28 and 2:21–25. One could call this a politics of equalization that simultaneously describes difference: man and woman are equal before God in that they are images of God in their relation to one another. Thus we see that human beings are valued as relational beings. But can one deduce from this that same-sex inclination should not lead to partnership? Is such a partnership not (also) in God's image? If homosexuality is polemicized with reference to the Bible, then it is polemicized against the background of a concept that has nothing to do with today's human-scientific, psychological concept of homosexuality.

---

7 For further details, see Thomas Hieke's contribution in this volume. For a brief overview, see Linn Marie Tonstad, *Queer Theology: Beyond Apologetics* (Eugene: Cascade Books, 2018), 13.

In essence, it has to be said that such appeals to biblical texts as a source of theological knowledge are lacking in hermeneutical complexity and are systematically fatal. The biblical texts owe their authorship to human beings, which means they are bound to their contemporary history. Therefore they have to be historically reconstructed, and the intention behind their message needs to be elucidated. But even when such work has indeed been done, one cannot simply establish an unambiguous, normative theological meaning. These texts developed out of the complex problems and knowledge contexts of their time, and therefore one cannot assume that they necessarily provide answers to the questions of other times. Hence, even if the biblical texts did condemn like-minded homosexual domestic partnerships, one would still have to ask whether such condemnations should be revised in the light of today's human-scientific knowledge. No text can establish normative claims without being questioned, and this also applies to texts that are considered sacred or are held up as part of a canon. Canonization processes can also be historically reconstructed.

With regard to the considerations I have presented here on the phenomenon of same-sex desire, however, these fundamental biblical hermeneutical considerations need not be made at all, since the texts from which the prohibition of active homosexual love is repeatedly derived address quite different issues. I would even go a step further: if one reads these texts precisely, one can derive from them a sharp critique of any theology that thinks it has the authority to condemn same-sex lovers. The issue at hand in these texts is what is expressed in modern terms as the concept of human dignity. When it comes to homosexual love, it is not the theological rhetoricians of sin who have the Bible on their side, but rather those who argue for the recognition of such love, even in the Church's sphere.

3 Evaluating the Arguments Against Recognizing Same-Sex Partnerships

It is scarcely comprehensible that homosexual partnerships are repeatedly devalued over against heterosexual ones because they are not open to the possibility of producing descendants. First, one must be permitted to say that there is hardly a lack of people in the world. Even if one wanted to consider the functional aspect of active sexuality in evaluating same-sex life, this argument would fall at the first hurdle due to a lack of empirical validity. This goes hand in hand with a question about references to the sacramentality of marriage between heterosexual partners, which assumes that such partnerships are in principle open to the possibility of producing descendants. Once again, one wonders how this can be justified. Simply falling back on Genesis 1:28 ("be fruitful and multiply") amounts to a reading of the Bible that recognizes no historical contingency and fails to grasp the contextual change which has taken place in terms of the global population. Being "fruitful" under our present conditions need not necessarily be equated with biological fertility. Could there be a sacramentality of partnership that renounces biological offspring, either voluntarily or because biological reproduction is impossible, as in the case of same-sex love?

Before I pursue this aspect of sacramentality further, however, we must first reflect on certain fundamental considerations regarding how lived human realities can be morally qualified at all under our present conditions of reflection. In theological contexts, such qualifications are widely presented under the auspices of an essentialist human nature. That which corresponds to this nature is identified with the will of God and is then set up as the standard by which lived realities are measured. However, it is also obvious that normative statements are made on the basis of biological descriptions without indicating precisely when one leaves the level of description in each case, or how and in which instances that which is described is subsequently standardized. This can also be observed in the "ecology of man" discourse.[8] First of all, the factual in and of itself cannot constitute the basis for normative claims. What is more, the factual does not actually exist in this way. In order to make it so, we would have to extend the concept of the factual until it is able to integrate plural phenomena. In this case, however, one could easily say that homosexual partnerships are also permissible and may be actively practiced simply because these orientations factually exist.

The explanatory structure of the arguments presented against same-sex sexuality in the sphere of the Roman Catholic Church is astonishing in view of the concurrent insistence on reason that one encounters over and over again. Of

---

8 See Benedict XVI, *The Listening Heart: Reflections on the Foundations of Law*, Apostolic Journey to Germany, 22–25 September 2011, Visit to the Bundestag, Address of His Holiness Benedict XVI (Rome: Vatican, 2011), https://www.vatican.va/content/benedict-xvi/en/speeches/2011/september/documents/hf_ben-xvi_spe_20110922_reichstag-berlin.html (accessed June 7, 2021): "there is also an ecology of man. Man too has a nature that he must respect and that he cannot manipulate at will. Man is not merely self-creating freedom. Man does not create himself. He is intellect and will, but he is also nature, and his will is rightly ordered if he respects his nature, listens to it and accepts himself for who he is, as one who did not create himself. In this way, and in no other, is true human freedom fulfilled." While it is anything but easy to understand the concept of nature Benedict employs here, nevertheless he obviously distinguishes nature from what he calls spirit and will. However, since we hear over and over again that God created humankind as man and woman, we may very well hear that same-sex love violates the "ecology of man." Thus heterosexuality is established as the only possible ecology.

course, one can argue about what is meant by the term reason – that is, on what basis and by which authority something may be presented as reasonable. And precisely herein lies the problem: the fact that one cannot make ethical deductions directly from "nature" should be obvious and has been pointed out repeatedly over decades.[9] It is precisely "the" nature of humankind not simply to exist (and in this sense, not to be "natural") but to possess the capacity for relative self-determination – that is, for freedom. And it is precisely for this reason that the moral and ethical dimension opens up. That which was previously simply the case can now be qualified. But then the way in which something is qualified becomes the sole decisive factor.

As I have already shown, magisterial theology still refers to that which it encapsulates as the order of creation or as natural law. However, one would like to know how exactly this order – or more specifically this law – is traced back to God himself. If one takes the potential for biological reproduction as a criterion, then one cannot avoid encountering the naturalistic fallacy. And even if God desired procreation (here we can leave aside the problem of whether and how evolutionary biology and creation theology can be understood alongside one another), which is certainly to be assumed, we cannot derive from this a sufficient argument against partnerships that either do not desire to transmit life or are not capable of doing so. Even more important is another argument: if everything that exists is determined to be in accordance with God's will, then one would have to know what God's will is. Otherwise we would be left with a circular argument. Of course, every understanding is circular, in the sense that there is no absolute starting point. But if I hypothesize that the free God desires people to shape their lives freely, appreciating one another and unconditionally recognizing other people's human dignity – and furthermore that human desire and partnership, if based on such a divine desire, should be practiced in accordance with these criteria, to which everything else is to be subordinated – then every argument against active same-sex love falls apart. Again, identifying God's will in such a way can only be hypothetical – we cannot know with sufficient certainty whether such a God exists. Nevertheless, I would like to respond by asking whether another God – one who does not respect human freedom, and with it the human dignity of every person, independently of how they feel and whom they desire – could be in any way acceptable within the framework of a moral coordinate system grounded in the human dignity of every person?

---

9 Cf. Christof Breitsameter, "Wie natürlich ist 'natürlich'?" in *Gender – Herausforderung für die christliche Ethik*, ed. Thomas Laubach, Katharina Klöcker, and Jochen Sautermeister (Jahrbuch für Moraltheologie 1; Freiburg im Breisgau: Herder, 2017), 69–91.

Whether the notion of the indissolubility of marriage, which magisterial theology repeatedly employs and attributes to Jesus can be understood as an objection to the theological acceptance of same-sex love and partnership is extremely questionable. It is already difficult to employ this notion in the debate over whether to allow remarried divorcees to receive the Eucharist, which has been going on for decades, since here too it is a matter of a different problem context – all the more so because we cannot deduce from this that Jesus categorically rejected same-sex partnerships. In fact, Jesus did not have such partnerships in mind, which is not at all surprising. He was a man of the cultural contexts of his time, and in these contexts the concept of homosexual inclination, which presupposes egalitarianism between people, did not yet exist – and of course, neither did human-scientific knowledge about the diverse configurations of human desire. However, in view of the deliberative politics that governed the thinking of Israel's theologians, which was concerned with the greatest possible freedom for individuals as long as basic rules were preserved to regulate a just coexistence – a politics that Jesus fearlessly pursued – it would be very surprising to find that he would have had problems with people who felt the same way under other conditions of knowledge.

4 Sacramental Partnership: A Systematic Approach

It is not necessary to abandon the concept of sacramental marriage. But on the basis of moral philosophy and recognition theory, and above all for theological reasons, it would be worth considering whether to develop a new, broader concept – that of sacramental partnership – in order to do justice to the insight, evident since biblical times, that the God of faith not only accepts human freedom, but actually desires it. If it is conceivable in terms of creation theology that God does not normatively prescribe the sexual constellations in which people may form partnerships, but rather that God's "law" is that people should be allowed to create and love in freedom, then such a life would be sacramental if it takes place under God's auspices – that is, on the basis of the promise he makes in Exodus: I am the one who will be there for you (Ex 3:14).[10] Thinking sacramentally in this way means developing an understanding of the sacramental from the inner core of faith, and in the logic of faith, this core consists of God's

---

10 For more on this topic, see Magnus Striet and Rita Werden, "Welcher Gott will welches Gesetz?" *Herder Korrespondenz* 69 (2015): 19 – 23.

love – which has existed since the beginning of creation – for his world and especially for humankind, who are made in his image, in the image of his freedom. According to Christian conviction, this is a love that has proven itself in God's incarnation, in a way that cannot be historically surpassed.[11] On the basis of this basic conviction of faith, of course, the question of what may be regarded as the consummation of the sacramental must be negotiated in historically contingent processes – but this does not mean we can leave it to arbitrariness. The criterion is faith, the core itself, and this core must also be defined. But does anything stand in the way of defining it as I have tried to do above, albeit in a condensed way?

In my opinion, there is nothing to be said against interpreting the name of God, which is expounded in the biblical text as God's self-attribution, in the way I have just done above, and then drawing the appropriate sacramental and theological conclusions. Or perhaps there is just one thing: the Roman Catholic Magisterium would then have to revision to its theology, to a tradition of theological thought which was invented in the nineteenth century and held up as constitutive of the Catholic. A tradition of the presumption of infallible certainty was established at this juncture. This is not to say that the Magisterium did not previously claim to have both the authority permission and the capacity to interpret Scripture authentically. But since then, corrections (even behind-the-scenes ones) have become increasingly difficult, because the Magisterium's authority is always at stake. In a certain sense, a magisterial self-imprisonment has obtained since then, which – in view of the dynamics of transforming societies – has led to a widening of the gap between what is taught and what is lived out in practice. Moreover, the further this process advances, the more resolutely the tradition of normativity is forged – a tradition which hardly stands up to historical scrutiny, and even less to systematic examination.

However, anyone who allows their thinking to become fixed and believes they cannot correct it without endangering their own authority – whether they are reflexively conscious of this or not (although the latter variant seems to me the more probable) – must not expect that people will allow their inclinations to be permanently constrained by this bind. Life demands to be lived, and neither the longing for love nor the desire for freedom can be permanently suppressed. Theologically, this longing for freedom and the will to emancipate oneself from unjust paternalism could be based on the biblically attested process of doing away with immaturity, which is anchored in God himself: the "I am who

---

11 On this topic, see Thomas Pröpper, *Erlösungsglaube und Freiheitsgeschichte. Eine Skizze zur Soteriologie* (2d rev. ed.; Munich: Kösel Verlag, 1988), 236 f.

will be there for you" essentially tempts people to risk freedom – to give in to their own longings and actually live them. Therefore granting God's blessing to same-sex lovers does not constitute blessing sin. It is simply expressly promising them, once again, the blessing under which they already live.

Stephan Goertz
From the Primacy of Nature to the Primacy of Love

Phases in the Assessment of Homosexuality in Moral Theology and the Roman Magisterium

In the magisterial proclamations of the Catholic Church, homosexuality is a relatively recent topic with a long moral-theological history. In the second half of the nineteenth century, this orientation and set of practices was given the term we are familiar with today. But it is only at the end of the twentieth century that it receives explicit attention in Roman magisterial documents. In the decades between this development and the Catholic statements on the topic, moral theology attempted either to uphold its centuries-old evaluation of same-sex sexual acts in the face of the new situation, or to revise it in the light of the shift in sexual morality. Since the end of the 1960s, moral-theological judgment of homosexuality has been in turmoil, and the Magisterium has not generally taken a positive view of the situation.

In this contribution, I will reconstruct and analyze the various phases in the moral-theological and magisterial assessment of homosexuality. This will bring to light the profound change in the moral-theological position on the one hand, and the ways in which the magisterium's attitude is out of sync with broader social, moral and scientific developments on the other.

As a first step, however, it is important to consider the changes in the way homosexuality and homosexuals have been treated that have taken place over the last 150 years. "Given the very substantial changes that have occurred in the scientific and cultural understanding of sexuality over the past several decades, it would be naïve for a church that expects to learn from nature [as the Catholic Church does] to assume that these changes would have no effect whatsoever on church doctrine."[1] In terms of theological categories, one could speak of a "sign of the times" which challenges the Catholic Church to take a stand.

---

1 Gerard Jacobitz, "Seminary, Priesthood, and the Vatican's Homosexual Dilemma," in *More than a Monologue: Sexual Diversity and the Catholic Church*, ed. J. Patrick Hornbeck and Michael A. Norko (New York: Fordham University Press, 2014), 86–105, here 105. Cf. Eberhard Schockenhoff, *Die Kunst zu lieben. Unterwegs zu einer neuen Sexualethik* (Freiburg im Breisgau: Herder, 2021), 13–74, 241–313.

https://doi.org/10.1515/9783110705188-007

1 Conceptualizing Homosexuality and Emancipating Homosexuals

The second half of the twentieth century saw a historically unprecedented emancipatory surge in the assessment of homosexuality, particularly in Western liberal democratic societies. Over the course of several decades, homosexuals' claims to protection from violence and discrimination obtained moral and legal recognition. As a normative principle, the conviction that intimate relationships between homosexuals represent "a legitimate form of relationship"[2] has largely prevailed – despite ongoing, widespread resentment of sexual diversity, which is also partly fed by religious traditions. At the same time, we should not conceal the fact that negative attitudes to and prejudices against homosexuality continue to be widespread. Homophobia is still very present.[3] If we take a global perspective, the history of "sodomy laws" since World War II reveals the following shift:

> Under the old regime, even consensual sodomy, that between adults in private, was conceived to be highly problematic, intermingling the wrong kinds of body parts with no hope of procreation. [...] By contrast, in the individualized global context [...] the locus of sex increasingly shifted from corporate entities (the family, the nation, the Church) to autonomous human persons. Individualization gave rise to expressive and pleasure-oriented definitions of sex [...]. Procreation ceased to be the legitimating goal of sexual activity, replaced by the rule of individual consent.[4]

The new view of same-sex sexuality begins in the mid-nineteenth century and is related to the modern project of "separating the guilty and the sinful from the sick."[5] In an effort to humanize the ways in which society handles deviation, those who were formerly considered sinners in need of punishment became sick people in need of treatment. In the words of Michel Foucault: "The sodomite had been a temporary aberration; the homosexual was now a species."[6] Thus the

---

2 Axel Honneth, *Das Recht der Freiheit. Grundriß einer demokratischen Sittlichkeit* (Berlin: Suhrkamp, 2011), 253.
3 Cf. Dennis Altman and Jonathan Symons, *Queer Wars* (Cambridge: Polity Press, 2016).
4 David John Frank, Steven A. Boutcher, and Bayliss Camp, "The Reform of Sodomy Laws From a World Society Perspective," in *Queer Mobilizations. LGBT Activists Confront the Law*, ed. Scott Barclay, Mary Bernstein, and Anna-Maria Marshall (New York: New York University Press, 2009), 123–141, here 137.
5 Peter Fiedler, *Sexuelle Orientierung und sexuelle Abweichung* (Weinheim: Beltz, 2004), 4.
6 Michel Foucault, *The History of Sexuality*, vol. I, *An Introduction*, trans. Robert Hurley, (New York: Pantheon Books, 1978), 43.

emerging human sciences entered into a hermeneutical competition with the established normative authorities: law and religion. However, categorizing something as a disease was by no means always conducive to the intended humanization of the sufferer – as evidenced, for example, by the struggle against "sexual deviation" in the form of (primarily male) masturbation, which sometimes involved extreme disciplinary practices and triggered "collective fear and guilt" well into the twentieth century.[7] Particularly since the mid-nineteenth century, both scientific and public interest have zeroed in on same-sex sexuality. Increasingly,

> German-language publications appear that deal with "fornication between two individuals of the male sex" and classify it in terms of forensic medicine and psychiatry. Until about 1914, an unprecedentedly dense sequence of publications [...] on the "contrary sexual instinct" emerges. The topic becomes the main subject of the new sexology. With the aid of medical justifications, criminal legislation is sharpened.[8]

The coining of the term homosexuality is attributed to Karl-Maria Benkert (1824 – 1882), who published under the pseudonym Karl-Maria Kertbeny (1869).[9] Since heterosexuality can easily be formulated as an antonym to homosexuality and both expressions are easily translatable into other languages, the new word soon spread throughout Europe and the United States, replacing other terms (such as contrary sexual instinct or inversion) and neologisms (such as uranism and uranian).

For almost a century thereafter, two schools of thought stood in opposition to one another: one saw homosexuality as a psychopathic condition, which the

---

7 Fiedler, *Sexuelle Orientierung*, 4.
8 Rüdiger Lautmann, *Soziologie der Sexualität. Erotischer Körper, intimes Handeln und Sexualkultur* (Weinheim: Juventa-Verlag, 2002), 393. It should be noted that in the 1810 French penal code, and subsequently in most countries in Latin Europe (including the Catholic ones!), same-sex sexual behavior was decriminalized. Under the influence of the British Empire, however, homosexuality became a criminal offense in many other countries. In the USA, laws punishing sodomy were repealed in various states beginning in the 1960s. Cf. the overview in Frank, Boutcher, and Camp, "The Reform of Sodomy Laws."
9 On the history of the term, see Magnus Hirschfeld, *Die Homosexualität des Mannes und des Weibes*, with a foreword by Bernd-Ulrich Hergemöller (2d rev. ed.; Berlin: De Gruyter, 2001), 3 – 16. The neologism uranism/uranian (first used in 1864) goes back to Karl Heinrich Ulrichs (1825 – 1895), who used it to allude to the goddess Aphrodite Urania and the fact that she originated directly from her father Uranus's love, which was interpreted as same-sex. Because (in today's terminology) the homosexual has different sexual desires by nature, Ulrichs rejects the idea of "unnatural fornication." The phrase "contrary sexual instinct" was coined by Carl Westphal (1833 – 1890) in 1869.

relevant sciences and the judiciary should address (a view which lead to all the negative consequences we are familiar with today); the other looked for a way out of the repression that went along with the designation of homosexuality as perversion or degeneration, and asserted an equivalence between different sexual sensations. Those who adhered to the second school of thought were helped by the fact that the newly emerging field of sexual science, as can be seen in the work of Sigmund Freud (1856–1939), was deconstructing the notion of normal sexuality.[10] For Freud, homosexuality is "nothing to be ashamed of,"[11] nor is it a vice or a disease. Sexually marginalized people discovered the liberating power of this critique of normality and set out on the long road of struggle for recognition and equal rights. The Kinsey Reports (*Sexual Behavior in the Human Male*, 1948; *Sexual Behavior in the Human Female*, 1953) gave this critique of normality a boost, bringing the intermediate stages and variations in sexual orientations into the public consciousness. This problematized the classification of homosexuality as a mental disorder. In 1973, the American Psychiatric Association removed homosexuality from its list of mental disorders. Criticism of this decision persisted until the 1980s – and continues in some circles even today – based on the assumption that homosexuality is accompanied by a "marked personality disorder."[12] From this perspective, the causes of homosexuality lay in the patient's dysfunctional psychosexual development and/or in various social developments.[13] We see the results of this perception of homosexuality in cultural criticism and an array of therapies.

---

10 Martin Dannecker, "Freuds Dekonstruktion der sexuellen Normalität," *Queer Lectures* 1 (2008): 79–107.
11 Sigmund Freud, "Letter to an American mother (1935)," reproduced in *American Journal of Psychiatry* 107 (1947): 786–787. Freud writes: "Homosexuality is assuredly no advantage but it is nothing to be ashamed of, no vice, no degradation, it cannot be classified as an illness; we consider it to be a variation of the sexual function produced by a certain arrest of sexual development. [...] It is a great injustice to persecute homosexuality as a crime and cruelty too."
12 Otto F. Kernberg, "Ein konzeptuelles Modell der männlichen Perversion," *Forum der Psychoanalyse* 1 (1985): 167–188, here 184. Cf. the psychoanalytically oriented contribution by Tony Anatrella, "Homosexualität und Homophobie," in *Lexikon Familie*, ed. Päpstlicher Rat für die Familie (Paderborn: Schöningh, 2007), 361–376, esp. 375: Homosexuality "is and remains a psychological complication and the symptom of a sexual immaturity that society cannot socially institutionalize and thus normalize." As early as 1966, in his article "Katholische Kirche und Homosexualität," *Werkhefte* 20 (1966): 91–95, Johannes Werres criticized the fact that many Catholic authors rely "indiscriminately and one-sidedly on speculations and theories from the psychoanalytic school, which can by no means be regarded as certain" (p. 94).
13 Anatrella, "Homosexualität," 365: "It is appropriate to note here that a certain contempt for the man and overvaluation of the woman, as can be observed particularly in Western societies in our era, at present almost challenges the [female] homosexual compensation." In general, every-

In the twentieth century, however, one could no longer pursue a definition of homosexuality while disregarding those affected. Homosexuals began to publicly demand their self-evident place in society. "Only since the 1970s have there been 'gays' in the sense of self-confident homosexuals."[14] The scientific focus shifted: homosexuality and its etiology were no longer of interest as a defect, but rather as a variant. The social and cultural sciences were replacing medicine and psychology as the leading sciences in the study of homosexuality. The ways in which different societies and cultures approached and addressed gender differences became more important than efforts to pinpoint what exactly the essence or identity of each gender is. In sum:

> Over the past century homosexuality has undergone a dramatic transformation, from the turn-of-the-century "disease of effeminacy" to the modern gay rights movement. We must be clear, however, that the modern social category and erotic identity signified by the term *gay* is [...] a unique development in human history.[15]

This lead to the recommendation that homosexuality as a permanent same-sex sexual orientation "deeply and unalterably linked to personality"[16] should be distinguished from same-sex behavior – men who have sex with men and women who have sex with women, respectively. Same-sex intimate contacts or relationships have been conceptualized in very different ways throughout history: as sodomy, as inversion, as homosexuality. Only the last of these concepts offers a basis on which to conceptualize homosexuality as a legitimate type of intimate love relationship. Since sexuality is a basic element of romantic love in

---

thing that "suppresses the formation of gender distinction" (including gender theory, for example) promotes the "homosexualization" of society. On Anatrella as an individual and his role in the Vatican's struggle against gender theory, see Mary Anne Case, "After Gender the Destruction of Man – The Vatican's Nightmare Vision of the 'Gender-Agenda' for Law," *Pace Law Review* 31, no. 3 (2011): 802–817.

14 Volkmar Sigusch, *Sexualitäten. Eine kritische Theorie in 99 Fragmenten* (Frankfurt am Main: Campus, 2013), 355.

15 Gilbert Herdt, "Homosexuality," in *The Encyclopedia of Religion*, vol. 6, ed. Mircea Eliade (New York: Macmillan, 1987), 445–453, here 451f. Cf. Lautmann, *Soziologie der Sexualität*, 396: "*As* a man engaging *a* man or *as* a woman engaging *a* woman in sexual interaction – that is what the gay or lesbian situation is. The reciprocity of desire is now also part of it. As an ideal type, this has not been historically proven for any period."

16 Martin Dannecker, "Homosexualität, 1. Zum Problemstand," in *Lexikon der Bioethik*, vol. 2, ed. Wilhelm Korff (Gütersloh: Gütersloher Verlag-Haus, 1998), 224–227, here 225. Cf. Hartmut Bosinski's contribution in the present volume.

the modern era[17] (love is not considered love if it does not take pleasure in physical closeness), and since the principle of equality demands that homosexuals should not be excluded from intimate love relationships as a form of sociality, sexuality in same-sex relationships is no longer considered a fundamental moral problem. In 2012, Carolin Emcke (b. 1967) articulated the self-assurance of a modern, emancipated homosexuality:

> I am not ashamed of the fact that I have a girlfriend, that I love as I love and desire as I desire. It gives me pleasure and makes me happy like I never thought I could be. I don't want to love or be loved in any other way than this. I don't care why it is this way, or whether my desire is innate, genetically encoded, or whether it has evolved. It may have been inherent in me, but I also chose to live this desire and this love. I am not proud, nor am I ashamed of it. I simply rejoice in it and am grateful for this happiness, as for an unexpected gift.[18]

Emcke finds the "labeling and classification" of homosexuals "weirdly inappropriate."[19] Such a crude conception of identity obstructs our view of individual and cultural differences. The deconstruction of normality does not end with homosexuality. According to Martin Dannecker, labelling a person as homosexual or heterosexual does not constitute "a significant statement."[20] In recent decades, homosexuals and heterosexuals have come so close to each other in terms of their sexuality and their romantic relationships (on issues such as subjectifying relationships, rejecting rigid gender roles, sexual liberalization, and new awareness of the body) that some have raised the question of whether it is possible to speak meaningfully about homosexual identity at all.[21]

While there is a cultural movement toward blurring the differences between homosexuality and heterosexuality, Catholic Christianity continues to emphasize the differences between the sexes and their identities, as well as between sexual

---

17 This is Niklas Luhmann's thesis in *Liebe. Eine Übung*, ed. André Kieserling (Frankfurt am Main: Suhrkamp, 2008), 42–45. This new connection between love and sexuality means that sexuality "can no longer be seen as a necessary evil(s) or as an earthly burden" (p. 44). The role sexuality plays in love goes far beyond its reproductive function.
18 Carolin Emcke, "So. Und nicht anders (2012)," in *Modern Love. Geschichten über die Liebe*, ed. Susanne Gretter (Berlin: Suhrkamp, 2013), 34–40, here 35 f.
19 Ibid., 36.
20 Dannecker, "Homosexualität," 225.
21 Cf. Mark D. Jordan, *The Silence of Sodom: Homosexuality in Modern Catholicism* (Chicago: University of Chicago Press, 2000).

orientations.[22] One way to explain this is with reference to the legacy of condemning same-sex sexuality as sodomy.

2 Traditional Judgment Prior to the Conceptualization of Homosexuality: Same-Sex Practice as a Grave Sin *contra naturam* (Phase 1)

Answering the question of how same-sex behavior was morally evaluated prior to the conceptualization of homosexuality is not difficult. There is a consensus among authors in this phase that a same-sex sexual act is a grave sin, because such sexual practice goes against the natural purpose of sexuality, which is procreation and raising offspring. Two traditions are responsible for this judgment:[23] a sexual pessimism that views sexual pleasure as a threat to a godly spiritual life and associates sexuality with impurity, and a sexual morality that is primarily oriented toward the natural purpose of sexual intercourse, which is understood to be God's will.[24] "Early Christianity assimilated a view that opposed all sexual pleasure and was generally antagonistic to homosexuality."[25] Any sexuality practiced for the sake of sexual pleasure – even in the context of a love relationship – was considered sinful. Following Genesis 19, same-sex sexual practice was referred to as the sin of sodomy.

---

22 See Bernard de Cock, "Homosexuality and Sexual Difference. An Introduction to the Thought of Xavier Lacroix," *Ephemerides Theologicae Lovanienses* 81, no. 4 (2005): 334–364; cf. Xavier Lacroix, *Le corps de l'esprit* (Paris: Éditions du Cerf, 2002).

23 On this point, see Christof Breitsameter and Stephan Goertz, *Vom Vorrang der Liebe. Zeitenwende für die katholische Sexualmoral* (Freiburg im Breisgau: Herder, 2020).

24 Cf. Augustine, *Confessions* 3.8: "Itaque flagitia, quae sunt contra naturam, ubique ac semper detestanda atque punienda sunt, qualia Sodomitarum fuerunt. Quae si omnes gentes facerent, eodum criminis reatu divina lege tenerentur, quae non sec fecit homines, ut hoc se uterentur modo" (Therefore are those foul offences which be against nature, to be everywhere and at all times detested and punished; such as were those of the men of Sodom: which should all nations commit, they should all stand guilty of the same crime, by the law of God, which hath not so made men that they should so abuse one another); for the English translation, see *The Confessions of Saint Augustine*, trans. Edward B. Pusey (Grand Rapids: Christian Classics Ethereal Library, 1999), 71, https://ccel.org/ccel/a/augustine/confess/cache/confess.pdf (accessed November 5, 2020).

25 Herdt, "Homosexuality," 447.

In the work of Thomas Aquinas (1224/1225–1274), the primary authority on Catholic sexual morality, the moral order of human sexuality is constructed (as it was by ancient authors as well) from the act's natural teleology toward the good. Semen must be spilled "for the purpose of generation (*ad generationis*), to which purpose the sexual act is directed (*ad quam coitus ordinatur*)" (*Summa contra gentiles* 3.122).[26] It follows "that every emission of semen, in such a way that generation cannot follow, is contrary to the good for man (*contra bonum hominis*)" (ibid.). Whoever does so intentionally necessarily commits a sin. Every ejaculation "apart from the natural union of male and female" constitutes a sin "contrary to nature (*peccata contra naturam*)." When semen is spilled without respect for its natural purpose, this act is "incompatible with the natural good; namely, the preservation of the species" (ibid.).[27] Thomas follows this up with a qualification that is momentous for the evaluation of sodomy: "Hence, after the sin of homicide whereby a human nature already in existence is destroyed, this type of sin appears to take next place, for by it the generation of human nature is precluded" (ibid.). He refers to Leviticus 18:22 and 1 Corinthians 6:9–11, whereby what he has said thus far is supported by "divine authority (*divina auctoritate*)." Anyone who seeks sexual pleasure in an unnatural act from which no procreation can result is unchaste (*Summa theologica* 2–2, q. 154, a. 11). More importantly, such an action is a particularly shameful transgression, because it not only violates the order of nature, but also wrongs God, the "Author of nature" (*Summa theologica* 2–2, q. 154, a. 12).[28] At the beginning of the nineteenth century, Johann Michael Sailer (1751–1832) wrote in the same tradition (albeit in different terms): "Every use of the sexual faculty against the purpose of nature thus makes the human person an instrument of pleasure, a mere

---

26 Thomas Aquinas, *Summa contra gentiles, Book 3: Providence, Part II*, trans. Vernon J. Bourke (Notre Dame: University of Notre Dame Press, 1956), 142–147. See also Thomas Aquinas, *De Malo* q. 15, a. 1.

27 The social function of marriage serves as a basis for criticizing extra-marital and same-sex relationships, including in Francis, *Post-Synodal Apostolic Exhortation Amoris laetitia* (Rome: Vatican, 2016), no. 52, https://www.vatican.va/content/dam/francesco/pdf/apost_exhortations/documents/papa-francesco_esortazione-ap_20160319_amoris-laetitia_en.pdf (accessed April 21, 2021): "No union that is temporary or closed to the transmission of life can ensure the future of society."

28 Cf. Augustine, *Confessions* 3.8: "Violatur quippe ipsa societas, quae cum deo nobis debet, cum eadem natura, cuius ille auctor est, libidinis perversitate polluitur." See also Henry Davis, *Moral and Pastoral Theology*, vol. 2 (2d ed.; London: n. p., 1936), 216: "Hoc peccatum est gravissimum, id quod patet ex eo quod est maxime contra naturam, et ex poenis gravissimis in iure antique et ab ipso Deo ob illud inflictis, et ex verbis S. Pauli (Rom. I, 26–28)."

means of pleasure against the purpose of pleasure."[29] Reproduction (preservation of the species) as a social excuse for sexuality, which is otherwise an object of suspicion, fails in principle when it comes to homosexual behavior.[30]

Because there was no concept of homosexuality as we understand it today – as a sexual orientation and a relational capacity – traditional judgment at this time solely focused on sexual acts between persons of the same sex, which as such cannot result in procreation and thus cannot achieve the purpose of sexuality. At first sight, the classification of same-sex behavior under the category of sins *contra naturam* was self-evident for moral theologians when it came to establishing norms. Further aspects only come into play when one thinks about the gravity of the sin of sodomy – also in comparison to other sins against nature.

Pierre Hurteau has interpreted post-Tridentine moral-theological discourses on sodomy as the missing link between the Thomistic position on the one hand, which was concerned with preserving nature's objective purpose, and the perception of the homosexual predisposition since the nineteenth century on the other.[31] His moral-historical analysis trains a sharper eye on moral-theological developments that are easily overlooked when one solely emphasizes the continuity of the established norms. The Council of Trent (1545 – 1563) decreed that the faithful "need to seek God's pardon" (Denzinger-Hünermann [DH] 1680) for all of their mortal sins at least once a year, which set the course for our topic. Because the Council was concerned with "diligent self-examination" (DH 1680) and with identifying the circumstances that mitigate the nature and gravity of the sin (DH 1681), the intentions of the subject who commits the action took primacy over a fixed, legalistic concept that focuses on the objective violation of order. In scholastic terms, what we encounter here is the ethically important distinction between the inherent goal of an action (*finis operis*) and the purpose of an action as established by an agent (*finis operantis*). The crux of the entire tradition of establishing norms with regard to same-sex behavior lies in

---

29 Johann Michael Sailer, *Handbuch der christlichen Moral*, vol. 2 (Sulzbach: Seidel, 1834), 51. Kant's thinking was the same on this point: sexuality that disregards the purpose of procreation is a "desecration (not merely degradation) of humanity in one's own person"; see *Metaphysik der Sitten*, AA 6, 424f.

30 Michael Brinkschröder offers "a brief overview of Christian anti-homosexuality" in *Sodom als Symptom. Gleichgeschlechtliche Sexualität im christlichen Imaginären – eine religionsgeschichtliche Anamnese* (Berlin: De Gruyter, 2006), 6 – 35; cf. previous works by David F. Greenberg and Marcia H. Bystryn, "Christian Intolerance of Homosexuality," *American Journal of Sociology* 88, no. 3 (1982): 515 – 548; Hubertus Lutterbach, "Gleichgeschlechtliches sexuelles Verhalten. Ein Tabu zwischen Spätantike und früher Neuzeit?" *Historische Zeitschrift* 267 (1998): 281 – 310.

31 Pierre Hurteau, "Catholic Moral Discourse on Male Sodomy and Masturbation in the Seventeenth and Eighteenth Centuries," *Journal of the History of Sexuality* 4 (1993): 1 – 26.

the fact that in this tradition, moral judgment considers only the *finis operis*, and sexuality is not appreciated in terms of the personal quality of its expression. Only those who consider the circumstances surrounding a homosexual act to be secondary can judge loving and loveless homosexuality as equally grave sins.

According to Hurteau, moral theology after Trent represents an early form of *scientia sexualis*, which conceptualizes the sexual agent in addition to the laws of the divine order of creation. This development took place at a time when morality in general was interiorized in the wake of political, economic, and religious upheavals and the new ethical questions that accompanied them. In such a context, the moral subject must be able to do more than simply obey traditional laws. Thus moral theology began to consider the details of and differences between various cases (casuistry), and the understanding of sin began to shift. Once again, the issue depends more on the inner person, on their sexual desires.[32] In contrast to previous definitions, moral theologians in the seventeenth and eighteenth centuries defined sodomy as sexual desire for the inappropriate sex (*ex affectu indebiti sexus*).[33] Admittedly, this desire was not yet attributed to an individual's particular constitution. This new definition allowed moral theologians to refer to individual same-sex sexual acts not as sodomy, but as *pollutio*, for example – provided such acts were not an expression of desire for the inappropriate sex.[34] From this perspective, sexuality is not merely physiology – it has intrapsychic significance as well. Since desire is what matters, some moral theologians refused to classify non-reproductive, improper heterosexual acts as sodomy, as was still customary well into the twentieth century.[35]

---

32 In this sense, masturbation could be classified as adultery (insofar as it involved fantasies about a person other than one's spouse), incest (insofar as the desire was directed toward a relative), or bestiality (insofar as it was directed toward a person of the same sex). Cf. Hurteau, "Catholic Moral," 12f.

33 On this point, see Henry Davis, *Commandments of God, Precepts of the Church*, vol. 2, *Moral and Pastoral Theology* (London: Sheed and Ward, 1936), 216: "Essentia sodomiae consistit in affect ad eundum sexum." See also Heribert Jone, *Katholische Moraltheologie* (Paderborn: Schöningh, 1941), 186: "*Malitia* sodomiae consistit in affectu ad sexum indebitum."

34 Thomas Slater, *A Manual of Moral Theology*, vol. 1 (2d ed.; New York: Benziger Brothers, 1908), 334: "Sodomia igitur consistit in concubitu cum sexu indebito cum pollution [...] sine affectu ad personam, et sine concubitu, habetur pollutio non sodomia." Cf. Jone, *Katholische Moraltheologie*, 186: "Si *deest* affectus ad personam indebitam [...] non habetur sodomia, etsi duae personae mutuis tactibus etc. se polluant."

35 The handbooks distinguished between *sodomia imperfecta* (anal or oral intercourse between a man and a woman) and *sodomia perfecta* (between persons of the same sex). In addition, there was the distinction between consummated (*sodomia consummata)* and unconsummated (*sodomia non consummata*) sodomy. The word had a broad meaning, and this was not only the case in the field of moral theology: "In Elizabethan English sodomy was not restricted to sexual inter-

In the history of Catholic moral teaching, the continuity of the established norms has gone hand in hand with various evaluations of the gravity of the sin of sodomy. In one of the rare papal statements on same-sex sexuality, in 1054 Leo IX (1049–1054) opposed the blanket punishment of clerics, as Peter Damianus (1007–1072/1073) – who was extremely rigorous in this matter – had called for. Trusting in "divine mercy," the pope stated that the circumstances surrounding such acts (which he also clearly condemned in moral terms) must be considered: Had this bad behavior become habitual? Were there several persons involved? Was the desire restrained? (DH 688) In a Decree of the Holy Office in 1665, Alexander VII (1655–1667) evaluated the opinion that in confession, it was unnecessary to distinguish between whether one had committed the sin of self-abuse, sodomy, or bestiality and judged it an error of laxity (DH 2044). Both papal pronouncements assume that sodomy is a sin but strive to moderate opinions which they perceive as extreme, in one direction or the other. The material history of sodomy includes Paul IV's (1555–1559) decision to grant the Roman Inquisition authority over allegations of sodomy in 1557. Under the reform-minded popes Paul IV and Pius V (1566–1572), sodomy came to be understood as a spiritual error with regard to correct sexuality, by analogy to heresy as an error of faith, and was drawn into the confessional controversies of the day with polemical intent.[36] As has frequently been the case throughout history, the accusation of sodomy became an instrument with which to discredit competing religious concepts on moral grounds.[37] As early as 1600, however, the Roman institutions seem to have lost any particular interest in the matter.[38]

In the sixteenth century, the goal of Peter Canisius's (1521–1597) influential catechisms was not to promote pastoral leniency, but rather to provoke revul-

---

course with the same sex and with beasts, but was applied to intercourse between unmarried human beings also"; George A. Barton, "Sodomy," in *Encyclopedia of Religion and Ethics*, vol. 11, ed. James Hastings (New York: Charles Scribner's Sons, 1920), 672–674, here 672. (This usage is attributed to English translations of Deut 23:18, among other verses.)

36 See also Maurizio P. Faggioni, "L'atteggiamento e la prassi della Chiesa in epoca medievale e moderna sull'omosessualità," *Gregorianum* 91, no. 3 (2010): 478–509, esp. 501: "La lotta alla sodomia del clero e dei laici fu un elemento costante fin dai primi tentativi di riforma cattolica."
37 Cf. Sita Steckel, "Perversion als Argument. Sex und Geschlechterordnung in innerkirchlichen Polemiken des lateinischen Hoch- und Spätmittelalters," in *"Als Mann und Frau schuf er sie"*. *Religion und Geschlecht*, ed. Barbara Stollberg-Rilinger (Würzburg: Ergon-Verlag, 2014), 47–85.
38 On this point, see Pierroberto Scaramella, "Sodomia," in *Dizionario storico dell'Inquisizione*, vol. 3, ed. Adriano Prosperi (Pisa: Edizioni della Normale, 2010), 1445–1450 (with thanks to my colleague in Mainz, Claus Arnold, for pointing me to this reference). The Spanish Inquisition and its activities would have to be considered separately; cf. Joseph Pérez, *La Inquisición española: crónica negra del Santo Oficio* (Madrid: Martínez Roca, 2005).

sion, particularly as he included sodomy – along with murder, oppressing the poor, and defrauding workers of the wages they had earned – among the "sins that cry out to heaven" (*peccata clamantia*, literally "screaming sins"), a theological category which had not been particularly common previously. The peculiarity of these sins is that they call for divine punishment and vengeance.[39] The effect of this has been devastating. "Since Peter Canisius, the destruction of the city of Sodom and the character of this sin as one that cries out to heaven have been the most popular arguments against homosexual acts in Northern European countries. The threat of God's vengeance can unconsciously induce panic, which manifests in a cruel ruthlessness that punishes the sinner, lest everyone be destroyed by the fire of heaven."[40] The moral uproar unleashed here is part of the oppressive legacy of the Christian tradition. Even decades after the conceptualization of homosexuality, one finds the following in an English-language handbook, with no critical commentary:

> [T]he distinguishing note of the so called *peccata clamantia* is violent suppression of certain natural instincts and conscious frustration of their ends and objects. [...] Sodomy is closely related to murder. Both crimes are directed against the preservation of the human race, and, moreover, cruelty and lust, heartlessness and debauchery, bloodthirst and unchastity (Sadism, Masochism) usually go hand in hand.[41]

The well-known 1933 *Lexikon für Theologie und Kirche* (Encyclopedia of Theology and the Church) renders the following judgment: homosexuality is, "so far as it is voluntary, a grave moral offense, a sin that 'cries out to heaven,' branded in the Holy Scriptures as an abomination (Lev 18:22), as worthy of death (Lev 20:13), as an unnatural aberration [...] and punished at Sodom and Gomorrah with destruction by fire and brimstone (Gen 19:24)."[42] Almost three decades later, the renowned German moral theologian Werner Schöllgen (1893–1985) wrote: "We emphasize [...] most emphatically that in the image of the natural human being as depicted in the Bible, homosexuality represents almost the

---

39 Biblical evidence includes Genesis 4:10 (murder); Genesis 18:20 and 19:13 (sodomy); and Exodus 3:7 (oppressing the poor).

40 Herman van de Spijker, *Die gleichgeschlechtliche Zuneigung. Homotropie: Homosexualität, Homoerotik, Homophilie – und die katholische Moraltheologie* (Olten: Walter-Verlag, 1968), 121.

41 Antony Koch, *A Handbook of Moral Theology*, vol. 2, adapted and edited by Arthur Preuss (St. Louis: B. Herder, 1919), 86–88.

42 Karl Hilgenreiner, "Homosexualität," in *LThK*, vol. 5, ed. Michael Buchberger (Freiburg im Breisgau: Herder, 1933), 130–131, here 130.

grimmest shadow, the utmost ethical darkness."[43] Two sentences later, he mentions Sodom and Gomorrah. With these quotations, we have already arrived at the phase which I will examine in more detail in the following section.

3 Handbooks of Moral Theology Since the Conceptualization of Homosexuality: The Unnatural Sin of Sodomy and Homosexual Perversion (Phase 2)

Until roughly the end of the nineteenth century, the moral-theological condemnation of same-sex behavior could proceed from the assumption – still unchallenged by science – that same-sex sexual acts constituted a perversion of the natural purpose of the male or female subject's sexuality. In the category of sins *contra naturam*, sodomy (along with bestiality) was considered a grave evil, but contraception and especially masturbation occupied much more space in the relevant handbooks, and in moral instruction in general.[44] These handbooks continued to treat sodomy/homosexuality comparatively briefly up to the early 1960s.[45]

---

43 Werner Schöllgen, "Der abnorme (homosexuelle) Mensch im Urteil der Moraltheologie," in *Konkrete Ethik*, ed. Werner Schöllgen (Düsseldorf: Patmos-Verlag, 1961), 406–414, here 410. Cf. Karl Hörmann, "Homosexualität," in *Lexikon der christlichen Moral*, ed. Karl Hörmann (Innsbruck: Tyrolia-Verlag, 1969), 643–648, esp. 646.
44 See, for example, Gregor Busl, *Katechetische Predigten Bd. 2: Von den Geboten*, ed. Karl Neumann (Regensburg: Habbel, 1899), 647–651.
45 Thomas Slater (*A Manual of Moral Theology*, vol. 1 [5th ed.; London: Burns Oates & Washbourne Ltd, 1925]) covers the subject in 22 lines of his 15 pages on the sixth and ninth commandments. Fritz Tillmann (*Die katholische Sittenlehre. Die Verwirklichung der Nachfolge Christi*, vol. 4.2, *Handbuch der katholischen Sittenlehre* [Düsseldorf: Patmos-Verlag, 1940]) devotes 16 lines to homosexuality over the course of 8 pages devoted to the "Sünden der Unkeuschheit" (Sins of Unchastity; pp. 117–124). Henry Davis (*Commandments of God, Precepts of the Church*, vol. 2, *Moral and Pastoral Theology* [London: Sheed and Ward, 1946]) requires just under one page out of a total of 52 pages on the sixth and ninth commandments. In Bernhard Häring (*Das Gesetz Christi* [Munich: Wewel, 1958]), the section on homosexuality covers about half a page out of 19 pages on unchastity (pp. 1135–1153). Joseph Mausbach and Gustav Ermecke (*Katholische Moraltheologie*, vol. 3 [Münster: Aschendorff, 1961]) grant the subject just five lines in the chapter on the "Sünden der Unkeuschheit" (pp. 380–390): "Sodomy is [...] lewd sexual intercourse between persons of the same sex [...]. It is often based on perverse drives or vicious brutalization." For a synopsis of the handbooks' stereotypical statements on sodomy/homosexuality, see van de Spijker, *Die gleichgeschlechtliche Zuneigung*, 125–143.

But how do these handbooks address the insight, conceptualized at the end of the nineteenth century, that same-sex behavior is the act of a person with a same-sex disposition? The modern concept of homosexuality is not compatible with the idea that a man or a woman perverts his or her natural sexuality by engaging in homosexual behavior. Such a notion – which lies behind the Pauline condemnation of same-sex behavior in the Letter to the Romans, for example[46] – becomes invalid if homosexuality is understood as an expression of a person's sexual identity. How does moral theology respond to this new situation?

Several decades elapsed before the term homosexuality was used at all in the relevant encyclopedias and handbooks. In the standard German-language theological lexicon of the time, there is no entry on homosexuality; instead, the "Sodoma" entry reminds the reader of the "grave degeneration" of unnatural sin and the "terrible judgment of God."[47] In the fifth edition of Thomas Slater's (1855–1928) handbook, printed in 1925, there is still no reference to homosexuality.[48] At the beginning of the twentieth century, the Viennese moral theologian Franz M. Schindler (1847–1922) was one of the first to mention the term homosexuality.[49] First, he condemns sodomy as the unnatural and particularly sinful "gratification of the sexual instinct with a person of the same sex."[50] After establishing these norms, Schindler points to contemporary efforts to abolish criminal punishment for (consummated) sodomy. In order to legitimize such efforts, one could invoke "pathological conditions of the sex drive," which one dubs homosexuality. "Such states can indeed be observed, partly as an individual psychopathic disposition, partly (in psychically normal persons) as a consequence of sexual debauchery." But ultimately it makes no difference: "Thereby, however, the unnaturalness of sodomy can in no way be denied."[51] Henry Davies (1866–1952) offers a typical juxtaposition of sodomy as sin and homosexuality as sexual perversion.[52] Homosexuality (*contraria sexualitas*) – like sadism, masochism, fetishism, or exhibitionism – stands outside the natural order of sexuality as *per-*

---

46 On Paul in general, see Ansgar Wucherpfennig, *Sexualität bei Paulus* (Freiburg im Breisgau: Herder, 2020).

47 Joseph Hergenröther and Franz Kaulen, eds., *Wetzer und Welte's Kirchenlexikon*, vol. 11 (Freiburg im Breisgau: Herder, 1899), col. 477.

48 On Slater, see James F. Keenan, *A History of Catholic Moral Theology in the Twentieth Century. From Confessing Sins to Liberating Consciences* (London: Continuum, 2010), 10–18.

49 Franz M. Schindler, *Lehrbuch der Moraltheologie*, vol. 3 (Vienna: Oplitz, 1914).

50 Ibid., 503.

51 All quotations taken from ibid.

52 Davis, *Commandments* (1936), 216–218. The passage on sodomy and homosexual perversion remains unchanged in all the editions until the end of the 1950s. Cf. Keenan, *A History of Catholic Moral Theology*, 18–25.

versio appetitus and, like these other conditions, could be either an inborn dis-position or the result of repeated lewd behavior. Homosexuals tended (*tendit*) to sodomy and pollution, and should be kept from opportunities to sin. Hierony-mus Noldin's (1838–1922) *Summa Theologiae Moralis* also deals with the subject along the same lines.[53] First, he condemns sodomy as a sin *contra naturam*; he then follows this with an appendix on sexual perversions, among which – in ad-dition to sadism, masochism, and fetishism – he counts "contrary sexual in-stinct," that is, homosexuality. Immediately following this, as in Davies's hand-book, he enumerates the sins associated with homosexuality: *pollutio*, sodomy, and pederasty. As a perversion, homosexuality can be but is not necessarily a sign of a mental defect. In principle, it is true that perverse desire can be re-pressed, and the person is therefore responsible for their actions, unless the mental defect is severe (*nisi defectus psychicus maiorem gradum attigerit*). In Bernhard Häring's (1912–1998) famous handbook, published at the end of the 1950s, homosexuality is once again classified among the sexual perversions. Concerning the causes, he states briefly: "Homosexuality is often the result of se-duction and complete sexual barbarity; but it can also be a bad, pathological dis-position. The act is the sodomy."[54] However, a pathological predisposition does not relieve the actor of moral responsibility. Homosexuals, like all other "forni-cators [...] are responsible according to the degree of freedom they retain."[55] Any attempt on the part of homosexuals to present their vice "as something natural" must be decisively contradicted.[56]

We cannot deny that the ways in which these handbooks address the phe-nomenon of homosexuality demonstrates an inner coherence, as has become clear above. If same-sex sexual practices are judged as "grave sin" in every case, and this judgment is never questioned, then it stands to reason that the predisposition or inclination to such practices is likewise evaluated negatively. Kleptomania sometimes serves as a comparison. Even if homosexuality is part of a person's individual nature, the traditional judgment of this behavior as un-

---

53 Hieronymus Noldin, *Summa Theologiae Moralis. Complementum: De Castitate*, Editio XXXIV, ed. G. Heinzel (Innsbruck: Felizian Rauch, 1952), 38–39, 41–43.
54 Häring, *Das Gesetz Christi*, 1148 (reproduced unchanged in the 7th edition in 1963). It takes Häring a long time to give up this negative judgment of homosexuality: "Our whole tradition holds the principle that persons with so strong a homosexual tendency that they are not fitted for marriage must abstain from all genital activity, just as other celibates are expected to do"; see *Free and Faithful in Christ. Moral Theology for Priests and Laity*, vol. 2 (New York: The Seabury Press, 1979), 563.
55 Häring, *Das Gesetz Christi*, 1148.
56 Ibid.

natural still stands, because the nature which homosexual behavior violates is the natural purpose of sexuality, the finality of the semen in the sexual act. Even for a person who is homosexual "by nature," homosexual behavior would be "against nature." Ulpian's (ca. 170 – 223/228) ancient definition of natural law is crucial to the position demonstrated in these handbooks: "Ius naturale est, quod natura omnia animalia docuit; nam ius istud non humani generis proprium, sed omnium animalium." Immediately thereafter, he addresses human sexuality and marriage: "Hinc descendit maris atque feminae coniunctio, quam nos matrimonium appellamus, hinc liberorum procreatio, hinc educatio" (*Institutiones* 1.2). Whether the sexual act has a humane meaning for the individual and their relationships beyond the sexual is a secondary question. In this tradition, the judgment of (homo)sexual behavior is based primarily on humankind's animal nature, which human beings have in common with animals and their *telos* (namely, the preservation of the species). Homosexuality is of interest to these moral theological authors more as the wrong kind of genital contact and as inappropriate ejaculation than as a personal encounter.[57] It is true that "[s]uch a belated awareness of the phenomenon [...] of homosexuality can hardly be explained other than with reference to a theology that [with the exception of confession] is not very oriented toward pastoral practice, high-handedly rejects dialogue with other sciences, and does not incorporate their findings into its theological thinking."[58] This rejectionist attitude is the result of the specific character of the sexual ethics in these handbooks. Contrary to all the emancipatory processes taking place on behalf of homosexuals,[59] these judgments – once formulated – were repeated unchanged until the 1960s. "With their pastoral purpose of training confessors as judges, the manuals were so entrenched in practice that nothing was going to change their basic approach." They "fully endorsed the spirit of neo-scholasticism, emphasizing the defensiveness of the Church and the failure to dialogue with the modern world."[60]

---

57 See van de Spijker, *Die gleichgeschlechtliche Zuneigung*, 163.

58 Ibid., 149. One notable exception is Theodor Müncker, *Die psychologischen Grundlagen der katholischen Sittenlehre*, vol. 3 of *Handbuch der katholischen Sittenlehre* (Düsseldorf: Mosella, 1940), 204 f.

59 Hilgenreiner, "Homosexualität," 130: "It is a sign of moral decay that homosexuality is [labelled] normal, a kind of justified sexual sensibility." See also Josef Mausbach, *Katholische Moraltheologie*, vol. 3, ed. Gustav Ermecke (Münster: Aschendorff, 1953), 121: "The excuse or defense [...] of homosexual offenses in modern times is one of the signs of sinking back into pagan immorality."

60 Charles E. Curran, *Catholic Moral Theology in the United States. A History* (Washington, DC: Georgetown University Press, 2008), 11.

4 A New Attitude Since the 1950s: Homosexuality Is a Problem that Precludes True Love (Phase 3)

The sparse and stereotypical information on homosexuality provided in these handbooks may suffice to instruct the confessor on how to judge a specific sexual act in moral terms. However, if the pastoral concern goes beyond the concrete context of confession, then priests will find "little help in the moral theology manuals when they are confronted with cases of homosexuality."[61] This observation prompted the Salesian and moral theologian John F. Harvey (1918–2010), based in the USA, to write a lengthy theological reflection that was published in the journal *Theological Studies* in 1955 under the evocative title "Homosexuality as a Pastoral Problem."[62] According to Harvey, the nature and complex causes of homosexuality should no longer be ignored. At the very beginning of his reflections, he opposes the conceptualization of homosexuality as a perversion of a heterosexual orientation, because such a definition makes the "inverts" (Harvey's term) unfairly responsible for their homosexual tendencies.[63] Catholic moral theology knows how to differentiate between an inclination to sin and its deliberate satisfaction. The distinction between a blameless disposition and a sinful activity is, as we shall see, also regularly employed in the magisterial documents on homosexuality.[64] Harvey argues that there is much more to homosexuality than the sexual act. The inversion reaches into the depths of the soul; the whole person is same-sex oriented. Therefore, in moral-theological terms, one should not concentrate on controlling lust. Rather,

---

61 John F. Harvey, "Homosexuality as a Pastoral Problem," *TS* 16 (1955): 86–108, here 86; see also idem, "Homosexuality," in *NCE*, vol. 7, ed. William J. McDonald (New York: McGraw-Hill, 1967), 116–119; idem, "The Controversy Concerning the Psychology and Morality of Homosexuality," *American Ecclesiastical Review* 167, no. 9 (1973): 602–629; idem, *The Homosexual Person: New Thinking in Pastoral Care* (San Francisco: Ignatius Press, 1987); idem, *The Truth about Homosexuality* (San Francisco: Ignatius Press, 1995).

62 This pattern of speech is by no means specifically Catholic; cf., for instance, Alfred Adler, *Das Problem der Homosexualität* (Munich: Ernst Reinhardt, 1917).

63 "It is necessary to distinguish between psychologically conditioned but involuntary homosexuality, and the deliberate formation [...] and the gratification of such impulses"; Harvey, "Homosexuality" (1967), 116.

64 Cf. Tillmann, *Die katholische Sittenlehre*, 124: "Today, it can no longer be denied that there are perverse dispositions given by nature, which entail misfortune for the individual, but not guilt. Yet a right to same-sex activity cannot be derived even from such a disposition, just as the kleptomaniac has no right to steal."

homosexuality is a problem of the person's entire emotional nature. Harvey's evaluation – which goes beyond the previous assessment grounded in natural law, which also he shared[65] – is momentous. It reads: "True heterosexual love – indeed all true love – is a going out of oneself, a gift of oneself, while homosexual love is the purest form of egoism."[66] Homosexuals narcissistically seek and love only what is their own in the other. This issue was not mentioned in previous condemnations of same-sex behavior. Thus in Harvey's contribution, the difference between heterosexuality and homosexuality becomes a difference in the capacity to love.

Harvey is somewhat more reticent on the etiology of homosexuality. From a psychological perspective, however, early childhood plays a significant role in psychosexual development. Nevertheless, it is impossible to make general statements about the treatment of homosexuality. As a theological preventive measure, Harvey recommends addressing the sacred character of sexuality's procreative function in sex education. With appropriate concern, he comments on attempts to justify homosexuality in contemporary culture. He observes that some would go so far as to suggest that homosexuals have a quasi-marital relationship. Contrary to such secularist attitudes, he asserts, Catholic morality remains committed to offering constructive measures to prevent homosexual acts. Moreover, "Catholic theology alone gives man the full truth about his nature, his destiny, and the means which he can use to attain his goal."[67] The invert is not exclusively psychically, but also morally ill, and this justifies the priest's spiritual guidance alongside the doctor's therapeutic work. In this instance, religious help consists in ascetic schemes to overcome the rebellion of the flesh; in the hope of and constant prayer for God's saving grace; in clear moral recognition of homosexual acts as mortal sins; in strengthening freedom against fatalism; and finally, in regularly receiving the sacraments of penance and the Eucharist.[68] In the best-case scenario, an outright conversion takes place. The sinful

---

65 In quite traditional terms, he writes: "The homosexual act by its essence excludes all possibility of transmission of life; such an act cannot fulfill the procreative purpose of the sexual faculty and is, therefore, an inordinate use of that faculty. Since it runs contrary to a very important goal of human nature, it is a grave transgression of the divine will"; see Harvey, "Homosexuality" (1967), 117.

66 Harvey, "Homosexuality" (1955), 88; cf. idem, "Homosexuality" (1967), 119: "All true love is a going-out of oneself, a self-giving; but, all unconsciously, homosexual love is bent back upon the self in a closed circle, a sterile love of self, disguised in apparent love for another. What seems like ideal love to the homosexual must be shown to be narcissism."

67 Harvey, "Homosexuality" (1955), 93.

68 Davis also recommends this pastoral strategy to counter the sins of unchastity in *Commandments* (1936), 202: "Boys and girls should be urged to go to confession frequently, and to Holy

habitual action does not have to have the last word. The priest's goal remains re-education: "Another manner of thinking, willing, and loving must replace the old."[69] The homosexual must break away from their homosexual friends and, at all costs, avoid occasions in which they might be tempted to sin. The priest can show the homosexual that their inverted love is self-destructive by its very nature, because it closes the way to the fullness of humanity and revolts against the law of God's love. In the end, the homosexual must reconstitute their love: "Love of God must become the driving motive in the life of the homosexual who, otherwise, will grow lonely for the kind of fellowship found in homosexual haunts – in which he had been formerly enslaved, to which he is still attracted, and in place of which a stronger love must be found."[70]

But if the cause of homosexual inclination is unclear, what does this mean for the homosexual's responsibility for their behavior? Harvey recommends a middle way: "Do not tell him that he is not responsible. Do not tell him that he is completely responsible."[71] As with alcoholism, there is always a margin of freedom. In principle, homosexuals are able to sublimate their inclinations, but women are more readily able to do so than men. According to Harvey, this is because the possibility of parenthood in the context of a stable family is more attractive to women than it is to men; it corresponds to their essential duties as women and mothers. Thus, at the end of his remarks, Harvey indicates that he is convinced there is a Christian solution to the problem of homosexuality. The norm of complete sexual abstinence, he claims, should not be seen as an excessive human demand or as a Catholic illusion. Others also think this way: "To deny that the power of God's grace enables homosexuals to live chastely is to deny, effectively, that Jesus has risen from the dead."[72]

In Harvey's case, we can see how same-sex behavior as a morally wrong act becomes a moral problem for the whole person after the conceptualization of homosexuality. The immorality of the homosexual act radiates out to the whole person, so to speak. Such a person is not merely required to abstain from individual acts, but is confronted with the expectation of conversion. The homosexual act is

---

Communion daily, if possible." This encounter with the (pure!) body of Christ is apparently supposed to guard against impurity, as through "the reception of the Holy Eucharist we become united to Christ, fount of purity as of all other virtues" (ibid., 173).

69 Harvey, "Homosexuality" (1955), 103.
70 Harvey, "Homosexuality" (1967), 119.
71 Harvey, "Homosexuality" (1955), 106.
72 Cardinal Francis George (Archbishop of Chicago), *Address to the Annual Meeting of the National Association of Catholic Diocesan Gay and Lesbian Ministries* (Chicago, 1998), as cited in Jeffrey Keefe, "Homosexuality," in *NCE*, vol. 7 (Detroit: Gale Group, 2003), 66–71, here 70.

not only contrary to love; the homosexual person is also incapable of love. Homosexuals must not merely change their actions, they must also change themselves – they must convert.[73]

The third phase, which Harvey initiated, pulls the "problem" of homosexuality off of the moral-theological sidelines, but it also fends off all attempts to reevaluate homosexuality morally and legally with the aid of traditionally established norms. This also applies to one of the first Catholic monographs on homosexuality, the Jesuit Michael J. Buckley's (1931–2019) *Morality and the Homosexual*, published in 1959.[74] In this book, Buckley does not conceal the fact that he is troubled by the view emerging in society that it is time to devise a "new moral code" for homosexuality because homosexuals cannot be morally culpable for their constitution.[75] In contrast, Buckley holds that society "should always condemn immoral sexual practices, and homosexual acts are included in this category."[76] He follows this up with a statement that is not found in the handbooks: "Yet if there be such a person as a congenital homosexual, then society should allow him to fulfil a useful purpose and not spurn him merely for what he is."[77] Of course, this changes nothing with regard to the established norms. The only morally acceptable way of life remains the path of abstinence. A distinction must be made between the homosexual "condition and homosexual practices."[78] This distinction is of "supreme importance," because whoever renounces it may think

---

73 In the Archdiocese of New York in 1980, at the initiative of Cardinal Terrence Cook, Harvey founded Courage (https://couragerc.org [accessed November 10, 2020]) – a pastoral ministry now operating in several countries with the goal of helping homosexuals in the Catholic Church to attempt to lead abstinent lives, such as by adhering to the program developed by Alcoholics Anonymous: "Courage moves to intimacy with Jesus Christ as the most cogent force in fostering interior chastity. It does not promote reorientation, leaving the choice of that goal to the individual. Instead it focuses on the member's spiritual life. Pope John Paul II has called Courage 'the work of God'" (Keefe, "Homosexuality," 70). Harvey accused the US Conference of Catholic Bishops of placing too little emphasis on church doctrine and too much on accepting homosexuality and spreading misconceptions about homosexual orientation. Harvey and Courage received support from cardinals Alfonso López Trujillo and Raymond Burke, both members of the Roman Curia, among others. Cf. Steve Weatherbe, "Remembering Father John Harvey," *National Catholic Register*, January 5, 2011, https://www.ncregister.com/news/remembering-father-john-harvey-8wh2r6vs (accessed September 28, 2020).
74 Michael J. Buckley, *Morality and the Homosexual. A Catholic Approach to a Moral Problem* (London: Sands & Co Ltd, 1959).
75 Buckley, *Morality and the Homosexual*, 2.
76 Ibid., 3 f.
77 Ibid., 4.
78 Ibid., 5 f.

that abstinence constitutes an impossible demand.[79] The assertion that the Church's moral commandments can never be too much for humankind to bear is an old means of warding off the question of whether the Church's moral teaching might demand the impossible.[80]

Buckley does not accept homosexuality as a condition of sexual orientation, because this would lead to the equal treatment of heterosexuality and homosexuality, which would be dangerous. Rather, homosexuality is to be understood as "psychosexual attraction."[81] It must not be considered another form of love. Echoing Harvey, Buckley writes: *"The obvious error involved in homosexuality lies in the homosexual's false concept of human love."*[82] Homosexuality is an "intellectual aberration,"[83] and therefore no one should consciously desire to persist in their homosexuality. There is no escape from this responsibility. This also means that efforts must be made to awaken in homosexuals the "desire to be cured,"[84] the "journey back to mental health."[85] This path back to normality requires self-denial and self-discipline. In the end, Catholic morality wins out: "Modern scientific theories are but mists which some moralists use in their attempts to obscure the teaching of the True Church. But we find that on closer examination these mists disappear leaving the old altars standing."[86]

5 The Upheavals of the 1960s and 1970s: A Time for Revision and a Re-evaluation of Homosexuality (Phase 4)

I have quoted the two theologians from the United States extensively above in order to gauge the comparative importance of the first German-language

---

79 Ibid., 7.
80 Cf. Augustine, *On Nature and Grace*, c. 43, n. 50 (CSEL 60, 270): *non igitur deus inpossibilia iubet*. In this tradition, "God desires our chastity! But if God desires our chastity, then it must also be possible! It is not conceivable or imaginable that something God desires would not be possible, not achievable. God gives us no commandment that cannot be kept," as Josef Wisdorf puts it in *Muß ein Junge daran scheitern?* (Düsseldorf: Altenberg, 1966), 62. The subject here is the gravely sinful "self-abuse."
81 Buckley, *Morality and the Homosexual*, 7.
82 Ibid., 141 (italics in the original).
83 Ibid., 154.
84 Ibid., 184.
85 Ibid., 186.
86 Ibid., 196.

moral-theological monograph on the subject. The study by the Dutch Capuchin Herman van de Spijker (b. 1936) makes one sit up and take notice, even in its title: *Die gleichgeschlechtliche Zuneigung* (Same-Sex Affection).[87] His reflections represent an important milestone in the Catholic evaluation of homosexuality.

Van de Spijker breaks away from the standard comparisons between natural and unnatural or normal and abnormal, both of which make a fact-based ethical debate difficult from the outset. From his perspective, homosexuality (or as he calls it: homotropy) includes three elements: constitution (biology), situation (social context), and position (the individual's opinion of their own sexuality). For the broader moral-theological debate, van de Spijker's theologically and exegetically reflective method of interpreting the relevant biblical texts is trailblazing in comparison to the handbooks. This is especially true with regard to the fateful Sodom narrative, which he de-homosexualizes, noting that the text does not even speak of same-sex affection in the contemporary sense.[88] He asks whether Genesis 19 is primarily about same-sex behavior at all, or whether it in fact concerns a violation of the right to hospitality. Strictly speaking, the Sodom narrative is a story about violently humiliating other men by means of same-sex behavior.[89] Nevertheless, there is no biblical text that condones homosexual acts – or more precisely, same-sex behavior. But as van de Spijker notes, the text's condemnation and disapproval of such behavior is no harsher than it is in the case of immoral heterosexual acts.

In contrast to the handbooks, van de Spijker's text includes extensive testimony gleaned from theological and Church history. In this way, he illuminates historical developments. For example, as he rightly points out, at that time it had only been a few decades since Catholic moral teaching had begun to appreciate sexuality within marital relationships as an expression of love. He then

---

87 The book dates back to his theological licentiate thesis (1966), supervised by Alfons Auer (1915–2005), author of the standard reference work *Autonome Moral und christlicher Glaube* (Autonomous Morality and the Christian Faith; 1st ed. 1971). Due to his position, which deviated from the previous tradition, the author encountered considerable resistance among the Würzburg faculty. He was forbidden to publish his work (private communication, September 28, 2015). In later publications, van de Spijker was able to formulate his plea for homosexuality's personalization more freely and decisively. Cf. Herman van de Spijker, *Homotropie. Menschlichkeit als Rechtfertigung. Überlegungen zur gleichgeschlechtlichen Zuneigung* (Munich: Manz, 1972); idem, *Omotropia nell'orizzonte della eterotropia. La realtà della sessualità umana* (Padua: CLEUP, 2014).

88 Van de Spijker, *Die gleichgeschlechtliche Zuneigung*, 73.

89 See, among others, Hugh Ross Williamson, "Sodom and Homosexuality," *Clergy Review* 48 (1963): 507–514.

makes a reference that opens a new perspective on the question of homosexuality:

> Discussions between theologians and married couples have contributed more than a little to this end. But when it comes to people who are inclined to a partner of the same sex, one obviously sees hardly any compelling reason to speak directly to the people concerned. [...] But one has to get to know these people in order to understand the problems in their lives and, together with them, to seek an answer to the question: "How is our life to be mastered and shaped?"[90]

If one speaks to homosexuals, then one realizes that sexuality can be lovingly practiced beyond the bounds of reproduction as the ultimate goal – even if, according to van de Spijker, the forms homosexual love takes are perhaps still foreign to us. Neither Harvey's nor Buckley's text comes close to van de Spijker's when he asserts: "You have to try to walk a mile in this person's shoes and to love him as he is, and to help him accept himself."[91]

How does van de Spijker evaluate same-sex affection? Let us begin with his view of homosexuality. Biblically as well as anthropologically, the encounter between man and woman is "the highest form of human intersubjectivity."[92] The complementary relationship between a man and a woman constitutes the ideal. Same-sex affection undercuts this "unity in diversity" and is therefore evaluated as "a lack, a diminishment of being, a restriction of the possibilities of existence" – that is, as an existential deficiency.[93] Hetero- and homosexuality are "not ontically equivalent."[94] The idea that homosexuals can change their inclination by an effort of will, as it were, is unrealistic. Therefore the issue is how homosexuals concretely shape their lives. Homosexual acts do not correspond to the order of creation for van de Spijker either. On this he initially remains within the traditionally established norms. For him as well, sublimation is the goal. But he does not break off his reflections at this point. Same-sex affection is human affection, and it can be personalized. Therefore van de Spijker does not consider a homophilic friendship to be evil – it is a *minus bonum*, but still a *bonum*.[95] Homosexuals should be recognized by both the Church and the state simply as they are. This is the basis on which van de Spijker criticizes § 175 of the German Crim-

---

90 Van de Spijker, *Die gleichgeschlechtliche Zuneigung*, 164.
91 Ibid., 165.
92 Ibid., 198.
93 Ibid.
94 Ibid., 200.
95 Ibid., 210.

inal Code as discrimination.[96] Furthermore, he states that the excessively negative evaluation of homosexuality in the history of moral theology also constitutes
morally unjustified unequal treatment.[97] Van de Spijker's nuanced evaluation is
as follows: "A distinction is made between same-sex acts and same-sex affection, between the same-sex act as an expression of love and as selfish gratification."[98] This second differentiation constitutes the novelty of his study. If we take
this idea further, we see that it has the potential to overcome the previous concept that undergirded the traditionally established norms. For why should a
same-sex act be evaluated negatively if it is an expression of love? At the end
of the 1960s, however, van de Spijker cannot yet openly state this conclusion.

Van de Spijker's work is significant because it forms a kind of blueprint for
the section "Zur Problematik der Homosexualität" (On the Issue of Homosexuality) in the working paper "Sinn und Gestaltung menschlicher Sexualität" (The
Meaning and Configuration of Human Sexuality), written by the so-called Würzburg Synod (1971–1975).[99] This paper follows his reasoning right down to the
level of word choice: "A holistic interpretation of homosexuality must start
from the assumption that same-sex affection is usually the result of a certain
inner constitution, an external situation, and a personal opinion provided by
the individual concerned."[100] While Van de Spijker speaks of homosexuality's
existential deficiency, the working paper notes a "limitation of existential possibilities," since the homosexual person misses out on the purpose of human sexuality, which is heterosexual love.[101] The working paper interprets this restriction
theologically – again as in van de Spijker's work – not as guilt, but as a sign of
"humankind's general need for redemption, caused by sin," which is analogous

---

96 Paragraph 175 of the German Criminal Code, according to the version in force between January 9, 1935 and January 9, 1969, provided for punishment (up to ten years in prison) for, among
other things, "a man over twenty-one years of age who entices a male person under twenty-one
years of age to commit fornication with him or to be abused by him for fornication." On the controversial discussion of Paragraph 175 in the Catholic Church and Catholic theology, see Stephan
Goertz, "Sünde und Strafe. Moraltheologische Positionen zur Reform des § 175," *Stimmen der
Zeit* 144 (2019): 837–846.
97 Van de Spijker, *Die gleichgeschlechtliche Zuneigung*, 225.
98 Ibid.
99 Kardinal Karl Lehmann, *Gemeinsame Synode der Bistümer in der Bundesrepublik Deutschland, Offizielle Gesamtausgabe* (Freiburg im Breisgau: Herder, 2012), 163*–183*, esp. 176*ff. on
homosexuality (the sections of the working paper are indicated in the text). According to van
de Spijker, "the text of the Würzburg Synod is largely [...] mine, as I had submitted critical
and acceptable suggestions for improvements to the synodal draft" (personal communication,
September 28, 2015).
100 Lehmann, *Gemeinsame Synode*, 4.4.3.
101 Cf. ibid., 4.4.4.

to "sickness, suffering, and death."[102] Like all other people, homosexuals are "affected by the consequences of original sin."[103] In its ethical evaluation, the working paper adheres to the well-known distinction between affection and behavior. The persons concerned must learn to live with the affection, which is to be shaped positively. As in van de Spijker's text, sublimation is regarded as a sensible form of homosexuality, and friendships are distinguished from promiscuity. "The individual who personalizes his same-sex affection tries to incorporate these drives into the whole person and to put them at the service of personality development."[104] There is no more talk of healing or of a return to normality.

During the counter-culture years of the 1960s and 1970s,[105] several countries saw the emergence of Christian homosexual groups, which came out into the open to advocate for a re-evaluation of homosexuality as well as a dialogue among Christians and within the Church.[106] In moral theology at that time, we see a revision of the previous judgment. Across the entire sphere of human sexuality, it is the quality of the relationship between two persons that is established as the new primary criterion. The primacy of nature's finality gives way to the primacy of the love between two people. Interest in homosexuality's etiology recedes into the background. In the work of Charles Curran (b. 1934), for example, which marks the beginning of this new phase, the experiential question of what exactly homosexuality is all about remains open as late as 1971.[107] Like van de Spijker, Curran prefers to emphasize the distinction between homosexuality in the context of a personal relationship and promiscuous or selfish homosexual behavior. Thus it follows, "for an irreversible or constitutional homosexual, [that] homosexual acts in the context of a loving relationship striving for perma-

---

102 Ibid.

103 Van de Spijker, *Die gleichgeschlechtliche Zuneigung*, 163.

104 Lehmann, *Gemeinsame Synode*, 4.4.5.2.

105 On the characterization of those years and their new sexual practices, see Andreas Reckwitz, *Das hybride Subjekt. Eine Theorie der Subjektkulturen von der bürgerlichen Moderne zur Postmoderne* (Weilerswist: Velbrück, 2006; rev. ed. Berlin: Suhrkamp, 2020).

106 In the USA, Dignity – a group for gay and lesbian Catholics – was formed as early as 1969; in France, David & Jonathan was founded in 1972; in Germany, the ecumenical working group *Homosexuelle und Kirche* (HuK) was founded in 1977.

107 Charles Curran, "Homosexuality and Moral Theology: Methodological and Substantive Considerations," *The Thomist* 35 (1971): 447–481, here 459. See the summary of the article in Curran, *Catholic Moral Theology*, 195: "Curran maintained that homosexual acts in a stable homosexual relationship fall short of the heterosexual ideal but can be justifiable and good for homosexual persons."

nency can be and are morally good."[108] Such sexual practice is not objectively disordered, nor is it merely a lesser evil. Within the context of a personal relationship, such practices "can be and are objectively, morally good."[109] For in such cases, Curran argues, the behavior corresponds to homosexual identity, thereby satisfying the scholastic axiom *agere sequitur esse*. One could also say that the desire for a person of one's own sex is a natural desire for homosexuals. At the same time, Curran wants to hold on to the morally relevant anthropological and theological distinctions between heterosexuality and homosexuality. This idea is taken up by Eberhard Schockenhoff (1953–2020), among others: "We must speak of a specific, objective deficiency of homosexual practice [...] insofar as here the possibility of begetting offspring, as one of the most elementary tasks arising from a heterosexual partnership, is excluded, as is [the possibility of] being shaped by having children together and by the experience of one's own motherhood or fatherhood."[110] Thus human sexuality finds its true purpose (as Curran puts it) or its original, comprehensive meaning (in Schockenhoff's terms) in the relationship between a man and a woman. Heterosexuality remains the "ideal meaning of human sexual relationships"[111] from the perspective of fully realizing sexuality's potential. Thus the familiar theological interpretation endures: "The psychic structure of the irreversible invert constitutes [...] a manifestation of sin in the world."[112]

How can the indisputable difference between heterosexuality and homosexuality be conceptualized in such a way that a moral inequality does not follow from a factual heterogeneity? My suggestion is that one could distinguish the majority variant of sexual orientation (heterosexuality), which is open to the possibility of reproduction under certain circumstances, from the minority variant of sexual orientation (homosexuality), which does not (naturally) correlate with reproduction. Homosexual acts as expressions of love are "completely adequate" personally, but not biologically.[113] To date we can only speculate about whether this distinction carries any evolutionary meaning. In any case, nature has pro-

---

108 Charles Curran, *Transition and Tradition in Moral Theology* (London: University of Notre Dame Press, 1979), 71.
109 Ibid., 73.
110 Eberhard Schockenhoff, "Sexualität, IV. Theologisch-ethisch," in *LThK*, vol. 9, ed. Walter Kasper (Freiburg im Breisgau: Herder, 2000), 518–524, here 523.
111 Curran, *Transition and Tradition*, 71.
112 Ibid., 76.
113 Ruben Schneider, "Gender-Metaphysik und Ontologie der Homosexualität," in *Freiheit ohne Wirklichkeit?* ed. Benedikt P. Göcke and Thomas Schärtl (Münster: Aschendorff-Verlag, 2020), 249–287, here 283.

duced another form of sexuality besides the desire inherently linked to hetero-sexual reproduction. Human beings need to configure this form of sexuality humanely, and while this configuration is not the same as heterosexuality in every respect, it is nevertheless morally equivalent – insofar as the personal level is decisive. No ethical difference can be directly derived from a difference in the reproductive potential of a sexual practice. The morality of sexual practice and the criteria that determine this (such as reciprocity and respect) can be transverse to the (potential) reproductive consequences. The inability to produce offspring cannot be a decisive criterion for sexual morality.[114] In this sense, homosexuality is morally neutral.

This new moral-theological phase in the evaluation of homosexuality, initiated primarily by theologians in the USA,[115] breaks with the traditionally established norm that there is no justification for same-sex sexuality. If a mutually binding and enduring relationship exists, then in principle there is no longer anything to be said against a positive moral evaluation of homosexuality. The criterion of personhood applies to sexual relationships in general, both morally and theologically, and not exclusively to marriage between a man and a woman. In this way, one can put an end to the unequal treatment of heterosexual and homosexual relationships in sexual ethics. Both are equally "under the law of responsibility and love for their partner and for the integrity of their behavior."[116] Such a step is only possible if the postulate of the inseparability of

---

114 Cf. Christof Breitsameter, *Liebe – Formen und Normen. Eine Kulturgeschichte und ihre Folgen* (Freiburg im Breisgau: Herder, 2017), 272–280.

115 See John J. McNeill, *The Church and the Homosexual* (Kansas City: Andrews and McMeel, 1976), esp. 3–9 on the first reform-oriented reflections by John J. McNeill, Peter Fink, Gregory Baum, et al. in the USA in the early 1970s; Philip S. Keane, *Sexual Morality: A Catholic Perspective* (New York: Paulist Press, 1977); Robert Nugent, ed., *A Challenge to Love: Gay and Lesbian Catholics in the Church* (New York: Crossroad, 1983). Important historical studies include D. Sherwin Bailey, *Homosexuality and the Western Christian Tradition* (New York: Longmans, 1955); John Boswell, *Christianity, Social Tolerance, and Homosexuality: Gay People in Western Europe from the Beginning of the Christian Era to the Fourteenth Century* (Chicago: University of Chicago Press, 1980). The US Conference of Catholic Bishops responded as early as 1973, with the statement *Principles to Guide Confessors in Questions of Homosexuality*, which was based primarily on Harvey's writings; cf. McNeill, *The Church and the Homosexual*, 7 f. On developments in the USA, see also Curran, *Catholic Moral Theology*, 195–199. On French-language theology, cf. Guy Ménard, *De Sodome à l'Exode. Jalons pour une théologie de la libération* (Montreal: Guy Saint-Jean, 1980).

116 Johannes Gründel, "Haben Homosexuelle Heimat in der Kirche?" in *Homosexuelle Männer in Kirche und Gesellschaft*, ed. Udo Rauchfleisch (Düsseldorf: Patmos-Verlag, 1993), 40–64, here 63; cf. Bernhard Fraling, *Sexualethik. Ein Versuch aus christlicher Sicht* (Paderborn: Schöningh, 1995), 242.

love and procreation loses its status as the highest criterion for sexual morali-ty.[117] Theological ethicists are beginning to ask whether 'partner reference' as a sexual dimension of meaning can also be independently realized[118] – since this also applies to instances of marital sexuality which are not open to the pos-sibility of procreation (due to sterility, old age, or the "natural" regulation of con-ception). Once the standard of evaluation is no longer the heterogenital comple-mentarity of a man and a woman, and the polyvalence of human sexuality is accepted, there is no longer any ethical argument for requiring homosexuals to commit to complete abstinence. Homosexuality is then no longer considered an inclination to an "intrinsically evil" behavior, which is therefore prohibited at all times and under all circumstances,[119] but can be recognized as an "existen-tial"[120] or a "pre-existent, basic disposition of human sexuality."[121] Consequent-ly, there is no longer any reason to oppress homosexuals with the expectation that they should undergo therapy or convert to heterosexuality.

If a homosexual orientation can be part of a person's identity and the asso-ciated behaviors can be morally good, then anything that stands in the way of homosexuals' self-discovery and self-acceptance is to be avoided. As the Italian moral theologian Martin M. Lintner (b. 1972) writes: "On the part of the Church [...] a pastoral care is called for that helps these people to develop a positive self-esteem, to escape their loneliness or isolation, from which they often suffer, and to overcome the pressure of suffering that is often built up by false feelings of guilt and shame."[122] Forms of subtle or overt violence, pathologization, social ex-clusion, or discrimination – which still exist today, and sometimes come clothed in religious garb – are what must truly be ethically condemned in the context of

---

117 The postulate of the inseparability of conjugal love and reproduction was used for the first time in 1968, in *Humanae vitae* no. 12; see Paul VI, *Encyclical Letter Humanae Vitae* (Rome: Vatican, 1968), http://www.vatican.va/content/paul-vi/en/encyclicals/documents/hf_p-vi_enc_25071968_humanae-vitae.html (accessed April 21, 2021).

118 Wilhelm Korff, "Homosexualität, III. Theologisch-ethisch," in *LThK*, vol. 5, ed. Walter Kas-par (Freiburg im Breisgau: Herder, 1996) 255–258, here 257f.

119 On this category, see Nenad Polgar and Joseph A. Selling, eds., *The Concept of Intrinsic Evil and Catholic Theological Ethics* (Lanham: Lexington Books/Fortress Academic, 2019).

120 Fraling, *Sexualethik*, 241.

121 Udo Rauchfleisch, "Homosexualität, I. Anthropologisch, II. Soziologisch," in *LThK*, vol. 5, ed. Walter Kaspar (Freiburg im Breisgau: Herder, 1996), 254–255, here 254.

122 Martin M. Lintner, *Den Eros entgiften. Plädoyer für eine tragfähige Sexualmoral und Bezie-hungsethik* (Brixen: Weger, 2012), 134. In the sphere of Italian theology, see Enrico Chiavacci, "Omosessualità. Un tema de ristudiare," *RTM* 167 (2010): 469–477; Beatrice Brogliato and Dam-iano Migliorini, *L'amore omosessuale. Saggi di psicoanalisi, teologia e pastorale. In dialogi per una nuova sintesi* (Assisi: Cittadella editrice, 2014). On the Spanish literature, see José Rafael Prada, "La Persona Homosexual," *StMor* 42 (2004): 293–335.

homosexuality. The moral gravity of this new perspective should not be taken lightly: "The critique of gender norms must be situated within the context of lives as they are lived and must be guided by the question of what maximizes the possibilities for a livable life, what minimizes the possibility of unbearable life or, indeed, social or literal death."[123]

The position that characterizes this new moral-theological phase is consistently formulated in Margaret A. Farley's (b. 1935) sexual ethics.[124] It is no longer homosexuality that is the problem, but rather discrimination against it and the fact that it is still an explosive issue in Christian and other religious communities. Farley makes it clear that the fundamental question is not whether same-sex relationships can be ethically justified, but rather how these relationships can be lived out in such a way that we can affirm them in moral terms. Sexual ethics should no longer make a fundamental distinction between heterosexual and homosexual relationships. As Farley summarizes her argument, love is just love "(1) when it does not falsify or 'miss' the reality of the person loved (either as human or as unique individual), (2) when it does not falsify or 'miss' the reality of the one loving, and (3) when it does not violate, distort, or ignore the nature of the relationship between them."[125] There is no special norm for homosexuals apart from this. The rule for them, as for everyone else, is that they must respect every person's dignity and rights, which excludes treating them selfishly, as a mere means to satisfy one's own needs. Homosexual relationships are also fruitful and life-giving (not directly and biologically, but indirectly and socially) through "love for others, care for others, making the world a better place for others than just the 'two of us.'"[126]

6 The Magisterium Breaks Its Silence: The *Persona Humana* Declaration (1975)

Approximately one hundred years elapsed between the conceptualization of homosexuality and the Roman Magisterium's first pronouncement on the subject. Over the course of this century – which was characterized by a struggle for

---

123 Judith Butler, *Undoing Gender* (New York: Routledge, 2004), 8.
124 Margaret A. Farley, *Just Love. A Framework for Christian Sexual Ethics* (New York: Continuum, 2006).
125 Farley, *Just Love*, 202; for an early treatment of this subject, see Margaret A. Farley, "An Ethic for Same-Sex-Relations," in *A Challenge to Love: Gay and Lesbian Catholics in the Church*, ed. Robert Nugent (New York: Crossroad, 1983), 93–106.
126 Farley, *Just Love*, 290.

the decriminalization, depathologization, and de-dramatization of homosexuality – we have been able to distinguish three moral-theological phases:[127] (1) In the first phase, the moral theology handbooks repeat the stereotypes inherent in the traditional judgment on same-sex behavior; use the term sodomy; emphasize the particular gravity of this sin *contra naturam*; and take little or no interest in insights from exegesis or the human sciences. (2) The second phase begins after World War II and addresses the phenomenon of homosexuality in more detail – probably at least in part because pastoral experiences and general cultural developments recommend this course of action; the first extensive moral-theological studies on the subject appear; and the distinction between an (abnormal, pathological) homosexual inclination and homosexual activity (which still constitutes a grave sin) is established. A new argument denies that homosexuals have the full human capacity to love, and homosexuality is still considered a problem. (3) Only in the third phase (since the end of the 1960s) does moral theology strive to make a differentiated assessment – of both sexual orientation and sexual behavior. Traditional semantics are critically assessed and abandoned; positive opportunities for homosexual life are spoken of for the first time, beyond healing or a return to normality; and the relevant biblical texts are approached in a hermeneutically sophisticated way. Under the banner of the primacy of love, the personal level becomes a morally authoritative measure of sexual morality.

The *Persona Humana* declaration, promulgated by the Congregation for the Doctrine of the Faith on December 29, 1975, is to be interpreted as a reaction to the upheavals in the spheres of sexual morality and gender relations in Western societies, which accelerated at the end of the 1960s and the beginning of the 1970s.[128] In the Congregation's judgment, as expressed at the very beginning of the document, this represents serious moral decay, which leaves Christian life "very much unsettled" and makes the proclamation of "sound doctrine" difficult.[129] In contrast to the last Council's teaching, *Persona Humana* considers respect for the natural goal of sexuality a primary moral principle in the sphere of

---

127 For a different breakdown of the development, albeit one that likewise amounts to a phase in which homosexuality came to be accepted, cf. James B. Nelson, "Homosexuality," in *The Westminster Dictionary of Christian Ethics*, ed. James F. Childress and John Macquarrie (Philadelphia: Westminster Press, 1986), 271–274.

128 Congregation for the Doctrine of the Faith, *Persona humana: Declaration on Certain Questions Concerning Sexual Ethics* (Rome: Vatican, 1975), http://www.vatican.va/roman_curia/con gregations/cfaith/documents/rc_con_cfaith_doc_19751229_persona-humana_en.html (accessed April 21, 2021).

129 Ibid., nos. 1 and 13, respectively.

sexuality. The law of nature is the law of God.[130] In *Persona Humana*, it is the "constitutive elements of human nature" that establish the moral order.[131] Homosexuality is by no means the central theme among the "abuses of the sexual faculty" discussed.[132] Masturbation is discussed in greater detail, as was customary in the past, and so is extramarital sexuality. The section on homosexuality comprises only one page.

The passage begins with the observation that in the present day, some people judge homosexual relationships leniently, or even excuse them completely: "This they do in opposition to the constant teaching of the Magisterium and to the moral sense of the Christian people."[133] In view of the fact that *Persona Humana* number 8 is the very first statement the Roman Magisterium makes on homosexuality, this is an astonishing remark. While one can speak of consistent, established moral-theological norms, the Magisterium shaped a consistent doctrine on homosexuality only after this declaration was made. Therefore, in contrast to the sections on masturbation, there are no references to earlier magisterial statements in *Persona Humana* number 8.

In this declaration, homosexuality is considered either a (curable) inclination or an (incurable) pathological "innate instinct."[134] However, this should by no means be taken as a basis – and we have already encountered this warning – for the justification of marriage-like homosexual relationships. In contrast to the positive identification of sexuality as a formative factor in human personhood, homosexuality is presented either as a (surmountable) inclination or as an innate, abnormal, pathological drive. The integrative understanding evident in *Persona Humana* number 1 – the idea that sexuality defines the whole human person – is still applied solely to heterosexuality.

The text addresses pastoral care only briefly. Homosexual people "must certainly be treated with understanding and sustained in the hope of overcoming their personal difficulties and their inability to fit into society," and thus "their culpability will be judged with prudence."[135] Nevertheless, it is also true that, "according to the objective moral order, homosexual relations are acts which lack an essential and indispensable goal. In Sacred Scripture they are condemned as a serious depravity and even presented as the sad consequence of

---

130 Cf. ibid., no. 5.
131 Ibid., no 4.
132 Ibid., no. 6.
133 Ibid., no. 8. This raises the question of whether those believers who cannot share the stance put forward in the declaration are not to be counted as part of the Christian people.
134 Congregation for the Doctrine of the Faith, *Persona Humana*, no. 8.
135 Ibid.

rejecting God."[136] The text cites Romans 1:24–27 – that is, the Pauline statement – as evidence from the New Testament to support its understanding of natural law.[137] However, there are no citations of Old Testament passages; the Sodom narrative no longer appears. Furthermore, the dramatic condemnation of "sodomy" as a "sin that cries out to heaven" is also avoided. In conclusion, the Congregation for the Doctrine of the Faith states that homosexuals are not generally to be held responsible for their condition, but notwithstanding this, the section concludes that homosexual acts are "intrinsically disordered and can in no case be approved of."[138]

In contrast to many previous statements on the subject, this text is comparatively moderate in its moral condemnation of homosexuality and quite traditional in the established norms it upholds. It omits casuistic considerations, and while it makes a distinction between inclination and action, it makes none between friendship and promiscuity. There is no positive statement about a homosexual lifestyle. *Persona Humana* aims at demarcation: not only with regard to the shift in social approaches to homosexuality, but also with reference to the human sciences, which it indicates are ultimately irrelevant to ethical questions.[139]

If we compare *Persona Humana* with the phases I have identified above, the influence of Harvey's and Buckley's positions is clearly recognizable (see phase 3). This prevents a differentiated assessment of homosexual acts, especially since the experience of the persons concerned is given no space in the official Catholic document. In *Humanae vitae* in 1968, Pope Paul VI postulates the God-given inseparability between sexual devotion in the context of marriage and procreation. This has a direct effect on the ethical assessment of homosexuality because it establishes a definitive norm, according to which humankind may not break the "connection [...] between the unitive significance and the procreative

---

136 Ibid.
137 Romans 1:26–27: "For this reason God gave them up to degrading passions. Their women exchanged natural intercourse for unnatural, and in the same way also the men, giving up natural intercourse with women, were consumed with passion for one another. Men committed shameless acts with men and received in their own persons the due penalty for their error." On this point, see Wucherpfennig, *Sexualität bei Paulus*, 106–115; see also Michael Theobald's contribution in this volume.
138 Congregation for the Doctrine of the Faith, *Persona Humana*, no. 8.
139 Cf. the critique in Alfons Auer, Wilhelm Korff, and Gerhard Lohfink, "Zweierlei Sexualethik. Kritische Bemerkungen zur 'Erklärung' der römischen Glaubenskongregation 'Zu einigen Fragen der Sexualethik,'" *ThQ* 156 (1976): 148–158. At that time, Hans Küng and Walter Kasper (among others) declared themselves to be in agreement with this Tübingen text.

significance" under any circumstances.[140] Homosexual behavior is always a violation of the objective moral order, and therefore an intrinsically evil act. This stance would not change in subsequent decades. Just three years after *Persona Humana* was published, on a pastoral trip to the USA, Pope John Paul II praised the bishops for their clear moral disapproval of homosexual acts.[141] Thus he became the first pope to speak out on homosexuality, asserting that understanding and compassion should not lead one to refuse to proclaim the truth – that is, the divine plan for human sexuality, according to the Magisterium's binding interpretation. The pope also drew homosexuality into the conflict he constructed between a Christian "culture of life" and an un-Christian "culture of death."

7 Confirming the Magisterial Position with New Accents (1978 to 2013)

During John Paul II's papacy (1978–2005),[142] various congregations and papal councils took positions on different aspects of homosexuality. The pope himself also affirmed the doctrine in his encyclical *Veritatis splendor*.[143] Thus a tradition was formed that reached back to *Persona Humana*, found its way into the Catechism of the Catholic Church, and influenced subsequent Catholic reactions,

---

140 Paul VI, *Humanae vitae*, no. 12. Karol Wojtyła's influence on this postulate is substantiated in Michael J. Barberi and Joseph A. Selling, "The Origin of *Humanae Vitae* and the Impasse in Fundamental Theological Ethics," *Louvain Studies* 37 (2013): 364–389. In 1967, Harvey had already noted: "As soon as one separates completely the procreative function of the reproductive organs and of the marital act from their personal and individual values, there remains no principle 'by which any mutual act of two people, married or unmarried, of opposite sexes, or of the same sex, can be condemned as immoral, if they simply state that this is the way they choose to express their mutual love' [J. Du Hamel, *The Catholic Church and Birth Control* (Paulist Press Pamphlet 1962), 17]"; see "Homosexuality" (1967), 117 f. In this version of Catholic sexual morality, the inseparability postulate ranks higher than the mutual love between two people.
141 See John Paul II, "Apostolic Journey to the United States of America. To the Bishops of the United States of America," *AAS* 71 (1979): 1218–1229, here 1224 f.
142 Cf. Magnus Striet and Stephan Goertz, eds., *Johannes Paul II. – Vermächtnis und Hypothek eines Pontifikats*, Katholizismus im Umbruch 12 (Freiburg im Breisgau: Herder, 2020).
143 John Paul II, *Encyclical: Veritatis splendor* (Rome: Vatican, 1993), http://www.vatican.va/content/john-paul-ii/en/encyclicals/documents/hf_jp-ii_enc_06081993_veritatis-splendor.html (accessed April 21, 2021). On this encyclical, which has been the subject of intense moral theological debate, see Dietmar Mieth, ed., *Moraltheologie im Abseits? Antwort auf die Enzyklika "Veritatis splendor"* (QD 153; Freiburg im Breisgau: Herder, 1994); Joseph A. Selling and Jan Jans, eds., *The Splendor of Accuracy* (Kampen: Kok Pharos, 1994); Raphael Gallagher, "The Reception of *Veritatis splendor* within the Theological Community," *StMor* 33, no. 2 (1995): 415–435.

even under Benedict XVI (2005–2013), who was instrumental in shaping the Vatican position on homosexuality as prefect of the Congregation for the Doctrine of the Faith from 1982 to 2005.[144]

7.1 The Congregation for Catholic Education

This process began with *Educational Guidance in Human Love*, published by the Congregation for Catholic Education in 1983.[145] Although, as we have seen above, the moral-theological debate had been gaining momentum since the 1970s and new assessment criteria had been established, the Congregation for Education essentially limits itself to repeating the statements made in *Persona Humana*. Homosexuality remains a serious, objective problem for the persons concerned, because it prevents them from developing mature interpersonal relationships. While this document once again expresses understanding and offers help, the idea of positive self-acceptance among homosexuals is nevertheless absent. The document is concerned with "encouraging the emancipation of the individual and his or her growth in self-control, promoting an authentic moral force towards conversion to the love of God and neighbour."[146] As we saw in the texts from the 1950s presented above, support from doctors and psychologists is deemed helpful only if they recognize and respect the Church's teaching.[147]

144 Cf. Patricia Beattie Jung, "The Roman Catholic Tradition," in *Homosexuality and Religion*, ed. Jeffrey S. Siker (Connecticut: Greenwood Press, 2007), 191–200. On Joseph Ratzinger's role, see Case, "After Gender," 806–817. Ratzinger holds gender theory jointly responsible for the acceptance of homosexuality, since from his perspective, whoever questions the difference between or duality of man and woman also regards heterosexuality and homosexuality as equal. See Congregation for the Doctrine of the Faith, *Letter to the Bishops of the Catholic Church on the Collaboration of Men and Women* (Rome: Vatican, 2004), no. 2, http://www.vatican.va/roman_curia/congregations/cfaith/documents/rc_con_cfaith_doc_20040731_collaboration_en.html (accessed April 21, 2021).
145 Congregation for Catholic Education, *Educational Guidance in Human Love: Outlines for Sex Education* (Rome: Vatican, 1983), http://www.vatican.va/roman_curia/congregations/ccatheduc/documents/rc_con_ccatheduc_doc_19831101_sexual-education_en.html (accessed April 21, 2021).
146 Ibid., no. 103.
147 Cf. ibid.

7.2 The Congregation for the Doctrine of the Faith

As the moral-theological discussion progressed in tandem with the Magisterium's pronouncements – which lagged behind theological, social, and human-scientific developments – the Congregation for the Doctrine of the Faith felt compelled to issue a more comprehensive statement in 1986, addressed to the bishops of the Catholic Church and published under the eloquent title *Homosexualitatis problema*.[148] Although the title also refers to the "pastoral care of homosexual persons," as in *Persona Humana*, the content of the document is primarily concerned with the formulation of a moral-theological doctrine. For the Congregation, the principle is as follows: "Only what is true can ultimately be pastoral," which means that "a truly pastoral approach will appreciate the need for homosexual persons to avoid the near occasions of sin."[149] This letter is a concerned reaction to the development of arguments and positions, even in Catholic circles, which view the "homosexual condition" favorably, or describe it as "neutral, or even good," and which are therefore "inconsistent with the teaching of the Catholic Church."[150]

By way of introduction, the text reminds the reader that comprehensive Catholic truth surpasses scientific findings.[151] Even if there is a contemporary push to treat homosexuality differently, from the perspective of Catholic morality it remains a problem. The entire letter is written under this banner. The distinction between "homosexual condition or tendency and individual homosexual actions" is restated and clarified in a way that will prove decisive for the subsequent decades: "Although the particular inclination of the homosexual person is not a sin, it is a more or less strong tendency ordered toward an intrinsic moral evil; and thus the inclination itself must be seen as an objective disorder."[152] The term "pathological constitution," used in *Persona Humana* number 8, is not taken up here. In contrast, the Congregation for the Doctrine of the Faith deals relatively extensively with the "gravely erroneous" view that Sacred Scripture "has nothing to say on the subject of homosexuality" or that its direc-

---

148 Congregation for the Doctrine of the Faith, "*Letter to the Bishops of the Catholic Church on the Pastoral Care of Homosexual Persons Homosexualitatis problema*," *AAS 79* (1987): 543–554. The letter is also available on the Vatican website, but interestingly without the subtitle *Homosexualitatis problema*: http://www.vatican.va/roman_curia/congregations/cfaith/documents/rc_con_cfaith_doc_19861001_homosexual-persons_en.html (accessed April 21, 2021).
149 Ibid., no. 15.
150 Ibid., nos. 3 and 1, respectively.
151 Ibid., no. 2.
152 Ibid., no. 3.

tives should be attributed to the cultural context of the time.[153] The hermeneutical rule applied to the subsequent biblical considerations is that, "to be correct," the interpretation of Scripture must be "in substantial accord" with that handed down by the Church.[154] Thus the traditionally established norm is affirmed. If the biblical texts that address same-sex behavior are to be read on the basis of the magisterial history of interpretation, then this would seem to render that interpretation immune to criticism.[155] According to the Congregation for the Doctrine of the Faith, the exegetical findings of the previous decades (together with their moral-theological reception) do not seem to be a relevant stage in the history of the interpretation of Holy Scripture.

The letter then turns to an interpretation of the biblical creation narrative in terms of the complementarity of man and woman, and the transmission of life. This truth is obscured as a result of original sin – a process which continues in the degeneration of the men of Sodom: "There can be no doubt of the moral judgement made there against homosexual relations."[156] This consistent, uninterrupted teaching is witnessed in Leviticus 18:22 and 20:13; 1 Corinthians 1:6 – 9; Romans 1:18 – 32; and 1 Timothy 1:10, and therefore constitutes a "theocratic law."[157] In contrast to the doubts and inquiries evident in both exegesis and moral theology, the Congregation is convinced that the Bible clearly condemns homosexual behavior. We can agree with the letter to the extent that same-sex behavior has indeed been condemned in the past, but this fact does not provide a conclusive answer to the question of how homosexuality should be evaluated ethically. Since the benchmark of magisterial sexual morality is opposite-sex behavior, the Congregation for the Doctrine of the Faith concludes that homosexuality can never be practiced in a morally responsible way. "Homosexual activity is not a complementary union, able to transmit life."[158] Moreover,

---

153 Ibid., no. 4. On the exegesis in the document, see Gerald D. Coleman, "The Vatican Statement on Homosexuality," *TS* 48 (1987): 727–734, esp. 728 – 731; on the document as a whole, see Jeannine Gramick and Pat Furey, eds., *The Vatican and Homosexuality* (New York: Crossroad, 1988).

154 Congregation for the Doctrine of the Faith, *Letter to the Bishops of the Catholic Church*, no. 5.

155 Jacobitz ("Seminary," 96) argues that the CDF "turns toward the Bible in a way that is completely strange to the Catholic natural law theory; that is, it employs an uncritical prooftexting reminiscent of Christian fundamentalism."

156 Congregation for the Doctrine of the Faith, *Letter to the Bishops of the Catholic Church*, no. 6.

157 Ibid.

158 Ibid., no. 7. The term complementarity appeared on the Catholic theological stage in the first half of the twentieth century; on the importance of Dietrich von Hildebrand and Edith Stein in this context, see Prudence Allen, "Man–Woman Complementarity: The Catholic Inspi-

homosexuals miss out on the essence of Christian self-giving: "This does not mean that homosexual persons are not often generous and giving of themselves; but when they engage in homosexual activity they confirm within themselves a disordered sexual inclination which is essentially self-indulgent."[159] The letter takes up the moral theology of the 1950s in its conclusion, stating that the unhappiness homosexuals experience is the result of their own actions, because they act in a way that is "contrary to the creative wisdom of God" and thus do not obey the order of creation.[160] The Congregation recognizes no social or ecclesiastical complicity in the suffering of homosexual persons.

Furthermore, the letter portrays groups – both within and outside the Church – that seek an ethical reassessment and social recognition of homosexuality as threatening. At this point, the letter becomes lachrymose and is not squeamish in its choice of words. Such groups have tried to manipulate the Church, have used "deceitful propaganda," and have claimed "that any and all criticisms of or reservations about homosexual people, their activity and lifestyle, are simply diverse forms of unjust discrimination."[161] Thus the letter discredits liberal attitudes,[162] insinuating that every defense of the Church's traditional attitude to homosexuality and every criticism of modern liberality in contemporary society is

---

ration," *Logos* 9, no. 3 (2006): 87–108. The complementarity of the sexes plays a central role in what John Paul II refers to as "new feminism"; cf. Léonie Caldecott, "Sincere Gift: The Pope's 'New Feminism,'" in *John Paul II and Moral Theology*, ed. Charles E. Currran and Richard A. McCormick (New York: Paulist Press, 1998), 216–234; Susan A. Ross, "The Bridegroom and the Bride. The Theological Anthropology of John Paul II and Its Relation to the Bible and Homosexuality," in *Sexual Diversity and Catholicism. Toward the Development of Moral Theology*, ed. Patricia Beattie Jung and Joseph A. Coray (Collegeville, MN: Liturgical Press, 2001), 39–59; Edward C. Vacek, "Feminism and the Vatican," *TS* 66 (2005): 159–177.

159 Congregation for the Doctrine of the Faith, *Letter to the Bishops of the Catholic Church*, no. 7.
160 Cf. Buckley, *Morality and the Homosexual*, 156: "This unhappiness follows, not so much from the condemnation of society as such, but from the unnaturalness of his whole attitude to life."
161 Congregation for the Doctrine of the Faith, *Letter to the Bishops of the Catholic Church*, no. 9.
162 Cf. Anatrella, "Homosexualität," 370–372. Anatrella speaks of an "idea police (political correctness) that uses homophobia as a byword to inject heterosexuals with feelings of sexual guilt" (p. 370). "A dictatorship of morals or of ideas is erecting itself on the basis of criteria that are incompatible with the spiritual and moral values that constitute the couple, the marriage, the family, and lines of descent. How can one fail to see that so-called democratic society is thus fragmenting social cohesion in favor of particular interests, and to the detriment of the general best interest, thus discouraging and depressing its citizens?" (p. 372). Here the mass media plays the "role of the moral censor" (p. 371). It is not surprising that Dignity USA protested when Anatrella was appointed to as a "collaborator" of the Special Secretary at the Third Extraordinary General Assembly of the Synod of Bishops in 2014, also known as the Synod on the Family.

morally condemned from the outset as discrimination (or later as homophobia). That such a strategy is indeed encountered in political debate is undeniable, but this is not a solid argument with regard to the issue at hand. If homosexuals are denied access to socially recognized institutions on the basis of a double standard of sexual morality, then this might indeed constitute unjustified discrimination and unequal treatment. Simply to assert that one does not wish to discriminate is by no means to address the dispute over which unequal treatment is justified and which is not. Thus the letter touches on a topic that will increasingly come to the fore in subsequent years: Should "civil-statutes and laws" be changed in the interests of emancipation and democratization? The letter recognizes no reason whatsoever for such changes.[163]

In one key passage, the text produces an explosive ambiguity. On the one hand, it deplores the fact "that homosexual persons have been and are the object of violent malice in speech or in action."[164] Such behavior is contrary to respect for human dignity. On the other hand, those who aggressively advocate a reassessment of homosexuality are indirectly made jointly responsible for "irra-

---

163 Congregation for the Doctrine of the Faith, *Letter to the Bishops of the Catholic Church*, no. 9; cf. Congregation for the Doctrine of the Faith, *Considerations Regarding Proposals to Give Legal Recognition to Unions Between Homosexual Persons* (Rome: Vatican, 2003), http://www.vatican.va/roman_curia/congregations/cfaith/documents/rc_con_cfaith_doc_20030731_ho mosexual-unions_en.html (accessed April 21, 2021): "There are absolutely no grounds for considering homosexual unions to be in any way similar or even remotely analogous to God's plan for marriage and family. Marriage is holy, while homosexual acts go against the natural law" (no. 4). "In those situations where homosexual unions have been legally recognized or have been given the legal status and rights belonging to marriage, clear and emphatic opposition is a duty" (no. 5). In view of Rome's clear position on this matter, Pope Francis's divergent statement, made public in October 2020 in the documentary film *Francesco* (directed by Yevgeny Afineyevsky), received worldwide attention: according to the pope, society should permit same-sex couples a "civil partnership" (as distinct from marriage). On the implications of this, see Hans Rotter, "Ehe und homosexuelle Partnerschaft. Vergleichbares und Unterscheidendes in moraltheologischer Sicht," in *Eingetragene Lebenspartnerschaft. Rechtssicherheit für homosexuelle Paare – Angriff auf Ehe und Familie?* ed. Harmut Bosinski et al. (Regensburg: Pustet, 2001), 30–44: "Against the background of our Christian tradition, the assessment of a homosexual relationship essentially depends on whether one considers this relationship to be sinful in itself, and therefore also immoral. If so, then one will of course also be against a legal revaluation. If not, then justice seems to require such a revaluation in some respects" (p. 44). On this topic, see also Stephan Goertz, "Zwischen Ablehnung und Anerkennung. Katholische Stellungnahmen zur gleichgeschlechtlichen Ehe in Deutschland, " *Family Forum* 7 (2017): 35–54 (open access); and, with a slightly different emphasis, Konrad Hilpert's contribution in this volume.
164 Congregation for the Doctrine of the Faith, *Letter to the Bishops of the Catholic Church*, no. 10.

tional and violent reactions."[165] This approach comes very close to what is known as victim-blaming: those in a disadvantaged position who advocate for the evolution of human rights seem to be complicit in the outcome when their cause meets with vigorous resistance.

The letter's religious proposition to homosexuals deserves particular theological attention. If homosexual persons believe in Christ, then they should realize that their suffering can be united with the "sacrifice of the Lord's Cross";[166] indeed, "you cannot belong to Christ unless you crucify all self-indulgent passions and desires" (Gal 5:24). Homosexuals who submit to God's will by following Christ will be saved from a life "which constantly threatens to destroy them."[167] But what does it mean "to sacrifice one's own will" in this context? This clearly relates to a particular sexual asceticism that is required of homosexuals. However, this connection between homosexuality and the sacrifice of Christ on the cross is only plausible if one concedes the premise that homosexuality is intrinsically disordered. The real question, however, is whether or not the burdens which the Church's moral teaching places on homosexuals are morally justified. Concealing the ethically dubious restrictions on homosexuals' lives and opportunities which the Church's moral teaching entails by characterizing them as a way of following Christ can open the door to spiritual abuse. However, if one understands the cross of Jesus as a manifestation of a divine empathy which does not shrink from human pain and suffering, as Paul G. Crowley does, then one comes to different conclusions.[168] Christ who was crucified is a witness to the love of God, who gave himself fully to humankind.[169] For all who believe, the cross is intrinsically connected to the message that Almighty God uses no means other than his love to win human hearts. The Christian mes-

---

165 Ibid.

166 Ibid., no. 12.

167 Ibid. Cf. Andrew Sullivan, "Alone Again, Naturally: The Catholic Church and the Homosexual (1994)," in *Theology and Sexuality*, ed. Eugene F. Rogers (Malden: Blackwell Publishing, 2007), 275–288, esp. 282, where Sullivan characterizes this passage from 1986 as an "ugly reference to HIV."

168 Cf. Paul G. Crowley, "Homosexuality and the Counsel of the Cross," *TS* 65 (2004): 500–529. After the Congregation for the Doctrine of the Faith requested a clarification, Crowley made the following statement in his paper "Homosexuality and the Counsel of the Cross: A Clarification," *TS 69* (2008): 637–640: "The article does not intend to deny the teaching of the magisterium about the objective disorder of homosexual inclination or homosexual acts. Rather, it intends to ask how the counsel of the Cross built on these formulations can speak with better effect and impart a sense of hope for those for whom it is intended" (p. 640).

169 Cf. Magnus Striet, *In der Gottesschleife. Von religiöser Sehnsucht in der Moderne* (Freiburg im Breisgau: Herder, 2014), 168 f.

sage to human beings – both heterosexual and homosexual – is a message of loving self-transcendence, not of physical self-denial.

One final reflection concerns a formulation that raises a new idea. The Congregation for the Doctrine of the Faith makes a point of speaking of the "homosexual person."[170] In doing so, it seeks to clarify that homosexuals are first and foremost persons, who also have a particular sexual orientation. To use the Congregation's own terminology, it is therefore the sexual inclination that is "disordered," not the person. A persons is thus more than a particular sexual being. Their "fundamental identity" as God's beloved creature subsumes all differences.[171] Making distinctions between people according to their sexual orientation or gender identity is therefore always secondary to their fundamental dignity as persons. But if the common dignity of all people constitutes the foundation of the Church's doctrine, then questions regarding the human rights of sexual minorities can also be answered differently than they have been in the magisterial documents to date. From the very beginning, the letter emphasizes that it does not seek to present an "exhaustive treatment of this complex issue,"[172] and therefore the theological discussion is not yet closed.

All things considered, the 1986 letter can be characterized as Janus-faced. It dispenses with the conventional language of natural law, but the established norms it embraces spring from the natural law mindset, which I have outlined above. It leans heavily on a biblical foundation, but it reactivates precisely those historically loaded biblical narratives (Sodom) and texts (Leviticus) which were not cited in *Persona Humana*. It speaks of the homosexual person, but simultaneously calls such persons to self-denial.[173] It states that it does not seek to discriminate, but it does not align itself with anti-discrimination policies. It distinguishes between inclination and action, but not between just (or loving) and unjust (or unloving) relationships. Taken together, this signifies that,

> [i]n the magisterial documents, a person's deepest and most important disposition (namely, their disposition to love and its physical expression) is unequivocally described as a permanent disposition toward intrinsic moral evil, inscribed in the deepest dimension of their being: According to the Church's teaching, homosexuals, in their disposition to love, are

---

170 Congregation for the Doctrine of the Faith, *Letter to the Bishops of the Catholic Church*, no. 16.

171 Ibid.

172 Ibid., no. 2.

173 Sullivan, "Alone Again," 282: "Ratzinger had guided the Church into two simultaneous and opposite directions: a deeper respect for homosexuals, and a sterner rejection of almost anything they might do."

intrinsically disposed to the ultimate abyss of separation from God – their love actually *is* the abyss that leads to perdition.[174]

7.3 The Catechism of the Catholic Church

The previous magisterial statements are condensed in the Catechism of the Catholic Church, promulgated in 1993. Evaluating this document requires a close reading. In the familiar language of natural law, the established norm is justified in that homosexual acts are designated as "contrary to the natural law," because homosexuality excludes the possibility of the transmission of life.[175] This reproductive deficit corresponds to a personal one, since homosexual relationships lack the aspect of complementarity that obtains in a relationship between a man and a woman. Moreover, Scripture characterizes such acts as "grave depravity."[176] A footnote refers to the familiar biblical texts, omitting the two passages from the book of Leviticus. This restatement of the established norm is followed by a shorter passage on homosexual inclination, which is not a choice. Therefore homosexuals "must be accepted with respect, compassion, and sensitivity. Every sign of unjust discrimination in their regard should be avoided."[177] Then, following the example of the 1986 declaration, the text makes reference to Jesus's sacrifice on the cross. Homosexuals are called to chastity, which for them – as for all unmarried people – means complete sexual abstinence.[178] Initially the Catechism avoids the concept of sin, contenting itself with the statement that homosexual behavior is "intrinsically disordered" (with reference to *Persona Humana* no. 8). However, in a subsequent section titled "In Brief," it states: "Among the sins gravely contrary to chastity are masturbation, fornication, pornography, and homosexual practices."[179]

Some of the statements in the Catechism seem to have been perceived as misleading, to the extent that a remarkable change occurred in the revised Latin version, published in 1997. Whereas previously homosexuality was described as a disposition not of one's own choosing, the revised document refers

---

174 Schneider, "Gender-Metaphysik," 269.
175 Catechism of the Catholic Church (Rome: Vatican, 1993), no. 2357, https://www.vatican.va/archive/ENG0015/__P85.HTM (accessed April 21, 2021).
176 Ibid.
177 Ibid., no. 2358.
178 Ibid., no. 2359.
179 Ibid., no. 2396.

to "deep-seated homosexual tendencies."[180] Additional wording from the letter *Homosexualitatis problema* (no. 3) has also been added, namely: "this inclination, which is objectively disordered."

Information on the intention behind these changes can be found in a commentary by Livio Melina, who worked in the Congregation for the Doctrine of the Faith between 1984 and 1991, and was appointed president of the Pontifical John Paul II Institute for Studies on Marriage and Family by Pope Benedict XVI in 2006. According to Melina, any impression that homosexuality should be placed on the same level as heterosexuality – which one might assume based on the reference to an innate disposition – must be avoided. There should be no doubt about the abnormality of homosexuality: "Psychoanalysts emphasize that gender identity is not so much a 'natural' capacity as it is the subject's response to an insufficient reality that raises questions."[181] Homosexuality thus becomes – albeit in quotation marks – a personal "statement" or "decision." Does this mean that the person is to be held responsible for their sexual orientation once again, and that homosexuality – as a "mindset" – is to be declared a sin after all?[182] One thing is clear: homosexuality should not be interpreted as a natural variant of sexual orientation. The "very concept of sexual orientation [...] has been downplayed by the Vatican in favor of an approach that treats homosexuality simply as a tendency or inclination immediately ordered to a set of specific genital acts,"[183] as in the old handbooks I have described above. That is why the magisterial texts do not state that there are persons who are homosexual. Instead, contrary to contemporary scientific findings, the text speaks of men and women with "deep-seated homosexual tendencies." The Roman Magisterium sees no symmetry whatsoever between homosexuality and heterosexuality – not on the level of the phenomenon itself, and certainly not on the level of moral evaluation.

Does the Magisterium consider homosexuality, as an "intrinsically disordered" act, a grave sin as well? The Catechism seems to be undecided on this

---

180 Ibid., no. 2358. Regarding this use of language, Harald Dreßing and his colleagues noted that "the idiosyncratic terminology used by the Church [...] such as that of 'deep-seated homosexual tendencies,' lacks any scientific basis"; see Harald Dreßing et al., *Sexueller Missbrauch an Minderjährigen durch katholische Priester, Diakone und männliche Ordensangehörige im Bereich der Deutschen Bischofskonferenz* (Mannheim: MHG, 2018), 17.

181 Livio Melina, *Liebe auf katholisch. Ein Handbuch für heute* (Augsburg: Sankt-Ulrich-Verlag, 2009), 123–128, here 126. The Italian edition is *Per una cultura della famiglia: il linguaggio dell'amore* (Venice: Marcianum Press, 2006), 124. The authors Melina mentions who consider homosexuality a psychopathological disorder include Kernberg, Anatrella, and Harvey.

182 Cf. ibid., 132.

183 Jacobitz, "Seminary," 88.

point. However, we can be in no doubt about John Paul II's judgment. In the 1984 *Post-Synodal Apostolic Exhortation Reconciliatio et paenitentia*, he makes reference to the various forms of fornication condemned in Leviticus 18:26 – 30, including same-sex behavior, which Church tradition classifies among the mortal sins.[184] The 1993 encyclical *Veritatis splendor*, number 49, refers back to this document. Thus John Paul II condemns homosexual behavior as a mortal sin, as had been done in the past. In general, it is worth our while to study *Veritatis splendor* numbers 47 – 50 more closely. Here the Magisterium defends itself against moral-theological critiques of its condemnation of contraception and homosexual relations, among other things.

> In the opinion of these same theologians, a morally negative evaluation of such acts fails to take into adequate consideration both man's character as a rational and free being and the cultural conditioning of all moral norms. In their view, man, as a rational being, not only can but actually *must freely determine the meaning* of his behaviour. [...] Love of neighbour would mean above all and even exclusively respect for his freedom to make his own decisions.[185]

The encyclical counters this with the assertion that a proper assessment of homosexuality must be based upon the "correct relationship between freedom and human nature, and in particular *the place of the human body in questions of natural law*."[186] It is not the person-to-person relationship that is decisive, but the relationship a person has to their own body. Those who do not consider homosexuality a problem also consider the human body "devoid of any meaning and moral values." For John Paul II, a person can discover in their body "the promise of the gift of self, in conformity with the wise plan of the Creator."[187] For the pope, every person – "in the unity of body and soul" – must respect their sexuality's orientation toward reproduction, which is ordained through either the male or the female body. It is not without reason that the encyclical speaks in scholastic terms of "the specific moral value of certain good towards which the person is naturally inclined (*inclinationes naturales*)" at this point.[188] In this context, the "good" is the preservation of the species. Whoever does not respect this good – for example, through homosexual behavior – "would fall into

---

184 John Paul II, *Post-Synodal Apostolic Exhortation: Reconciliation and Penance* (Rome: Vatican, 1984), no. 17, http://www.vatican.va/content/john-paul-ii/en/apost_exhortations/docu ments/hf_jp-ii_exh_02121984_reconciliatio-et-paenitentia.html (accessed April 21, 2021).
185 John Paul II, *Veritatis splendor*, no. 47, italics in the original.
186 Ibid., no. 48, italics in the original.
187 Ibid.
188 Ibid.

relativism and arbitrariness."[189] As in the works of Thomas Aquinas and in the handbooks, a short theological passage is appended to the ethical argumentation, which makes reference to the two authorities of Scripture and tradition, which unanimously (with reference to 1 Cor 6:9–10, 19 as well as the Council of Trent [DH 1544]) classify homosexuality as a mortal sin that excludes one from the kingdom of God.[190]

That which is presented here as the harmony of nature and freedom[191] is in fact the continuation of the traditional primacy of nature in sexual morality – or more precisely, the primacy of the natural pursuit of the preservation of the species. All the other purposes which sexuality might serve – for example, the expression and promotion of love – are subordinated to this function, as usual. It seems inconceivable to John Paul II or to Joseph Ratzinger/Benedict XVI that the complementary body for which a homosexual person longs in their unity of body and soul is the body of a person of their own sex.[192] The Magisterium believes that whoever refuses to condemn homosexuality in moral terms is thinking in dualistic terms, because such a person ignores the human body's moral message. But one can also turn the tables here: if the Magisterium calls homosexuals to abstinence because homosexual orientation is contrary to nature, then it dualistically disregards the connection between sexuality and personhood, which is natural for homosexuals as well as for heterosexuals.[193]

On the whole, the mindset exemplified by John Paul II and Joseph Ratzinger/ Benedict XVI, which shaped Church documents and policy between 1978 and 2013, remains within the moral-theological phase that developed in the 1950s. The concept of homosexuality as a standard variant of human sexuality is not approved. Homosexuality remains a problem first and foremost, and as such it represents a trial for the homosexual person. From this perspective, homosexuals are incapable of forming a true love relationship, because true love can only arise in the context of the complementary relationship between a man and a woman. On this issue, the Church offers its clear knowledge of moral truth and its spirituality as support. Anything that could lead to the moral or legal recognition of homosexuality is rejected. The traditional judgment of same-sex be-

---

189 Ibid.
190 Ibid., no. 49.
191 Ibid., no. 40.
192 Cf. Todd A. Salzman and Michael Lawler, *Sexual Ethics. A Theological Introduction* (Washington, DC: Georgetown University Press, 2012), 62–83; see also the contribution by the same authors in this volume.
193 Cf. Schneider, "Gender-Metaphysik," 281 f.

havior must not be criticized or altered. Homosexuality is not considered to be part of God's plan for creation.[194]

In contrast with the Church's previous position, Joseph Ratzinger/Benedict XVI emphasizes the personhood of homosexuals. This is the basis for the criticism of disrespectful behavior toward gay and lesbian people; their dignity should not be attacked in practice. Homosexuals are respected in their personhood, but at the same time, they are denied the capacity to realize a true love relationship. The dignity of homosexuals is to be respected, but their rights of self-determination are curtailed.[195] It is presumed that, as homosexuals, they cannot deal responsibly with their sexuality. Therefore they are obliged to practice complete abstinence. From a modern sexual-ethical point of view, the verdict would be different: consensual, mutually respectful homosexual behavior recognizes the person's moral self-determination and does no harm to anyone. From the Magisterium's perspective, however, this violates the natural purpose of sexuality and the God-given complementarity of the sexes.

From whatever angle one examines this issue, the rigorous moral assessment of homosexuality as intrinsically disordered and as a grave sin can only be maintained within the framework of an ethics in which the natural purpose takes priority over sexuality's personal dimension of meaning. This is how Karol Wojtyła/John Paul II always viewed the issue: "Thus, the conjugal act considered with complete objectivity is not only a union of persons, of a man and a woman, in their reciprocal relation, but also is by its nature (essence) a union of persons in relation to procreation."[196] Under John Paul II, the Church attempts to prevent the open, moral-theological discussion of this sexual-moral norm and

---

194 Benedict XVI, *Light of the World* (San Francisco: Ignatius Press, 2010), 151 f.: "We could say, if we wanted to put it like this, that evolution has brought forth sexuality for the purpose of reproducing the species. The same thing is true from a theological point of view as well. The meaning and direction of sexuality is to bring about the union of man and woman and, in this way, to give humanity posterity, children, a future. This is the determination internal to the essence of sexuality. Everything else is against sexuality's intrinsic meaning and direction. This is a point we need to hold firm, even if it is not pleasing to our age." Homosexuality "remains contrary to the essence of what God originally willed." Thus the theological interpretation follows the moral judgment. At the same time, in a circular argument, the moral evaluation is presented as a consequence of the theological insight.
195 Cf. Stephan Goertz, "Streitfall Diskriminierung. Die Kirche und die neue Politik der Menschenrechte," *HerKorr* 67 (2013): 78–83.
196 Karol Wojtyła, *Love and Responsibility* (Boston: Pauline Books & Media, 2013), 211. See also Paul VI, *Humanae vitae*, no. 8: "As a consequence, husband and wife, through that mutual gift of themselves, which is specific and exclusive to them alone, develop that union of two persons in which they perfect one another, cooperating with God in the generation and rearing of new lives."

regards it as an expression of a lack of faith or an erroneous concept of love. Thus the Magisterium does not receive, and in fact rejects and regularly sanctions the moral-theological developments in the evaluation of homosexuality that one can observe in society more broadly since the end of the 1960s.[197]

8 No Longer A Problem? Developments Under Pope Francis

The question of whether there will be a change in the Vatican's assessment of homosexuality during Pope Francis's papacy cannot be answered with a simple yes or no. There are several reasons for this. First, the explicitly magisterial documents issued under Francis's tenure contain only a few passages on the subject of homosexuality. However, the pope has expressed himself somewhat more extensively in certain press conferences and interviews.[198] These remarks reveal new emphases but do not yet constitute a well-formulated concept. On the other hand, the Roman documents issued in recent years do not contain a clear message: the old familiar perspectives stand alongside new ones. This leaves room for different interpretations.

A number of documents seem to hand down the Vatican's previous position in an unbroken chain. We have seen that the Roman concept of the complementarity between man and woman is one reason for the Church's negative view of homosexuality. Gender theory is accused of disregarding this complementarity, on which the happiness of marriage and family is founded. The argument con-

---

197 Cf. Congregation for the Doctrine of the Faith on John McNeill, "The Church and the Homosexual (1978)," in *Dialogue about Catholic Sexual Teaching*, ed. Charles E. Curran and Richard A. McCormick (Readings in Moral Theology 8; New York: Paulist Press, 1993), 491–497; Congregation for the Doctrine of the Faith, "Letter regarding the suspension of Father Carlo Curran from the teaching of Theology," *AAS* 79 (1987): 116–118; Congregation for the Doctrine of the Faith, "Notification regarding Sister Jeannine Gramick, SSND, and Father Robert Nugent, SDS," *AAS* 91 (1999): 821–825; Congregation for the Doctrine of the Faith, "Notification regarding certain writings of Fr. Marciano Vidal, C.Ss.R.," *AAS* 93 (2001): 545–555; Committee on Doctrine, United States Conference of Catholic Bishops, *Inadequacies in the Theological Methodology and Conclusions of* The Sexual Person: Toward a Renewed Catholic Anthropology *by Todd A. Salzman and Michael Lawler*, September 15, 2010, http://www.usccb.org/about/doctrine/publications/upload/Sexual_Person_2010-09-15.pdf (accessed October 7, 2020); Congregation for the Doctrine of the Faith, "Notification on the book *Just Love. A Framework for Christian Sexual Ethics* by Sr. Margaret A. Farley, R.S.M.," *AAS* 104 (2012): 505–511.
198 See the documentation in Luciano Moia, *Chiesa e Omosessualità* (Milan: San Paolo, 2020), 31–44.

cludes that it is this disregard for the duality of the sexes that leads to the legitimization of homosexual relationships. As the Congregation for Catholic Education's 2019 document *Male and Female He Created Them* states in a key passage:

> Therefore, in the light of a *fully human and integral ecology,* women and men will understand the real meaning of sexuality and genitality in terms of the intrinsically relational and communicative intentionality that both informs their bodily nature and moves each towards the other mutually.[199]

The footnotes to numbers 30 – 35 in this document make reference to corresponding statements by John Paul II, Benedict XVI, and Francis. In his encyclical *Laudato si'*, the latter is concerned that one should learn to value "one's own body in its femininity or masculinity."[200] Gender theory starts from the individual person's options, "determining his or her sexual tendencies without having to take account of the reciprocity and complementarity of male–female relationships, nor of the procreative end of sexuality."[201] On the subject of gender, we can discern no relevant change under Francis, as compared to his predecessors.

There is also continuity on the question of whether homosexuality is compatible with the priestly vocation. In 2005, the Congregation for Catholic Education deems it necessary

> to state clearly that the Church, while profoundly respecting the persons in question, cannot admit to the seminary or to holy orders those who practise homosexuality, present deep-seated homosexual tendencies or support the so-called "gay-culture." Such persons, in fact, find themselves in a situation that gravely hinders them from relating correctly to men and women. One must in no way overlook the negative consequences that can derive from ordination of persons with deep-seated homosexual tendencies.[202]

---

199 Congregation for Catholic Education, *Male and Female He Created Them: Towards a Path of Dialogue on the Question of Gender Theory in Education* (Rome: Vatican, 2019), http://www.vatican.va/roman_curia/congregations/ccatheduc/documents/rc_con_ccatheduc_doc_20190202_maschio-e-femmina_en.pdf (accessed April 21, 2021), italics in the original.
200 Pope Francis, *Encyclica Laudatio si'* (Rome: Vatican, 2015), no. 155, http://www.vatican.va/content/francesco/en/encyclicals/documents/papa-francesco_20150524_enciclica-laudato-si.html (accessed April 21, 2021).
201 Congregation for Catholic Education, *Male and Female He Created Them*, no. 10.
202 Congregation for Catholic Education, *Instruction Concerning the Criteria for the Discernment of Vocations with regards to Persons with Homosexual Tendencies in view of their Admission to the Seminary and to Holy Orders* (Rome: Vatican, 2005), no. 2, http://www.vatican.va/roman_curia/congregations/ccatheduc/documents/rc_con_ccatheduc_doc_20051104_istruzione_en.html. (accessed April 21, 2021).

The last sentence obviously conveys the intention to establish a connection between sexual abuse and homosexual clerics. These Roman guidelines were heavily criticized, and not only because they groundlessly placed homosexuality in proximity to pedophilia.[203] Nevertheless, in 2016 the section quoted above is included unchanged in a document by the Congregation for the Clergy.[204]

The third example concerns the central question of the moral evaluation of homosexual behavior. Here it becomes difficult to determine the pope's attitude precisely. It is true that Francis no longer repeats the explicit condemnation of homosexuality as a grave sin, but when it comes to pastoral dealings with homosexuals and there is talk of mercy, integration, and non-judgment, the question of how Francis evaluates homosexual practice itself remains up in the air.[205] The well-known statement: "If someone is gay and is searching for the Lord and has good will, then who am I to judge him?"[206] leaves open the issue of whether this also means: Who am I to judge it (meaning homosexual behavior, or homosexual relationships)? One cannot exclude the possibility that this is simply a reminder of the distinction between the sin as an act and the sinner as a person. Even if the sinner is not to be condemned, provided they repent, "seek the Lord and have good will," is it still the case that homosexual behavior is a sin? So far, the pope has failed to give a clear answer to this question. The fact that he refers neither to Scripture nor to natural law on this subject could be interpreted as a sign that he no longer finds the grounds for the previous condemnation convincing. Nor is there any more talk of an "intrinsically evil" act in this context; in fact, John Paul II's central moral-theological document, the 1993 encyclical *Veritatis splendor*, in which the rigorous judgments of Catholic sexual morality are

---

203 Cf. the commentary in Hanspeter Heinz, "Erklärungsbedürftige Erklärung. Zur römischen Instruktion über die Priesterweihe Homosexueller," *HerKorr* 60 (2006): 21–25. The text "betrays some connotations that must be discriminatory against homosexual persons. For example, anyone who has taken note of the human sciences literature of recent decades will not claim that homosexuals living in committed partnerships are incapable of conducting proper relationships with men and women, or that people with an inclination to homosexuality are severely handicapped in this" (p. 23).

204 Congregation for the Clergy, *The Gift of the Priestly Vocation: Ratio Fundamentalis Institutionis Sacerdotalis* (Rome: Vatican, 2016), no. 199, http://www.clerus.va/content/dam/clerus/Ratio%20Fundamentalis/The%20Gift%20of%20the%20Priestly%20Vocation.pdf (accessed April 21, 2021).

205 Altman and Symons, *Queer Wars*, 103: "While the Catholic Church under Pope Francis has moderated its language on homosexuality, this is a shift in emphasis rather than doctrine."

206 Francis, "Apostolic Journey to Rio de Janeiro: Press Conference of Pope Francis during the Return Flight," July 28, 2013, http://www.vatican.va/content/francesco/en/speeches/2013/july/documents/papa-francesco_20130728_gmg-conferenza-stampa.html (accessed September 25, 2020).

defended as unshakable truths, is hardly mentioned at all – a fact which has not gone unnoticed by the pope's critics.[207] The pope's choice not to repeat something can send a strong message; disregard can be interpreted as delegitimization. The goal of initiating change is also served by the method of selectively quoting previous documents. For example, when asked about the issue of homosexuality, Francis refers to the Catechism several times; however, he never refers to number 2357 (which contains the phrases "grave depravity" and "contrary to the natural law"), but always to number 2358: "They must be accepted with respect, compassion, and sensitivity. Every sign of unjust discrimination in their regard should be avoided." Nevertheless, Francis has not yet changed the Catechism either.

If one is aware of the moral-theological history of the term problem as applied to homosexuality, then one pricks up one's ears when Francis says: "The problem is not having this tendency [...]. The problem is in making a lobby of this tendency."[208] Is this a reappearance of the old stereotype of homosexuals forming their own "clubs" – as some used to put it? On the other hand, Francis is the first pope to use the word "gay," and thus seems to respect homosexuals' modern self-image.

In contrast to the past, this is where a change is clearly recognizable. Francis strikes a self-critical note when he talks about the Christian and ecclesiastical treatment of homosexuality; homosexuals have been insulted and ostracized – for which one must not only apologize, but also ask forgiveness.[209] Like his predecessor, he wants to see homosexuals' dignity respected, though without adopting Joseph Ratzinger/Benedict XVI's harsh judgments on homosexual relation-

---

207 On this topic, see Antonio Autiero and Stephan Goertz, "A proposito di dubbia, errori e distinzioni. Una postfazione," in *Amoris laetitia. Un punto di svolta per la teologia morale?*, ed. Stephan Goertz and Caroline Witting (Milan: San Paolo, 2017), 257–269.

208 Francis, "Press Conference," July 28, 2013. Thus we see that even Francis cannot escape the term tendency.

209 Francis, "Apostolic Journey of His Holiness Pope Francis to Armenia: In-Flight Press Conference of His Holiness Pope Francis from Armenia to Rome," June 26, 2016, http://www.vatican.va/content/francesco/en/speeches/2016/june/documents/papa-francesco_20160626_armenia-conferenza-stampa.html (accessed September 28, 2020). On this point, the pope explicitly refers to a statement made by Cardinal Reinhard Marx (Munich), the then-president of the German Bishops' Conference: "Until 'very recently,' the church, but also society at large, had been 'very negative about gay people [...] it was the whole society. It was a scandal and terrible,' he [Cardinal Marx] told *The Irish Times* after speaking at a conference held in Trinity College"; see Patsy McGarry, "Church must apologise to gay people, pope's adviser declares," *The Irish Times*, June 23, 2016, https://www.irishtimes.com/news/social-affairs/religion-and-beliefs/church-must-apologise-to-gay-people-pope-s-adviser-declares-1.2697089 (accessed September 28, 2020).

ships.[210] Because self-criticism is required, a more open discussion of the moral-theological assessment of homosexuality is permitted. Bishops have begun to publicly and frankly address their own Church's prejudices against homosexuality and homosexuals, as well as the consequences of such prejudices.[211] A theological discussion of whether to bless same-sex couples has been permitted.[212] The Catholic taboo on homosexuality seems to be crumbling at the magisterial level as well.

The potentially decisive point that could result in an about-face on the subject of homosexuality is Francis's decision to favor a theology of love over a theology of the body in relation to the morality of marriage. In the extensive, central fourth chapter of *Amoris laetitia*, which is devoted to "Love in Marriage,"[213] the pope writes:

> Love inspires a sincere esteem for every human being and the recognition of his or her own right to happiness. I love this person, and I see him or her with the eyes of God, who gives us everything "for our enjoyment" (1 Tim 6:17). As a result, I feel a deep sense of happiness and peace.[214]

Anyone who loves another person should be concerned about their welfare and dignity. In love, desire is not to be conquered, but cultivated: "Yet we believe that God loves the enjoyment felt by human beings: he created us and 'richly furnishes us with everything to enjoy' (1 Tim 6:17)."[215] Marriage between a man and a woman is considered the most perfect form of human partnership because it includes the possibility of procreation. But according to Francis's theology of love, couldn't homosexual relationships also be understood as a form of love? In any case, the possibility of arriving at this conclusion seems to be less obstructed than it was in the past, when the complementarity of male and female bodies completely dominated Catholic doctrine. From this point of view, Francis's papacy could perhaps turn out to be the beginning of a new, long overdue phase in the magisterial assessment of homosexuality.

---

210 Francis, *Amoris Laetitia*, no. 250.
211 Cf. the comment by the Bishop of Essen (Germany), Franz-Josef Overbeck, "Vorurteile überwinden," *HerKorr* 73, no. 2 (2019): 6.
212 Cf. the attitude of the bishops Franz-Josef Bode (Osnabrück, Germany) and Stefan Heße (Hamburg, Germany), "Zum Geleit," in *Mit dem Segen der Kirche? Gleichgeschlechtliche Partnerschaft im Fokus der Pastoral*, ed. Stephan Loos, Michael Reitemeyer, and Georg Trettin (Freiburg im Breisgau: Herder, 2019), 13–14.
213 Francis, *Amoris laetitia*, nos. 89–164.
214 Ibid., no. 96.
215 Ibid., no. 149.

9 A Summary

Over the past one hundred years, moral theology has passed through various phases in its assessment of homosexuality. In retrospect, the two decades following the mid-1950s proved to be particularly productive. Not only did the first major works on the subject emerge during this period, but the end of the 1960s also saw a significant change in the evaluation of homosexuality. Whereas previously the negative judgment had always been fixed because homosexual behavior was considered a grave sin against nature, moral theologians in this phase began to distinguish between loving (responsible) and unloving (irresponsible) relationships. This marks the decisive turning point, when personal characteristics (such as consensus, reciprocity, and commitment) became the moral standard. Thus the concept of sexual self-determination as a human right enters moral-theological thought. The deep traditional skepticism regarding the enjoyment of sexual pleasure is overcome. One is no longer concerned about pleasure as such, but about its integration into morally responsible relationships. However, the fact that many theologians still cling to the traditional negative judgment is also part of recent moral-theological history. New arguments no longer seem to emerge; one circles around the same two authorities (Scripture and the Magisterium) and the same two ideas (the lack of reproduction and of complementarity).

The Roman Magisterium does not officially enter the debate until the mid-1970s, at a time when the first moral theologians were revising the previous position, and the depathologization and decriminalization of homosexuality were making significant gains. The Vatican response to the cultural upheavals that have taken place since the 1950s has primarily been to reaffirm the negative judgment of homosexual behavior. Homosexuality remains a problem in the magisterial documents – an objective disorder – because the possibility that life will be transmitted is excluded when the complementarity of man and woman is disregarded. The Magisterium becomes the guardian of a lost conception of moral order. In this sense, it becomes reactionary in the 1970s – and remains so for decades. In questions of sexual morality, the Magisterium sees itself as a soldier "in the front line in a lively battle for the dignity of man,"[216] but moral and sexual

---

216 Karol Wojtyła, *Sign of Contradiction* (New York: Seabury Press, 1979), 124, in his Lenten retreat for Paul VI in 1976. The then-Archbishop of Krakow adds: "One has only to recall the contestation of the Encyclical *Humanae vitae*, or that provoked by the latest Declaration by the Sacred Congregation for the Doctrine of the Faith, *Persona humana*."

self-determination are not considered expressions of this dignity. On the contrary, they are considered incompatible with the Catholic faith.[217]

Things could have been different. In its doctrine on marriage, the Second Vatican Council (1962–1965) arrived at formulations that could have heralded a new doctrinal phase. Sexuality is practiced humanely within the framework of love "from one person to another," as it says in the pastoral constitution *Gaudium et Spes*, no. 49: "The actions within marriage by which the couple are united intimately and chastely are noble and worthy ones. Expressed in a manner which is truly human, these actions promote that mutual self-giving by which spouses enrich each other with a joyful and a ready will."[218] From the moral-theological point of view, is not love between one person and another a higher form of dignity than that which naturally occurs between a male and a female body? Is it not the respect for the other's freedom that justifies the humanity of sexual consummation, rather than respect for a natural law of human reproduction? Based on the person-to-person principle, an ecclesiastical recognition of homosexual relations would certainly not be unthinkable. The question remains open as to whether, either under or after Pope Francis – as a result of the influence of his theology of love, as expounded in *Amoris laetitia* – we will see an appropriate correction of the undifferentiated negative judgment of homosexual relationships. What is certain is that the topic will not disappear from the Church's agenda.

This would by no means lead to a departure from natural law, as some fear. It is not the intention behind the natural law mindset that is at issue, but rather a certain form of this thought pattern in the sphere of sexual morality. At the beginning of the 1960s, the philosopher Ernst Bloch (1885–1977) got to the heart of the problem that arises here. According to Ulpian's definition (*Ius naturale est, quod natura omnia animalia docuit*), which he himself – and with him many Christian theologians – relates to sexuality, natural law loses its "human sparkle and pride,"[219] and by extension diminishes itself. In doing so, the choice to

---

217 Cf. Stephan Goertz, "'Freiheit? Welche Freiheit?' Der eigentümliche Kampf von Johannes Paul II. um die Würde der menschlichen Person," in *Johannes Paul II. – Vermächtnis und Hypothek eines Pontifikats*, ed. Stephan Goertz and Magnus Striet (Katholizismus im Umbruch 12; Freiburg im Breisgau: Herder, 2020), 85–113.
218 Second Vatican Council, Pastoral Constitution on the Church in the Modern World: *Gaudium et Spes* (Rome: Vatican, 1965), no. 49, http://www.vatican.va/archive/hist_councils/ii_vatican_council/documents/vat-ii_cons_19651207_gaudium-et-spes_en.html (accessed April 21, 2021).
219 Ernst Bloch, *Natural Law and Human Dignity*, trans. Dennis J. Schmidt (Cambridge, MA: MIT Press, 1986), 22; the original German edition is *Naturrecht und menschliche Würde*, vol. 6, *Werkausgabe* (Frankfurt am Main: Suhrkamp, 1961).

damn homosexual relationships may be fashioned as particularly natural. As Bloch writes, those who counteract the factual conditions with the concept of human dignity, "the establishment of honesty and uprightness," are following natural law's "genuine intentions."[220] Natural law constructed conditions in which "degradation and insult ceased."[221] Such a natural law desires "emancipation into the free space."[222] This natural law understands human dignity as the dignity of free subjects who do not have to submit their animal nature to a purpose, a sacralized biological lawfulness (and its ecclesiastical interpretation). It is interested in how human beings deal with their own sexuality and its various characteristics in such a way that the well-being and dignity of the person are respected and protected in the process. Thus modern natural law thinking develops into human rights thinking, and it does not shun the topics of sexuality, gender identity, marriage, and family.

In the post-*Persona Humana* era, the Catholic Magisterium sees itself as the guardian of traditional values (the natural asymmetry of the sexes and marriage as the exclusive location of legitimate human sexuality) when it comes to homosexuality.[223] Catholicism is threatening to become a breeding ground for prejudice against homosexuals. The appreciation of liberal values (individuality, autonomy, equality), which increased after World War II, is unilaterally perceived as a threat, rather than as the legacy of Christian concepts of human dignity. The democratization of gender relations collides with the Catholic Church's hierarchical organization of gender.[224] Thus in many parts of the world, the Catholic Church is becoming a countercultural institution, and its concepts of sexuality and gender identity are finding less and less resonance. Those who cling to a tottering order will also falter. In the past, homosexuality itself was considered a problem; today, it is addressing homosexuality that has become a problem for the Catholic Church.

---

220 Ibid., xxviii.
221 Ibid., xxix.
222 Ibid., xxx.
223 Cf. Helen M. Alvaré, "From Rome to Cairo and Beijing: John Paul II on Family and Human Rights," in *New Catholic Encyclopedia, Jubilee Volume: The Wojtyla Years*, ed. Gale Group (Washington, DC: Catholic University of America, 2001), 53–61. Many people, both Christians and non-Christians alike, considered John Paul II "a champion of traditional family values and relationships" (p. 53).
224 Cf. Linda Woodhead, *Geschlecht, Macht und religiöser Wandel in westlichen Gesellschaften* (Freiburg im Breisgau: Herder, 2018).

Bibliography

Adler, Alfred. *Das Problem der Homosexualität*. Munich: Ernst Reinhardt, 1917.

Allen, Prudence. "Man-Woman Complementarity: The Catholic Inspiration." *Logos 9*, no. 3 (2006): 87–108.

Altman, Dennis, and Jonathan Symons. *Queer Wars*. Cambridge: Polity Press, 2016.

Alvaré, Helen M. "From Rome to Cairo and Beijing: John Paul II on Family and Human Rights." In *New Catholic Encyclopedia, Jubilee Volume: The Wojtyla Years*, ed. Gale Group, 53–61. Washington, DC: Catholic University of America, 2001.

Anatrella, Tony. "Homosexualität und Homophobie." In *Lexikon Familie*, ed. Päpstlicher Rat für die Familie, 361–376. Paderborn: Schöningh, 2007.

Aquinas, Thomas. *Summa contra gentiles, Book 3: Providence, Part II*. Translated by Vernon J. Bourke. Notre Dame: University of Notre Dame Press, 1956.

Aquinas, Thomas. *Summa theologica*. Translated by Fathers of the English Domincan Province. New York: Benziger Bros., 1947. https://www.ccel.org/ccel/aquinas/summa.i.html. Accessed April 21, 2021.

Auer, Alfons, Wilhelm Korff, and Gerhard Lohfink. "Zweierlei Sexualethik. Kritische Bemerkungen zur 'Erklärung' der römischen Glaubenskongregation 'Zu einigen Fragen der Sexualethik'." *ThQ* 156 (1976): 148–158.

Autiero, Antonio, and Stephan Goertz. "A proposito di dubbia, errori e distinzioni. Una postfazione." In *Amoris laetitia. Un punto di svolta per la teologia morale?*, ed. Stephan Goertz and Caroline Witting, 257–269. Milan: San Paolo, 2017.

Bailey, D. Sherwin. *Homosexuality and the Western Christian Tradition*. New York: Longmans, 1955.

Barberi, Michael J., and Joseph A. Selling. "The Origin of *Humanae Vitae* and the Impasse in Fundamental Theological Ethics." *Louvain Studies* 37 (2013): 364–389.

Barton, George A. "Sodomy." In *Encyclopedia of Religion and Ethics*, vol. 11, ed. James Hastings, 672–674. New York: Charles Scribner's Sons, 1920.

Beattie Jung, Patricia. "The Roman Catholic Tradition." In *Homosexuality and Religion*, ed. Jeffrey S. Siker, 191–200. Connecticut: Greenwood Press, 2007.

Benedict XVI. *Light of the World*. San Francisco: Ignatius Press, 2010.

Bloch, Ernst. *Natural Law and Human Dignity*. Translated by Dennis J. Schmidt. Cambridge, MA: MIT Press, 1986; original German edition: *Naturrecht und menschliche Würde*, vol. 6, *Werkausgabe*. Frankfurt am Main: Suhrkamp, 1961.

Bode, Franz-Josef, and Stefan Heße. "Zum Geleit." In *Mit dem Segen der Kirche? Gleichgeschlechtliche Partnerschaft im Fokus der Pastoral*, ed. Stephan Loos, Michael Reitemeyer, and Georg Trettin, 13–14. Freiburg im Breisgau: Herder, 2019.

Boswell, John. *Christianity, Social Tolerance, and Homosexuality: Gay People in Western Europe from the Beginning of the Christian Era to the Fourteenth Century*. Chicago: University of Chicago Press, 1980.

Breitsameter, Christof, and Stephan Goertz. *Vom Vorrang der Liebe. Zeitenwende für die katholische Sexualmoral*. Freiburg im Breisgau: Herder, 2020.

Breitsameter, Christof. *Liebe – Formen und Normen. Eine Kulturgeschichte und ihre Folgen*. Freiburg im Breisgau: Herder, 2017.

Brinkschröder, Michael. *Sodom als Symptom. Gleichgeschlechtliche Sexualität im christlichen Imaginären – eine religionsgeschichtliche Anamnese*. Berlin: De Gruyter, 2006.

Brogliato, Beatrice, and Damiano Migliorini. *L'amore omosessuale. Saggi di psicoanalisi, teologia e pastorale. In dialogi per una nuova sintesi.* Assisi: Cittadella editrice, 2014.

Buckley, Michael J. *Morality and the Homosexual. A Catholic Approach to a Moral Problem.* London: Sands & Co Ltd, 1959.

Busl, Gregor. *Katechetische Predigten Bd. 2: Von den Geboten*, ed. Karl Neumann. Regensburg: Habbel, 1899.

Butler, Judith. *Undoing Gender.* New York: Routledge, 2004.

Caldecott, Léonie. "Sincere Gift: The Pope's 'New Feminism'." In *John Paul II and Moral Theology,* ed. Charles E. Currran and Richard A. McCormick, 216–234. New York: Paulist Press, 1998.

Case, Mary Anne. "After Gender the Destruction of Man – The Vatican's Nightmare Vision of the 'Gender-Agenda' for Law." *Pace Law Review* 31, no. 3 (2011): 802–817.

Chiavacci, Enrico. "Omosessualità. Un tema de ristudiare." *RTM* 167 (2010): 469–477.

Cock, Bernard de. "Homosexuality and Sexual Difference. An Introduction to the Thought of Xavier Lacroix." *Ephemerides Theologicae Lovanienses* 81, no. 4 (2005): 334–364.

Coleman, Gerald D. "The Vatican Statement on Homosexuality." *TS* 48 (1987): 727–734.

Committee on Doctrine, United States Conference of Catholic Bishops. *Inadequacies in the Theological Methodology and Conclusions of* The Sexual Person: Toward a Renewed Catholic Anthropology by *Todd A. Salzman and Michael Lawler.* September 15, 2010. http://www.usccb.org/about/doctrine/publications/upload/Sexual_Person_2010-09-15.pdf. Accessed October 7, 2020.

Congregation for Catholic Education. *Educational Guidance in Human Love: Outlines for Sex Education.* Rome: Vatican, 1983. http://www.vatican.va/roman_curia/congregations/cca theduc/documents/rc_con_ccatheduc_doc_19831101_sexual-education_en.html. Accessed April 21, 2021.

Congregation for Catholic Education. *Instruction Concerning the Criteria for the Discernment of Vocations with regards to Persons with Homosexual Tendencies in view of their Admission to the Seminary and to Holy Orders.* Rome: Vatican, 2005. http://www.vat ican.va/roman_curia/congregations/ccatheduc/documents/rc_con_ccatheduc_doc_ 20051104_istruzione_en.html. Accessed April 21, 2021.

Congregation for Catholic Education. *Male and Female He Created Them: Towards a Path of Dialogue on the Question of Gender Theory in Education.* Rome: Vatican, 2019. http:// www.vatican.va/roman_curia/congregations/ccatheduc/documents/rc_con_ccatheduc_ doc_20190202_maschio-e-femmina_en.pdf. Accessed April 21, 2021.

Congregation for the Clergy. *The Gift of the Priestly Vocation: Ratio Fundamentalis Institutionis Sacerdotalis.* Rome: Vatican, 2016. http://www.clerus.va/content/dam/cle rus/Ratio%20Fundamentalis/The%20Gift%20of%20the%20Priestly%20Vocation.pdf. Accessed April 21, 2021.

Congregation for the Doctrine of the Faith. "Declaration on certain questions concerning sexual ethics: *Persona humana.*" *AAS* 68 (1976): 77–96.

Congregation for the Doctrine of the Faith on John McNeill. "The Church and the Homosexual (1978)." In *Dialogue about Catholic Sexual Teaching,* Readings in Moral Theology 8, ed. Charles E. Curran and Richard A. McCormick, 491–497. New York: Paulist Press, 1993.

Congregation for the Doctrine of the Faith. "Letter to the Bishops of the Catholic Church on the Pastoral Care of Homosexual Persons *Homosexualitatis problema.*" *AAS* 79 (1987):

543 – 554. http://www.vatican.va/roman_curia/congregations/cfaith/documents/rc_con_ cfaith_doc_19861001_homosexual-persons_en.html. Accessed April 21, 2021.

Congregation for the Doctrine of the Faith. "Letter regarding the suspension of Father Carlo Curran from the teaching of Theology." *AAS* 79 (1987): 116 – 118.

Congregation for the Doctrine of the Faith. "Notification regarding Sister Jeannine Gramick, SSND, and Father Robert Nugent, SDS." *AAS* 91 (1999): 821 – 825.

Congregation for the Doctrine of the Faith. "Notification regarding certain writings of Fr. Marciano Vidal, C.Ss.R." *AAS* 93 (2001): 545 – 555.

Congregation for the Doctrine of the Faith. *Considerations Regarding Proposals to Give Legal Recognition to Unions Between Homosexual Persons.* Rome: Vatican, 2003. http://www. vatican.va/roman_curia/congregations/cfaith/documents/rc_con_cfaith_doc_20030731_ homosexual-unions_en.html. Accessed April 21, 2021.

Congregation for the Doctrine of the Faith. *Letter to the Bishops of the Catholic Church on the Collaboration of Men and Women.* Rome: Vatican, 2004. http://www.vatican.va/roman_ curia/congregations/cfaith/documents/rc_con_cfaith_doc_20040731_collaboration_en. html. Accessed April 21, 2021.

Congregation for the Doctrine of the Faith. "Notification on the book *Just Love. A Framework for Christian Sexual Ethics* by Sr. Margaret A. Farley, R.S.M." *AAS* 104 (2012): 505 – 511.

Crowley, Paul G. "Homosexuality and the Counsel of the Cross." *TS* 65 (2004): 500 – 529.

Crowley, Paul G. "Homosexuality and the Counsel of the Cross: A Clarification." *TS* 69 (2008): 637 – 640.

Curran, Charles. "Homosexuality and Moral Theology: Methodological and Substantive Considerations." *The Thomist* 35 (1971): 447 – 481.

Curran, Charles. *Transition and Tradition in Moral Theology.* London: University of Notre Dame Press, 1979.

Curran, Charles E. *Catholic Moral Theology in the United States. A History.* Washington, DC: Georgetown University Press, 2008.

Dannecker, Martin. "Freuds Dekonstruktion der sexuellen Normalität." *Queer Lectures* 1 (2008): 79 – 107.

Dannecker, Martin. "Homosexualität, 1. Zum Problemstand." in *Lexikon der Bioethik.* vol. 2, ed. Wilhelm Korff, 224 – 227. Gütersloh: Gütersloher Verlag-Haus, 1998.

Davis, Henry. *Commandments of God, Precepts of the Church.* Vol. 2, *Moral and Pastoral Theology.* London: Sheed and Ward, 1936.

Davis, Henry. *Commandments of God, Precepts of the Church.* Vol. 2, 5th ed., *Moral and Pastoral Theology.* London: Sheed and Ward, 1946.

Dreßing, Harald, et al. *Sexueller Missbrauch an Minderjährigen durch katholische Priester, Diakone und männliche Ordensangehörige im Bereich der Deutschen Bischofskonferenz.* Mannheim: MHG, 2018.

Emcke, Carolin. "So. Und nicht anders (2012)." In *Modern Love. Geschichten über die Liebe,* ed. Susanne Gretter, 34 – 40. Berlin: Suhrkamp, 2013.

Faggioni, Maurizio P. "L'atteggiamento e la prassi della Chiesa in epoca medievale e moderna sull'omosessualità." *Gregorianum* 91, no. 3 (2010): 478 – 509.

Farley, Margaret A. "An Ethic for Same-Sex-Relations." In *A Challenge to Love: Gay and Lesbian Catholics in the Church,* ed. Robert Nugent, 93 – 106. New York: Crossroad, 1983.

Farley, Margaret A. *Just Love. A Framework for Christian Sexual Ethics.* New York: Continuum, 2006.

Fiedler, Peter. *Sexuelle Orientierung und sexuelle Abweichung.* Weinheim: Beltz, 2004.

Foucault, Michel. *The History of Sexuality.* Vol. 1, *An Introduction.* Translated by Robert Hurley. New York: Pantheon Books, 1978.

Fraling, Bernhard. *Sexualethik. Ein Versuch aus christlicher Sicht.* Paderborn: Schöningh, 1995.

Frank, David John, Steven A. Boutcher, and Bayliss Camp. "The Reform of Sodomy Laws From a World Society Perspective." In *Queer Mobilizations. LGBT Activists Confront the Law,* ed. Scott Barclay, Mary Bernstein, and Anna-Maria Marshall, 123–141. New York: New York University Press, 2009.

Francis. "Apostolic Journey of His Holiness Pope Francis to Armenia: In-Flight Press Conference of His Holiness Pope Francis from Armenia to Rome." June 26, 2016. http://www.vatican.va/content/francesco/en/speeches/2016/june/documents/papa-francesco_20160626_armenia-conferenza-stampa.html. Accessed September 28, 2020.

Francis. "Apostolic Journey to Rio de Janeiro: Press Conference of Pope Francis during the Return Flight." July 28, 2013. http://www.vatican.va/content/francesco/en/speeches/2013/july/documents/papa-francesco_20130728_gmg-conferenza-stampa.html. Accessed September 25, 2020.

Francis. Post-Synodal Apostolic Exhortation *Amoris Laetitia.* Rome: Vatican, 2016. https://www.vatican.va/content/dam/francesco/pdf/apost_exhortations/documents/papa-francesco_esortazione-ap_20160319_amoris-laetitia_en.pdf. Accessed April 21, 2021.

Freud, Sigmund. "Letter to an American mother (1935)." Reproduced in: *American Journal of Psychiatry* 107 (1947): 786–787.

Gallagher, Raphael. "The Reception of Veritatis splendor within the Theological Community." *StMor* 33, no. 2 (1995): 415–435.

Goertz, Stephan. "Streitfall Diskriminierung. Die Kirche und die neue Politik der Menschenrechte." *HerKorr* 67 (2013): 78–83.

Goertz, Stephan. "Zwischen Ablehnung und Anerkennung. Katholische Stellungnahmen zur gleichgeschlechtlichen Ehe in Deutschland." *Family Forum* 7 (2017): 35–54

Goertz, Stephan. "Sünde und Strafe. Moraltheologische Positionen zur Reform des § 175." *Stimmen der Zeit* 144 (2019): 837–846.

Goertz, Stephan. "'Freiheit? Welche Freiheit?' Der eigentümliche Kampf von Johannes Paul II. um die Würde der menschlichen Person." In *Johannes Paul II. – Vermächtnis und Hypothek eines Pontifikats,* Katholizismus im Umbruch 12, ed. Stephan Goertz and Magnus Striet, 85–113. Freiburg im Breisgau: Herder, 2020.

Goertz, Stephan, and Magnus Striet, eds. *Johannes Paul II. – Vermächtnis und Hypothek eines Pontifikats.* Katholizismus im Umbruch 12. Freiburg im Breisgau: Herder, 2020.

Gramick, Jeannine, and Pat Furey, eds. *The Vatican and Homosexuality.* New York: Crossroad, 1988.

Greenberg, David F., and Marcia H. Bystryn. "Christian Intolerance of Homosexuality." *American Journal of Sociology* 88, no. 3 (1982): 515–548.

Gründel, Johannes. "Haben Homosexuelle Heimat in der Kirche?" In *Homosexuelle Männer in Kirche und Gesellschaft,* ed. Udo Rauchfleisch, 40–64. Düsseldorf: Patmos-Verlag, 1993.

Häring, Bernhard. *Das Gesetz Christi.* Munich: Wewel, 1958.

Häring, Bernhard. *Free and Faithful in Christ. Moral Theology for Priests and Laity.* Vol. 2. New York: The Seabury Press, 1979.

Harvey, John F. "Homosexuality as a Pastoral Problem." *TS* 16 (1955): 86–108.

Harvey, John F. "Homosexuality." In *NCE*. vol. 7, ed. William J. McDonald, 116–119. New York: McGraw-Hill, 1967.

Harvey, John F. "The Controversy concerning the Psychology and Morality of Homosexuality." *American Ecclesiastical Review* 167, no. 9 (1973): 602–629.

Harvey, John F. *The Homosexual Person: New Thinking in Pastoral Care.* San Francisco: Ignatius Press, 1987.

Harvey, John F. *The Truth about Homosexuality.* San Francisco: Ignatius Press, 1995.

Heinz, Hanspeter. "Erklärungsbedürftige Erklärung. Zur römischen Instruktion über die Priesterweihe Homosexueller." *HerKorr* 60 (2006): 21–25.

Herdt, Gilbert. "Homosexuality." In *The Encyclopedia of Religion*, vol. 6, ed. Mircea Eliade, 445–453. New York: Macmillan, 1987.

Hilgenreiner, Karl. "Homosexualität." In *LThK*, vol. 5, ed. Michael Buchberger, 130–131. Freiburg im Breisgau: Herder, 1933.

Hirschfeld, Magnus. *Die Homosexualität des Mannes und des Weibes.* With a foreword by Bernd-Ulrich Hergemöller. 2d rev. ed. Berlin: De Gruyter, 2001.

Honneth, Axel. *Das Recht der Freiheit. Grundriß einer demokratischen Sittlichkeit.* Berlin: Suhrkamp, 2011.

Hörmann, Karl. "Homosexualität." In *Lexikon der christlichen Moral*, ed. Karl Hörmann, 643–648. Innsbruck: Tyrolia-Verlag, 1969.

Hurteau, Pierre. "Catholic Moral Discourse on Male Sodomy and Masturbation in the Seventeenth and Eighteenth Centuries." *Journal of the History of Sexuality* 4 (1993): 1–26.

Jacobitz, Gerard. "Seminary, Priesthood, and the Vatican's Homosexual Dilemma." In *More than a Monologue: Sexual Diversity and the Catholic Church*, ed. J. Patrick Hornbeck and Michael A. Norko, 86–105. New York: Fordham University Press, 2014.

John Paul II. "Apostolic Journey to the United States of America. To the Bishops of the United States of America." *AAS* 71 (1979): 1218–1229.

John Paul II. *Encyclical Veritatis splendor.* Rome: Vatican, 1993. http://www.vatican.va/content/john-paul-ii/en/encyclicals/documents/hf_jp-ii_enc_06081993_veritatis-splendor.html. Accessed April 21, 2021.

Jone, Heribert. *Katholische Moraltheologie.* Paderborn: Schöningh, 1941.

Jordan, Mark D. *The Silence of Sodom: Homosexuality in Modern Catholicism.* Chicago: University of Chicago Press, 2000.

Keane, Philip S. *Sexual Morality: A Catholic Perspective.* New York: Paulist Press, 1977.

Keefe, Jeffrey. "Homosexuality." In *NCE*, vol. 7, 66–71. Detroit: Gale Group, 2003.

Keenan, James F. *A History of Catholic Moral Theology in the Twentieth Century. From Confessing Sins to Liberating Consciences.* London: Continuum, 2010.

Kernberg, Otto F. "Ein konzeptuelles Modell der männlichen Perversion." *Forum der Psychoanalyse* 1 (1985): 167–188.

Koch, Antony. *A Handbook of Moral Theology*, vol. 2. Adapted and edited by Arthur Preuss. St. Louis: B. Herder, 1919.

Korff, Wilhelm. "Homosexualität, III. Theologisch-ethisch." In *LThK*, vol. 5, ed. Walter Kaspar, 255–258. Freiburg im Breisgau: Herder, 1996.

Lacroix, Xavier. *Le corps de l'esprit.* Paris: Éditions du Cerf, 2002.

Lautmann, Rüdiger. *Soziologie der Sexualität. Erotischer Körper, intimes Handeln und Sexualkultur.* Weinheim: Juventa-Verlag, 2002.

Lehmann, Karl. *Gemeinsame Synode der Bistümer in der Bundesrepublik Deutschland, Offizielle Gesamtausgabe.* Freiburg im Breisgau: Herder, 2012.

Lintner, Martin M. *Den Eros entgiften. Plädoyer für eine tragfähige Sexualmoral und Beziehungsethik.* Brixen: Weger, 2012.

Luhmann, Niklas. *Liebe. Eine Übung,* Ed. André Kieserling. Frankfurt am Main: Suhrkamp, 2008.

Lutterbach, Hubertus. "Gleichgeschlechtliches sexuelles Verhalten. Ein Tabu zwischen Spätantike und früher Neuzeit?" *Historische Zeitschrift* 267 (1998): 281–310.

Mausbach, Joseph, and Gustav Ermecke. *Katholische Moraltheologie,* vol. 3. 9th ed. Münster: Aschendorff, 1953.

Mausbach, Joseph, and Gustav Ermecke. *Katholische Moraltheologie,* vol. 3. 10th ed. Münster: Aschendorff, 1961.

McGarry, Patsy. "Church must apologise to gay people, pope's adviser declares." *The Irish Times,* June 23, 2016. https://www.irishtimes.com/news/social-affairs/religion-and-be liefs/church-must-apologise-to-gay-people-pope-s-adviser-declares-1.2697089. Accessed September 28, 2020.

McNeill, John J. *The Church and the Homosexual.* Kansas City: Andrews and McMeel, 1976.

Melina, Livio. *Liebe auf katholisch. Ein Handbuch für heute.* Augsburg: Sankt-Ulrich-Verlag, 2009; original Italian edition: *Per una cultura della famiglia: il linguaggio dell'amore.* Venice: Marcianum Press, 2006.

Ménard, Guy. *De Sodome à l'Exode. Jalons pour une théologie de la libération.* Montréal: Guy Saint-Jean, 1980.

Mieth, Dietmar, ed. *Moraltheologie im Abseits? Antwort auf die Enzyklika "Veritatis splendor".* QD 153. Freiburg im Breisgau: Herder, 1994.

Moia, Luciano. *Chiesa e Omosessualità.* Milan: San Paolo, 2020.

Müncker, Theodor. *Die psychologischen Grundlagen der katholischen Sittenlehre.* Vol. 3, *Handbuch der katholischen Sittenlehre.* Düsseldorf: Mosella, 1940.

Nelson, James B. "Homosexuality." In *The Westminster Dictionary of Christian Ethics,* ed. James F. Childress and John Macquarrie, 271–274. Philadelphia: Westminster Press, 1986.

Noldin, Hieronymus. *Summa Theologiae Moralis. Complementum: De Castitate,* Editio XXXIV. Edited by Godefridus Heinzel. Innsbruck: Felizian Rauch, 1952.

Nugent, Robert, ed. *A Challenge to Love: Gay and Lesbian Catholics in the Church.* New York: Crossroad, 1983.

Overbeck, Franz-Josef. "Vorurteile überwinden." *HerKorr* 73 (2/2019): 6.

Paul VI. Encyclical *Humanae Vitae.* Rome: Vatican, 1968. http://www.vatican.va/content/paul-vi/en/encyclicals/documents/hf_p-vi_enc_25071968_humanae-vitae.html. Accessed April 21, 2021.

Pérez, Joseph. *La Inquisición española: crónica negra del Santo Oficio.* Madrid: Martínez Roca, 2005.

Polgar, Nenad, and Joseph A. Selling, eds. *The Concept of Intrinsic Evil and Catholic Theological Ethics.* Lanham: Lexington Books/Fortress Academic, 2019.

Prada, José Rafael. "La Persona Homosexual." *StMor* 42 (2004): 293–335.

Rauchfleisch, Udo. "Homosexualität, I. Anthropologisch, II. Soziologisch." In *LThK*, vol. 5, ed. Walter Kaspar, 254–255. Freiburg im Breisgau: Herder, 1996.

Reckwitz, Andreas. *Das hybride Subjekt. Eine Theorie der Subjektkulturen von der bürgerlichen Moderne zur Postmoderne.* Weilerswist: Velbrück, 2006.

Ross, Susan A. "The Bridegroom and the Bride. The Theological Anthropology of John Paul II and Its Relation to the Bible and Homosexuality." In *Sexual Diversity and Catholicism. Toward the Development of Moral Theology*, ed. Patricia Beattie Jung and Joseph A. Coray, 39–59. Collegeville, MN: Liturgical Press, 2001.

Rotter, Hans. "Ehe und homosexuelle Partnerschaft. Vergleichbares und Unterscheidendes in moraltheologischer Sicht." In *Eingetragene Lebenspartnerschaft. Rechtssicherheit für homosexuelle Paare – Angriff auf Ehe und Familie?*, ed. Harmut Bosinski et al., 30–44. Regensburg: Pustet, 2001.

Sailer, Johann Michael. *Handbuch der christlichen Moral*, vol. 2. Sulzbach: Seidel, 1834.

Salzman, Todd A., and Michael Lawler. *Sexual Ethics. A Theological Introduction.* Washington, DC: Georgetown University Press, 2012.

Scaramella, Pierroberto. "Sodomia." In *Dizionario storico dell'Inquisizione*, vol. 3, ed. Adriano Prosperi, 1445–1450. Pisa: Edizioni della Normale, 2010.

Schindler, Franz M. *Lehrbuch der Moraltheologie*, vol. 3. Vienna: Oplitz, 1914.

Schneider, Ruben. "Gender-Metaphysik und Ontologie der Homosexualität." In *Freiheit ohne Wirklichkeit?*, ed. Benedikt P. Göcke and Thomas Schärtl, 249–287. Münster: Aschendorff-Verlag, 2020.

Schockenhoff, Eberhard. "Sexualität, IV. Theologisch-ethisch." In *LThK*, vol. 9, ed. Walter Kasper, 518–524. Freiburg im Breisgau: Herder, 2000.

Schockenhoff, Eberhard. *Die Kunst zu lieben. Unterwegs zu einer neuen Sexualethik.* Freiburg im Breisgau: Herder, 2021.

Schöllgen, Werner. *Konkrete Ethik.* Düsseldorf: Patmos-Verlag, 1961.

Selling, Joseph A., and Jan Jans, eds. *The Splendor of Accuracy.* Kampen: Kok Pharos, 1994.

Sigusch, Volkmar. *Sexualitäten. Eine kritische Theorie in 99 Fragmenten.* Frankfurt am Main: Campus, 2013.

Slater, Thomas. *A Manual of Moral Theology*, vol. 1. 2d ed. New York: Benziger Brothers, 1908.

Slater, Thomas. *A Manual of Moral Theology*, vol. 1. 5th ed. London: Burns Oates & Washbourne Ltd, 1925.

Spijker, Herman van de. *Die gleichgeschlechtliche Zuneigung. Homotropie: Homosexualität, Homoerotik, Homophilie – und die katholische Moraltheologie.* Olten: Walter-Verlag, 1968.

Spijker, Herman van de. *Homotropie. Menschlichkeit als Rechtfertigung. Überlegungen zur gleichgeschlechtlichen Zuneigung.* Munich: Manz, 1972.

Spijker, Herman van de. *Omotropia nell'orizzonte della eterotropia. La realtà della sessualità umana.* Padua: CLEUP, 2014.

Steckel, Sita. "Perversion als Argument. Sex und Geschlechterordnung in innerkirchlichen Polemiken des lateinischen Hoch- und Spätmittelalters." In *"Als Mann und Frau schuf er sie". Religion und Geschlecht*, ed. Barbara Stollberg-Rilinger, 47–85. Würzburg: Ergon-Verlag, 2014.

Striet, Magnus. *In der Gottesschleife. Von religiöser Sehnsucht in der Moderne.* Freiburg im Breisgau: Herder, 2014.

Sullivan, Andrew. "Alone Again, Naturally: The Catholic Church and the Homosexual (1994)." In *Theology and Sexuality*, ed. Eugene F. Rogers, 275–288. Malden: Blackwell Publishing, 2007.

Tillmann, Fritz. *Die katholische Sittenlehre. Die Verwirklichung der Nachfolge Christi.* Vol 4.2 of *Handbuch der katholischen Sittenlehre.* Düsseldorf: Patmos-Verlag, 1940.

Vacek, Edward C. "Feminism and the Vatican." *TS* 66 (2005): 159–177.

Weatherbe, Steve. "Remembering Father John Harvey." *National Catholic Register*, January 5, 2011. https://www.ncregister.com/news/remembering-father-john-harvey-8wh2r6vs. Accessed September 28, 2020.

Werres, Johannes. "Katholische Kirche und Homosexualität." *Werkhefte* 20 (1966): 91–95.

Williamson, Hugh Ross. "Sodom and Homosexuality." *Clergy Review* 48 (1963): 507–514.

Wisdorf, Josef. *Muß ein Junge daran scheitern?* Düsseldorf: Altenberg, 1966.

Wojtyła, Karol. *Sign of Contradiction.* New York: Seabury Press, 1979.

Wojtyła, Karol. *Love and Responsibility.* Boston: Pauline Books & Media, 2013.

Woodhead, Linda. *Geschlecht, Macht und religiöser Wandel in westlichen Gesellschaften.* Freiburg im Breisgau: Herder, 2018.

Wucherpfennig, Ansgar. *Sexualität bei Paulus.* Freiburg im Breisgau: Herder, 2020.

Todd A. Salzman and Michael G. Lawler
Reconstructing Complementarity as a Foundational Catholic Sexual Ethical Principle

The First Letter to Timothy, written around the year 100,[1] issues a standard Jewish command: "Let a woman learn in silence in all submissiveness. I permit no woman to teach or to have authority over men; she is to keep silent" (1 Tim 2:11–14; 1 Cor 14:34). This hierarchical stratification of power and authority between women and men, unjust already in the first century, continues to be unjust in the twenty-first century and has been eroticized in the specifically sexual sector of social life. The cultural cues that women and men learn, in both society and the Catholic Church, are that men are powerful and dominant and that women are weak and submissive to men. This teaching is further solidified in the Church by the pervasive image of God as a powerful male/father and ordained male clerics as his sacramental representations. Almost fifty years ago, feminist theologian Mary Daly highlighted the obvious analogical equation, "if God is male, then the male is God."[2] Another early feminist theologian, Rosemary Radford Ruether, argued that the hierarchy of patriarchal rule was established and is daily reinforced by the metaphor of male monotheism literally interpreted.[3]

In 1981, in his response to the Synod on Marriage and Family, Pope John Paul II introduced the term *complementarity* into official magisterial sexual teaching.[4] Since its introduction, complementarity has been allied to the twentieth-century unitive-procreative sexual principle to fashion a foundational Catholic sexual ethical principle defending the morality of heterosexual marital intercourse of a reproductive kind and condemning as immoral homosexual unions

---

1 Robert A. Wild, "The Pastoral Letters," in *The New Jerome Biblical Commentary*, ed. Raymond E. Brown, Joseph A. Fitzmyer and Roland E. Murphy (Englewood Cliffs, NJ: Prentice Hall, 1990), 891–902, 893.
2 Mary Daly, *Beyond God the Father: Toward a Philosophy of Women's Liberation* (Boston: Beacon, 1973), 19.
3 Rosemary Radford Ruether, *Sexism and God-Talk: Toward a Feminist Theology* (Boston: Beacon, 1983).
4 John Paul II, *Familiaris Consortio*, 1981, n. 19, http://www.vatican.va/content/john-paul-ii/en/apost_exhortations/documents/hf_jp-ii_exh_19811122_familiaris-consortio.html [accessed 22.10.2020].

https://doi.org/10.1515/9783110705188-008

and intercourse. Complementarity as presented by John Paul II and the Magisterium, we submit, is difficult to sustain in the real world in the face of the social, and ecclesially-approved, subordination of women to men and, if the principle cannot stand, then neither can the prescriptive and proscriptive sexual norms derived from it. In this essay, based on consideration of the sexual human person "integrally and adequately considered,"[5] we propose a reconstructed understanding of complementarity. We argue in three cumulative sections that the Magisterium's complementarity principle, grounded as it is primarily in the male and female biological genital organs, is inadequate as a principle for the construction of a sexual ethic for the human *person* integrally and adequately considered. First, we present the Magisterium's complementarity principle; second, we deconstruct this principle on the basis of historical and sexual anthropological considerations; third, we reconstruct a principle of *holistic complementarity* based on considerations of the sexual human person integrally and adequately considered.

1 Magisterial Teaching and the Primacy of Biological Complementarity

The term *complementarity* introduced in *Familiaris Consortio* has been incorporated into other magisterial documents, including the *Catechism of the Catholic Church*[6] and the Congregation for the Doctrine of the Faith's (henceforth cited as CDF) "Considerations Regarding Proposals to Give Legal Recognition to Unions Between Homosexual Persons" (henceforth cited as CRP).[7] The CDF articulates the principle that "sexual relations are human when and insofar as they express and promote the mutual assistance of the sexes in marriage and are open to the transmission of new life."[8] This is the standard Catholic unitive-procreative principle. The CDF explains the term sexual complementarity in relation to this prin-

---

5 See Louis Janssens, "Artificial Insemination: Ethical Considerations," *Louvain Studies* 8 (1980): 3–29.
6 *Catechism of the Catholic Church.* Second Edition, revised in accordance with the official Latin text promulgated by Pope John Paul II (Vatican City: Libreria Editrice Vaticana, 1994), n. 2333.
7 Congregation for the Doctrine of the Faith, *Considerations Regarding Proposals to Give Legal Recognition to Unions Between Homosexual Persons* [CRP], 2003, nn. 2–4, https://www.vatican.va/roman_curia/congregations/cfaith/documents/rc_con_cfaith_doc_20030731_homosexual-unions_en.html [accessed 22.10.2020].
8 Ibid., 7.

ciple and, on this foundation, defends heterosexual marriage and condemns homosexual unions and acts.

Neither John Paul II nor the magisterial documents that followed him specifically define complementarity, but we offer the following definition that reflects its use in these documents. Complementarity suggests that two realities belong together in the created order and that together they produce a whole which neither can produce alone. The idea of complementarity has predecessors in religious and philosophical traditions, in the *yin* and *yang* symbols of Taoism, for instance, and in the early Gnostic teaching that the divine was a joining of male and female opposites.[9] The term *complementarity*, however, does not have such an ancient history. A web search for the term reveals no results prior to 1975 and many after that.[10] In magisterial documents, complementarity has two general meanings, biological and personal, with subcategories within each (Table 1). The definition of what constitutes a moral sexual act depends on how biological and personal complementarity are defined each in themselves and in relation to one another. We consider each in turn.

Biological complementarity is subdivided into *heterogenital* and *reproductive* complementarities. The CDF describes heterogenital complementarity this way: "Men and women are equal as persons and complementary as male and female. Sexuality is something that pertains to the physical-biological realm and has also been raised to a new level – the personal level – where nature and spirit are united."[11] Heterogenital complementarity pertains to the physical-biological realm, to the biological-genital distinction between male and female. Biological genitalia are necessary for moral sexual acts, but they are not sufficient to realize such acts; they must also function properly. If they cannot function complementarily, neither heterogenital nor reproductive complementarity is possible, and in that case Canon Law prescribes that a valid marriage and sacrament are also not possible. "Antecedent and perpetual impotence to have intercourse, whether on the part of the man or of the woman, which is either absolute or relative, of its very nature invalidates marriage."[12] Only sexual acts where the penis is inserted into the vagina and (male) orgasm takes place in the vagina are suitable for moral sexual acts. All other sexual acts that lead to orgasm, masturbation, oral sex, sodomitical acts, are considered immoral. Three biological criteria,

---

9 See Tobias S. Haller, *Reasonable and Holy: Engaging Same Sexuality* (New York: Seabury, 2009), 37 ff.

10 Jean Baptiste Michel et al., "Quantitative Analysis of Culture Using Millions of Digitized Books," *Science* 331 (2011): 176 – 182.

11 CRP, n. 3.

12 *Code of Canon Law* (Vatican City: Libreria Editrice Vaticana, 1983), Canon 1084, 1.

Table 1

The Meanings of Complementarity	
I. Biological Complementarity	
Title	**Definition**
Hetero-Genital Complementarity	The physically functioning male and female sexual organs (penis and vagina) used in sexual acts
Reproductive Complementarity	The physically functioning male and female reproductive organs used in sexual acts to biologically reproduce
II. Personal Complementarity	
Title	**Definition**
Communion Complementarity	The two-in-oneness within a hetero-genital complementary marital relationship that is created and sustained by sexual acts
Affective Complementarity	The integrated emotional, psychological, spiritual, relational dimensions of the human person grounded in hetero-genital complementarity.
Parental Complementarity	Hetero-genitally complementary parents who fulfill the second dimension of reproductive complementarity, namely, the education of children.

therefore, biological genitalia, biologically functioning genitalia, and biological location of orgasm, must be met before one can even begin to consider whether a sexual act is a moral act.

Heterogenital complementarity is the foundation for human reproduction and "therefore, in the Creator's plan, sexual complementarity and fruitfulness belong to the very nature of marriage."[13] Heterogenital and reproductive complementarity, however, are to be distinguished. While the Magisterium teaches that a couple must complement each other genitally, it also teaches that it is not necessary that they biologically reproduce. Infertile couples and couples who choose not to reproduce for the duration of the marriage "for serious reasons"[14] can still enter into a valid and sacramental marital relationship. Reproductive complementarity, therefore, necessarily entails heterogenital complementarity, but heterogenital complementarity does not necessarily entail reproductive com-

---

13 CRP, n. 3.
14 Paul VI, *Humanae Vitae*, 1968, n. 10, http://www.vatican.va/content/paul-vi/en/encyclicals/documents/hf_p-vi_enc_25071968_humanae-vitae.html [accessed 22.10.2020].

plementarity. Heterogenital complementarity is distinct from and can stand alone from reproductive complementarity in the service of personal complementarity.

The CDF does refer to complementarity on the "personal level—where nature and spirit are united,"[15] and divides this personal complementarity into several subcategories. First, there is what we call *communion complementarity*. In the marital relationship, "a communion of persons is realized involving the use of the sexual faculty."[16] The use of male and female genitals in heterosexual marital acts expresses and contributes to a communion of persons. Without heterogenital complementarity, according to the CDF, communion complementarity is not possible, a point underscored in its statement on the morality of homosexual unions.

There are absolutely no grounds for considering homosexual unions to be in any way similar or even remotely analogous to God's plan for marriage and family. Marriage is holy, while homosexual acts go against the natural moral law. Homosexual acts 'close the sexual act to the gift of life. They do not proceed from a genuine affective and sexual complementarity. Under no circumstances can they be approved.'[17]

Second, there is *affective personal* complementarity. Citing the *Catechism of the Catholic Church*, the CDF asserts without proof that affective complementarity is lacking in homosexual acts and, therefore, these acts can never be approved. It does not clarify here exactly what it means by affective complementarity, but we can glean some insight from other magisterial sources. The Congregation for Catholic Education teaches that, "affective sex education must consider the totality of the person and insist on the integration of the biological, psycho-affective, social and spiritual elements."[18] Since affective sex education seeks to integrate the biological and personal, affective complementarity must similarly integrate the biological and personal in the two persons engaging in a heterosexual act. Given the Magisterium's teaching on the immorality of gay and lesbian acts, it is clear it regards heterogenital complementarity as a *sine qua non* for personal complementarity in sexual acts. Without heterogenital complementarity, complementarity in the sexual act is not possible.

---

15 CRP, n. 3.

16 Ibid.

17 Ibid., n. 4.

18 Congregation for Catholic Education, *Educational Guidance in Human Love: Outlines for Sex Education*, 1983, n. 35, http://www.vatican.va/roman_curia/congregations/ccatheduc/documents/rc_con_ccatheduc_doc_19831101_sexual-education_en.html [accessed 22.10.2020].

Third, the CDF refers to *parental complementarity.*[19] Parental complementarity designates heterogenitally complementary parents who fulfill the second dimension of reproductive complementarity, namely, the education of children. It argues against same-sex unions based on the scientifically demonstrated false claim that, "as experience has shown, the absence of sexual complementarity in these unions creates obstacles in the normal development of children who would be placed in the care of such persons."[20] The CDF provides no scientific evidence, here or elsewhere, to substantiate this claim and, since there is substantial social scientific data that contradicts it, the question remains unresolved whether or not parental complementarity is as intrinsically linked to heterogenital complementarity as the Magisterium claims. Social scientific data strongly support the claim that the communion and affective complementarity of the spouses greatly facilitate parental complementarity.

Heterogenital complementarity alone is insufficient to justify moral sexual acts. Rape, incest, and adultery all take place in a heterogenitally complementary way, but no one would argue they also express and generate personal complementarity. Complementarity is not either/or, either heterogenital or personal, but both/and, both heterogenital and personal. Though the Magisterium posits an intrinsic relationship between biological, heterogenital, and personal, affective complementarities, heterogenital complementarity is prioritized over personal complementarity. Functioning male and female genitals are the *sine qua non* of personal complementarity and moral sexual acts. When heterogenital complementarity is assured, it must be situated within the marital, interpersonal context to assure that sexual acts are moral. When heterogenital complementarity is not assured, as it is not assured in gay and lesbian sexual acts, the acts are by definition "intrinsically disordered...do not proceed from a genuine affective and sexual complementarity. Under no circumstances can they be approved" as moral sexual acts creating personal complementarity.[21]

---

19 CRP, n. 3.

20 Ibid., n. 7.

21 Catechism, n. 2357; see also CDF, *Persona Humana: Declaration on Certain Questions concerning Sexual Ethics*, 1975, n. 8, https://www.vatican.va/roman_curia/congregations/cfaith/documents/rc_con_cfaith_doc_19751229_persona-humana_en.html [accessed 22.10.2020].

2 The Deconstruction of Complementarity

2.1 Divinely Instituted Complementarities

Prior to the revision of Canon Law in 1983, religious and denominational complementarity, found in the marriage between two Catholics, were required for valid marriage in the Catholic Church. Religious non-complementarity, the marriage between a Catholic and a non-baptized person, and denominational non-complementarity, the marriage between a Catholic and a non-Catholic Christian, were strictly forbidden in the 1917 *Code of Canon Law*.[22] In the conceptual world of early twentieth-century theology and canon law, it would be correct to say that "religious complementarity" and "denominational complementarity" were instituted by God and were strict requirements for any valid Catholic marriage. In the 1983 *Code*, however, these canons were revised. "*Without the express permission of the competent authority*, marriage is forbidden between two baptized persons, one of whom was baptized in the Catholic Church...and the other of whom is a member of a Church or ecclesial community which is not in full communion with the Catholic Church."[23] The revised *Code* continues to declare that interreligious marriages are invalid,[24] though they can be permitted and validated if certain prescribed conditions are fulfilled.[25] Strict religious and denominational complementarity were relaxed in the Catholic tradition and in other traditions.

Though the Catholic Church never explicitly condemned interracial marriages, other Christian denominations did and, in the United States up to 1967, racial-complementarity in marriage was enforced through miscegenation laws which prohibited interracial marriage as "unnatural" and prohibited by divine sanction. For example, in 1878 the Virginia Supreme Court declared the following: "the moral and physical development of both races...require that they should be kept distinct and separate...that connections and alliances so unnatural that God and nature seem to forbid them, should be prohibited by positive law, and be subject to no evasion."[26] Racial complementarity was defended

---

22 *Code of Canon Law* (Rome: Typis Polyglottis Vaticanis, 1917), Canon 1060 and Canons 1070, 1071.

23 Code of Canon Law (1983), Canon 1124 [emphasis added].

24 Ibid., Canon 1086.

25 Ibid., Canons 1125, 1126.

26 See Virginia Supreme Court of Appeals, *Kinney v. the Commonwealth* (October 3, 1878), https://www.encyclopediavirginia.org/Kinney_v_The_Commonwealth_October_3_1878 [accessed 22.10.2020].

both legislatively and religiously for many Christian denominations as a reflection of God's will and the natural order. Such complementarity is now seen for what it truly is, racist bigotry.

Throughout most of its history, the Catholic tradition posited a strict role complementarity in marriage justified by its biological, historical, and socially conditioned interpretation of gender in the creation story in Genesis.[27] Wives are described as essentially nurturing childbearers, subservient to husbands who are described as essentially active protectors and providers. These traditional gender roles have been seriously challenged in recent theological writings and mildly challenged in recent magisterial teaching, but residual influences remain. While admitting that women's roles have been too narrowly defined historically "as wife and mother, without adequate access to public functions, which have generally been reserved for men," John Paul II goes on to note the following: "On the other hand, the true advancement of women requires that clear recognition be given to the value of their maternal and family role, by comparison with all other public roles and all other professions."[28] Men's roles are never defined primarily in terms of husband and father; more emphasis is given to their social roles.

Positing such hierarchical role-complementarity in marriage perpetuates imbalances in power that limit women's creativity and contributions in the public realm. That power imbalance is theologically reinforced by the literal interpretation of the analogy of God as male/Father. Again, Mary Daly's analogical equation, "if God is male, then the male is God."[29] If we are ever to erase the power imbalances between women and men and the sexual violence against women to which it leads, we must erase the literal interpretation of God as male/Father by teaching consistently that it is an analogy and not a literal description, for it underlies, creates, and sustains the eroticization of male power which, in turn, underlies, creates, and sustains sexual violence against women, both within and without the Catholic Church. Contemporary gender analysis demonstrates that the power imbalances between women and men in marriage and society are

---

27 Genesis 2:18 reports that "Then the Lord God said, 'it is not good that man should be alone; I will make him a helper ['ezer] fit for him.'" The Hebrew 'ezer does not carry the hint of subordination that the English helper carries and, in fact, is frequently applied to God (e. g. Ex 18:4; Ps 30:10; Ps 33:20; Heb 13:6). Any effort to construe helper with a subordinate meaning, including John Paul II's, is incorrect. See Phyllis Trible, "Eve and Adam: Genesis 2–3 Reread," in Womanspirit Rising: A Feminist Reader in Religion, ed. Carol P. Christ and Judith Plaskow (San Francisco: Harper and Row, 1979), 74–83.

28 John Paul II, Familiaris Consortio, n. 23.

29 Daly, Beyond God the Father, 19.

more socio-historically than divinely constructed. For this reason, most Catholic theologians now argue that traditional perceptions of role-complementarity in marriage are unjust toward women and should be abandoned. We ask now what would warrant the displacement of heterogenital complementarity as the primary consideration for moral sexual acts in magisterial teaching?

2.2 Historical Developments in Catholic Teaching on Marriage

Though biological complementarity, heterogenital and reproductive, has long been accepted as the foundational principle in Catholic teaching for valid marriage and moral sexual acts, several developments in that teaching necessitate a redefinition of its status. First, in his encyclical on marriage, *Casti Connubii*, Pope Pius XI affirms the Thomistic primary and secondary ends of marriage. "The primary end of marriage is the procreation and the education of children;" the secondary end includes "mutual aid, the cultivating of mutual love, and the quieting of concupiscence."[30] Pius, unexpectedly, also shows a deepening appreciation of the secondary end. The mutual love of spouses "can in a very real sense...be said to be the chief reason and purpose of matrimony provided matrimony be looked at not in the restricted sense as instituted for the proper conception and education of the child, but more widely as the blending of life as a whole and the mutual interchange and sharing thereof."[31] Further, Pius agrees with Augustine: "it is wrong to leave a wife that is sterile in order to take another by whom children may be had."[32] The renewed emphasis on the secondary end of marriage and the recognition of the validity and sacramentality of infertile marriages combine to challenge the primacy of biological over personal complementarity.

Second, Pope Pius XII assured Italian midwives in 1951 that "serious reasons, such as those that not rarely arise from medical, eugenic, economic, and social indications, may exempt husband and wife from the obligatory positive debt [of procreating] for a long period or even for the entire period of matrimonial life."[33] Pope Paul VI repeated that same teaching in *Humanae Vitae*.[34] In

---

30 Pius XI, *Casti Connubii*, 1930, nn. 17 and 59, http://www.vatican.va/content/pius-xi/en/en cyclicals/documents/hf_p-xi_enc_19301231_casti-connubii.html [accessed 22.10.2020].
31 Ibid., n. 24.
32 Ibid., n. 36.
33 Pius XII, *Address to Midwives on the Nature of Their Profession*, 1951, https://www.papal encyclicals.net/pius12/p12midwives.htm [accessed 22.10.2020].

such cases, Paul VI taught, the marital act does not "cease to be legitimate even when, for reasons independent of their will, it is foreseen to be infertile."[35] On the basis of this teaching, a couple can intentionally eliminate the possibility of biological reproduction from their sexual intercourse through natural but not artificial family planning, and their sexual act can be moral.

Third, the vast majority of the Bishops of Vatican II affirmed what was logically implicit in earlier magisterial teaching, namely, since reproduction is not essential for a sacramental and valid marriage, it was illogical to continue to teach procreation as the primary end of marriage. *Gaudium et Spes* eliminated the primary end-secondary end terminology; procreation is no longer the primary end of marriage. Marriage and conjugal love, the Council teaches, "are by their very nature ordained to the generation and education of children," but that "does not make the other ends of marriage of less account," and "marriage is a communion of life" even when biological reproduction is impossible.[36] The Council also replaced the traditional, juridical term *contract* to describe the marital relationship with the biblically based, interpersonal term *covenant*.[37] These shifts are significant in that they emphasize personal and relational over biological complementarity.

Fourth, Paul VI abandoned the primary end-secondary end terminology with respect to sexual intercourse and defined intercourse, rather, as having two intrinsic *meanings*, one procreative and the other unitive.[38] Procreation, it is to be noted, is not equivalent to *actual* reproduction in *Humanae Vitae* or earlier magisterial documents; rather, it is defined as being "capable of generating new life."[39] A question to be posed to *Humanae Vitae* and its act-centered approach to human sexuality is whether it is illogical to claim that "each and every marriage act must remain open to the transmission of life."[40] In the cases of infertile couples, couples who legitimately intend not to have any children, couples who practice natural family planning with the specific intention of avoiding the transmission of life, and couples where the wife is post-menopausal, this statement is morally ambiguous at best, and morally meaningless at

---

34 Paul VI, Humanae Vitae, n. 10.
35 Ibid., n. 11
36 Second Vatican Council, *Gaudium et Spes*, 1965, n. 50, http://www.vatican.va/archive/hist_councils/ii_vatican_council/documents/vat-ii_const_19651207_gaudium-et-spes_en.html [accessed 22.10.2020].
37 Ibid., n. 48.
38 Paul VI, Humanae Vitae, n. 12.
39 Ibid.
40 Ibid., n. 11.

worst. In all these cases, it seems that the procreative meaning of the marital act, if indeed it exists at all, is elided into its unitive meaning and personal complementarity is the primary meaning of the act.

This evolution in sexual teaching with its growing appreciation for the centrality of conjugal love in the marital relationship and the sexual act, and the elimination of procreation as the primary end of marriage and the sexual act, have implications for complementarity. They justify the displacement of biological complementarity by personal complementarity as the primary meaning of complementarity. These teachings combined seem to indicate the *de facto* primacy of personal complementarity in marriage and the marital act since a marriage is still valid and sacramental when a couple cannot biologically reproduce or chooses not to reproduce for the duration of the marriage. Elsewhere, the Magisterium offers a sexual anthropology that further warrants the displacement of the traditional primacy of heterogenital complementarity.

2.3 Development in Sexual Anthropology

The Magisterium's sexual anthropology, in dialogue with the scientific community, has evolved in recent years. According to the CDF,

> The human person, present-day scientists maintain, is so profoundly affected by sexuality that it must be considered one of the principal formative influences of a man or woman. In fact, sex is the source of the biological, psychological, and spiritual characteristics which make a person male or female and which thus considerably influence each individual's progress towards maturity and membership of society.[41]

An important dimension of the human sexual person is the person's integrated relationship to self and, to be moral, a sexual act must to be integrated with the whole self. The Congregation for Catholic Education teaches that sexuality "is a fundamental component of personality, one of its modes of being, of manifestation, of communicating with others, of feeling, of expressing and of living human love. Therefore, it is an integral part of the development of the personality and of its educative process."[42] The integration of the sexual self and its moral expression in sexual acts requires that we know the sexual self, and the Magisterium's teaching on sexual orientation has furthered this self-knowledge.

---

41 CDF, Persona Humana, n. 1.
42 Congregation for Catholic Education, Educational Guidance in Human Love, n. 4.

The Magisterium recognizes both that homosexual orientation and homosexual acts are morally distinct and that homosexual orientation is a given factor in personal sexuality. This recognition has profound implications for any discussion of the primacy of heterogenital complementarity as a foundational sexual ethical principle. The meaning of the phrase *sexual orientation* is complex, but the Magisterium provides Catholics with a concise description. It distinguishes between "a homosexual tendency, which proves to be transitory, and homosexuals who are definitively such because of some kind of innate instinct."[43] In light of this distinction, the United States Council of Catholic Bishops (USCCB) continues that "it seems appropriate to understand sexual orientation (heterosexual or homosexual) as a *deep-seated* dimension of one's personality and to recognize its relative stability in a person. A homosexual orientation produces a stronger emotional and sexual attraction toward individuals of the same sex, rather than toward those of the opposite sex."[44] We define sexual orientation as an innate condition of humans characterized by an emotional, psychosexual attraction to persons of the opposite sex or same sex or both, depending on whether the orientation is heterosexual. homosexual, or bisexual.

Concerning the genesis of homosexual orientation, the USCCB notes what is agreed on in the scientific community, namely, that it has as yet no isolated single cause. The experts point to a variety of factors, biological, genetic, hormonal, psychological, social, that may contribute to its rise, a combination of nature and nurture. That there is a biological basis to sexual orientation is suggested by the experience of transgender persons who claim a gender that matches neither their biological structure nor their socialization. Nature, the sciences suggest, produces a greater diversity in sex and sexual desire than the accepted sexual binary allows. Whatever its origin, homosexual orientation is personally experienced as a given, something not freely chosen, and therefore, since morality presumes the freedom to choose, not sinful. The Magisterium teaches, however, that "this inclination...is objectively disordered" and, therefore, homosexual acts, to which it leads, are "intrinsically disordered."[45] They are intrinsically disordered because they "are contrary to the natural law. They close the sexual act to the gift of life. They do not proceed from a genuine affective and sexual complementarity."[46]

---

43 United States Council of Catholic Bishops, "Always Our Children," *Origins* 28, 7 (July 2, 1998): 100; CDF, Persona Humana, n. 8.
44 Ibid.
45 CDF, Persona Humana, n. 8; Catechism, n. 2357. See "Vatican List of Catechism Changes," *Origins* 27, 15 (September 25, 1997): 257.
46 Catechism, n. 2357.

3 The Reconstruction of Complementarity

3.1 Pope Francis and Complementarity

In his opening speech to a CDF-hosted interfaith colloquium on "The complementarity of Man and Woman in Marriage" in 2014, Pope Francis opened up the possibility for thinking anew about complementarity as a foundational anthropological, sexual idea. He opens his treatment with a generic description, which "refers to situations where one of two things adds to, completes, or fulfills a lack in the other," importantly adding that complementarity "is much more than that."[47] He provides four nuances for us to think theologically about that *more*.

The first nuance is a scriptural nuance that celebrates the fact that "the Spirit has endowed each of us with different gifts so that – just as the human body's members work together for the good of the whole – everyone's gifts can work together for the benefit of each (cf. 1 Cor 12)." For the followers of Christ, he adds, this Spirit-giftedness is the "deepest meaning" of complementarity and the essential root of what he calls the "human ecology" of human relationships.[48] All complementarities emanate from this fundamental Spirit-giftedness which impels humans to create harmony and unity, to overcome division and exclusion, to acknowledge and affirm the Spirit-created varieties of human relationships with God, neighbor, and self. Francis correctly emphasizes that complementarity assumes many forms, since every man and woman brings their own personal contribution – "personal richness," their own "charisma" – to the marriage.[49] The complementarity between spouses, therefore, is *a*, not *the*, root of marriage and family, but the contribution of marriage to society is "indispensable." Given the crises in contemporary marriages and families, this positive affirmation of marriage as a particular anthropological and theological expression of the general harmony of God's creation is a necessary and welcome prophetic statement, but the complementarity of woman and man is only one of the many harmonies of which Francis speaks.

Francis' second nuance, an emphasis on complementarity as a dynamic and evolving idea rather than a "simplistic notion 'that all the roles and relations of

---

47 See Vatican Radio, "Pope Francis: Marriage and Family are in Crisis," 17.11.2014, http://www.archivioradiovaticana.va/storico/2014/11/17/pope_francis_marriage_and_the_family_are_in_crisis/en-1111371 [accessed 22.10.2020].
48 Ibid.
49 Ibid.

the two sexes are fixed in a single, static pattern'" is a critical nuance.[50] It reflects his shift from a classicist to an historically conscious worldview. A classicist worldview asserts that reality is static, fixed, and universal. The method utilized, anthropology formulated, and norms taught in this worldview are timeless, universal, and immutable, and the acts condemned by those norms are always so condemned. An historically conscious worldview, on the other hand, fundamentally challenges this classicist view of reality by positing that reality is dynamic, evolving, and particular. The method utilized, anthropology formulated, and norms taught in this worldview are contingent, particular, and changeable, and the acts judged by those norms are morally evaluated in light of evolving human knowledge and understanding. John Paul and the Magisterium use the term complementarity in a classicist way, defining it to reflect culturally determined gender roles grounded in the biological distinction between male and female required for reproduction.

Francis' third nuance addresses the "ecological crisis" plaguing marriage and family. *Ecology* is originally a biological concept referring to the relations between living organisms and their environment, but it has been extended in our time to include relations between human groups, the social patterns those relationships create, and the material resources available to them.[51] Francis clearly has in mind this contemporary meaning of ecology, the inclusion of the idea of complementarity in that human ecology, and the role of complementarity in the present crisis in that ecology. He invites us to reflect upon complementarity in light of how social sins limit its full realization and impact in order to "foster a new human ecology."[52] These social sins, which create a social ecology that restricts the full impact of complementarity on people, include poverty, racism, sexism, homophobia, discrimination, patriarchy, and every other social reality that frustrates, and does not facilitate, human dignity and relationship. Francis issues an invitation to find a more dynamic definition of complementarity that simultaneously exposes those threats to social, marital, and familial harmony and responds to them.

Francis' fourth nuance of complementarity is a focus on family as an "anthropological fact," which "we cannot qualify with ideological concepts which are compelling at only one moment in history, and then decline."[53] World-

---

50 Ibid.
51 See Pope Francis' holistic and detailed understanding of "integral ecology" in *Laudato Si'*, 2015, chapter 4, http://www.vatican.va/content/francesco/en/encyclicals/documents/papa-fran cesco_20150524_enciclica-laudato-si.html [accessed 22.10.2020].
52 Vatican Radio, Pope Francis.
53 Ibid.

wide experience shows that family is defined and influenced historically, culturally, socially, and legally. While one can certainly conceive and present an idealized concept of family as one man, one woman, and their children, the historical reality of family is more complex. There are now two-parent families, single-parent families, step-parent families, adoptive-parent families, foster-parent families, polygamous-parent families, and same-sex parent families.[54] In each of these cases, family is family and we must engage the reality we find, not what we would like it ideally to be. We must also evaluate the nature of the relationship between parents and their children based on sound scientific evidence, not on unjustified speculative prejudgment.

This legitimate demand for evidence can be directed toward the USCCB's 2006 statement on homosexuality. Speaking of a homosexual inclination, avoiding the term orientation, the USCCB declares that it "predisposes one toward what is truly not good for the human person."[55] The predisposition is towards gay and lesbian sexual acts that are "not ordered toward the fulfillment of the natural ends of human sexuality" and therefore "acting in accord with such an inclination simply cannot contribute to the true good of the human person." The statement that gay and lesbian sexual acts, by definition, cannot contribute to the good of the human person is at variance with the scientifically-demonstrated relational experiences of committed, monogamous, gay and lesbian couples. Lawrence Kurdek has done extensive research on these couples and notes the following characteristics when comparing them with married heterosexual couples. Gay and lesbian couples tend to have a more equitable distribution of household labor, demonstrate greater conflict resolution skills, have less support from members of their own families but greater support from friends, and, most significantly, experience similar levels of relational satisfaction compared to heterosexual couples.[56] Empirical studies also challenge the CDF's claim that, "as

---

54 Just recently, in a documentary Pope Francis states that "homosexuals have a right to be a part of the family. They're children of God and have a right to a family. Nobody should be thrown out, or be made miserable because of it…. What we have to create is a civil union law. That way they are legally covered." See Catholic News Agency, "Pope Francis' Call for Civil Union Law for Same-Sex Couples, in Shift from Vatican Stance," 21.10.2020, https://www.catholicnewsagency. com/news/pope-francis-calls-for-civil-union-law-for-same-sex-couples-in-shift-from-vatican-stance-12462 [accessed 22.10.2020].

55 United States Council of Catholic Bishops, *Ministry to Persons with a Homosexual Inclination: Guidelines for Pastoral Care* (Washington, DC: United States Conference of Catholic Bishops, 2006), p. 5.

56 Lawrence A. Kurdek, "What Do We Know about Gay and Lesbian Couples?" *Current Directions in Psychological Science* 14 (2005): 251–254, 251; "Differences between Partners from Heterosexual, Gay, and Lesbian Cohabiting Couples," *Journal of Marriage and Family* 68 (2006): 509–

experience has shown, the absence of sexual complementarity in these [homosexual] unions creates obstacles in the normal development of children...[and] would actually mean doing violence to these children."[57] That unsupported claim is also contradicted by experience and scientific analysis of experience.

Pope Francis' speech focused on complementarity as it applies to man and woman in marriage, but the four nuances he introduces open up the possibility of ongoing theological and anthropological reflection on the concept and its relevance to all human relationships. The challenge is to discern the implications of these nuances for an historically conscious sexual ethic and an evolving notion of complementarity which seeks ecological harmony in all human relationship and is relevant to the lived reality of all sexual persons. We argue that to judge moral sexual acts only on the basis of biological heterogenital complementarity is a reductive and inadequate consideration of a significant number of sexual human persons.

3.2 Holistic Complementarity

In light of the various senses of complementarity explored in the foregoing, we argue that a moral sexual act must be a mutual, free, just, and loving sexual act and an expression of what we call *holistic complementarity* (see Table 2). Holistic complementarity is the authentic *integration* of biological, personal, and orientation complementarities.

In holistic complementarity, biological complementarity alone is an inadequate foundational principle for moral sexual acts; orientation and personal complementarities are the cofoundational principles. It is only in light of these cofoundational complementarities that we can assess the appropriate nature of biological complementarity within a sexual relationship and morally assess a sexual act. Certainly genitalia are essential for human sexual acts; their moral use, however, must be assessed in terms of the human sexual person adequately considered. It is this personalist interpretation of genital complementarity, which sees the physical genitals as organs of the whole person, including his or her sexual orientation, which allows us to expand the definition of a moral sexual act to include both heterosexual and homosexual sexual acts. In couples of heterosexual orientation, personal complementarity is manifested, nurtured,

---

528; Jimi Adams and Ryan Light, "Scientific Consensus, the Law, and Same Sex Parenting Outcomes," *Social Science Research* 53 (2015): 300–310.
57 CRP, n. 7.

Table 2

Holistic Complementarity

Biological
(Genital,
Reproductive)
Complementarity

Moral
Sexual
Act

Sexual
Orientation
Complementarity

Personal
(Affective,
Communion,
[Parental])
Complementarity

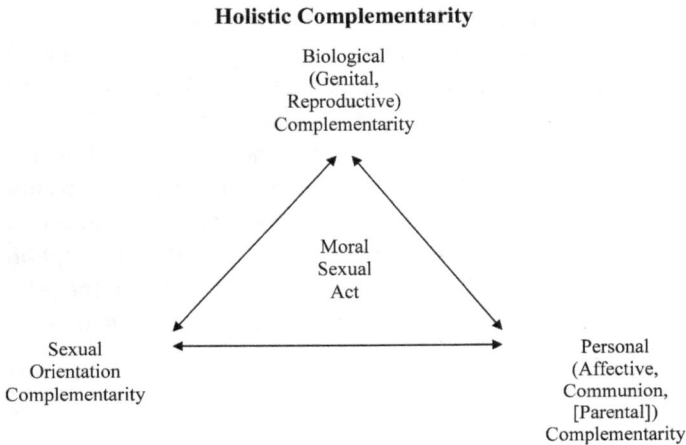

and strengthened through male and female genital activity; in couples of homosexual orientation, it is equally manifested, nurtured, and strengthened through male and female genital activity. If one takes heterogenital complementarity as the *primary* principle for a moral sexual act, one defines a person's potential for a moral sexual act in terms of a single, physical dimension, namely, the biological genitals. This mono-dimensional perspective, we argue, does not acknowledge and embrace the complexity of the human sexual person. Holistic complementarity embraces all human persons and understands biological genitality to be in dialogue with and at the service of personal and orientation complementarity.

Moral sexual acts can be defined only in the context of this complex biological, personal, and orientation interrelationship. As it would be an immoral and unnatural sexual act for a heterosexual person to engage in sexual acts with a person of the same sex, so also it would be an immoral and unnatural sexual act for a gay or lesbian person to engage in sexual acts with a person of the opposite sex. It would be immoral and unnatural not because of physical genitals alone, but because of the individual's personhood, sexuality, and sexual orientation. Recognizing, embracing, and internalizing personal sexuality facilitates a deeper realization of self in relation to not only that other with whom a person enters into intimate sexual relationship but also to God who so created the person. If we shift the *sine qua non* foundation for a moral sexual act from heterogenital complementarity to an integrated, holistic personal, orientation, and biological complementarity, the principle for what constitutes a moral sexual act becomes more personal and can be formulated as follows. A moral sexual act is a mutual, free, just, and loving sexual act that is an authentic expression of holistic complementarity. Such acts are in accord with a person's sexual orientation and facilitate a deeper appreciation, integration, and sharing of a person's relational embodied self with another relational embodied self, which may or may not result in reproduction. The principle of holistic complementarity allows for the morality of *some* homosexual sexual acts and *some* heterosexual sexual acts, depending on the interrelationship of its three dimensions and their meaning for the human persons involved. It may also allow for other sexual acts that are absolutely prohibited by the Magisterium, such as artificial contraception and reproductive technologies. Pope Francis' and our reconstruction of the principle of complementarity, we believe, reflects a more adequate human and Christian sexual anthropology and ethic.

Bibliography

Adams, Jimi and Ryan Light. "Scientific Consensus, the Law, and Same Sex Parenting Outcomes." *Social Science Research* 53 (2015): 300–310.

Catechism of the Catholic Church. Second Edition, revised in accordance with the official Latin text promulgated by Pope John Paul II (Vatican City: Libreria Editrice Vaticana, 1994).

Catholic News Agency. "Pope Francis' Call for Civil Union Law for Same-Sex Couples, in Shift from Vatican Stance," 21.10.2020, https://www.catholicnewsagency.com/news/pope-fran cis-calls-for-civil-union-law-for-same-sex-couples-in-shift-from-vatican-stance-12462 [accessed 22.10.2020].

Code of Canon Law. Rome: Typis Polyglottis Vaticanis, 1917.

Code of Canon Law. Vatican City: Libreria Editrice Vaticana, 1983.

Congregation for the Doctrine of the Faith. *Persona Humana: Declaration on Certain Questions concerning Sexual Ethics,* 1975, https://www.vatican.va/roman_curia/con gregations/cfaith/documents/rc_con_cfaith_doc_19751229_persona-humana_en.html [accessed 22.10.2020].

Congregation for Catholic Education. *Educational Guidance in Human Love: Outlines for Sex Education,* 1983, http://www.vatican.va/roman_curia/congregations/ccatheduc/docu ments/rc_con_ccatheduc_doc_19831101_sexual-education_en.html [accessed 22.10.2020].

Congregation for the Doctrine of the Faith. *Considerations Regarding Proposals to Give Legal Recognition to Unions Between Homosexual Persons,* 2003, https://www.vatican.va/ roman_curia/congregations/cfaith/documents/rc_con_cfaith_doc_20030731_ homosexual-unions_en.html [accessed 22.10.2020].

Daly, Mary. *Beyond God the Father: Toward a Philosophy of Women's Liberation.* Boston: Beacon, 1973.

Francis. *Laudato Si',* 2015, http://www.vatican.va/content/francesco/en/encyclicals/docu ments/papa-francesco_20150524_enciclica-laudato-si.html [accessed 22.10.2020].

Haller, Tobias S. *Reasonable and Holy: Engaging Same Sexuality.* New York: Seabury, 2009.
Janssens, Louis. "Artificial Insemination: Ethical Considerations." *Louvain Studies* 8 (1980): 3–29.
John Paul II. *Familiaris Consortio,* 1981, http://www.vatican.va/content/john-paul-ii/en/apost_
    exhortations/documents/hf_jp-ii_exh_19811122_familiaris-consortio.html [accessed 22.10.2020].
Kurdek, Lawrence A. "Differences between Partners from Heterosexual, Gay, and Lesbian Cohabiting Couples." *Journal of Marriage and Family* 68 (2006): 509–528.
Kurdek, Lawrence A. "What Do We Know about Gay and Lesbian Couples?" *Current Directions in Psychological Science* 14 (2005): 251–254.
Michel, Jean Baptiste et al. "Quantitative Analysis of Culture Using Millions of Digitized Books." *Science* 331 (2011): 176–182.
Paul VI. *Humanae Vitae,* 1968, http://www.vatican.va/content/paul-vi/en/encyclicals/docu
    ments/hf_p-vi_enc_25071968_
    humanae-vitae.html [accessed 22.10.2020].
Pius XI. *Casti Connubii,* 1930, http://www.vatican.va/content/pius-xi/en/encyclicals/docu
    ments/hf_p-xi_enc_19301231_casti-connubii.html [accessed 22.10.2020].
Pius XII. *Address to Midwives on the Nature of Their Profession,* 1951, https://www.papal
    encyclicals.net/pius12/p12midwives.htm [accessed 22.10.2020].
Ruether, Rosemary Radford. *Sexism and God-Talk: Toward a Feminist Theology.* Boston: Beacon, 1983.
Second Vatican Council, *Gaudium et Spes,* 1965, http://www.vatican.va/archive/hist_councils/
    ii_vatican_council/documents/vat-ii_const_19651207_gaudium-et-spes_en.html [accessed 22.10.2020].
Trible, Phyllis. "Eve and Adam: Genesis 2–3 Reread." In *Womanspirit Rising: A Feminist Reader in Religion,* ed. Carol P. Christ and Judith Plaskow, 74–83. San Francisco: Harper and Row, 1979.
United States Council of Catholic Bishops. "Always Our Children." *Origins* 28, 7 (July 2, 1998): 100.
United States Council of Catholic Bishops. *Ministry to Persons with a Homosexual Inclination: Guidelines for Pastoral Care.* Washington, DC: United States Conference of Catholic Bishops, 2006.
"Vatican List of Catechism Changes," *Origins* 27, 15 (September 25, 1997): 257.
Vatican Radio. "Pope Francis: Marriage and Family are in Crisis," 17.11.2014, http://www.ar
    chivioradiovaticana.va/storico/2014/11/17/pope_francis_marriage_and_the_family_are_
    in_crisis/en-1111371 [accessed 22.10.2020].
Virginia Supreme Court of Appeals. *Kinney v. the Commonwealth* (October 3, 1878), https://
    www.encyclopediavirginia.org/Kinney_v_The_Commonwealth_October_3_1878 [accessed 22.10.2020].
Wild, Robert A. "The Pastoral Letters." In *The New Jerome Biblical Commentary,* ed. Raymond E. Brown, Joseph A. Fitzmyer and Roland E. Murphy, 891–902. Englewood Cliffs, NJ: Prentice Hall, 1990.

Socio-Ethical Challenges

Konrad Hilpert
Same-Sex Partnership and Marriage

1 Reconstructing the Socio-Ethical Issue

Two motivational strands intertwine around the issue of same-sex marriage, each with its own long, tumultuous history. One of these is the effort to gain access to marriage as an institutionalized way of life and model of responsibility; the other is the demand for public recognition of the practiced and socially observed behaviors and lifestyles of people oriented toward persons of the same sex as themselves.

Both historically and culturally, neither access to institutionalized marriage nor the free choice of a partner and the decision to have children together is as self-evident as it seems to most citizens of liberal constitutional states today. Indeed, for long periods of history, marriage bans existed with regard to criteria such as lineage, economics, or ethnicity. In addition, family associations and interests imposed severe restrictions, which individuals – with all of their wishes and feelings – only rarely managed to oppose with any prospect of success. In isolated cases along the present-day cultural spectrum, marriages may still be arranged by parents or guardians, or require the approval of an official government authority, and coercion may even be employed. Nevertheless, there is a broad consensus, partly based on human rights, that such restrictions can in no way be justified and therefore should not occur. The only legitimate, meaningful restriction is the age of majority, which is concretized in the respective legislation and recognized as the external criterion of marriageability.

The struggle for public recognition of same-sex sensibilities, behaviors, and lifestyles has primarily been a campaign against their disqualification as "unnatural," and thus as a choice for which the subjects were culpable, or as "pathological" – views which had been firmly enculturated for centuries. The social consequences of these outdated perspectives included severe legal restrictions and prohibitions as well as *de facto* stigmatization. However, the threat of sanctions and the risk of social contempt also triggered strenuous efforts on the part of those affected to conceal their homosexual inclinations and practices from others and/or to move them into closed, secret spaces, which in turn often provoked intense mutual suspicion and gave rise to the idea that persons who frequented such milieus might be susceptible to blackmail. Since the 1960s, efforts to gain public recognition of same-sex orientation and its specific forms of expression have primarily focused on the right to a self-determined lifestyle,

https://doi.org/10.1515/9783110705188-009

which was essentially made possible by the expansion of medical and psychological knowledge about human sexuality and its development.

On the one hand, based on the logic of eliminating unjustified restrictions on access to the institution of marriage, the problem of same-sex civil partnership presents itself as the question of whether the right to marry can continue to be reserved for unions between a man and a woman, or whether it must be extended or opened up to other constellations of persons. On the other hand, based on the logic of a person's right to a self-determined lifestyle, the demand that marriage should also be opened up to partners of the same sex is seen as a potential consequence of equal treatment for same-sex and opposite-sex oriented citizens. At the present moment, when the two strands of this debate are coming together, the following questions need to be clarified: 1) the question of the concept underlying the institution of marriage; 2) the question of the reason(s) why certain domestic partnerships require special protection; and 3) the question of the relationship between church and state in terms of their power to define and their jurisdiction over "marriage."

This contribution will explore these questions. First, however, I will outline the developments that have taken place with regard to so-called "equal marriage" and analyze the normative guiding principles that underpin it.

2 Social Changes and Legal Developments in Germany

Since the German Parliament's decision in June 2017, the current legislative situation in Germany entails that marriage – as defined in Section 1353 (1) of the Civil Code – can be entered into as a life-long relationship not only by two persons of different sexes, but also by persons of the same sex. Those politicians who promoted this change, as well as a large segment of the German population – particularly the younger demographic – and the media, interpreted this change as a long-overdue legal confirmation of a social shift that had already taken place.[1] On the other hand, those who opposed the decision, along with a different segment of the population – particularly the older demographic – perceived (and still perceive) it as a decisive break in both cultural and legal history.

---

1 See, among others, Anna Katharina Mangold, "Stationen der Ehe für alle in Deutschland," Bundeszentrale für politische Bildung, August 9, 2018, https://www.bpb.de/gesellschaft/gen der/homosexualitaet/274019/stationen-der-ehe-fuer-alle-in-deutschland (accessed April 21, 2021).

These two interpretations of the situation are not necessarily mutually exclusive, although they each emphasize different points: while the second focuses primarily on the continuity of marriage as an institution as well as its normative character, the first presumes the need to legally recognize sociological findings on the forms of cohabitation that exist in practice. Precisely because the outcome of the 2017 decision stands in such sharp contrast to previous conventions, the change also seems justified and urgent as both the result and the endpoint of comprehensive, decades-long social, political, and juridical debates.

These social, political, and juridical debates took place in the German public sphere in three major phases. The first was entirely defined by the struggle against the infamous Paragraph 175 of the German Criminal Code. In 1957, the Federal Constitutional Court declared that the stricter version of this law, which had been passed during the National Socialist era, conformed to the constitution,[2] and it stipulated penalties for any sexual contact between men. Even before the Criminal Code was reformed in 1969 and the relevant aspects of this crime were clarified and curtailed, the reasons given to justify this paragraph had been problematized as prejudicial, and reference had been made to the ways in which the prohibition inevitably pressured the relevant minority to live in hiding.[3] This battle against Paragraph 175 came to an end in 1994, when homosexuality was completely decriminalized in the course of legislative harmonization between the Federal Republic of Germany and the former German Democratic Republic.

The second phase of the debate is characterized by the so-called gay (and lesbian) movement. In the 1970s and 1980s, this movement – following the model of a civil rights movement – branded the unequal treatment of persons with a homosexual orientation in many existing legal provisions as scandalous and organized a series of initiatives and civil actions aimed at obtaining equal treatment for homosexual and heterosexual people in various legal spheres (such as housing, information, representation, insurance, naturalization, and emergency care),[4] and at the same time fought to be recognized as a group within society. Adopting the previously pejorative classifications "gay" and (later also) "lesbian" as demonstratively self-confident self-designations, as a declara-

---

2 Bundesverfassungsgericht, judgment from May 10, 1957, AZ 1 BvR 550/52, https://dejure.org/dienste/vernetzung/rechtsprechung?Text=1%20BvR%20550/52 (accessed April 21, 2021).
3 See, among others, Fritz Bauer et al., eds., *Sexualität und Verbrechen: Beiträge zur Strafrechtsreform* (Frankfurt am Main: Fischer, 1963).
4 On this topic, see, for example, the chapter on "life as a minority group in the Federal Republic of Germany and the German Democratic Republic" in Hans-Georg Stümke, *Homosexuelle in Deutschland: Eine politische Geschichte* (Munich: Beck, 1989), 132–171.

tion of war on the deeply held, firmly anchored prejudices that permeated society, was important for this effort. Nevertheless, this combative self-confidence was strongly challenged by the appearance of the (at the time fatal) immunodeficiency disease HIV/AIDS in the 1980s. Although it soon became clear that the infection could also be transmitted to sexual partners via heterosexual activity and to infants via infected mothers, and that everyday social encounters with infected persons carried no risk, homosexuals – among whom the infection had first been observed – found themselves bearing the brunt of social fears around the issue, along with drug users. This triggered calls for those infected to be locked away and treated in isolation. Widespread debate on this issue succeeded in breaking down this constriction and exposing the associated dangers of legitimizing discrimination and stigmatization.[5] At the same time, the political emphasis on education and prevention prevailed. As an alternative to promiscuity, the focus shifted to the question of cultivating sexuality and respectful behavior in partnership – which is a challenge for all people, regardless of whether they are homosexual or heterosexual, and which cannot be guaranteed by legal means or by any other externally imposed standards.

Finally, it is not only the emergence and proliferation of non-marital lifestyles (such as non-marital domestic partnerships of various kinds, as well as single life), but primarily the rapid tolerance these lifestyles came to enjoy across various regions, denominations, segments of the population that has made the possibility of same-sex partnerships a topic of public debate.[6] This question is the characteristic feature of the third phase of the debate. However, the issue is no longer simply the demand for acceptance and the right to shape one's own life according to individual preferences and ideas, but particularly the right to determine one's own lifestyle, family structures, and forms of coexistence as well.

This is precisely the point at which the demand for recognition of same-sex oriented persons and the demand for unrestricted access to marriage and family intersect. However, the goal of equality is not achieved all at once – particularly in a social context in which institutionalized marriage is dominant and enjoys strong legal protection – but only in a series of steps. One of these steps is the legal recognition of same-sex couples' right to adopt children. Another is the es-

---

5 See, for example, Johannes Gründel, "Aids – Anlass zur Enttabuisierung ethischer Fragestellungen," in *AIDS – Herausforderung an Gesellschaft und Moral*, ed. idem (Düsseldorf: Patmos, 1987), 80–106, here 94–95.

6 On the population's attitude to this, see Beate Küpper, Ulrich Klocke, and Lena-Carlotta Hoffmann, *Einstellungen gegenüber lesbischen, schwulen und bisexuellen Menschen in Deutschland: Ergebnisse der bevölkerungsrepräsentativen Studie* (Baden-Baden: Nomos, 2017).

tablishment of registered civil partnership in many nation-states as a separate option specifically for same-sex couples, by which they can enter into an institutionally regulated and publicly recognized form of domestic partnership. Yet another step is lesbian or (with somewhat more complex challenges) gay couples becoming parents, by means of either sperm donation or reproductive medicine. Here as well, *de facto* practice demands the development of legal regulations even in contexts in which the legislature has declared its intention to prevent such parental constellations for the sake of the child's presumed best interests.

3 From Criticism of Discrimination to Anti-Discrimination

In all the phases of the debate described above, the same goal was at stake – namely, the establishment of equal rights. However, the political thrust was different in each case and left its particular mark on the respective phase. Another feature is the role that moral arguments played in each of these debates.

One common thread running through these three phases is the allegation of discrimination, which is legitimized by nothing more than a reference to the other sexual orientation. According to this allegation, such "justified" discrimination severely restricts freedom and social participation. This realization leads to the demand for measures suited to eliminating such discrimination individually, institutionally, and also culturally.

Corresponding to the three phases of the debate outlined above, efforts to resist discrimination first concentrated on problematizing the outdated assessment of homosexuality as an act worthy of punishment, and thus also as immoral. If homosexual sensibility and perception is an element of certain individuals' identity and cannot be chosen or overridden by acts of volition, then homosexual practices cannot be classified as criminal offenses, nor can the threat of punishment be justified. As a consequence, the prohibition was gradually reversed and limited to certain asymmetric constellations, until the offense was completely abolished from the criminal code.

During the second phase, various activities aimed to make the diversity of gender orientations (homosexual and bisexual, in addition to the dominant heterosexual) visible throughout society, thus "normalizing" people with same-sex orientations who had previously been forced into dissimulation or driven underground. Both the self-image and the organizational appearance of homosexuals and bisexuals as groups or minorities were essential to this effort. Those affected by discrimination are visible and audible only as a group, and only in this way do they secure a platform from which they can participate in shaping the rules of social coexistence. Here as well, the institutional return on these investments is not a single legal statute, but a whole series of explicit improvements in favor of persons with same-sex orientations in the areas of tenancy, inheritance, custody, insurance, naturalization law, and so on. This phase also entailed an important qualitative leap in the formal prohibition of discrimination, which came into force in Germany with the General Act on Equal Treatment in 2006.[7] In forbidding discrimination with reference to the equal dignity of human beings, it specifically prohibits a person being reduced to a predetermined characteristic and consequently treated unequally on the basis of this characteristic. In the present context, this is primarily a question of the characteristic of sexual orientation, which has been added to the list of characteristics long recognized as potential grounds for discrimination, including "sex, race, colour, ethnic or social origin, genetic features, language, religion or belief, political or any other opinion, membership of a national minority, property, birth, disability, [and] age."[8]

The third phase is centrally and normatively concerned with a person's freedom to choose their lifestyle and domestic partnership arrangements. Institutionally, this initially manifested in the highly controversial establishment of a separate form of legally regulated community of responsibility specifically for same-sex couples: the registered civil partnership. This new designation as well as the special modalities for entering into such an agreement were also intended to clarify the difference between this form of partnership and the existing institution of marriage. However, several high court rulings have eliminated the existing regulatory differences and harmonized the regulations, and the distance which the legislature originally intended to preserve has been deemed to constitute a disadvantage.[9] In the long run, however, with no substantial differences in the respective rights associated with these two institutionalized communities of responsibility, it becomes difficult to justify why two such institutions should exist at all. Apart from the relatively minimal differences in (joint) adoption and access to reproductive medicine, which is solely subject to medical guidelines, only the difference in the sex of those who decide to marry and the corre-

---

7 See the text of the Allgemeines Gleichbehandlungsgesetz (AGG), available in English at: https://www.gesetze-im-internet.de/englisch_agg/index.html (accessed April 21, 2021).
8 Cf. Article 21 (1) of the Charter of Fundamental Rights of the European Union, https://www. europarl.europa.eu/charter/pdf/text_en.pdf (accessed April 21, 2021).
9 This is fully documented in Ferdinand Wollenschläger's expert report on constitutional law, in Wollenschläger and Dagmar Coester-Waltjen, *Ehe für alle: Die Öffnung der Ehe für gleichgeschlechtliche Paare aus verfassungsrechtlicher und rechtsvergleichender Perspektive* (Tübingen: Mohr Siebeck, 2018), 21–44.

sponding designation linked to each arrangement remain as substantial differences. This could then plausibly be construed by a significant portion of the public as well as the majority of members of parliament, spanning the political leanings of the various parties, as a disadvantage for same-sex couples.[10]

This became possible because conventional marriage between a man and a woman – to put it bluntly – was presented as a union between two people, each with a heterosexual orientation. Only under these conditions can the accusation of discrimination apply, because discrimination exists only if and to the extent that a fundamental equality is violated.[11] As such, the debate presents us with a concept of our common humanity. The concept of marriage as a union between a man and a woman, on the other hand, assumes that "the" human being always exists concretely in one of two manifestations – either as a man or as a woman – and that this is an elemental, irrevocable difference (which nevertheless does not exclude the principle of equal dignity). This is why the EU Charter of Fundamental Rights mentions both gender and sexual orientation in the list of prohibited grounds for discrimination: rather than being redundant, this represents the identification of two entirely different violations.[12] The same principle applies when we consider Article 20, which states that "everyone is equal before the law," alongside Article 23, which explicitly enshrines "equality between men and women."[13]

Thus the demand for same-sex marriage,[14] which until recently was quite controversial, has become superfluous due to the delegitimization of presumed heterosexuality as an unjustified privilege – a development which is described as an "opening." The fact that the legal situation in many Western countries has recently changed (for example, the Netherlands, Belgium, Spain, Canada,

---

10 Symptomatic of this is the question posed in an opinion piece in the daily press in 2015 on the grounds for upholding the "marriage ban for same-sex couples"; see Robert Roßmann, "Fast gleiches Recht für alle," *Süddeutsche Zeitung*, October 15, 2015, https://www.sueddeutsche.de/ politik/lebenspartnerschaften-fast-gleiches-recht-fuer-alle-1.2691970 (accessed April 21, 2021).
11 On the normative content of the prohibition of discrimination, see, for example, Susanne Baer, "Gleichheitsgebot und Diskriminierungsverbot," in *Menschenrechte: Ein interdisziplinäres Handbuch*, ed. Arnd Pollmann and Georg Lohmann (Stuttgart/Weimar: J. B. Metzler, 2012), 261–264; Annette Hilscher et al., "Art. Diskriminierung," in *StL* vol. 1, 8th ed. (Freiburg im Breisgau: Herder, 2018), 1424–1435; Andreas Foitzik, "Einführung in theoretische Grundlagen: Diskriminierung und Diskriminierungskritik," in *Diskriminierungskritische Schule: Einführung in theoretische Grundlagen*, ed. idem and Lukas Hezel (Weinheim: Beltz, 2019), 12–39.
12 See, for example, Article 21 (1) of the Charter of Fundamental Rights of the European Union.
13 See ibid., articles 20 and 23.
14 See the constitutional literature cited in Wollenschläger and Coester-Waltjen, *Ehe für alle*, 2–3.

the USA, and Ireland) has played a considerable role in the rapid shift in public opinion.

4 Same-Sex Domestic Partnership and the Church Magisterium

The Catholic Church's position on homosexuality is complicated and fraught. In parallel with the social problematization arising in numerous countries and international organizations, and with indirect or explicit reference to these developments, the Church has made a series of official statements.[15] In retrospect, it must be said that these statements succeeded neither in connecting to current knowledge in the human sciences at the time nor in meeting pastoral needs and expectations. On the contrary, the Catholic Church's stance is widely regarded today as an example – or even the epitome – of a homophobic position. This may also be due to the thought patterns, argumentation, and language evident in these statements – such as the Church's way of talking about "the" meaning of sexuality, assuming that humankind has a fixed "nature," or appealing to the wording of isolated biblical passages without considering their contextuality.

---

15 Congregation for the Doctrine of the Faith, *Persona Humana: Declaration on Certain Questions Concerning Sexual Ethics* (Rome: Vatican, 1975), https://www.vatican.va/roman_curia/con gregations/cfaith/documents/rc_con_cfaith_doc_19751229_persona-humana_en.html (accessed April 21, 2021); idem, *Letter to the Bishops of the Catholic Church on the Pastoral Care of Homosexual Persons* (Rome: Vatican, 1986), http://www.vatican.va/roman_curia/congregations/cfaith/documents/rc_con_cfaith_doc_19861001_homosexual-persons_en.html (accessed April 21, 2021); idem, *Some Considerations Concerning the Response to Legislative Proposals on the Non-Discrimination of Homosexual Persons* (Rome: Vatican, 1992), http://www.vatican.va/roman_curia/congregations/cfaith/documents/rc_con_cfaith_doc_19920724_homosexual-persons_en.html (accessed April 21, 2021); idem, *Considerations Regarding Proposals to Give Legal Recognition to Unions Between Homosexual Persons* (Rome: Vatican, 2003), http://www.vatican.va/roman_curia/congregations/cfaith/documents/rc_con_cfaith_doc_20030731_homosexual-unions_en.html (accessed April 21, 2021); Catechism of the Catholic Church (Rome: Vatican 1993), nos. 2357–2359, http://www.vatican.va/archive/ENG0015/_INDEX.HTM (accessed April 21, 2021); Congregation for Catholic Education, *Instruction Concerning the Criteria for Discernment of Vocations with regard to Persons with Homosexual Tendencies in view of their Admission to the Seminary and to Holy Orders* (Rome: Vatican, 2005), *http://www.vatican.va/roman_curia/con gregations/ccatheduc/documents/rc_con_ccatheduc_doc_20051104_istruzione_en.html* (accessed April 21, 2021); Francis, *Post-Synodal Apostolic Exhortation: Amoris laetitia* (Rome: Vatican, 2016), nos. 250–251, https://www.vatican.va/content/dam/francesco/pdf/apost_exhortations/documents/papa-francesco_esortazione-ap_20160319_amoris-laetitia_en.pdf (accessed April 21, 2021).

Nevertheless, it is not correct to assert that these statements merely reiterate the old positions the Church has always held.

In fact, the Church's official position has undoubtedly shifted, at least in the following respects: For some time, the Church has recognized that homosexual people "do not choose their homosexual condition."[16] In the revised 1997 edition of the Catechism, however, this statement was weakened when it was revised to speak of "deep-seated homosexual tendencies" and to qualify this as an "inclination," thus attributing it to an individual development instead of an innate predisposition.[17] Furthermore, the text makes a distinction between sexual orientation and the person who has this orientation. And not only that – it also emphasizes that same-sex oriented people possess the same human dignity and are called to fulfill God's will in and through their lives, just like everyone else.[18] Therefore sexual orientation – and this applies to homosexually as well as to heterosexually oriented people – is not constitutive of a person, but is only one of their characteristics. Finally, we should not overlook the prominent statements made in the context of the 2014 and 2015 family synods: these renounce the classification of homosexuality as sin and speak appreciatively of homosexual people's gifts and qualities.[19] In another context, Pope Francis responded to a question about an individual's homosexuality by saying, "Who am I to judge him?"[20] Furthermore in October 2020, in quite an unusual situation – namely, in a documentary film – the pope spoke out in favor of the legal recognition of homosexual couples, asserting they were children of God and had a right to have a family.[21] These elements do not yet constitute a coherent doctrine, but they are fragments of a perspective – or at least an appreciation – that may be developed.

---

16 Catechism, no. 2358.

17 Cf. also the reference to this change in Stephan Goertz's contribution in this volume.

18 Catechism, no. 2358.

19 See the interim report from October 2014 in Sekretariat der Deutschen Bischofskonferenz, ed., *Die pastoralen Herausforderungen der Familie im Kontext der Evangelisierung. Texte zur Bischofssynode 2014 und Dokumente der Deutschen Bischofskonferenz* (Bonn, 2014), 117–140, nos. 50–52; see also Synod of Bishops, *The Pastoral Challenges of the Family in the Context of Evangelization: Relatio Synodi* (Rome: Vatican, 2014), http://www.vatican.va/roman_curia/synod/documents/rc_synod_doc_20141018_relatio-synodi-familia_en.html (accessed April 21, 2021).

20 As stated in an interview in Antonio Spadaro, *Das Interview mit Papst Franziskus,* ed. Andreas R. Batlogg (Freiburg im Breisgau: Herder, 2013), 49–50; see also http://www.vatican.va/content/francesco/en/speeches/2013/july/documents/papa-francesco_20130728_gmg-conferenza-stampa.html (accessed March 22, 2021).

21 See the details in the report by Christoph Paul Hartmann, "Papst Franziskus befürwortet Lebenspartnerschaften Homosexueller," katholisch.de, October 21, 2020, https://katholisch.de/

Above all, Church documents that speak to the subject of homosexuality have been concerned with delegitimizing discrimination based on sexual orientation – and this, at least, they do unequivocally.[22] They explicitly state that the effects of such discrimination include difficulty, trial, and injustice.[23]

Nevertheless, the earlier statements – most prominently the 1992 and 2003 letters issued by the Congregation for the Doctrine of the Faith – strongly criticized the political and legislative initiatives that aimed to eliminate inequalities between the legal status of heterosexual marriage and family structures on the one hand, and same-sex unions on the other. The ostensible reason for this is that homosexual relationships do not "proceed from a genuine affective and sexual complementarity."[24] The more recent of the aforementioned doctrinal letters raises logical, anthropological, social, and legal concerns.[25] More precisely, these concerns address a tense opposition to nation-states' expressed commitment to the promotion of marriage, the belief that children's successful development requires the experience of bipolar parenthood, the profound changes to the previous concept of marriage, and the public interest in the common-good function of opposite-sex married couples, insofar as they guarantee the existence of successive generations. While the first of the above-mentioned arguments cannot generally be said to cohere with the findings of sexual medicine and psychology, the other four objections definitely refer to the international debate and represent substantial points of discussion. However, we will not follow this discussion point by point, but will touch on these issues in the following three systematic or thematic sections.

---

artikel/27298-papst-franziskus-befuerwortet-lebenspartnerschaften-homosexueller (accessed October 22, 2020).

22 Catechism, no. 2358. On the avoidance or reduction of discrimination as a goal of internal efforts at Church reform, see Stephan Goertz, "Streitfall Diskriminierung: Die Kirche und die neue Politik der Menschenrechte," *Herder Korrespondenz* 67 (2013): 78–83.

23 Catechism, no. 2358.

24 As also in Catechism, no. 2357.

25 Congregation for the Doctrine of the Faith, *Considerations Regarding Proposals to Give Legal Recognition*, nos. 6–9.

5 Between Autonomous and Institutional "Forms of Life"[26]

Like all other citizens, homosexuals have the right to a self-determined lifestyle. The fact that their equal rights and their claim to social respect are no longer subject to question, in contrast to the discrimination they faced in the past, is one of the achievements of liberal democracies today.

Romantic relationships and domestic partnerships are essential elements of self-determined lifestyles. Unlike communities of fate such as school classes, study groups, or workforces, the formation of such relationships is based on an act of free and mutual choice.

In contrast to the system that obtained until the late nineteenth century, today the decisive basis of such relationships is mutual affection. However, all romantic and domestic partnerships must be lived under the conditions set by immutable shifts in social processes and the inexorable march of time. Consequently, the existence and persistence of such relationships also depend on the partners' willingness to support each other, not only in moments and phases of effortless agreement and happiness, but also in those characterized by antagonism, crisis, or strain due to illness, hardship, or stress. This also entails the abllity to rely on one's partner in the face of a future that remains unknown to either partner. Through informal or formal vows, partners can assure each other of their readiness to face such challenges by freely committing themselves to one another, demonstrating their desire to establish a relationship with the other, independent of mutable or momentary emotional states, interests and sensitivities.

According to all the knowledge we now have about forms of homosexuality and relationships between same-sex persons, we cannot and must not deny, either en masse or on the basis of speculation, that gay and lesbian couples are also capable of such committed romantic and domestic partnerships – if they desire to make such commitments, and if the necessary conditions obtain.

Almost every social and legal system recognizes the institution of solidarity and future-oriented domestic partnership in the form of marriage between a man and a woman (in the singular or also in the plural). The institutional character of this arrangement initially provides a framework for the union of certain people, with recognized structures which are familiar to all. It establishes a sphere of ex-

---

26 For further details on the concept and analysis of "forms of life," see Rahel Jaeggi, *Critique of Forms of Life*, trans. Ciaran Cronin (Cambridge, MA: Harvard University Press, 2018).

perience and action, defines claims and tasks, and specifies the modalities of the transition from one protected familial or self-determined status to a new status – one which nevertheless faces many uncertainties. The adoption and individual appropriation of this framework also admittedly has the effect of encouraging others to treat this concrete domestic partnership with acceptance, recognition, and a readiness to provide assistance. In the course of the modern era, the institution of marriage also developed into a bulwark against the claims of landlords, official authorities, and parents who wanted to harness marriageable but dependent young women and men to their own interests and plans. In principle, the fundamental right to marriage guaranteed young people the chance to defend themselves against such desires, but only together with their partner – as a couple. However, the institution as such could not protect them from the general risks of life, from bitter disappointments, or from their partner's infidelity. At best, it could entitle them to partial relief or provision and, through precautionary arrangements in the event of separation, it could erect obstacles so that the vows made previously could not be withdrawn in private and without consequences.

In this context, there remains an open question: What genuine interest does the state have in domestic partnership? This question becomes all the more acute when such a partnership is based on mutual affection, as is generally the case today. The starting point for a conclusive answer to this question is the observation that some legal systems, including the German one, explicitly state that marriage (i. e., not only the family) "shall enjoy the special protection of the state" (see Article 6 [1] of the German Constitution, for example[27]).

However, this special protection, which the state promises and to which it commits itself in the formulation of laws and in politics, does not primarily apply to a person's self-determination of their lifestyle, because this would constitute a particularizing repetition of the general right to autonomy or self-determination. Nor does it apply solely to the consolidation of affection between the two persons who have decided to enter into such a partnership, because affection cannot be subject to legal obligation. It is therefore all the more astonishing that the justifications for the laws that have opened up marriage to same-sex couples in many countries explicitly mention – in addition to the goal of eliminating unequal treatment – the goal of strengthening reliability in same-sex re-

---

27 An English translation is available on the German Federal Government's website: https://www.bundesregierung.de/breg-en/chancellor/basic-law-470510 (accessed April 21, 2021).

lationships.[28] According to the prevailing opinion, the state's protection of marriage (as conventionally understood) was primarily intended to safeguard (socially, economically, and legally) the possibility attributed to a man and a woman in their respective concrete domestic partnership that children would someday be born of their union and would then have to be cared for, supported, and brought up over many years. Thus the main reason why many state constitutions promise or guarantee special protection to the institution of marriage is the possibility that the man–woman constellation will become a family with joint children, and only then and for the sake of supporting this decades-long, demanding task does the guarantee of protection also extend to the stability of the parental unit. This guarantee of protection applies from the moment at which a couple is married – that is, even before a pregnancy has occurred or a joint child has been born – and it remains effective for couples who do not have children together, for those for whom such a possibility it excluded at the outset (due to age, for example), and even for those who choose not to exercise the option of having children.

Traditionally, state protection is also granted based on the prospect of society's continued existence in the distant future. It is true that a liberal state such as Germany is not supposed to pursue an active demographic policy, especially against the background of the politics experienced between 1933 and 1945. Nevertheless, marriage between a man and a woman remains the only location in liberal societies that has to do with the readiness for parenthood, procreation, pregnancy, birth, care, and upbringing, and thus with different generations caring for each other. In this respect, marriage and family remain closely tied together, even if in today's society they tend to develop into discrete phenomena, and transitions into marriage and from there to family are more difficult and more protracted, and the risks entailed in such a lifelong project are greater than ever before.

6 The Problem of the Appropriate Legal Form

State legislation in Germany, as in neighboring European countries and in the USA, has followed the path laid down by supreme court rulings to open up the legal institution of marriage between a man and a woman, which has existed

---

28 On the corresponding legal situation in Europe and worldwide, see Dagmar Coester-Waltjen's comprehensive presentation of the issue in Wollenschläger and Coester-Waltjen, *Ehe für alle*, 133–252.

for thousands of years (and has certainly varied considerably within that period), to same-sex couples This is a remarkable process in two respects. On the one hand, the protection of marriage, as an institution in which two partners unite, was thought to be so self-evident in its application to the constellation of a relationship between a man and a woman that it was simply unnecessary to explicitly address this issue. In this respect, the opening that has been achieved marks a caesura in the history of marriage law, even though some commentators would like to interpret this opening as a confirmation and a strengthening of this institution and the model of life it enshrines. On the other hand, at least since the introduction of registered civil partnerships in most countries, a second institution had emerged alongside marriage, guaranteeing same-sex partnerships – if they so wished – a recognized status under public law and rights similar to those already enjoyed by married couples. However, this alternative was abolished in most countries when marriage was opened up "for all".[29]

There were also alternatives to this development, although it was presented as an imperative in the media and by international interest groups and networks, while critical objections were reflexively classified as deep-seated resentment or as an anachronism. The majority of courts and parliaments adopted the logic of dismantling existing discrimination against same-sex persons as a minority group and providing recognition by permitting them to participate in the prestige associated with the established institution of marriage. However, this was only one of two possible paths.

Another option would have been to start with the differences between the two manifestations of the human being – man and woman – and from there to inquire into the potential unique features of opposite-sex and same-sex domestic partnerships, respectively. One such unique feature of opposite-sex domestic partnerships is the basic biological possibility that the couple will produce their own children. This is also the central object of protection.

Only a man and a woman, in mutual cooperation, are able to produce a child. This applies, of course, to so-called "normal" procreation by means of sexual union between a man and a woman. But even when reproductive assistance

---

29 This was the case most recently in Switzerland, in the parliamentary decision of June 2020; see also Konrad Hilpert, "Ehe für alle wirft kulturelle Fragen auf," *Schweizerische Kirchenzeitung* 188 (2020): 254–255. The explanatory statement that accompanied the German law establishing the right of same-sex persons to marry (Gesetzes zur Einführung des Rechts auf Eheschließung für Personen gleichen Geschlechts, Deutscher Bundestag, Drucksache 18/6665, November 11, 2015, 7 ff) expressly emphasized "marriage as a community of support and responsibility, independent of the family," and stressed the distance between this concept and the understanding of marriage in the Weimar Constitution, which was aimed at establishing a family.

procedures are applied, this fundamental condition for human procreation still obtains, because such procedures also require gametes from both a woman and a man. Furthermore, these cells can only develop into a child if the living being created from these gametes is implanted in a woman's uterus, where it is then protected and cared for over many months and is able to mature. Finally, the pregnant woman must give birth to the child. The interaction of male and female elements, on the one hand, and the growth of the embryo and the mother's act of bearing and giving birth to the child, on the other, are so fundamental to life in the world and such an enduring feature of the whole of human existence that – without exception – every human being is the child of a very specific genetic pair of parents, as well as of a very specific biological mother, however the subsequent social aspects of parenthood may have been organized. The fact that genetic and biological parentage is anything but insignificant or negligible for a person's identity is also confirmed by the intensive efforts to find their biological parents made by people who grew up with non-genetic or non-biological parents, some of which extend over many years.

Any reference to the potential to produce children as a unique feature and a distinguishing characteristic is often criticized for its supposedly naturalistic and exclusive focus on biological relationships. From this perspective, these connections are no longer socially compelling for us today, because there have long been ways to have children other than sexual procreation – namely, legal adoption or procreation by means of reproductive assistance.

What is often ignored is that these two alternative paths are "merely" substitutive and will remain so for the foreseeable future. This means nothing more than that they are also dependent – directly or indirectly – on the fundamental man–woman constellation. Adoption can only take place at all if and insofar as a child exists who was once conceived in a "natural" way and then "given up" by their parents or their mother after birth, or if a child has lost their parents. The reasons for and circumstances surrounding such situations almost always involve difficult events or severe conflicts and crises that cannot be resolved in any other way, which can also place a strain on the child's further development, and indeed their entire biography. Therefore international consensus has established that the decisive factor in the decision of whether to entrust a child to adults who are willing to adopt is the well-being of the child concerned, not the adults' desire to obtain a child in this way.[30] In this sense adoption is, in both principle and intent, a form of substitute parenthood for the ben-

---

30 See, for example, Article 20 (3) of the UN Convention on the Rights of the Child, https://www.unicef.org/child-rights-convention/convention-text (accessed April 21, 2021).

efit of children who would otherwise have to grow up without parents or under extremely stressful conditions, not a means of having children that one can choose from the outset.

Reproductive medical assistance, for its part, does not consist in the production and provision of children for couples with a desire to have children, but is limited to supporting and engendering a pregnancy, and to overcoming any obstacles that stand in the way of creating such a pregnancy. The basic biological conditions are not abolished, but rather optimized and supported. In the case of a same-sex couple wishing to have a child, procreation remains dependent on the cooperation of at least one person of a different sex, who is not a life partner. In the female–female constellation, this is a male sperm donor; in the male–male constellation, it is a surrogate mother who must make herself available for the desired child's conception, gestation, and birth. Sperm donation and access to sperm banks are not prohibited in many countries because they also benefit opposite-sex couples and single people, but they cannot eliminate the need for the child conceived in this way to know about his or her biological origins. Surrogacy, on the other hand, is banned in many countries because it can foreseeably lead to profound parental conflicts and often only takes place in a context in which dependence is accepted and economic hardship is exploited. In both cases, the concern that procreation, pregnancy, and birth are qualitatively different than goods and services that can be exchanged for money must also be taken into account.

These considerations yield two reflections: First, both adoption and reproductive assistance procedures confirm the natural biological basis of childbearing, rather than invalidating or relativizing it. Second, childbearing in homosexual contexts is only possible by extending the chain of procreation and involving actors outside the domestic partnership who are used as "donors" or as "surrogates" for a successful pregnancy. In the interests of the child, this necessitates a number of additional regulations to secure the child's right to know about their origins as an aspect of their identity, as well as to be cared for, educated, and nurtured; to establish parental responsibility; and to demarcate family relationships (for example, defining "mother" in lesbian partnerships). Once again, these considerations confirm the substitutive nature of these other means of having a child and could constitute an argument for special status, and thus for civil partnership as a distinct institution alongside marriage.

Of course, it would be utopian to wait or work for such considerations to lead to a revision of the legal situation that has just been achieved and enforced, namely "equal marriage." Nevertheless, the expectations associated with this opening up are probably set too high. On the one hand, the old homophobic mindsets, prejudices, and disparaging terms are unlikely to evaporate simply as a result of the practice of opening up marriage to same-sex couples. Rather, such a development will require efforts in education, training, and knowledge that go far beyond what can be legally regulated. On the other hand, there is a risk that the strong focus on stabilizing attachment and recognition could weaken the so-called institutional guarantee of marriage in legal doctrine, and one day even call it into question in favor of private legal agreements. Relationships and "forms of life" would then become primarily private affairs, and the state would only be called upon as a notary and a guarantor of that which individuals have contractually agreed.[31]

The alternative path of maintaining and strengthening a second institution of domestic partnership would at least have offered the further possibility of providing a reliable legal framework for other, hitherto unprotected cohabitation arrangements in which people care for and assume responsibility for one another (such as household communities, multigenerational households, residential communities for the inclusion of people with disabilities or for rehabilitation after serving a prison sentence, and also spiritual communities). After all, these also constitute specific minority groups of vulnerable persons.

Finally, one could also argue in favor of this duality of domestic partnership institutions that it keeps the concept of marriage concise. Even if more recent discussions about gender have led to greater ambiguity in place of oppositions that were previously taken for granted, and even if we must concede that the influence of social conventions in shaping gender roles is greater than we previously assumed, the tension and fateful burden (pregnancy, birth, and care, at least in infancy) granted or induced by the biological manifestations of man and woman is of fundamental anthropological, existential, social, and cultural significance.

---

31 The question of the meaning of and justification for the special protection of marriage has long been raised in legal literature. The driving force behind the depletion of such protection could be, of all things, the principle of equality, which enforces equal legal treatment of the various forms of domestic partnership and thus undermines the special standing of marriage. Constitutional imperatives such as the special protection of marriage can also change "silently." On the general problem, see, for example, Jörg Benedict, "Die Ehe unter dem besonderen Schutz der Verfassung: Ein vorläufiges Fazit," *Juristen-Zeitung* 68 (2013): 477–487. With regard to the debate on same-sex marriage, which was still under discussion at the time, Benedict comes to the dogmatic constitutional conclusion that "Article 6 (1) of the Basic Law [...] is obsolete with regard to the extraordinary protection of 'marriage'" (p. 486). The two expert opinions commissioned by the Bavarian state government to examine the constitutionality of the adopted law also address not only the question of whether the different sexes of the spouses is one of the structural features that the constitution prescribes to the legislature, but also (and extensively) the question of the constitution's stability and dynamics; see Wollenschläger and Coester-Waltjen, *Ehe für alle.*

A society that refuses to acknowledge this tends toward uniformity, artificiality, and in many places, structural carelessness. Last but not least, models of normality are also important from a socio-psychological point of view, because in a world that is becoming increasingly diverse and mobile, they offer people a basic point of orientation in their various developmental phases, and they also offer a perspective on life – one which they may have to differentiate later, but which can also motivate them. Heterosexual orientation and marriage-based family structures are the reality or the ideal for the vast majority of the population. The legitimate concern to protect minorities and their lifestyles should neither obscure nor attempt to problematize this.

7 Tasks for the Church

Traditionally, the Church and Christian theology have always maintained that the different sexes of the partners are an essential characteristic of marriage. So is exclusivity, the partners' mutual consent, the intention of maintaining the marital relationship until one of the partners dies, and the commitment to mutual love. This is why, in the liturgical celebration of the wedding, in the context of the marriage vows, the question of whether the couple was willing to have children and to care for them was asked quite explicitly. Even if one would like to formulate the readiness to reproduce somewhat more broadly today, it is still a matter of concern that the partnership should be open to generations to come, and that it demonstrates consideration for these potential lives.

In any case, the recent change in the civil legal situation regarding marriage is a challenge that the Church and Christian theology must face up to, because the term marriage is no longer understood in the same way in the different spheres of church and state. As I have said above, hoping that the state will revise these decisions would be just as futile as protesting against them – it would achieve nothing. On the contrary, at this point the Church and Christian theology are clearly discovering that the power to define and control social developments has slipped away from them, at least with regard to this question. In this respect, it is now up to them to position themselves in relation to the changes that have taken place.

The lack of congruence between these views on marriage will not simply even out on its own at some point, and if this incongruence remains unprocessed, sooner or later it will lead to tensions and misunderstandings among the faithful, in terms of awareness and expectations. These persons are both citizens and members of the Church, and in this dual role they must integrate the civil and the ecclesiastical perspective. If the Church does not wish to adopt the view that now obtains in the state sphere, then it will come under increasing pressure to justify itself and to explain the "added value" of its perspective in concrete terms.

What is already clear, however, is that in responding to the changed legal situation in the state sphere, it is no longer an option for the Church to return to its earlier condemnation and exclusion of same-sex predisposition, same-sex expression, and same-sex relationships; both the level of knowledge that the human sciences have achieved in the meantime[32] and respect for the people concerned prevents this. Consequently, the only remaining option is to recognize that, in addition to marriage – which is open to the possibility of procreation – there are other domestic partnerships that must not only be accepted, but also respected, because they are also undertaken with the serious intention of taking responsibility for the other partner and working to ensure that the relationship has a future.

In principle, the Church has already recognized some of the tasks that arise from this realization and has repeatedly declared its commitment to these issues over many years. This is certainly true of the necessity to offer pastoral care to homosexual persons, as well as of the struggle against existing prejudices and social disadvantages.[33]

In addition, there is a clear need for theological clarification. In particular, there is a need to systematically reflect anew on what it is that actually constitutes the sacramentality of marriage and how much weight is given to enabling new human life to be created, as well as the readiness to support and accompany such lives over a long period of time. Points which can be clarified theologically include the act of creating new life together as well as unconditional acceptance. Ethically, the findings of the human sciences with regard to homosexuality, the diversity of relationships, and the variability of gender roles, as well as the reasons why relationships might fail must be accepted, even if this creates tensions with established tradition. In theological ethics, this revision is currently in full swing,[34] but it must also be quickly followed by a clear correction of the official statements – in the Catechism, for example – precisely because a large portion of

---

32 Cf. Hartmut Bosinski's contribution in this volume.

33 See Congregation for the Doctrine of the Faith, *Letter to the Bishops of the Catholic Church on the Pastoral Care of Homosexual Persons*; see also Francis, *Amoris laetitia*, no. 250.

34 See my own attempts to address the issue: "Partnerschaftliche Lebensformen im Plural? Fundamentalethische Überlegungen," *Kerygma und Dogma* 61 (2015): 181–194; "Art. Homosexualität: Sozialethische Überlegungen," in *StL*, vol. 3, 8th ed., 76–80; "Homosexuality from the Perspective of Theological Ethics: An Analysis of the Problem," *Marriage, Families and Spirituality* 25 (2019): 136–147.

the public identifies the Catholic Church with its earlier, entirely negative position.

An important aspect of pastoral care is blessing cohabiting couples when they begin their domestic partnership, or when those who are already living together in this way explicitly promise to commit to each other and to their future together. Some same-sex couples explicitly desire such a blessing. The desire for recognition, also on the part of the Church as an institution – and perhaps also after and in contrast to numerous negative and hurtful experiences – may be at play here. But the wish can also be an expression of the need to integrate their particular partnership into their individual biographical context and their own religious self-understanding. In this case, a blessing could help them to accept their same-sex orientation.

A liturgical blessing always has two aspects – the individual one, which offers solace in the form of God's support for this very specific relationship between two particular individuals, and the public one, which entails the act of blessing as an official act on the part of the ecclesial community. In other words, the blessing occurs with and on behalf of the community.[35] All of this seems to be "theologically responsible and pastorally appropriate,"[36] even at the present stage of reflection – that is, before the question of whether such a blessing constitutes a sacrament or is "merely" a symbolic sacramental and in-

---

35 Therefore the practice of blessing such unions should be preceded by a meaningful correction of the official Church statements on homosexuality in practice. Several volumes have recently been published on the issues involved in offering such blessings in the Church sphere, two of which have come out of academic conferences, namely: Stephan Loos and Georg Trettin, eds., *Mit dem Segen der Kirche? Gleichgeschlechtliche Partnerschaft im Fokus der Pastoral* (Freiburg im Breisgau: Herder, 2019); Ewald Volgger and Florian Wegscheider, eds., *Benediktion von gleichgeschlechtlichen Partnerschaften* (Regensburg: Friedrich Pustet, 2020); Julia Knop and Benedikt Kranemann, eds., *Segensfeiern in der offenen Kirche: Neue Gottesdienstformen in theologischer Reflexion* (Quaestiones disputatae 305; Freiburg im Breisgau: Herder, 2020). A good overview of the debate in a broader context can be found in Julia Knop, *Beziehungsweise: Theologie der Ehe, Partnerschaft und Familie* (Regensburg: Friedrich Pustet, 2019), 280 – 291. Also worthy of attention is the volume on the state of this discussion in Old Catholic theology by Andreas Krebs and Matthias Ring, eds., *Mit dem Segen der Kirche: Die Segnung gleichgeschlechtlicher Partnerschaften in der Diskussion* (Bonn: Alt-Katholischer Bistumsverlag, 2018), including a contribution by Jochen Sautermeister on the central types of argumentation from a theological-ethical perspective (pp. 111 – 122).

36 These are the "common" assessment criteria based on the reflections of the German bishops in *Die pastoralen Herausforderungen der Familie im Kontext der Evangelisierung* (2014) in the run-up to the two synods of bishops on the topic of the family; see Sekretariat der Deutschen Bischofskonferenz, *Die pastoralen Herausforderungen*, 42 – 76.

tercessional act has been theologically clarified.[37] Such a blessing would be for the success of the partnership, for mutual fidelity, and for a solidarity in which each partner is willing to share the other's burdens and problems. Actions that hurt one's partner, including infidelity, violence, exploitation, repudiation when another opportunity presents itself, breaking the mutual vow, or failing to provide attention and care – all of which can occur in same-sex relationships just as in heterosexual ones – are by no means approved. Thus blessing in no way entails neutralizing guilt.[38]

Realistically, we can assume that efforts to introduce such a practice of blessing same-sex unions in the Catholic Church (as many Protestant churches have done) will encounter difficulties, and that some of the faithful will reject such a move. Much will depend on explaining this practice beforehand and on proceeding with tact when introducing it.

8 A Contextual Note to Conclude

Part of the peculiarity of the debate on opening up marriage is that it is conducted neither as merely theoretical – for instance, in the sense of improving the coherence and consistency of the legal system – nor as primarily pragmatic, in the sense of seeking to provide a viable, acceptable path for a relatively small minority. Instead, this debate takes place in a social and political environment in which strong forces (such as lobbyists and solidarity organizations) operate, strong emotions (such as fear, hatred, questions of identity, or a sense of victimhood) are present, and strong accusations that invite generalizations (such as homophobia, archaic moral standards, racism, or gender ideology) co-determine arguments, perceptions, and decisions.

Outrage and "active counter-perspectives" are certainly suitable if the goal is to put a debate on the agenda or to speed up a pending decision. But they can also contaminate arguments and perspectives, creating a climate in which political correctness or an unequivocal commitment to one of two "camps" seems to be more important than careful reflection and weighing the pros and cons. One would hope that this situation will not be repeated in the forthcoming continuation of the debate in the Church sphere.

---

37 On this topic explicitly, see Knop, *Beziehungsweise*, 211–221.
38 On this topic, see also Jochen Sautermeister, "Angebotene Wirklichkeit: Theologisch-ethische Skizzen zum Verhältnis von Segen und Moral," in *Segensfeiern in der offenen Kirche: Neue Gottesdienstformen in theologischer Reflexion*, ed. Julia Knop and Benedikt Kranemann (Quaestiones disputatae 305; Freiburg im Breisgau: Herder, 2020), 320–339.

Bibliography

Baer, Susanne. "Gleichheitsgebot und Diskriminierungsverbot." In *Menschenrechte: Ein interdisziplinäres Handbuch*, ed. Arnd Pollmann and Georg Lohmann, 261–264. Stuttgart/Weimar: J. B. Metzler, 2012.
Bauer, Fritz, et al., eds. *Sexualität und Verbrechen: Beiträge zur Strafrechtsreform*. Frankfurt am Main: Fischer, 1963.
Benedict, Jörg. "Die Ehe unter dem besonderen Schutz der Verfassung: Ein vorläufiges Fazit." *Juristen-Zeitung* 68 (2013): 477–487.
Catechism of the Catholic Church. Rome: Vatican 1993. http://www.vatican.va/archive/ ENG0015/_INDEX.HTM. Accessed April 21, 2021.
Congregation for the Doctrine of the Faith. *Persona Humana: Declaration on Certain Questions Concerning Sexual Ethics*. Rome: Vatican, 1975. https://www.vatican.va/ roman_curia/congregations/cfaith/documents/rc_con_cfaith_doc_19751229_persona-hu mana_en.html. Accessed April 21, 2021.
Congregation for the Doctrine of the Faith. *Letter to the Bishops of the Catholic Church on the Pastoral Care of Homosexual Persons*. Rome: Vatican, 1986. http://www.vatican.va/ roman_curia/congregations/cfaith/documents/rc_con_cfaith_doc_19861001_homosexual-persons_en.html. Accessed April 21, 2021.
Congregation for the Doctrine of the Faith. *Some Considerations Concerning the Response to Legislative Proposals on the Non-Discrimination of Homosexual Persons*. Rome: Vatican, 1992. http://www.vatican.va/roman_curia/congregations/cfaith/documents/rc_con_ cfaith_doc_19920724_homosexual-persons_en.html. Accessed April 21, 2021.
Congregation for the Doctrine of the Faith. *Considerations Regarding Proposals to Give Legal Recognition to Unions Between Homosexual Persons*. Rome: Vatican, 2003. http://www. vatican.va/roman_curia/congregations/cfaith/documents/rc_con_cfaith_doc_20030731_ homosexual-unions_en.html. Accessed April 21, 2021.
Congregation for Catholic Education. *Instruction Concerning the Criteria for Discernment of Vocations with regard to Persons with Homosexual Tendencies in view of their Admission to the Seminary and to Holy Orders*. Rome: Vatican, 2005. http://www.vatican.va/roman_ curia/congregations/ccatheduc/documents/rc_con_ccatheduc_doc_20051104_istruzione_ en.html. Accessed April 21, 2021.
Foitzik, Andreas. "Einführung in theoretische Grundlagen: Diskriminierung und Diskriminierungskritik." In *Diskriminierungskritische Schule: Einführung in theoretische Grundlagen*, ed. idem and Lukas Hezel, 12–39. Weinheim: Beltz, 2019.
Francis. *Post-Synodal Apostolic Exhortation: Amoris laetitia*. Rome: Vatican, 2016. https:// www.vatican.va/content/dam/francesco/pdf/apost_exhortations/documents/papa-fran cesco_esortazione-ap_20160319_amoris-laetitia_en.pdf. Accessed April 21, 2021.
Goertz, Stephan. "Streitfall Diskriminierung: Die Kirche und die neue Politik der Menschenrechte." *Herder Korrespondenz* 67 (2013): 78–83.
Gründel, Johannes. "Aids – Anlass zur Enttabuisierung ethischer Fragestellungen." In *AIDS – Herausforderung an Gesellschaft und Moral*, ed. idem, 80–106. Düsseldorf: Patmos, 1987.
Hartmann, Christoph Paul. "Papst Franziskus befürwortet Lebenspartnerschaften Homosexueller." *Katholisch.de*, October 21, 2020. https://katholisch.de/artikel/27298-

papst-franziskus-befuerwortet-lebenspartnerschaften-homosexueller. Accessed October 22, 2020.

Hilpert, Konrad. "Partnerschaftliche Lebensformen im Plural? Fundamentalethische Überlegungen." *Kerygma und Dogma* 61 (2015): 181–194.

Hilpert, Konrad. "Art. Homosexualität: Sozialethische Überlegungen." In *StL*, vol. 3, 8th ed., 76–80. Freiburg im Breisgau: Herder 2019.

Hilpert, Konrad. "Homosexuality from the Perspective of Theological Ethics: An Analysis of the Problem." *Marriage, Families and Spirituality* 25 (2019): 136–147.

Hilpert, Konrad. "Ehe für alle wirft kulturelle Fragen auf." *Schweizerische Kirchenzeitung* 188 (2020): 254–255.

Hilscher, Annette, et al. "Art. Diskriminierung." In *StL*, vol. 1, 8th ed., 1424–1435. Freiburg im Breisgau: Herder 2017.

Jaeggi, Rahel. *Kritik von Lebensformen*. Berlin: Suhrkamp, 2014.

Knop, Julia. *Beziehungsweise: Theologie der Ehe, Partnerschaft und Familie*. Regensburg: Friedrich Pustet, 2019.

Knop, Julia, and Benedikt Kranemann, eds. *Segensfeiern in der offenen Kirche: Neue Gottesdienstformen in theologischer Reflexion*. Quaestiones disputatae 305. Freiburg im Breisgau: Herder, 2020.

Krebs, Andreas, and Matthias Ring, eds. *Mit dem Segen der Kirche: Die Segnung gleichgeschlechtlicher Partnerschaften in der Diskussion*. Bonn: Alt-Katholischer Bistumsverlag, 2018.

Küpper, Beate, Ulrich Klocke, and Lena-Carlotta Hoffmann. *Einstellungen gegenüber lesbischen, schwulen und bisexuellen Menschen in Deutschland: Ergebnisse der bevölkerungsrepräsentativen Studie*. Baden-Baden: Nomos, 2017.

Loos, Stephan, and Georg Trettin, eds. *Mit dem Segen der Kirche? Gleichgeschlechtliche Partnerschaft im Fokus der Pastoral*. Freiburg im Breisgau: Herder, 2019.

Mangold, Anna Katharina. "Stationen der Ehe für alle in Deutschland." *Bundeszentrale für politische Bildung*, August 9, 2018. https://www.bpb.de/gesellschaft/gender/homo sexualitaet/274019/stationen-der-ehe-fuer-alle-in-deutschland. Accessed October 22, 2020.

Roßmann, Robert. "Fast gleiches Recht für alle." *Süddeutsche Zeitung*, October 15, 2015. https://www.sueddeutsche.de/politik/lebenspartnerschaften-fast-gleiches-recht-fuer-alle-1.2691970. Accessed November 26, 2020.

Sautermeister, Jochen. "Segnung gleichgeschlechtlicher Paare: Strukturanalytische Beobachtungen zentraler Argumentationstypen aus theologisch-ethischer Sicht." In *Mit dem Segen der Kirche: Die Segnung gleichgeschlechtlicher Partnerschaften in der theologischen Diskussion*, ed. Andreas Krebs and Matthias Ring, 111–122. Bonn: Alt-Katholischer Bistumsverlag, 2018.

Sautermeister, Jochen. "Angebotene Wirklichkeit: Theologisch-ethische Skizzen zum Verhältnis von Segen und Moral." In *Segensfeiern in der offenen Kirche: Neue Gottesdienstformen in theologischer Reflexion*, ed. Julia Knop and Benedikt Kranemann, 320–339. Quaestiones disputatae 305. Freiburg im Breisgau: Herder, 2020.

Sekretariat der Deutschen Bischofskonferenz, ed. *Die pastoralen Herausforderungen der Familie im Kontext der Evangelisierung. Texte zur Bischofssynode 2014 und Dokumente der Deutschen Bischofskonferenz*. Bonn, 2014.

Spadaro, Antonio. *Das Interview mit Papst Franziskus.* Edited by Andreas R. Batlogg. Freiburg im Breisgau: Herder, 2013.

Stümke, Hans-Georg. *Homosexuelle in Deutschland: Eine politische Geschichte.* Munich: Beck, 1989.

Volgger, Ewald, and Florian Wegscheider, eds. *Benediktion von gleichgeschlechtlichen Partnerschaften.* Regensburg: Friedrich Pustet, 2020.

Wollenschläger, Ferdinand, and Dagmar Coester-Waltjen. *Ehe für alle: Die Öffnung der Ehe für gleichgeschlechtliche Paare aus verfassungsrechtlicher und rechtsvergleichender Perspektive.* Tübingen: Mohr Siebeck, 2018.

Gerhard Marschütz
Same-Sex Parenthood
Theological and Ethical Reflections on a Contentious Debate

1 Points of Departure

1.1 Lifestyle Pluralization

The general pluralization of lifestyles that began in the final third of the twentieth century increasingly called attention to homosexual lifestyles as well. Initially, public perception and social scientific research focused on the differentiation of contexts of life and meaning, which had previously been predominantly
concentrated in marriage and nuclear family structures, into a variety of heterosexual forms of familial and non-familial cohabitation. Until the 1960s, the institutional normality of marriage and family, which most people had deeply inter-
nalized as part of their own biographies, was accompanied by a pronounced
intolerance for alternative lifestyles. Since then, the diversification of heterosexual lifestyles has increasingly come to be tolerated and accepted. As early as
1988, the sociologist Hartmann Tyrell stated, "What was sure to cause offense
twenty years ago upsets no one today. [...] Sexuality before or outside marriage
has largely been freed from moral discrimination."[1]

This attitude has expanded to encompass homosexual lifestyles as well, albeit with a time lag and in a weaker form, as many people continue to flatly reject lesbian and gay parenthood in particular – primarily with the argument that
this family structure goes against the child's best interests. Nevertheless, one
cannot ignore the fact that in Western Europe, since the 1990s at the latest –
and to some extent in many other countries around the world as well – there
has been a sustained shift in societal awareness of the issue of homosexuality,
which has also been successively reflected in legal changes. As a first step, numerous laws that adversely affected homosexual persons were repealed on the
basis of advances in scientific knowledge. Then in a second step, legally en-
shrined rights for lesbian and gay people were gradually established – with re-

---

1 Hartmann Tyrell, "Ehe und Familie – Institutionalisierung und Deinstitutionalisierung," in
Die "postmoderne" Familie. Familiale Strategien und Familienpolitik in einer Übergangszeit, ed.
Kurt Lüscher et al. (Konstanz: Univ.-Verl. Konstanz, 1988), 145–156, here 154.

https://doi.org/10.1515/9783110705188-010

gard to partnership arrangements, these were recognized either by opening up marriage to same-sex couples or by instituting the independent legal institution of registered civil partnership, which is similar to marriage. To this day, however, legal recognition of same-sex families remains controversial.

1.2 Legal Developments

I do not have sufficient space here to present an overview of the development of the legal recognition of same-sex couples, and particularly of so-called "rainbow families," which is proceeding very unevenly in numerous countries.[2] Focusing on Western Europe, the foundation for this development over the past two decades has been Article 14 (prohibition of discrimination) in conjunction with Article 8 (right to respect for private and family life) of the European Convention on Human Rights (ECHR).[3] Non-discrimination as a consequence of respect for human dignity, which now specifically includes sexual orientation, is also a central aspect of the EU Treaty of Lisbon, which entered into force on December 1, 2009, and the Treaty on the Functioning of the European Union, which was annexed to it.[4] Similarly, the EU Charter of Fundamental Rights explicitly refers to sexual orientation in Article 21, which addresses non-discrimination.[5]

---

2 For a preliminary overview of these subjects, see: https://en.wikipedia.org/wiki/Same-sex_marriage; https://rainbowfamilies.org; https://en.wikipedia.org/wiki/LGBT_parenting (accessed April 21, 2021).

3 Article 14 of the ECHR states: "The enjoyment of the rights and freedoms set forth in this Convention shall be secured without discrimination on any ground such as sex, race, colour, language, religion, political or other opinion, national or social origin, association with a national minority, property, birth or other status." With regard to Article 8 of the ECHR, the European Court of Human Rights (ECtHR) has ruled several times (for example, with regard to Austria in the judgment of June 24, 2010 – 30141/04) that same-sex couples also have a right to respect for family life and thus a right to establish a family.

4 Article 2 of the Treaty on European Union states: "The Union is founded on the values of respect for human dignity, freedom, democracy, equality, the rule of law and respect for human rights, including the rights of persons belonging to minorities. These values are common to the Member States in a society in which pluralism, non-discrimination, tolerance, justice, solidarity and equality between women and men prevail." Article 10 of the Treaty on the Functioning of the European Union states: "In defining and implementing its policies and activities, the Union shall aim to combat discrimination based on sex, racial or ethnic origin, religion or belief, disability, age or sexual orientation."

5 Article 21 (1) of the EU Charter of Fundamental Rights states: "Any discrimination based on any ground such as sex, race, colour, ethnic or social origin, genetic features, language, religion

Based on these articles, particularly Article 14 and Article 8 of the ECHR, European Court of Human Rights (ECtHR) case law is currently consistent in identifying distinctions made solely on the basis of sexual orientation as prohibited discrimination. Therefore, in conjunction with the principle of equality, from a legal perspective, there are no longer any significant discernible differences between a marriage and a registered civil partnership. This also applies to the question of children.

For example, the Austrian Constitutional Court, in its ruling on adoption rights for same-sex couples,[6] states that there is "no apparent objective justification for legally denying registered partners joint adoptive parenthood of an adopted child *per se*" (para. 50). Therefore, whereas legislators had previously differentiated between people "on the basis of the characteristic of sexual orientation" (para. 43), this approach can no longer be upheld because "there must be exceptional reasons, both with regard to the principle of equality and to Art. 14 of the ECHR, to justify statutory unequal treatment that is linked to characteristics which are suspected to be subject to discrimination" (para. 38).

The same line of argument underlies the Austrian Constitutional Court's ruling on lesbian couples' use of reproductive medicine.[7] In this case as well, the court points out that, according to ECtHR case law, "particularly convincing and weighty reasons must exist in order for a differentiation not to constitute discrimination, and thus a violation of Art. 14 of the ECHR" (para. 38). Restricting access to artificial insemination solely to opposite-sex marriages and cohabiting couples, however, constitutes an "encroachment on the scope of protection of Art. 14 in conjunction with Art. 8 of the ECHR with regard to the desire of women living in a same-sex domestic partnership to have children," and this is "not justified by sufficiently weighty reasons and [is] therefore disproportionate, because it effectively excludes this group of persons in general from artificial heterologous intrauterine insemination" (para. 54).

Thus the obligation to respect human rights – which the ECtHR consistently reinforces and which, according to current legal opinion, also includes sexual

---

or belief, political or any other opinion, membership of a national minority, property, birth, disability, age or sexual orientation shall be prohibited."

6 Österreichischer Verfassungsgerichtshof, Entscheidung vom 11. Dezember 2014, G119 – 120/ 2014 – 12, https://www.vfgh.gv.at/downloads/VfGH_G_119-120-2014_Adoptionen_EP_Entscheidung. pdf (accessed April 21, 2021).

7 Österreichischer Verfassungsgerichtshof, Entscheidung vom 10. Dezember 2013, G 16/2013 – 16, G 44/2013 – 14, https://www.vfgh.gv.at/downloads/VfGH_G_16-2013_G_44-2013_Fortpflanzungs medizing.pdf (accessed April 21, 2021).

self-determination as a central object of protection[8] and consequently considers discrimination on the basis of sexual orientation to be unacceptable – in connection with the principle of equality, leads to the progressive equality of homosexual and heterosexual lifestyles in family matters as well.

1.3 Resistance

These remarkable legal developments, which are taking place in many countries around the world, have also encountered opposition, of course – some of which has been vehemently expressed. Apart from the fact that there are still numerous countries in which the human rights of lesbian and gay (as well as bisexual and transgender) people are restricted or violated, even in countries where homosexual people and lifestyles now find (varying levels of) legal recognition, a socio-cultural climate of reservations about or even rejection of homosexuality continues to exist, particularly when it comes to equal legal recognition of life or marriage partners, or of same-sex families. Central to this resistance are those perspectives that paint homosexuality and related lifestyles as unnatural and immoral, arguing that such lifestyles lack the natural prerequisites for children's healthy development because every child needs a parental relationship with a mother and a father.

The magisterial statements of the Roman Catholic Church in particular testify to an equally persistent and emphatic resistance to the legal recognition of homosexual unions. Since the Church believes, on the basis of natural law and the Bible, that any homosexual inclination is already an "objective disorder," the "living out of this orientation in homosexual activity" therefore cannot be a "morally acceptable option."[9] While it is true that homosexual persons should not be discriminated against "in word, in action [or] in law,"[10] at the same time it must be noted that homosexual unions "are totally lacking in the biological and anthropological elements of marriage and family which would be the basis, on

---

8 Cf. Claudia Lohrenscheit, ed., *Sexuelle Selbstbestimmung als Menschenrecht* (Baden-Baden: Nomos Verlag, 2009).
9 Congregation for the Doctrine of the Faith, *Letter to the Bishops of the Catholic Church on the Pastoral Care of Homosexual Persons* (Rome: Vatican, 1986), no. 3, http://www.vatican.va/roman_curia/congregations/cfaith/documents/rc_con_cfaith_doc_19861001_homosexual-persons_en.html, (accessed April 21, 2021).
10 Ibid., no. 10.

the level of reason, for granting them legal recognition."[11] Specifically, these missing elements are the natural possibility of procreation and the natural complementarity of the sexes, which exists only in marriage, the absence of which also implies "obstacles in the normal development of children."[12]

Due to these fundamental differences between heterosexual and homosexual unions – which are ultimately rooted in God's plan for his creation[13] – it is also impossible to invoke "the principles of respect and non-discrimination" in favor of same-sex unions.[14] A letter from the Congregation for the Doctrine of the Faith addressed to the bishops in the USA does state that "homosexual persons, as human persons, have the same rights as all persons." However, insofar as these rights are "not absolute," they can rightly be restricted on the basis of "objectively disordered external conduct,"[15] since "it is accepted that the state may restrict the exercise of rights, for example, in the case of contagious or mentally ill persons, in order to protect the common good."[16] Moreover, "'sexual orientation' does not constitute a quality comparable to race, ethnic background, etc. in respect to non-discrimination,"[17] and therefore it cannot constitute the basis for legal demands for the social recognition of homosexual partnerships. In addition, for lack of the missing elements mentioned above and for the sake of the general welfare, the letter asserts that "not even in a remote analogous sense do homosexual unions fulfil the purpose for which marriage and family deserve specific categorical recognition."[18]

---

11 Congregation for the Doctrine of the Faith, *Considerations Regarding Proposals to Give Legal Recognition to Unions Between Homosexual Persons* (Rome: Vatican, 2003), no. 7, http://www. vatican.va/roman_curia/congregations/cfaith/documents/rc_con_cfaith_doc_20030731_homo sexual-unions_en.html, (accessed April 21, 2021).
12 Ibid.
13 See ibid., no. 2: "Marriage is not just any relationship between human beings. It was established by the Creator with its own nature, essential properties and purpose." Therefore, as number 4 emphasizes, according to God's plan, "marriage is holy, while homosexual acts go against the natural moral law."
14 Ibid., no. 8.
15 Congregation for the Doctrine of the Faith, *Some Considerations Concerning the Response to Legislative Proposals on the Non-Discrimination of Homosexual Persons* (Rome: Vatican, 1992), no. 12, http://www.vatican.va/roman_curia/congregations/cfaith/documents/rc_con_cfaith_ doc_19920724_homosexual-persons_en.html, (accessed April 21, 2021).
16 Ibid.
17 Ibid., no. 10.
18 Congregation for the Doctrine of the Faith, *Considerations Regarding Proposals to Give Legal Recognition*, no. 8.

Much more subtly but equally unequivocally, in the post-synodal letter *Amoris Laetitia*, Pope Francis also states that there are "absolutely no grounds for considering homosexual unions to be in any way similar or even remotely analogous to God's plan for marriage and family."[19]

Thus the Catholic point of view – which is based on certain creation-theological foundations as well as on biological and anthropological factors derived from arguments grounded in natural law – emphasizes an essential inequality between heterosexual marriage and family structures over against homosexual partnerships, both with and without children. The Church asserts that this does not contradict the principle of equality, since it states not only that what is essentially the same is to be treated equally, but also that what is essentially different is to be treated unequally. What is disputed, however, is the extent to which the opposite-sex essence of marriage, in its natural openness to the possibility of procreation and family, correctly indicates the substantial inequality which stands in the way of equality for same-sex unions.

In any case, the Catholic position on this issue – which the Church shares with other actors as well – is that same-sex couples and family structures are fundamentally different from heterosexual married couples in terms of their potential to procreate and produce a family. This also justifies the unequal treatment of same-sex couples with regard to adoption law or access to reproductive medicine, especially when one considers the best interests of the child. But do these constitute "particularly convincing and weighty reasons" – as the above-mentioned Austrian judicial decisions demand – that could legitimize a differentiation based on the characteristic of sexual orientation?

2 Conflicting Arguments

It is not only the existence of rainbow families, but also (and even more so) their legal recognition that unsettles deep-seated cultural convictions regarding gender relations, sexuality, reproduction, and raising children. It is therefore not surprising that protests against legal developments that increasingly seem to relativize the natural foundations of parenthood are taking shape. One cannot deny that only a sexual relationship between a man and a woman, hitherto exclusively recognized in the legal institution of marriage, has the active potential to pro-

---

19 Francis, *Post-Synodal Apostolic Exhortation: Amoris Laetitia* (Rome: Vatican, 2016), no. 251, https://www.vatican.va/content/dam/francesco/pdf/apost_exhortations/documents/papa-fran cesco_esortazione-ap_20160319_amoris-laetitia_en.pdf (accessed April 21, 2021).

duce offspring, which also guarantees a supra-individual purpose to this relationship – namely the continuation of human society. Moreover, this is true not only in quantitative, but also in qualitative terms: as a rule, natural-biological parents also want to ensure the best possible development for their children, and within this parental framework – which is also social – they make an irreplaceable contribution to the development of human capital.

On the other hand, late-modern discussions of the pluralization of family structures obscure the fact that, in a longer-term historical comparison, this marks a "return to diversity" in Western Europe.[20] Such a discussion can only be meaningfully introduced in relation to the "golden age of the family" (statistically speaking) from the mid-1950s to the mid-1960s, and could perhaps be construed in an alarmist fashion, as a scenario of decay. But even pre-industrial times were characterized by "a colorful variety of very different family structures, which were probably much more differentiated in their diversity than [they are] in the present."[21] Thus divided parenthood has always existed in both biological and social terms; it deviated from the norm, but was nevertheless tolerated or had to be tolerated, albeit only in a heterosexual context. Only more recent modernization processes have enabled the growing public awareness of the reality of homosexual parenthood. At the core of the dispute about the recognition of such family structures, therefore, is less the issue of divided parenthood, and more the rupture that arises from the detonation of heterosexual thought patterns.

Thus the central arguments against same-sex parenthood culminate in the argument that (1) such parenthood lacks the necessary natural educational prerequisites, which (2) inevitably entails a danger to children in terms of their emotional, social, and sexual development. For this reason, numerous comparative studies, particularly in the Anglo-American world, have been devoted to the question of the extent to which these counterarguments can be empirically verified.

---

20 Trutz von Trotha, "Zum Wandel der Familie," *Kölner Zeitschrift für Soziologie und Sozialpsychologie* 42 (1990): 452–473, here 453 f.
21 Michael Mitterauer, "Entwicklungstrend der Familie in der europäischen Neuzeit," in *Handbuch der Familien- und Jugendforschung 1*, ed. Rosemarie Nave-Herz and Manfred Marefka (Neuwied: Luchterhand, 1989), 179–194, here 179.

2.1 Comparative Studies

Two American meta-analyses, which evaluated more than 100 scientific publications over a period of more than 30 years,[22] as well as the study published by Marina Rupp on behalf of the German Federal Ministry of Justice (hereinafter referred to as the Rupp study),[23] broadly agree that homosexual parents are by no means less suitable to raise children and enable their healthy development than heterosexual parents are. In this regard, the research "has found no reasons to believe lesbian mothers or gay fathers to be unfit parents. On the contrary, results of research suggest that lesbian and gay parents are as likely as heterosexual parents to provide supportive home environments for children."[24]

Contrary to the fears frequently expressed, these studies contain no relevant evidence that cohabiting homosexual couples would exhibit comparably more frequent behavioral disorders, that such partnerships would in principle be of shorter duration, or that the children of gay parents would be at higher risk of sexual abuse. Nor is the central concern – that the lack of opposite-sex relationships would have a negative effect on children's development –empirically verifiable. Rather, the research repeatedly points out that the child's well-being depends far more on factors such as a reliable, loving parental relationship and the family's social and economic resources than on the parents' sexual orientation.

> Many studies have assessed the developmental and psychosocial outcomes of children whose parents are gay or lesbian and note that a family's social and economic resources and the strength of the relationships among members of the family are far more important variables than parental gender or sexual orientation in affecting children's development and well-being.[25]

Similarly, the Rupp study concludes

> that children and adolescents from civil partnerships differ little from children and adolescents growing up in other family structures in terms of the quality of relationships with both parents and in their psychological adjustment. [...] The decisive factor in children's

---

22 These are the American Psychological Association (APA) publication "Lesbian & Gay Parenting," http://www.apa.org/pi/lgbt/resources/parenting-full.pdf (accessed April 21, 2021), issued in conjunction with three other associations in 2005; as well as the American Academy of Pediatrics (AAP) report edited by Ellen C. Perrin et al., "Promoting the Well-Being of Children Whose Parents Are Gay or Lesbian," *Pediatrics* 131 (2013): e1374–e1383.
23 Marina Rupp, ed., *Die Lebenssituation von Kindern in gleichgeschlechtlichen Lebenspartnerschaften* (Cologne: Bundesanzeiger-Verl.-Ges, 2009).
24 APA, "Lesbian & Gay Parenting," 8.
25 Perrin et al., "Promoting the Well-Being of Children," e1377.

development is not the family structure, but the quality of intra-family relationships. Thus, with regard to the developmental dimensions of children and adolescents considered, it turned out not to be significant whether they grow up with a single parent, two mothers or fathers, or with a father and a mother, but rather what the quality of the relationship is in these families.[26]

In particular, the gender development of children and adolescents in rainbow families also indicates no negative effects with regard to gender identity or gender-typical role-related behavior, nor any significant differences with regard to sexual orientation.[27] Thus children in rainbow families develop a gender identity corresponding to their biological sex: they see themselves as women or men and exhibit a comparable degree of female or male role-related behavior. These results call into question the monopoly on interpretation enjoyed by traditional psychoanalytic developmental models, because the "importance of representatives of both sexes as primary (parental) caregivers for healthy psychosexual development is [...] in no way confirmed."[28] Likewise, the results indicate no statistically relevant difference with regard to sexual orientation. Young adults raised in lesbian families describe themselves as homosexually oriented just as rarely as their peers raised in heterosexual families.[29]

Despite the fact that these studies primarily emphasize "uniformity," they also substantiate differences. For example, children and adolescents raised in rainbow families are more often exposed to stigmatization and discrimination (especially to teasing and exclusion, and very rarely to severe violence) in their social environment, particularly among their peers. However, the idea that such experiences have solely negative effects on the child's development (resulting in social isolation, anxiety, or depression, for example) is generally not true at all. To the extent that homosexual parents talk to their children about these discriminatory experiences, the children are able to cope with them adequately. This even results in the majority of children raised in rainbow families acquiring a more differentiated capacity for reflection, handling conflict,

---

26 Rupp, *Die Lebenssituation von Kindern*, 308.
27 Cf. APA, "Lesbian & Gay Parenting," 8–10.
28 Elke Jansen and Melanie C. Steffens, "Lesbische Mütter, schwule Väter und ihre Kinder im Spiegel psychosozialer Forschung," *Verhaltenstherapie & psychosoziale Praxis* 38 (2006): 643–656, here 648.
29 Cf. Nanette K. Gartrell, Henny M.W. Bos, and Naomi G. Goldberg, "Adolescents of the U.S. National Longitudinal Lesbian Family Study: Sexual Orientation, Sexual Behavior, and Sexual Risk Exposure," *Archives of Sexual Behavior* 40, no. 6 (2011): 1199–1209; Susan Golombok and Fiona Tasker, "Do parents influence the sexual orientation of their children? Findings from a longitudinal study of lesbian families," *Developmental Psychology* 32 (1996): 3–11.

and linking tolerance with high self-esteem, as compared to their peers raised in other families.[30] Moreover, it is the intolerant reactions of people in the child's social environment that constitute the source of such humiliations – as can also be demonstrated, for example, with regard to migrant families or economically disadvantaged families. Therefore no relevant argument against rainbow families can be derived from this finding. Other differences – such as the fact that homosexual parents tend to practice a more egalitarian division of labor than heterosexual parents, both professionally and in their joint commitment to the children, or that heterosexual young people raised in rainbow families are more open to their own same-sex experiences than other young people – can only be briefly mentioned here.

Taken together, these studies prove that rainbow families demonstrate more similarities than differences to opposite-sex families. Nevertheless, scientific understandings of rainbow families are a relatively recent historical phenomenon, and we should not overlook the fact that the data on this topic "is still scanty overall."[31] Furthermore, "there is a lack of more comprehensive longitudinal studies on children's development in same-sex partnerships."[32] In addition, such studies are usually comparative in nature and interpret differences primarily in terms of whether or not deficits exist. Repeated statements to the effect that rainbow families might even be superior to conventional families usually contribute little to a differentiated understanding of the respective family structures.

2.2 Defensive Strategies

Even though scientific studies have demonstrated that lesbian and gay people are just as capable of raising children as heterosexual parents are and that no demonstrable harm arises from such arrangements in principle, it is also impossible to overlook the fact that many people – and by no means only those who

---

30 Cf. Rupp, *Die Lebenssituation von Kindern*, 296–298; Judith Stacey and Timothy T. Biblarz, "(How) Does the sexual orientation of parents matter?" *American Sociological Review* 66 (2001): 159–183.
31 Bernd Eggen, "Gleichgeschlechtliche Lebensgemeinschaften ohne und mit Kindern. Soziale Strukturen und künftige Entwicklungen," in *Die gleichgeschlechtliche Familie mit Kindern. Interdisziplinäre Beiträge zu einer neuen Lebensform*, ed. Dorett Funke and Petra Thorn (Bielefeld: Transcript, 2010), 37–60, here 54.
32 Marina Rupp and Andrea Dürnberger, "Wie kommt der Regenbogen in die Familie?," in *Die gleichgeschlechtliche Familie mit Kindern. Interdisziplinäre Beiträge zu einer neuen Lebensform*, ed. Dorett Funke and Petra Thorn (Bielefeld: Transcript, 2010), 61–98, here 63.

are bound to a religion – nevertheless have not changed their perspective on homosexual parenthood as something to be rejected because every child requires a mother and a father for healthy psychosexual development. According to this viewpoint, lesbian and gay people, no matter how competent and loving they may be, are not suited to be parents. But are there particularly convincing and weighty arguments to justify this rejection, particularly in the light of the available comparative studies?

First, one can argue in principle that ethical-normative judgments cannot be directly derived from empirical findings. This would constitute a naturalistic fallacy, disregarding the independence of practical reason, which seeks to fathom moral obligations. An increase in empirical knowledge does not automatically produce a higher level of ethics. In its independent action, however, practical reason does not exist in a vacuum – it never operates beyond, but always in the midst of empirical knowledge, and thus in relation to it. Therefore every material-ethical judgment represents a mediation between values and factual insights, a concrete combination of normative and descriptive elements. Thus there is always the question of how empirical factual insights are relevant to ethical judgment.

In view of this, one defensive strategy would be to minimize the relevance of empirical studies to the greatest extent possible – for instance, by criticizing their methodological and theoretical weaknesses, and thus questioning their quality and significance in terms of both ethical considerations and legal conclusions. That such minimizations of relevance are subject to strict scientific criteria should be self-evident. After all, any serious study with a clearly formulated research design which is conducted in accordance with scientific standards also contains statements on external validity – that is, on the validity of generalizable conclusions drawn on the basis of the study. For example, the Rupp study is "backed up by good target group representation" and can therefore "be regarded as representative."[33] Nevertheless, the fact that telephone interviews were used as the primary method in this case (as in many other related studies) rightly leads many critics, particularly those on the Catholic–conservative spectrum, to question the results; as a representative example, the director of the German

---

33 Rupp, *Die Lebenssituation von Kindern*, 282, 309. This study is based on a survey of parents and experts as well as a study of children. Although the latter is not representative, it is made up of "a sample of 97 children, which is large compared to other such studies and is therefore extremely robust."

Institute for Youth and Society (DIJG), Christl Ruth Vonholdt, questioned "how reliable and objective interviewees' self-assessments are."[34]

A differentiated clarification of this issue can ultimately only be achieved by placing empirical social sciences research in an interdisciplinary dialogue. It is clear, however, that if one criticizes this methodology, then that criticism should apply to every study conducted in the same way. Thus Vonholdt's statement is itself open to criticism, because a study by the American psychiatrist Robert L. Spitzer "on the question of whether homosexual orientation can be changed" was published on the same page of the DIJG website – a study which was also based on telephone interviews, and thus methodologically identical to the Rupp study, but which does not receive any criticism.[35] This exemplifies the fact that the scientification of an argument based on certain research findings often violates scientific standards when studies that reinforce one's own position are prominently cited, while other studies that would call one's position into question are either ignored or presented and rejected in a one-sided manner, often in an abbreviated or distorted form. It is precisely such "inconsistency and selectivity in the search for exclusionary factors" that constitute "indications of prejudice and bias."[36]

Second, such prejudices and biases are also evident in argumentative defenses against and questionings of same-sex partnering and parenting. For example, in her critique of the Rupp study, Vonholdt refers to an American study from 2009,[37] according to which "the incidence of mental illness is significantly

---

34 Christl Ruth Vonholdt, "Das Kindeswohl nicht im Blick," *Bulletin DIJG, Sonderdruck Herbst 2009* (2009): 2–4, here 3.

35 Robert L. Spitzer's study (an unpublished paper presented at an APA symposium on May 9, 2001) on whether it was possible to change a person's homosexual orientation was available on the DIJG website until 2018

36 Guido Pennings, "Gleichgeschlechtliche Elternschaft und das moralische Recht auf Familiengründung," in *Die gleichgeschlechtliche Familie mit Kindern. Interdisziplinäre Beiträge zu einer neuen Lebensform*, ed. Dorett Funke and Petra Thorn (Bielefeld: Transcript, 2010), 225–249, here 232. It is fitting that the DIJG homepage fails to mention that in May 2012, Spitzer officially withdrew the study he presented in 2001 because it had been repeatedly misinterpreted, including by the DIJG. In doing so, he apologized "to any gay person who wasted time and energy undergoing some form of reparative therapy because they believed that I had proven that reparative therapy works with some 'highly motivated' individuals." Cf. Amber Moore, "Psychiatrist Sorry for Gay Reparative Therapy Study," *Medical Daily*, May 9, 2012, http://www.medical daily.com/psychiatrist-sorry-gay-reparative-therapy-study-240498 (accessed April 21, 2021).

37 Cf. Christine E. Grella et al., "Influence of gender, sexual orientation, and need on treatment utilization for substance use and mental disorders. Findings from the California Quality of Life Survey," *BMC Psychiatry* 9, no. 52 (2009): http://www.biomedcentral.com/1471-244X/9/52 (accessed September 15, 2020).

higher among homosexually active men and women than among heterosexually active people."[38] However, she does not mention that this higher prevalence of mental illness was studied in the context of alcohol and drug consumption and thus cannot be directly transferred to the distinct target group of studies on rainbow families. Such transference errors frequently occur in references to studies that indicate higher promiscuity among gay men, based on which their fundamental inability to enter into and sustain lasting relationships is inferred and sometimes psychoanalytically substantiated.[39] Admittedly, several studies indicate a comparatively higher degree of promiscuity, mental disorders, depression, or risk of suicide among persons with a same-sex orientation, but this is mostly likely not primarily due to sexual orientation as such, but rather to ongoing experiences of social discrimination.[40] Nevertheless, these (and other) characteristics are identified as factors that would exclude persons with a homosexual orientation from the possibility of "cultivating relational capacity,"[41] which in a family context also implies a danger to the child's welfare. Ultimately, however, this line of argumentation can only be sustained by a premeditated but scientifically untenable minimization of the relevance of studies on the rainbow family, and it usually proves to be inconsistent and selective. For if

> these characteristics were indeed so common in homosexuals, they would influence the findings on their children. The evidence, however, is that the psychosocial development of children and the quality of parenting in homosexual families does not differ from that of heterosexual families.[42]

---

38 Vonholdt, "Das Kindeswohl nicht im Blick," 4

39 From a psychoanalytic perspective, Gerhard Amendt – among others – seeks to question the partnering and parenting capacities of persons with a same-sex orientation "on the basis of a pathological narcissism that knows only itself and no one else." The resulting "limited capacity for empathy" implies, for example, that since a lesbian woman has "problems with her sons and their masculinity" in principle, her sons must grow up with a woman "whose femininity is dominated by unconscious fear and by a rejection of the masculine – that is, the body, the penis, and its symbolizations"; see Gerhard Amendt, "Kultur, Kindeswohl und homosexuelle Fortpflanzung," *Leviathan* 30 (2002): 161–174, here 165 and 169.

40 Cf. Michael King et al., "A systematic review of mental disorder, suicide, and deliberate self harm in lesbian, gay and bisexual people," *BMC Psychiatry* 8, no. 70 (2008): http://www.bio medcentral.com/1471-244X/8/70 (accessed September 15, 2020); Theo G. M. Sandfort et al., "Same-sex behavior and psychiatric disorders. Findings from the Netherlands Mental Health Survey and Incidence Study (NEMESIS)," *Archives of General Psychiatry* 58 (2001): 85–91.

41 Amendt, "Kultur, Kindeswohl und homosexuelle Fortpflanzung," 168.

42 Pennings, "Gleichgeschlechtliche Elternschaft," 232.

The third and central defensive strategy is based on arguments about the child's best interests. This is not surprising, given the deeply rooted conviction that children should grow up with their natural parents – and that this arrangement is usually in the best interests of the child. Although it is generally admitted that even natural-biological families can present a danger to the child's well-being, and therefore that so-called "state guardians" must intervene if necessary (especially in cases of child neglect, maltreatment, and sexual abuse), it is nevertheless argued that this is not comparable to the situation of rainbow families, since in such cases the child is expected to be "intentionally deprived of a father or a mother."[43] Does this constitute a fundamental threat to the child's best interests?

From a scientific point of view, we must emphasize from the outset that the concept of "the best interests of the child" is a "definitional disaster," as Harry Dettenborn puts it. The phrase is predominately used in the judicial context as an "indeterminate legal concept" that must be (re)interpreted in each individual case. At the same time, the concept transcends a purely legal perspective – which is why, according to Dettenborn, any jurist "who uses the concept of the best interests of the child exceeds his or her competence," since he or she is "compelled to include psychological aspects that go beyond legal aspects and the value aspects they imply."[44] Thus the concept of the best interests of the child would require an interdisciplinary definition, in which primarily psychological, pedagogical, medical, and sociological, as well as ethical aspects would have to be taken into account. This would naturally involve a level of complexity that would probably never allow the concept to take on a precise scientific definition. In formal terms, the concept of the best interests of the child is a construction based on empirical findings and normative values. It is thus necessarily subject to historically conditioned socio-cultural modes of understanding – which is why, for example, in comparison to earlier perspectives, no one today would understand corporal punishment as acting in the best interests of the child.

---

43 Vonholdt, "Das Kindeswohl nicht im Blick," 3.
44 Harry Dettenborn, *Kindeswohl und Kindeswille. Psychologische und rechtliche Aspekte* (Munich: Reinhardt, 2007), 47. Similarly, Friederike Walper states that in legal practice, it is unavoidable that "the best interests of the child, as an indeterminate legal concept, is a container that can be filled with very different contents, and that its interpretation is influenced not only by social change, but often also by the prior understandings of the persons authorized to make decisions"; see Friederike Walper, "Gleichgeschlechtliche Lebensgemeinschaften mit Kindern. Verfassungsrechtliche Rahmenbedingungen," in *Die gleichgeschlechtliche Familie mit Kindern. Interdisziplinäre Beiträge zu einer neuen Lebensform*, ed. Dorett Funke and Petra Thorn (Bielefeld: Transcript, 2010), 115–159, here 130.

In abstract terms, however, there is a general consensus that the best interests of the child encompass the child's physical, mental, and spiritual dimensions. What this means in concrete terms, however, cannot be uniformly stated; it depends on various normative preconceptions, which is why the distinction in family law between an optimal and a minimal standard of the child's welfare is both helpful and necessary. While the optimal standard can be formulated differently in relation to cultural and religious perspectives, and thus cannot rely on unanimously agreed guidelines, the minimal standard focuses on those conditions which are indispensable for the child's well-being, which is why falling short of these conditions also represents a threat to the child's well-being.

> Therefore a risk to the child's well-being in the legal sense cannot be presumed to exist merely because the child's upbringing is not optimal, i.e., if the child's living conditions are stressful for social or economic reasons, or if the child is not being supported in the best possible way according to educational standards.[45]

Otherwise the state would have to intervene on a permanent basis.

Therefore, with regard to the research findings mentioned above, from a legal perspective there is no serious reason to assume that this minimal standard would not be met by lesbian or gay parental guardians. Nevertheless, these findings "should not be interpreted to mean that it does not matter for children's upbringing whether they live in an opposite-sex or a same-sex family."[46] Apart from the fact that almost all children will *de facto* continue to depend on the traditional father–mother–child constellation – although increasing numbers of them will not grow up in this constellation permanently – there is sufficient evidence to date to suggest that the child's experience of the difference between mother and father is significant for the child's psychosexual development.[47] For several decades, however, research findings related to attachment theory have been relativizing such evidence, in that the importance of primary caregivers in terms of the child forming secure attachments in their first years of life does not necessarily imply that these persons must be the natural mother (a mother–child relationship) or the natural parents (a mother–father–child relationship). Therefore

---

45 Walper, "Gleichgeschlechtliche Lebensgemeinschaften mit Kindern," 128.
46 Ibid., 132.
47 Cf. Karin Grossmann and Klaus E. Grossmann, *Bindungen – Das Gefüge psychischer Sicherheit* (Stuttgart: Klett-Cotta, 2014); Lothar Schon, *Sehnsucht nach dem Vater. Die Dynamik der Vater-Sohn-Beziehung* (Stuttgart: Klett-Cotta, 2000); Kornelia Steinhardt, Wilfried Datler, and Johannes Gstach, eds., *Die Bedeutung des Vaters in der frühen Kindheit* (Gießen: Psychosozial-Verlag, 2002).

in the current literature on developmental psychology, the terms mother and father are used sparingly; instead, experts predominantly speak of one or more primary or even secondary caregivers.[48] Thus we see that even this more fluid set of findings does not permit us to infer that same-sex parenting should be excluded as a possibility *per se* based on the child's best interests.

One must also note that same-sex parenthood arrangements exist *de facto*, and thus legal recognition does not establish a new family, but rather improves the child's legal position – which is certainly in the child's best interests – for example, with regard to custody, or to maintenance or inheritance claims in cases in which civil partnerships are dissolved through separation or death. From the child's perspective, the joint adoption of a child who is not the biological child of one of the partners also improves his or her situation by promoting his or her physical, mental, and spiritual well-being. In contrast, the establishment of a rainbow family by means of assisted reproduction certainly implies other ethical problems – primarily in the context of the discourse on reproductive medicine – whereby the extent to which the child's best interests can be meaningfully used as an argument in the case of a child who has not yet been conceived is questionable in principle. Irrespective of these issues, one must also note that adoption by a single parent is also legally permissible without its being assumed to endanger the child's best interests. Finally, beyond the same-sex context, one would have to include the question of the extent to which, for example, the absence of a father in single-parent families demonstrably results in serious harm to the child. All of this must be taken into account for the sake of argument, even if it has been and can be reasonably argued that the parental constellation of a mother and a father increases the chances for the child's well-being. Nevertheless, one cannot reasonably argue that the child's best interests should only be measured against the optimal standard when it comes to same-sex parenthood.

It is noteworthy, therefore, that Guido Pennings emphasizes that the best interests of the child argument is only bona fide in the discourse if, beyond the focus on sexual orientation, other characteristics that have either a positive or a negative "demonstrable effect on the well-being of the child" are also considered.[49] Empirically demonstrated negative effects include low family income, which "can have long-term effects on physical and mental health during childhood that linger into adulthood," as well as being a victim of child abuse, since "people who were abused as children show a much higher risk of abusing

---

48 See, for example, Laura E. Berk, *Entwicklungspsychologie* (Munich: Pearson Studium, 2011).
49 Pennings, "Gleichgeschlechtliche Elternschaft," 242.

their own children. Up to 50 percent of parents who were abused as a child abuse their children."[50] So we might ask, in the interest of the child's welfare, whether all potential parents should be examined according to criteria including their economic resources or their history of abuse, and if necessary prohibited from realizing their desire to have a child? Yet why should sexual orientation be the breaking point, particularly since no studies to date have shown any demonstrable negative effects on the child's well-being?

2.3 Conflicting Thought Patterns

Based on what I have said thus far, it becomes clear that the requirements stipulated by the Austrian Constitutional Court rulings mentioned above – namely, "particularly convincing and weighty reasons" for a general refusal to legally recognize rainbow families – do not exist, provided we reject an inconsistent, selective line of argumentation as a justification solely based on the characteristic of sexual orientation. Such a justification is indeed rejected as discriminatory and thus inadmissible in the thought patterns of a liberal democracy, which – out of a respect for human dignity – seeks to protect the fundamental rights and freedoms of the individual (as well as of minorities) against potential claims on the part of the majority. This continues to be opposed by a certain thought pattern grounded in natural law, which continued to effectively legitimize patterns of social order until well into the middle of the last century. According to this view, heterosexuality was considered natural, and the family was recognized as the natural nucleus of human society – and by no means only in Catholic discourse. In social settings, the natural was established as the normal, which is why homosexuality was primarily associated with the unnatural and the abnormal.

The social modernization processes of recent decades, however, have established a "flexible normalism"[51] – in other words, the previously narrow spectrum of normality over against broad swathes of abnormality and a severe logic of exclusion has given way to a broad spectrum of normality with significantly fewer spheres of abnormality, thanks to a highly intentional logic of inclusion. Taking sexuality as an example, many sexualities which were previously considered abnormal – such as homosexuality – are now integrated into the broad spectrum of normality, even though distinctions do exist along this spectrum; we do not have

---

50 Ibid., 242, 243.
51 Cf. Jürgen Link, *Versuch über den Normalismus. Wie Normalität produziert wird* (Göttingen: Vandenhoeck & Ruprecht, 2013).

to assume that everything that is not placed at the center of what constitutes normality automatically qualifies as abnormal. Thus the multiplication of normality is not only an empirical fact; it is also based on a shift in moral convictions.

Many people see this broadening of the spectrum as the loss of normality's previous lack of ambiguity. However, people often overlook the fact that the natural law thought pattern that traditionally underlies the narrow spectrum of normality is by no means the objective, inherently unambiguous foundation for normative statements that it is generally assumed to be. What the term nature means is not naturally unambiguous. Therefore its ethical relevance cannot simply be determined on the basis of nature, but only as a result of human reasoning. Since nature is interpreted by human beings, it always remains bound to their respective ways of understanding themselves and the human world, as well as to established power relations. Consequently, shifts in understanding and power structures also bring about changes in human conceptions of natural law.

In this way, to put it more succinctly, modern critical approaches to natural law developed in the wake of the Enlightenment and the accompanying sociopolitical upheavals, emphasizing the inherently equal freedom and autonomy of all people. This led to the development of fundamental and human rights based on human dignity, which are now regarded as the central standard of ethical judgment. The essence of natural law is thus understood as human rights, which in its dynamic interpretation now explicitly includes sexual self-determination. In contrast to this development, the Catholic Church's thought patterns with regard to natural law, which had dominated society until the Enlightenment, remain largely unchanged today. Consequently, the Church emphasizes an essentialist concept of nature, which is increasingly losing relevance as a point of orientation with regard to marriage, family, and sexual norms, since this understanding of natural law conflicts with the understanding that starts from the dignity of the person and is primarily grounded in the determination of the relationship between the person and nature or reason and nature. Therefore, whoever "refers to natural law today, beyond the claim to autonomy, loses the connection to the political and legal dynamics of modern morality. Such a natural law is perceived as ahistorical, as a mode of thought from a bygone era."[52]

Thus we can understand why the ethical discourse on same-sex parenthood remains so irreconcilable, despite enormous argumentative efforts on the part of both opponents and proponents, because every argument is based – often im-

---

52 Stephan Goertz, "Naturrecht und Menschenrecht. Viele Aspekte der kirchlichen Sexualmoral werden nicht mehr verstanden," *Herder Korrespondenz* 68 (2014): 509–514, here 513.

plicitly – on conflicting thought patterns. Consequently the ethical debate often becomes a kind of "shadow boxing," as Pennings puts it. Thus, for example, one contender deploys the argument about the child's best interests to thundering applause from the spectators, but in reality only manages to strike their opponent's shadow, while the opponent's body – the thought pattern underlying the argument – remains unaffected. As Pennings remarks, "We should not be surprised that the other person does not go down."[53] From an ethical point of view, an image of a boxing match is perhaps less relevant than one of an open dialogue about the thought patterns underlying the arguments – a dialogue which, in Jürgen Habermas's sense, would have to be committed to communicative rather than strategic reasoning, to reaching toward mutual understanding.

3 Theological and Ethical Remarks

From a confessional point of view, in the German-speaking world "Protestantism is most likely to have assimilated the findings of the modern human and sexual sciences regarding same-sex living arrangements, as well as the openings in legal policy."[54] Since the turn of the millennium, same-sex partnerships both with and without children have seldom been understood as a "core issue of Christian creed" for Protestants.[55] For this reason, same-sex partnerships can be blessed in churches in an increasing number of German federal states, and under certain conditions, homosexually oriented persons can even be ordained as pastors. In contrast, the Roman Catholic Church (according to Hartmut Kreß) continues to uphold "traditional reservations against homosexuality," viewing it "as intrinsically wicked, reprehensible, and sinful" – a position which "nowadays undermines the normative logic of fundamental rights and the concept of non-discrimination."[56]

---

53 Pennings, "Gleichgeschlechtliche Elternschaft," 229.
54 Hartmut Kreß, "Gleichgeschlechtliche Partnerschaften und gleichgeschlechtliche Familien mit Kindern. Rechtsethische Grundlagen – aktuelle Diskussionspunkte – Fortentwicklung von Rechtsnormen," *Zeitschrift für Evangelische Ethik* 56 (2012): 279–291, here 284. Cf. Hartmut Kreß, "Gleichgeschlechtliche Partnerschaften ohne und mit Kindern. Persönlichkeits- und Kinderrechte als Maßstab der Ethik – Probleme der Kirchen," *Evangelische Theologie* 73 (2013): 364–376; Siegfried Keil and Michael Haspel, eds., *Gleichgeschlechtliche Lebensgemeinschaften in sozialethischer Perspektive* (Neukirchen-Vluyn: Neukirchener, 2000).
55 Kreß, "Gleichgeschlechtliche Partnerschaften und gleichgeschlechtliche Familien mit Kindern," 284.
56 Ibid., 285.

278 — Gerhard Marschütz

Ultimately, this is because the Catholic Church continues to see the issue of homosexuality as a key moral issue for the Christian faith. In view of the relevant doctrinal documents on the subject, a change is not to be expected in the foreseeable future. Grounded in biblical evidence and an unbroken tradition, the Church's consistent rejection of homosexual practice is defended as a central aspect of crucial Christian moral teaching, which must not be abandoned.

But what constitutes a decisive feature of Christianity? In his fundamental theology, Hans-Joachim Höhn distinguishes between two thought patterns on this issue. According to the first, that which is decisively Christian asserts itself as distinct. Thus it is "to be determined by unique features," which are defined by "differences and distinctions."[57] By contrast, the second thought pattern sees the decisive features of Christianity as "that which unites all human beings and makes them equal to one another: their co-creativity, their being made in the image of God, their position as recipients of God's universal will to save."[58] Both thought patterns have always been part of the Catholic tradition. In recent church history, however, it is only since the Second Vatican Council that the dominance of the first pattern, as exemplified in Neo-Scholasticism, has been overcome. Yet even today, the two patterns often coexist without mediation, and this has a particular impact on moral questions.

The first thought pattern is usually based on an instructive-theoretical understanding of revelation, according to which God primarily conveys doctrine to humankind – that is, truths about himself that enable a precise knowledge of "what God has decreed for the sake of humankind's salvation and has put into effect – ultimately through the Church's Magisterium – as an absolutely binding 'law of faith.'"[59] With regard to moral law, the argumentation has primarily been based on natural law, but insofar as the natural law of behavior finds its objective expression in God's order of creation, this too was regarded as the absolutely binding will of God. In view of the subject at hand, therefore, homosexuality can only stand in contradiction to the creation-theological order of marriage and sexuality reflected in nature. Consequently, "[i]t is only in the marital relationship that the use of the sexual faculty can be morally good. A person engaging in homosexual behaviour therefore acts immorally."[60]

---

57 Hans-Joachim Höhn, *Gott – Offenbarung – Heilswege. Fundamentaltheologie* (Würzburg: Echter, 2011), 26.
58 Ibid., 25.
59 Jürgen Werbick, *Den Glauben verantworten. Eine Fundamentaltheologie* (Freiburg im Breisgau: Herder, 2000), 299.
60 Congregation for the Doctrine of the Faith, *Letter to the Bishops of the Catholic Church*, no. 7.

This is not the place to get into the epistemological problems with this thought pattern, particularly with regard to the premises of natural law, which I have hinted at above. What must be addressed, however, is its immanent logic of exclusion, insofar as any practice that deviates from the truth of divine law must be designated immoral, sinful, or unnatural, and thus excluded as an intolerable error. This concept of truth is the basis of a far-reaching differentiation from scholarly insights to the contrary. For example, recent exegetical findings on the subject of homosexuality, which would allow a modification of the traditional ethical judgment, are met with the undifferentiated reference to "the solid foundation of a constant Biblical testimony."[61] Furthermore, human sciences research on homosexuality, which almost uniformly understands it as "a natural variation of human sexuality,"[62] as distinct from disease and the need for therapy – see, for example, the World Medical Association's statement, issued in October 2013 – are at best only partially received. Instead, based on research undertaken by authors whose work is only marginally accepted in the scientific community, the Church tends to emphasize the pathological dimension of homosexuality.[63] Finally, contrary to (empirically demonstrable) experiences of happiness in same-sex partnerships, the Church refers to the affective deficit caused by a lack of gender complementarity[64] and further explains that a "disordered sexual inclination [...] is essentially self-indulgent," which is why "homosexual activity prevents one's own fulfillment and happiness."[65]

In extreme cases, this logic of exclusion provokes fundamentalist conspiracy theories, according to which "a small minority of the population whose sexual inclinations deviate from those of the vast majority [has] succeeded in making

---

61 Ibid., no. 5. Cf. also Congregation for the Doctrine of the Faith, *Considerations Regarding Proposals to Give Legal Recognition*, no. 4.

62 The World Medical Association expressed its views along these lines in an October 2013 statement; see World Medical Association, "WMA Statement on Natural Variations of Human Sexuality," October 2013, https://www.wma.net/policies-post/wma-statement-on-natural-varia tions-of-human-sexuality/ (accessed April 21, 2021). The depathologization of homosexuality has a longer history, however; homosexuality was removed from the official Diagnostic and Statistical Manual of Mental Disorders (DSM) by the American Psychiatric Association in 1973, and then from the International Classification of Diseases (ICD) by the WHO in 1990.

63 To clarify this point: Of course a homosexual (as well as a heterosexual) orientation can be associated with disease-related characteristics. However, affirming this is different from saying that homosexuality is itself, either in principle or predominantly, a disease.

64 Cf. Congregation for the Doctrine of the Faith, *Considerations Regarding Proposals to Give Legal Recognition*, no. 4: homosexual acts "do not proceed from a genuine affective and sexual complementarity. Under no circumstances can they be approved."

65 Congregation for the Doctrine of the Faith, *Letter to the Bishops of the Catholic Church*, no. 7.

their interests the dominant theme of a global culture war," which is now being waged "as a top-down revolution" on the initiative of the UN and the EU, and which is pursuing a "massive social re-education program."[66] Since such theories are primarily based on a pathological understanding of homosexuality, it remains difficult to understand how a

> very small number of people, all of them suffering from a mental defect (?!), should succeed in producing so many influential, renowned people in science, jurisprudence, and politics that they could convince an absolute majority of heterosexuals worldwide, apparently by eliminating their independent, reasonable powers of judgment, of things that are allegedly untenable. One may absolutely expect such a scenario in the kingdom of the Antichrist, but in attaching it to one's homosexual fellow human beings, one should at the very least not describe it as scientific.[67]

The second thought pattern is based on a communicative-theoretical understanding of revelation, which presumes that, rather than communicating individual truths about himself, God conveys himself as love, as the "reality of unconditional devotion to which Jesus the God–Man witnessed."[68] However, speaking of God in this way implies that

> the "decisive feature" of Christianity [is] not simply identical to the differences that are emphasized vis-à-vis people of other faiths and non-believers. The decisive feature of Christianity consists in the message that all people without exception are the recipients of God's

---

66 Gabriele Kuby, *Die globale sexuelle Revolution. Zerstörung der Freiheit im Namen der Freiheit* (Kißlegg: Fe-Medienverlag, 2012), 216, 87. The latter quotation is taken from the cover blurb. Cf. my critical discussion, published under the title "Wachstumspotenzial für die eigene Lehre" in *Herder Korrespondenz* 68 (2014): 457–462; on Kuby's statement ("Eine Top-down Revolution," ibid., 590–593), see my clarification, available at: https://www.herder.de/hk/hefte/ar chiv/2014/9-2014/wachstumspotenzial-fuer-die-eigene-lehre-zur-kritik-an-der-vermeintlichen-gender-ideologie/ (accessed September 17, 2020).

67 Valeria Hink, "Wie allwissend ist Wissenschaft im Namen des Allmächtigen. Kritische Anfragen an die Advokaten der Heilungspsychologie," *Zwischenraum*, January 1, 2003, https://www.zwischenraum.net/heilung/wie-allwissend-ist-wissenschaft-im-namen-des-allmaechtigen/ (accessed September 17, 2020).

68 Höhn, *Gott – Offenbarung – Heilswege*, 177, 242. The Second Vatican Council's Dogmatic Constitution on Divine Revelation: Dei Verbum ([Rome: Vatican, 1965], no. 2, http://www.vatican.va/archive/hist_councils/ii_vatican_council/documents/vat-ii_const_19651118_dei-verbum_en.html [accessed April 21, 2021]), as a doctrinal correction of an instructive-theoretical understanding of revelation, reads: "Through this revelation, therefore, the invisible God (see Col. 1;15, 1 Tim. 1:17) out of the abundance of His love speaks to men as friends (see Ex. 33:11; John 15:14–15) and lives among them (see Bar. 3:38), so that He may invite and take them into fellowship with Himself."

unconditional devotion. Its identity lies in bringing to bear something that unites all people in this universalism.[69]

From this perspective, that which is decisively Christian does not distinguish it-self by delimiting and determining differences, but rather by emphasizing the commonality that transcends these differences. Distinctions made in the name of differentiation cause inequalities to arise, and these quickly establish them-selves as discriminations. Therefore, whoever

> operates on the basis of material differences will also work formally on the basis of exclu-sions and will ultimately seek to implement them in society. Emphasizing one's differences from outsiders may have an "inward" identity-strengthening effect – and yet one already has one foot stuck in the ideology trap. Ideologies exist primarily for the purpose of making their adherents look superior by defining their differences over against others. Whoever deals with differences in such a way works on behalf of those who turn them into discrim-inations.[70]

Handling differences in this way is advantageous for those persons, groups, or institutions which have the power to define differences. But as Höhn rightly ob-serves, "[i]t becomes precarious for those who have to hear from others about how they are not like them and the reasons why they cannot be equal to them."[71] Insofar as the normality of heterosexuality corresponds with the differ-ential dynamics involved in the exclusion of homosexuality, this creates precari-ous situations for those who are excluded in this way. In Catholic terminology, this means that with regard to the order of creation, homosexual persons belong to the realm of the objectively disordered, and they are also given no opportunity to participate in God's intended order, since it is not only homosexual practice, but the homosexual "inclination itself [which] must be seen as an objective dis-order."[72]

How is this compatible with the second thought pattern, according to which the decisive feature of Christianity consists in the fact that all people without ex-ception are recipients of God's unconditional devotion? How can one concretely convey to a homosexual person God's desire that all people should be saved? In any case, such a thought pattern leaves no room for a theology of precarity – that is, it must not place same-sex oriented persons in a precarious situation before

---

69 Höhn, *Gott – Offenbarung – Heilswege*, 315.
70 Ibid., 319.
71 Ibid., 312.
72 Congregation for the Doctrine of the Faith, *Letter to the Bishops of the Catholic Church*, no. 3.

God. Beyond a logic of exclusion, but also beyond an undifferentiated logic of inclusion, the decisive feature of Christianity can only be realized when the Church as the people of God – that is, all believers – "also take as their cause that which God has taken as his very own cause: the dignification of human-kind."[73]

Such an appreciation requires constant dialogue and an understanding-oriented approach to communication, which in turn includes the willingness to listen. Only in this way can that which unites all people come to the fore; at the same time, that which distinguishes people is pushed into the background without being erased. Only on the basis of such appreciation can we reduce bias and prejudice against same-sex oriented people and promote an understanding that sexual orientation need not constitute a breaking point with regard to the desire for partnership and family. Such an understanding would hardly permit sweeping claims that same-sex couples do not have suitable parenting skills, or that the child's well-being would be endangered by the mere absence of parental heterosexuality.

Differences do exist, but they can only be properly identified within the horizon of this common basis which unites all people. These differences are based above all on the fact that what is understood as nature or natural, despite the many interpretational difficulties involved, constitutes a lasting regulative principle in human self-understanding. Therefore we can say, despite all the emphasis on lack of discrimination, that same-sex partnerships and families are also different and are experienced differently, without making these differences the basis for a hierarchical assessment. In view of this otherness, there are good reasons not to open the traditional understanding of marriage – in which the heterosexuality of a man and a woman implies the natural potential for parenthood – to include same-sex couples. However, the legal recognition of such relationships as another form of domestic partnership does not affect – at least in the sense of the current interpretation of Article 8 of the ECHR (right to respect for private and family life) – their right to found a family, which is to be understood as both a positive and a negative right. However, the extent to which same-sex family formation beyond foster care and adoption should also be permissible by means of reproductive medicine, since there are no analogies to the natural potentiality of parenthood, remains a central ethical question with regard to multiple parenthood and child welfare. From a legal perspective, since the characteristic of sexual orientation is not a legitimate criterion, this question cannot

---

73 Werbick, *Den Glauben verantworten*, 396.

be settled in any other way than to allow homosexual couples the same access as heterosexual couples.

Regardless of how we may identify and further discuss differences according to the regulative principles of nature, we can confidently state the following: To begin with, these principles do not question the traditional family structure, since same-sex families do not compete with this model. What is more, they do not justify a logic of exclusion, which is often only able to emphasize that which unites all people in abstract terms. What we need is a concrete recognition of difference in which same-sex families are acknowledged as an independent family structure. Like all ethics, theological ethics is committed to thinking about happiness and what constitutes a good life. Only a dignified life can be a good life.

Bibliography

Amendt, Gerhard. "Kultur, Kindeswohl und homosexuelle Fortpflanzung." *Leviathan* 30 (2002): 161–174.

American Psychological Association (APA) et al. "Lesbian & Gay Parenting." http://www.apa. org/pi/lgbt/resources/parenting-full.pdf. Accessed April 21, 2021.

Berk, Laura E. *Entwicklungspsychologie*. Munich: Pearson Studium, 2011.

Dettenborn, Harry. *Kindeswohl und Kindeswille. Psychologische und rechtliche Aspekte*. Munich: Reinhardt, 2007.

Eggen, Bernd. "Gleichgeschlechtliche Lebensgemeinschaften ohne und mit Kindern. Soziale Strukturen und künftige Entwicklungen." In *Die gleichgeschlechtliche Familie mit Kindern. Interdisziplinäre Beiträge zu einer neuen Lebensform*, ed. Dorett Funke and Petra Thorn, 37–60. Bielefeld: Transcript, 2010.

Francis. *Post-Synodal Apostolic Exhortation: Amoris Laetitia*. Rome: Vatican, 2016. https:// www.vatican.va/content/dam/francesco/pdf/apost_exhortations/documents/papa-fran cesco_esortazione-ap_20160319_amoris-laetitia_en.pdf. Accessed April 21, 2021.

Gartrell, Nanette K., Henny M. W. Bos, and Naomi G. Goldberg. "Adolescents of the U.S. National Longitudinal Lesbian Family Study: Sexual Orientation, Sexual Behavior, and Sexual Risk Exposure." *Archives of Sexual Behavior* 40, no. 6 (2011): 1199–1209.

Goertz, Stephan. "Naturrecht und Menschenrecht. Viele Aspekte der kirchlichen Sexualmoral werden nicht mehr verstanden." *Herder Korrespondenz* 68 (2014): 509–514.

Golombok, Susan, and Fiona Tasker. "Do parents influence the sexual orientation of their children? Findings from a longitudinal study of lesbian families." *Developmental Psychology* 32 (1996): 3–11.

Grella, Christine E., et al. "Influence of gender, sexual orientation, and need on treatment utilization for substance use and mental disorders. Findings from the California Quality of Life Survey." *BMC Psychiatry* 9, no. 52 (2009): http://www.biomedcentral.com/1471-244X/9/52. Accessed September 15, 2020.

Grossmann, Karin, and Klaus E. Grossmann. *Bindungen – Das Gefüge psychischer Sicherheit*. Stuttgart: Klett-Cotta, 2014.

Hink, Valeria. "Wie allwissend ist Wissenschaft im Namen des Allmächtigen. Kritische Anfragen an die Advokaten der Heilungspsychologie," *Zwischenraum*, January 1, 2003. https://www.zwischenraum.net/heilung/wie-allwissend-ist-wissenschaft-im-namen-des-all maechtigen/. Accessed September 17, 2020.

Höhn, Hans-Joachim. *Gott – Offenbarung – Heilswege. Fundamentaltheologie.* Würzburg: Echter, 2011.

Jansen, Elke, and Melanie C. Steffens. "Lesbische Mütter, schwule Väter und ihre Kinder im Spiegel psychosozialer Forschung." *Verhaltenstherapie & psychosoziale Praxis* 38 (2006): 643–656.

Keil, Siegfried, and Michael Haspel, eds. *Gleichgeschlechtliche Lebensgemeinschaften in sozialethischer Perspektive.* Neukirchen-Vluyn: Neukirchener, 2000.

King, Michael, et al. "A systematic review of mental disorder, suicide, and deliberate self harm in lesbian, gay and bisexual people." *BMC Psychiatry* 8, no. 70 (2008): http://www.biomedcentral.com/1471-244X/8/70. Accessed September 15, 2020.

Congregation for the Doctrine of the Faith. *Letter to the Bishops of the Catholic Church on the Pastoral Care of Homosexual Persons.* Rome: Vatican, 1986. http://www.vatican.va/roman_curia/congregations/cfaith/documents/rc_con_cfaith_doc_19861001_homosexual-persons_en.html. Accessed April 21, 2021.

Congregation for the Doctrine of the Faith. *Some Considerations Concerning the Response to Legislative Proposals on the Non-Discrimination of Homosexual Persons.* Rome: Vatican, 1992. http://www.vatican.va/roman_curia/congregations/cfaith/documents/rc_con_cfaith_doc_19920724_homosexual-persons_en.html. Accessed April 21, 2021.

Congregation for the Doctrine of the Faith. *Considerations Regarding Proposals to Give Legal Recognition to Unions Between Homosexual Persons.* Rome: Vatican, 2003. http://www.vatican.va/roman_curia/congregations/cfaith/documents/rc_con_cfaith_doc_20030731_homosexual-unions_en.html. Accessed April 21, 2021.

Kreß, Hartmut. "Gleichgeschlechtliche Partnerschaften und gleichgeschlechtliche Familien mit Kindern. Rechtsethische Grundlagen – aktuelle Diskussionspunkte – Fortentwicklung von Rechtsnormen." *Zeitschrift für Evangelische Ethik* 56 (2012): 279–291.

Kreß, Hartmut. "Gleichgeschlechtliche Partnerschaften ohne und mit Kindern. Persönlichkeits- und Kinderrechte als Maßstab der Ethik – Probleme der Kirchen." *Evangelische Theologie* 73 (2013): 364–376.

Kuby, Gabriele. *Die globale sexuelle Revolution. Zerstörung der Freiheit im Namen der Freiheit.* Kißlegg: Fe-Medienverlag, 2012.

Link, Jürgen. *Versuch über den Normalismus. Wie Normalität produziert wird.* Göttingen: Vandenhoeck & Ruprecht, 2013.

Lohrenscheit, Claudia, ed. *Sexuelle Selbstbestimmung als Menschenrecht.* Baden-Baden: Nomos Verlag, 2009.

Marschütz, Gerhard. "Wachstumspotenzial für die eigene Lehre." *Herder Korrespondenz* 68 (2014): 457–462. https://www.herder.de/hk/hefte/archiv/2014/9-2014/wach stumspotenzial-fuer-die-eigene-lehre-zur-kritik-an-der-vermeintlichen-gender-ideologie/. Accessed September 17, 2020.

Mitterauer, Michael. "Entwicklungstrend der Familie in der europäischen Neuzeit." In *Handbuch der Familien- und Jugendforschung 1*, ed. Rosemarie Nave-Herz and Manfred Marefka, 179–194. Neuwied: Luchterhand, 1989.

Moore, Amber. "Psychiatrist Sorry for Gay Reparative Therapy Study." *Medical Daily*, May 19, 2012. http://www.medicaldaily.com/psychiatrist-sorry-gay-reparative-therapy-study-240498. Accessed April 21, 2021.

Österreichischer Verfassungsgerichtshof. Entscheidung vom 11. Dezember 2014, G119 – 120/2014 – 12. https://www.vfgh.gv.at/downloads/VfGH_G_119-120-2014_Adoptio nen_EP_Entscheidung.pdf. Accessed April 21, 2021.

Österreichischer Verfassungsgerichtshof. Entscheidung vom 10. Dezember 2013, G 16/2013 – 16, G 44/2013 – 14. https://www.vfgh.gv.at/downloads/VfGH_G_16-2013_G_44-2013_Fortpflanzungsmedizing.pdf. Accessed April 21, 2021.

Pennings, Guido. "Gleichgeschlechtliche Elternschaft und das moralische Recht auf Familiengründung." In *Die gleichgeschlechtliche Familie mit Kindern. Interdisziplinäre Beiträge zu einer neuen Lebensform*, ed. Dorett Funke and Petra Thorn, 225 – 249. Bielefeld: Transcript, 2010.

Perrin, Ellen C., et al. "Promoting the Well-Being of Children Whose Parents Are Gay or Lesbian." *Pediatrics* 131 (2013): e1374 – e1383.

Rupp, Marina, and Andrea Dürnberger. "Wie kommt der Regenbogen in die Familie?" In *Die gleichgeschlechtliche Familie mit Kindern. Interdisziplinäre Beiträge zu einer neuen Lebensform*, ed. Dorett Funke and Petra Thorn, 61 – 98. Bielefeld: Transcript, 2010.

Rupp, Marina, ed. *Die Lebenssituation von Kindern in gleichgeschlechtlichen Lebenspartnerschaften*. Cologne: Bundesanzeiger-Verl.-Ges, 2009.

Sandfort, Theo G. M., et al. "Sam-sex behavior and psychiatric disorders. Findings from the Netherlands Mental Health Survey and Incidence Study (NEMESIS)." *Archives of General Psychiatry* 58 (2001): 85 – 91.

Schon, Lothar. *Sehnsucht nach dem Vater. Die Dynamik der Vater-Sohn-Beziehung*. Stuttgart: Klett-Cotta, 2000.

Second Vatican Council. *Dogmatic Constitution on Divine Revelation: Dei Verbum*. Rome: Vatican, 1965. http://www.vatican.va/archive/hist_councils/ii_vatican_council/docu ments/vat-ii_const_19651118_dei-verbum_en.html. Accessed April 21, 2021.

Stacey, Judith, and Timothy T. Biblarz. "(How) Does the sexual orientation of parents matter?" *American Sociological Review* 66 (2001): 159 – 183.

Steinhardt, Kornelia, Wilfried Datler, and Johannes Gstach, eds. *Die Bedeutung des Vaters in der frühen Kindheit*. Gießen: Psychosozial-Verlag, 2002.

von Trotha, Trutz. "Zum Wandel der Familie." *Kölner Zeitschrift für Soziologie und Sozialpsychologie* 42 (1990): 452 – 473.

Tyrell, Hartmann. "Ehe und Familie – Institutionalisierung und Deinstitutionalisierung." In *Die "postmoderne" Familie. Familiale Strategien und Familienpolitik in einer Übergangszeit*, ed. Kurt Lüscher et al., 145 – 156. Konstanz: Univ.-Verl. Konstanz, 1988.

Vonholdt, Christl Ruth. "Das Kindeswohl nicht im Blick." *Bulletin DIJG, Sonderdruck Herbst 2009* (2009): 2 – 4.

Walper, Friederike. "Gleichgeschlechtliche Lebensgemeinschaften mit Kindern. Verfassungsrechtliche Rahmenbedingungen." In *Die gleichgeschlechtliche Familie mit Kindern. Interdisziplinäre Beiträge zu einer neuen Lebensform*, ed. Dorett Funke and Petra Thorn, 115 – 159. Bielefeld: Transcript, 2010.

Werbick, Jürgen. *Den Glauben verantworten. Eine Fundamentaltheologie*. Freiburg im Breisgau: Herder, 2000.

World Medical Association. "WMA Statement on Natural Variations of Human Sexuality."
October 2013. https://www.wma.net/policies-post/wma-statement-on-natural-variations-of-human-sexuality/. Accessed April 21, 2021.

List of Contributors

Hartmut A. G. Bosinski (b. 1956), Doctor of Medicine, Professor of Sexual Medicine; sexual health physician and psychotherapist with a medical practice in Kiel, Germany.

Stephan Goertz (b. 1964), Doctor of Theology, Professor of Moral Theology at the Faculty of Catholic Theology, Johannes Gutenberg University Mainz, Germany.

Thomas Hieke (b. 1968), Doctor of Theology, Professor of Old Testament at the Faculty of Catholic Theology, Johannes Gutenberg University Mainz, Germany.

Konrad Hilpert (b. 1947), Doctor of Theology, Professor Emeritus of Moral Theology at the Faculty of Catholic Theology, Ludwig Maximilian University of Munich, Germany.

Micheal G. Lawler (b. 1933), Doctor of Theology, Professor Emeritus of Systematic Theology at the Department of Catholic Theology, Creighton University, Omaha, USA.

Gerhard Marschütz (b. 1956), Doctor of Theology, Professor of Theological Ethics at the Institute of Systematic Theology in the Catholic Theological Faculty, University of Vienna, Austria.

Claudia Niedlich (b. 1988), Doctor of Philosophy, Research Associate at the Department of Social Psychology, University of Koblenz Landau, Landau Campus, Germany.

Todd A. Salzmann (b. 1964), Doctor of Theology, Professor of Theological Ethics at the Department of Catholic Theology, Creighton University, Omaha, USA.

Melanie Caroline Steffens (b. 1969), Doctor of the Natural Sciences, Professor of Social Psychology, University of Koblenz Landau, Landau Campus, Germany.

Magnus Striet (b. 1964), Doctor of Theology, Professor of Fundamental Theology at the Faculty of Catholic Theology, Albert Ludwig University, Freiburg im Breisgau, Germany.

Michael Theobald (b. 1948), Doctor of Theology, Professor Emeritus of New Testament Exegesis at the Faculty of Catholic Theology, Eberhard Karls University of Tübingen, Germany.